The Sleuth Book For Genealogists

The Sleuth Book for Genealogists

Strategies for more successful family history research

Emily Anne Croom

BETTERWAY BOOKS
CINCINNATI, OHIO
www.familytreemagazine.com

About the Author

Emily Croom is a popular lecturer for societies and community groups and teaches genealogy at the Houston (Texas) Community College. She holds a masters degree in history, writes articles for several genealogy periodicals, and is an active researcher. She is the author of the widely-acclaimed *Unpuzzling Your Past*, *The Unpuzzling Your Past Workbook*, and *The Genealogist's Companion & Sourcebook*.

The Sleuth Book for Genealogists. Copyright © 2000 by Emily Anne Croom. Manufactured in the United States of America. All rights reserved. No part of this book may be reproduced in any form or by any electronic or mechanical means including information storage and retrieval systems without permission in writing from the publisher, except by a reviewer, who may quote brief passages in a review. Published by Betterway Books, an imprint of F&W Publications, Inc., 1507 Dana Avenue, Cincinnati, Ohio 45207. (800) 289-0963. First edition.

Other fine Betterway Books are available from your local bookstore or on our Web site at www.familytreemagazine.com.

04 03 02 01 00   5 4 3 2 1

Library of Congress Cataloging-in-Publication Data

Croom, Emily Anne
   The sleuth book for genealogists / by Emily Anne Croom.
     p. cm.
   Includes bibliographical references (p.) and index.
   ISBN 1-55870-532-5 (alk. paper)
    1. Genealogy. 2. United States—Genealogy—Handbooks, manuals, etc. I. Title.

CS16 .C85   2000
929'.1'072073—dc21
                                                             99-088395
                                                                     CIP

Editor: Sharon DeBartolo Carmack, CG
Production editor: Christine Doyle
Cover designer: Stephanie Redman
Cover photography by Hal Barkan/ Photo Art
Interior designer: Sandy Conopeotis Kent

Icons Used in This Book

Brick Wall Buster
How to turn dead ends into opportunities

Reminder
"Don't-Forget" items to keep in mind

Case Study
Examples of this book's advice at work

Research Tip
Ways to make research more efficient

For More Info
Where to turn for more in-depth coverage

See Also
Where in this book to find related information

Idea Generator
Techniques and prods for further thinking

Sources
Where to go for information, supplies, etc.

Important
Information and tips you can't overlook

Technique
How to conduct research, solve problems, and get answers

Internet Source
Where on the web to find what you need

Timesaver
Shaving minutes and hours off the clock

Notes
Thoughts, ideas and related insights

Tip
Ways to make research more efficient

Printed Source
Directories, books, pamphlets and other paper archives

Warning
Stop before you make a mistake

Quotes
Useful words direct from the experts

Table of Contents At-a-Glance

Table of Contents

On your mark, get set, go.

Foreword

Genealogy is the adventure of piecing together a puzzle of ancestors: the lives they lived and the people with whom they associated. The process of working the puzzle presents many questions and challenges to the researcher. Some of these are more readily answered than others, but all searches involve two basic elements: methods and sources. Generally, more success comes to genealogists who apply techniques of good research and use enough sources to find or propose answers. Obviously, some pieces of the puzzle may never be found, but success is often determined by the extent to which the researcher employs sound methods and legitimate sources.

Basic sources and techniques are the focus of my books *Unpuzzling Your Past* and *The Unpuzzling Your Past Workbook*. United States sources are the focus of *The Genealogist's Companion & Sourcebook*. Now, *The Sleuth Book for Genealogists* concentrates on methods and strategies for more successful research. Major topics include organizing, focusing on a specific research question, planning the research, practicing cluster genealogy, gathering and documenting evidence, analyzing data, evaluating the big picture, arranging ideas into progress reports, and sharing success in case studies. Reports from successful research on "tough cases" appear as the final three chapters, all focusing on the ultimate genealogical question of identifying a parent generation. The research examples throughout the book come from my research though not always my lineages, and from that of several friends. The final chapter is from my research on my own family.

This book is for any genealogist, regardless of experience, for we never stop learning and can often benefit from hearing how someone else "does genealogy" successfully. The book's down-to-earth approach includes advice and encouragement from many people, particularly selected literary sleuths such as Sherlock Holmes and Belgian detective Hercule Poirot, whose unraveling of mysteries often involves the same principles and techniques as our genealogical research. When asked by a tourist to explain his methods, Hercule Poirot responded,

> It is a little like your puzzle, Madame. One assembles the pieces. . . . and every strange-shaped little piece must be fitted into its own place. . . . And sometimes it is like that piece of your puzzle just now. One arranges very methodically the pieces of the puzzle—one sorts the colours—and then perhaps a piece of one colour that should fit in with—say, the fur rug, fits in instead in a black cat's tail.[1]

Notes

Endnotes for the foreword are on page 250.

The goal of *The Sleuth Book* is to spark in the minds of genealogists a variety of ideas or perspectives from which to view their own research, study their own data, mull over a research dilemma, or tackle a tough question. The research principles presented here are not new. The novelty and the fun are in letting literary sleuths and others tell us things we may already know but forget, or in hearing an idea expressed in a new or different way so that we look at our own research with new eyes.

Indeed. This throws new light upon the matter.
—*Sherlock Holmes*[2]

In the spirit of documenting sources and crediting direct quotes, endnotes identify the source of each quotation from the literary sleuths and others. These notes will also assist those who would like to read the stories and books from which the quotations come. Three of the books that even have a genealogical twist are Agatha Christie's *The Clocks*, *Elephants Can Remember*, and *Sleeping Murder*. In addition, a number of these sleuths are portrayed on public and cable television. (In genealogy, the use of footnotes is the preferred format for citing references. Here, as in many other disciplines such as history, endnotes are used for the ease of production. Because the notes are an important component of the text, readers are urged to read them along with the text.)

If asked whether I have a favorite sleuth, I must say that I have several. My early favorite was Dorothy Sayers's Lord Peter Wimsey, for whom one of my cats was aptly named: a bit arrogant but confident, charming, and in control of each situation in which he found or placed himself. Although not quoted in the book because he did not discuss his methods with his associates the way others did, my all-time favorite is Ellis Peters's Brother Cadfael, the eleventh century Benedictine monk. The others quoted in this book have provided much enjoyable reading time.

I want to express appreciation to family and friends for encouragement and advice for this book and to the loyal readers around the country who read and use my other books. It is wonderful to have researcher friends willing to share their own work; John Dorroh, Garrett and Dory Graham, and Franklin Smith contributed their research for use in chapters five, nine, and ten, respectively. Several other genealogists merit an individual thank-you: for manuscript reading and constructive suggestions, Mary Smith Fay, CG, FASG, Margaret Mathies, Tom Mathies, and Betty Goodrum; for reference assistance, manuscript reading, and constructive suggestions, Gay E. Carter, reference librarian at the University of Houston-Clear Lake; for research assistance, manuscript reading, constructive suggestions, and good cooking during the process, my husband, Robert T. Shelby.

Introduction:
Why the Sleuths?

These fellows are sharper than I expected.
They seem to have covered their tracks.

—*Sherlock Holmes*[1]

W hat genealogist has not accused ancestors of the same evasiveness, even conspiracy? One friend even accuses his ancestors of setting fire to the courthouse every time they moved away, for his ancestors from the time of the American Revolution until Reconstruction lived in counties that have had major loss of records due to fires.

Literary detectives constantly face the dilemma, What have I learned and where do I go from here? The same is true for genealogists. We can learn from these experts when we realize the extent to which our pursuits are similar.

Many parallels exist between literary sleuths and genealogists. Both gather and unravel sets of facts and circumstances. We try to answer unanswered questions. We seek to place people in a given place at a given time, reconstruct events, and understand their causes and results. Like detectives, genealogists want to determine who was where when, doing what and with whom, why they came or left, and where they are when we need to find them. Both literary sleuths and genealogists look for missing persons and sometimes need to identify skeletons in closets. Being a detective or a genealogist requires a certain amount of innate curiosity and the courage to talk to strangers, go to new places, and try new approaches. Both activities involve the skill of observation, the need to discriminate between things observed, and the ability to analyze and draw conclusions. We both tend to become thoroughly engrossed in what we are doing, to the neglect of house and yard work.

Obviously, the two disciplines have their differences. Genealogists are not usually trying to solve a crime or identify a criminal. Genealogists do not always need to figure out who had a motive and an opportunity to commit a crime or an act and who could benefit from it. Certainly, genealogists do not tend to

Notes

Endnotes for the introduction are on page 250.

1

put themselves in harm's way to the degree that detectives do. Although we all accumulate paper in the course of our investigations, we genealogists are the ones who, because of it, frequently lose the use of our dining room tables and spare beds. And genealogists unfortunately do not usually have the opportunity to confront and question their "suspects" when they are found.

Since the early nineteenth century, many sleuths have worked the pages of literature, and some have shared with their colleagues, and therefore with us, the methods and secrets of their successes. Since the disciplines of genealogy and sleuthing share considerable common ground, **why can't we genealogists learn from the sleuths**, make ourselves better at what we do, and have fun in the process? All of us can continue to grow in skill and understanding. And all of us would like to solve, during our lifetimes, some of our tough questions, to get beyond some of the proverbial brick walls.

As the incomparable Sherlock Holmes said, "There is a mystery about this which stimulates the imagination."[2] *This* can be a crime waiting to be solved or an ancestor waiting to be found. *This* may be one newly discovered fact or the whole process of genealogy. Whichever it is at any given time, we genealogists are more likely to be successful with it when we let our imaginations roam, when we question and ponder in the spirit of the sleuth, and when we remain open to imitate the sleuths.

Idea Generator

I have an idea! . . . This time it is an idea gigantic! Stupendous! And you—*you*, my friend, have given it to me!
—*Hercule Poirot to Captain Hastings*[3]

ONE

Putting a Down Payment on Success

He is insane, of course. I imagine that the family history has become a mania with him.

—*Hercule Poirot*[1]

Nongenealogists, especially those related to us, sometimes use the word *insane* to describe us and our passion for the search. We interpret their use of the word to mean that they do not understand why we spend beautiful Saturdays bending over microfilm readers or hot summer noons having picnic lunches in cemeteries. Nevertheless, their feelings need not stop us from enjoying and benefiting from what we do.

Yes, we benefit. We learn. That enriches us. We discover. That energizes us. We exercise the brain. That's healthy. We chuckle. That too is healthy. We meet other wonderful people. That's fun. We uncover and preserve the past. That's a legacy we pass down. We are enthusiastic about something. That adds zest to life. Perhaps we even develop perspective. That can have a balancing influence in life. And it is especially gratifying when one of the nongenealogical relatives calls to ask for ancestor information because "daughter Alice has a school project to do a family tree, and we don't have a clue."

Why do we do genealogy? In enlisting the support of Belgian detective Hercule Poirot for a particular investigation, a woman characterized Poirot in a way that could apply to genealogists as well: "You like finding out things. Things that you can't see the reason for at first. I mean, that nobody can see the reason for."[2]

Whatever drew us individually into the adventure of genealogy, we discover before long that it is a continual learning process. That is why we attend lectures, seminars, and classes. That is why we subscribe to journals and read books such as this one. That is why we hone our skills by asking questions and trying different approaches.

Notes

Endnotes for this chapter begin on page 250.

FOCUS OF THE BOOK

Much of what we do in research involves the sources where we find information. However, **the level of our success may well depend on the quality of our methods.** Methods determine (1) whether we get the most benefit from the sources, (2) whether we make decisions that can propel our research toward answers, and (3) whether our efforts exhibit high standards of quality. The process naturally divides itself into compartments of activity that are the focus of this book:

- organizing for the search
- focusing on the question at hand
- planning the search
- gathering and documenting adequate data
- interpreting and analyzing the results
- evaluating the big picture to determine where you are in your research and where to go next
- repeating the process for a new part of the search

These steps are things we do over and over again as we research. Even after long experience and even if the process has become second nature to us, it is helpful to review the steps when we begin to research a new line or new project.

Appropriately, Agatha Christie's Captain Hastings once said of the eccentric Hercule Poirot: "That is the worst of Poirot. Order and Method are his gods. He goes so far as to attribute all his success to them."[3] We can learn from Poirot even if we never approach his extraordinary ability.

If you are new to genealogy or feel that you need a refresher about the very basic tenets of genealogy and research, please stop here and read appendix A on page 203. We will wait here for you, and you will benefit more from the rest of the book once you have that background.

WHAT'S THE ANSWER?

And what after all *is* the matter on hand?
—"I" [Dupin's friend][4]

What the professor wanted was, "What is the question?"

A friend of mine had a philosophy professor in college who wrote a question on the chalkboard the first day of class. He announced that whoever could answer it would get an A in the class without having to come back to class the rest of the semester. Nobody could respond. The teacher asked, "What is the answer?" What would you have said? (See the sidebar at left for the response the professor wanted.)

For the rest of the semester, the professor focused on the reality that we have to be able to ask the right questions. We have to define the question or define the problem before we can look for an answer. When we face a large or complex set of information, as genealogists eventually do, we must break it down into manageable pieces. We must identify one small question to try to solve. Then we work on other small questions one at a time. Eventually we have only one piece of the original set left to handle.

This process is much like working a jigsaw puzzle: categorizing the colors and the straight edges, then working out a system to test pieces and begin to fit them together. It is also what we genealogists must do in trying to unpuzzle our pasts. We amass information (the puzzle pieces), but what do we do with it once we have it? How can we deal effectively with all of it? Hercule Poirot gave part of his answer to this question when he said, "It may occur to you that I am eccentric, perhaps mad. Nevertheless I assure you that behind my madness there is—as you English say—a method."[5] Method is what we hope to learn from him and other sleuths.

FIRST THINGS FIRST: GETTING ORGANIZED

> To work with method, one must begin from the beginning.
> —*Hercule Poirot*[6]

Before you start a do-it-yourself project, you prepare and get organized: You plan or draw the project, collect the tools and supplies, clear the work space, lay out materials, take measurements ("measure twice, cut once"), and do other preliminary tasks. Sometimes, getting ready takes longer than the project itself. In genealogy, preparation is just as necessary but not always as lengthy.

Method in a genealogist's madness implies, first, an organization process which allows the researcher to keep up with the accumulation of data. The sleuths do not talk much about committing evidence to paper; they seem to carry much of it around in their heads. Genealogists must not try to do that. We must accept the television commercial warning "Do not try this at home."

Most genealogists have at least a rudimentary system for organizing their efforts. Some systems are more sophisticated than others. Perhaps some resemble Adelaide Adams in *Murder à la Richelieu*: "Not much escapes my eyes and ears and nothing escapes my memory, although I may mislay it for a while."[7] Other systems may be like the study that lady detective Loveday Brooke observed in 1893: "The room was comfortably furnished, but presented an appearance of disorder from the books and manuscripts scattered in all directions. A whole pile of torn fragments of foolscap sheets, overflowing from a wastepaper basket beside the writing-table, seemed to proclaim the fact that the scholar had of late grown weary of, or else dissatisfied with his work, and had condemned it freely."[8]

Choices for Organizing

Most genealogists change organizing systems at some point in an effort to refine and strengthen their ability to find things. Therefore, there are at least twice as many systems as there are genealogists. However, certain constants pervade these systems. We generally divide our files according to surname, then location. After that, the individualism takes over.

Everybody keeps their stuff somewhere. Omitting the dining room table as a

Printed Source

For more on organizing your genealogy, see *Organizing Your Family History Search* by Sharon De-Bartolo Carmack (Cincinnati: Betterway Books, 1999).

viable option, many use a filing cabinet or file boxes with a folder for each person. For years, I had no money or space for a filing cabinet, so I needed something different. Alas, I did have a dining room table, for a while, but I also had bookcases.

Learning from my own mistakes in the first few months of research, I realized that spiral notebooks, even when subject-divided and indexed, are not the answer to organizing genealogy; there had to be a better way. Thus, my choice was and remains three-ring binders. I begin with one binder for each surname, divided into sections by state or county. As the binder fills, it can be divided into several notebooks for that surname in particular states or counties, depending on the situation of the individual family: Bennett—Louisiana, or Coleman—Cumberland County, Virginia. Using binders of consistent size leads to consistent use of the same size paper. The 8½″×11″ (21.6cm×27.9cm) size also conveniently matches paper size from photocopy machines.

The same principles work with organization systems using file folders. We divide by surname or full name: one folder per surname or per individual. Then we divide by location.

As the search progresses, each state or county binder is organized into sections by category: research plans, reference materials and maps, family charts, correspondence, state and county history, and types of records—census, land, marriage, tax, probate, cemetery, etc. The combining of like records helps me because I look for a given piece of information according to the type of record in which it occurred. In other words, I think in terms of deeds, cemeteries, marriage records, letters, etc. These divisions also allow me to keep track of several generations or siblings as they interact with each other, with a minimum of cross-referencing or filing copies of a document in several folders or notebooks.

Almost any adequate filing system means that each page of notes deals with only one surname. Some researchers speed up their note taking with laptop computers. If I did that, I would have to print out the notes for study and evaluation. Maybe it is a generational attitude, but I study data better when I can see my original note pages, document copies, and charts spread out all at once.

My other motivation for using binders is time. When I return home from research, I do not have time to transcribe notes or file pages in individual folders. I take the notebook(s) for the day's efforts to the research facility and put the notes right into the notebook section where they belong, and the filing is done. It works for me, and it allows me to use the dining room table for other things.

Some people feel that a computer is all they need for taking notes and storing material. Of course, thousands use genealogy software that links related individuals and prints out many useful and interesting charts. The use of this software is not what we mean by *organizing*. This software use is more for storage and presentation of completed research once it is known to be accurate.

Ideas for Organizing

In addition to an overall organizing system, many genealogists work out their own individual tricks of the trade to help them stay organized. Some researchers color code their binders or folders into the four grandparent lineages, or the eight great-grandparent lines, for easy identification. Some maintain a master

Idea Generator

card file on all ancestors as a quick reference to binders or folders or as a handy summary of events in ancestors' lives. Others dedicate one binder as an index to ancestors and the known events in their lives. Some do this master index alphabetically; some use ahnentafel numbers.

Ahnentafel is a German word meaning "family table" or "family tree." The numbers are a logical method of giving each ancestor an identification number. The beauty of this system is that you can add as many ancestors as you find without having to change anyone's number. Many pedigree charts use these numbers. If you chart your own ancestors, you are number one. Your father is double your number, or two. Your mother is double your number, plus one, or three. Double any person's number to get the father's number; double the number and add one to get the mother's number. Thus, fathers are even numbers; mothers are odd numbers. You can reach back as far as you need to go with these convenient numbers. Figure 1 on page 8 shows a sample ahnentafel chart.

One-page indexes and master lists are easy to take with you for reference when you research, especially if you prefer not to lug around heavy binders. Some genealogists keep an alphabetical list of ancestors by state so that they can check data at a glance while working on that state. Others prefer a complete listing of everyone. Most researchers who use these lists want basic vital statistics listed for each person as a frame of reference. On lists of ancestors in a given state, it is helpful to add their dates of residence in the state so that you look for each one in the correct time period. One friend prints from the computer a master list of research names and vital statistics but uses a light shading on the direct ancestors to spot them easily. Many binders have covers with insert pockets that are convenient places for your ancestor reference lists.

Some researchers code and number each page of notes in the binders and use these page numbers as references on family group sheets and other charts. One genealogist told me she uses different colored pages for notes on different surnames; if one sheet of the wrong color shows up in a set of notes, she immediately knows where to file it.

Customize Your Organization

You have to devise the system that works best for you, given your time, money, patience, and the way you think. Combining aspects of several systems may work well for you. Whatever you choose, the purpose is to (1) develop an efficient and systematic way to store research data on ancestors, (2) be able to access any given piece of it relatively quickly, and (3) have an effective way to pull materials together for comparison and study. Even those who use genealogy software to link related individuals will still need to use paper and pencil as they gather and evaluate material.

Let's take a piece of advice from an Eleanor Roosevelt mystery in which adviser Louis Howe said to President Franklin Roosevelt: "A disordered mind is unlikely ever to be made up."[9] His observation has a valid genealogical application: A genealogist with disordered research is unlikely to make much prog-

Sources

Emily Croom's *The Unpuzzling Your Past Workbook* (Cincinnati: Betterway Books, 1996) provides two kinds of five-generation pedigree charts: one with numbers 1–31 provided; one with blanks for you to fill in your own ahnentafel numbers so that you can keep the numbers consistent regardless of who is first on the chart.

Ahnentafel Table for No. 1	Roselda Greenapple		
Double a person's number to find the father. Double the number and add 1 to find the mother.			
Paternal Line		Maternal Line	
Parents			
2	Elderberry Greenapple	3	Cora Thorne
Grandparents			
4	Gouldsberry G. Greenapple	6	Royal Thorne
5	Rose Berry	7	Charity Ball
Great-Grandparents			
8	Huckleberry Greenapple	12	Woodrow "Woody" Thorne
9	Mary "Molly" Middlebury	13	Penny Royal
10	Logan Berry	14	Royal Ball
11	Mary Flora Rose	15	Charity House
Great-Great-Grandparents			
16	Granberry Greenapple	24	Major Thorne
17	Marietta Gouldsberry	25	Vienna Wood
18	Septimus Middlebury	26	Royal
19	Philadelphia Parks	27	Tinney Bell
20	Green Berry	28	T. Ball
21	Logan	29	Florida Foote
22	Hardy Rose	30	Green House
23	Virginia T. Rose	31	Patience Honey
The chart can expand to include as many generations as necessary.			

Figure 1 Sample Ahnentafel Chart

ress because much is in disarray and the overall picture is blurry. Therefore, organization is imperative, even if only in the lines chosen for study.

AT ANY BEGINNING—FOCUS

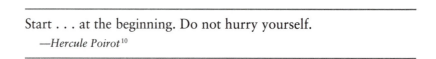

Start . . . at the beginning. Do not hurry yourself.
— *Hercule Poirot* [10]

Genealogists encounter many beginning points. Each time we identify a wife or mother, we are at the beginning of a new lineage in our story. Each discovery of a husband or father begins a new generation of that family. In a sense, we have many opportunities to start fresh with improvements in our organization and in our methods.

We generally do better when we concentrate on one or two lines at a time. This limit allows us to become intimately acquainted with members of the focus group and study their problems with an in-depth approach. Remember, ancestors did not live in a vacuum but among a group of friends, relatives, and neighbors. To study ancestors' lives and lineages, we often need to study their children, their siblings, and others in their lives as well.

Research Tip

> Perhaps when an historian was covering a field as large as the Middle Ages and the Renaissance he had no time to stop and analyse detail.
> —*Investigator Alan Grant*[11]

Grant's statement has an obvious genealogical application: When we try to cover all our ancestors at once, we have no time to stop and analyze detail. Without limitation to our research and without this study of detail, we make mistakes. Worst of all, we run the risk of claiming the wrong ancestors.

Before rushing out to tackle a new ancestor or new focus, update your family group sheets for that nuclear family and each sibling's family within that line. This effort confirms the vital statistics you already know. Then, list in chronological order all the known events in the life of the target ancestor. Include vital statistics and anything else you have, including such events as military service, land sales and purchases, church membership, and births of children. Even Sherlock Holmes asked, "Do you know anything about her history?"[12]

A chronology is most helpful when it gives the date and brief description of the event, the age (if known) of the person at the time of the event, and the sources for that information. The updated group sheets and chronology together show you what you have and help you determine the focus of the next research. With each piece of new information, keep the group sheet and/or chronology up-to-date to aid in the evaluation of your progress.

Sources

Chronology forms and family group sheets with space for documentation are available in Emily Croom's *The Unpuzzling Your Past Workbook.*

WHAT'S THE PROBLEM?

> The first step is to identify correctly the problem.
> —*Click and Clack, The Tappet Brothers*[13]

An engineer friend of mine sometimes trains new employees, fresh out of college, in the work that his company needs them to do. He has found over the years that the biggest problem facing these young employees is that they have not yet learned to look at a set of data and identify the problem. They are proficient at taking a given problem to the computer to find a solution, but they have trouble seeing the problem in the first place. Learning to "see" becomes part of their training.

Even Hercule Poirot had this problem with young detectives. To one he said, "Ah—but it is impossible, the way you never ask the right questions! As a result you know nothing of what is important."[14] Genealogists need this skill of questioning as well! That's why we talk about methods, sources, evaluating evidence, and planning the next step. If we can break down the information we have—including the holes and the blanks—and identify the questions, we are on our way to getting answers.

What are these genealogical questions? They work like a telescope, narrowing the view to address more and more specific issues. Initially, they are rather obvious because they address the holes in our information on family group sheets, pedigree charts, and chronologies. They generally ask *who*, *what*, *when*, and *where*:

- Who was his first wife, or her first husband?
- Who were the wife's parents? Or the husband's parents? Do you have names of potential parents and want to find out if they are indeed the correct ones?
- Who were the other children? Is the list of children complete?
- What was the wife's maiden name?
- When was the wife born?
- When and where did the couple marry?
- When and where were the three older children in the family born?
- Where was the husband really born? Do you have conflicting birthplaces for him?
- Where was this family in 1870?

These are the first kinds of questions we need to ask as we begin to define the research problem on which to focus. Two pieces of advice emerge here.

- It is usually better to work first on the nuclear family nearest in time to you to complete their entries on the charts before going back to earlier generations. In our rush to move backward, we often overlook our own parent and grandparent generations. When we study them, we often learn much, including information to send us more knowledgeably into research on previous generations.
- Choosing the next research focus depends, of course, on what we already know. When we say "what we already know," we mean "what we can prove" or "what we can back up with specific source information." Later chapters will discuss proof and documentation.

On a second level, the questions we must ask are specific to a given research problem, such as discovering a birthplace or a death date. These questions help develop a plan of research. Their answers actually direct the search. Our goal at this level is to identify activities in the ancestor's life, such as land purchase, jury or military service, appearance in censuses, or writing a will. Such events often created documents that may give us either our missing information or clues to help figure it out. Chapter two addresses this kind of questioning.

On a third level, the questions we ask help evaluate very specific parts of the search. These questions primarily focus on the *why*, *how*, and *what if*. If the research problem is to determine where Great-Grandpa was born, we may find ourselves asking questions such as these: Why did Uncle Henry swear his grandpa was born in Illinois? Why do the census records show him born in

Kentucky and Missouri? How can we explain the presence of the three states in connection with his birth? There is a reason. What if he was born in Kentucky and spent some childhood time in Illinois before moving to Missouri? These kinds of questions as evaluation tools are discussed more fully in chapters five through eleven.

In review, as we begin any new part of our research, we must

- organize for that specific search
- choose a focus person or couple
- update and study what we know about their lives and activities
- record the sources that back up these facts
- narrow the focus to specific missing information, i.e., identify the problem

Important

My dear fellow, there lies the problem.
—*Sherlock Holmes*[15]

TWO

Planning for Research

Notes

Endnotes for this chapter are on page 251.

Part I: Developing a Plan

I always think, you know, that one should have a plan.
—*Miss Marple*[1]

SPONTANEITY

Genealogy, like life, has to have a certain degree of spontaneity. While you are browsing in the library stacks, you want to be free to look through a book that strikes your fancy, especially if it may contain something vital on a family currently simmering on your back burner. Only you can decide whether you have time for this diversion or digression. Most of us find it hard to resist the temptation and have found great stuff this way. Besides, if you do not write down at the time the title, call number, and reason for wanting to use it, you may forget all about it. As long as you have to stop to write something, you may as well write down or photocopy whatever attracted your attention in the first place. Regardless of your plan for the day's research, sometimes it is beneficial to stop and insert something else.

However, if you want to progress on your focus family, you probably should succumb to this kind of spontaneity in moderation. Research plans have a way of keeping us focused, keeping our search on track, and motivating us to persevere. They are something like a shopping list, especially one generated over several days, with thought and planning. When we stray too much from the list, we pick up items that we do not need, add items that are already in the pantry that we forgot we had, and may even forget the main item on the list because we got sidetracked.

PRELIMINARY PLANNING

What is our plan of campaign?
—*Captain Hastings to Hercule Poirot*[2]

Many genealogists plan their searches without being conscious of going through any particular steps. However, when we dissect and understand the process, we often make better use of it. The overall goal is to zero in on a specific research problem in a way that may lead to a solution. Granted, some genealogical questions cannot be answered, but many tough ones can be, with an appropriate research plan and a dose of luck. Ultimately, good planning should help the researcher make good choices about procedures and sources to try. Good planning should help prevent unnecessary expenses and wasted time and effort.

Chapter one discussed the initial steps in this process:

1. Identify your focus family or person.
2. For this family, update family group sheets, pedigree charts, and chronological profiles. This represents what you know to be accurate at this time.
3. From these charts, determine the holes in your information.
4. From these holes, choose a focus. What specific information are you trying to find?

From specific questions, it is easier to plan for finding answers. The ultimate question for most searches is "Who were the parents?" However, between identifying the child (maybe as an older adult) and identifying the parents may lie other more specific questions that must be answered on the road to finding the parents. The road may be short or long, straight or winding. Each search is different. The plan will have to be tailored to each specific search, and the plan may change along the way. Much depends on what is found and what it means, or what is not found.

MAPPING OUT A PLAN

[W]e must map out our plan of campaign.
—*Hercule Poirot*[3]

Mapping is an appropriate word, for it reminds us that location plays as important a part in our planning as in our researching. We should remember that *mapping* also means outlining, defining, or planning. In mapping a research strategy, we have to consider all these definitions.

1. Outlining Ancestral Locations

Everything in genealogical research takes place in the context of location and time. Where was the focus ancestor at the time of the events in the chronological profile? Were several locations represented? Just as people today are mobile, ancestors often were born in one state, colony, or country and moved to or through several others during their lifetimes. Mark these changes clearly or list them in chart form, for your research will take place in the records of each place where the ancestor lived. This is part of the step of listing what you already know about the person. Each location will have its own plan.

Research Tip

Figure 2 shows the events and locations identified in Edmund Bennett's life by the time he became the focus of a concentrated search. These were the first places where research would focus. If there is only one known location, the search begins there.

Known Locations for Edmund Bennett (not necessarily all residences)		
Place	Event	Date
Georgia	born	c 1785–86
part of Jackson County, Georgia that became Walton County	"early resident"	
Walton County, Georgia	tax roll	1819
Walton County, Georgia	census	1820
Early County, Georgia	drew lots	
Irwin County, Georgia	drew lots	
Talbot County, Georgia	cenusus	1830
Marion County, Georgia	signed petition	c 1836–37
Talbot County, Georgia	census	1840
Natchitoches Parish, Louisiana	census	1850

Figure 2 Outlining Ancestral Locations

2. Defining the Framework for Research

When you isolate the ancestor's known locations, does the list include a state or country whose records you have not researched before? To research effectively in those records, it is advisable (1) to read some basic history of the place, (2) to learn about the sources available for research of the area, and (3) to learn about sources unique to that location.

University libraries and larger public libraries have state and regional histories, but one good reference for the United States is *Ancestry's Red Book: American State, County & Town Sources*, Alice Eichholz, editor (Salt Lake City: Ancestry, 1992, revised edition). State by state, the book surveys basic history, genealogical sources, parent counties, establishment of present counties, and major research facilities. Each chapter also includes an excellent map with current county boundaries, a bibliography of published histories, and a bibliography of materials helpful to genealogists. These reference lists often include published guides to genealogical research in that state. Each state differs slightly from others in its region in the way courts, counties, or towns are organized and where older records are kept. Thus, researchers save time and money by learning, before beginning research, about the state's records of genealogical value and where to find them.

Another helpful reference for basic state and county information is *The Handy Book for Genealogists* (Logan, UT: The Everton Publishers, Inc., latest edition). This book also includes a number of countries other than the United States. Another state-by-state guide is *The Hidden Half of the Family: A Sourcebook for Women's Genealogy*, by Christina Schaefer (Baltimore: Genealogical Publishing Company, 1999), which focuses on the search for women but includes ideas useful for genealogical searches in general.

3. Maps to Clarify Boundary Changes

Maps help us visualize boundary changes and the formation of new counties and new states. Two books cited above, *Ancestry's Red Book* and *The Handy Book for Genealogists*, both list the formation dates of United States counties and the names of parent counties or territories. County and state historical atlases can also help identify minor boundary changes that affected smaller numbers of residents. An excellent source of historical maps is William Thorndale and William Dollarhide's book *Map Guide to the U.S. Federal Censuses, 1790–1920* (Baltimore: Genealogical Publishing Company, 1987). The maps represent the counties existing in each state in each census year. The design of these maps helps researchers visualize county boundary changes between censuses. Comparing such maps with residence information for the family can help the researcher determine whether the family moved between censuses, they became part of a newly created county, or their county boundary changed for some other reason.

4. Maps As Research Tools

Every genealogist needs maps of ancestral counties. Knowing only the name of a county is not enough. When researching any county, the genealogist needs to know its location and the names of adjoining counties at the time the ancestors lived there. It is also helpful to be familiar with other geographic features, such as creeks and rivers, towns, and the county seat. Why does it matter? Political boundaries are often arbitrary and invisible lines, not fenced barriers. Thus, ancestors sometimes did business or had relatives in the nearest community, even if it was across a county or state line. Consider typical examples:

- Couples often married in the bride's county of residence. If the groom was not from the same county, he may have been from a neighboring county.
- Ancestors and extended family members often lived in an area where three or four counties came together, so records involving a focus ancestor could be located in more than one of the counties.
- If the focus county was on a state boundary, the focus ancestor could be mentioned in documents located in the neighboring county of the other state.
- Ancestors sometimes moved to neighboring counties, even across a state line.

By owning and studying state and county maps, the researcher can often locate where ancestors lived or the communities that were nearest the family. Clues to their residence are often identified in land and tax records, wills and estate records, or census records. For one early-nineteenth-century family, the county deed and tax records indicated residences of a potential father and son along two watercourses. One owned land crossing both branches of Tearwallet Creek, and the other owned land on the east fork of Bear Creek. A detailed county map showing the creeks indicated that these two men lived quite close to each other. This information was additional circumstantial evidence that they may have been father and son.

Sources

Such county maps are usually available from the state's department of transportation or highway department. These maps usually identify cemeteries, current roads and railroads, historical and tourist attractions, watercourses, towns, other landmarks, and townships and ranges for the states surveyed in that manner. Atlases of county maps for eleven states have been published by County Maps (Puetz Place, Lyndon Station, WI 53944). The printed atlases include Arkansas, Florida, Indiana, Kentucky, Michigan (no longer readily available), Ohio, Pennsylvania, South Carolina, Tennessee, West Virginia, and Wisconsin. County maps for Mississippi (with townships and ranges) have been published in atlas form by the University Press of Mississippi in Jackson.

Topographic maps from the U.S. government are widely available from map stores and from the United States Geological Survey, an agency of the Department of the Interior. They are also available for most states in atlas form through the DeLorme Mapping Company (P.O. Box 298, Yarmouth, ME 04096) and the booksellers who carry their *Atlas & Gazetteer* series. Each "topo" map covers a territory smaller than most counties and may cover portions of several counties because of the grid format. Thus, they are not set up county by county but do show features that transcend county boundaries, such as rivers, elevations, and roads. Although we genealogists are conditioned to think in terms of counties, it is helpful to see the broader area around the ancestral neighborhood. Topographic maps do not show the survey grid of townships and ranges that county maps often do, but together, the two kinds of maps can help genealogists locate ancestral homesites and burying grounds.

Because the rectangular survey system (townships and ranges) is so important in pinpointing ancestral property and studying ancestral neighborhoods in federal land states and other areas surveyed in a similar manner, maps that show these grids are perhaps the most useful. Most of the county maps available from the state highway or transportation departments have this feature, where applicable. One product that combines genealogically pertinent features of the topographic and county maps is the atlas series of Shearer Publishing (406 Post Oak Road, Fredericksburg, TX 78624; (800) 458-3808). Their atlases cover Arkansas, Colorado, Louisiana, New Mexico, North Carolina, Oklahoma, South Carolina, and Texas. The rectangular grids appear in the Colorado, Louisiana, and Oklahoma volumes.

Mapping ideas
Several other mapping ideas have proven useful to genealogists trying to locate or identify ancestors. One tactic is to get an outline map of the ancestral state showing the counties. (Maps such as those in *Ancestry's Red Book*, *The Handy Book for Genealogists*, and *Map Guide to the U.S. Federal Censuses*, cited above, are useful because they can fit on 8½″×11″ [21.6cm×27.9cm] paper.) To identify groups of counties where clusters of relatives may have lived, shade in with colored pencil the counties where a particular surname appears in a given census year or other statewide index. You could use different colors for surname locations shown in different indexes, such as marriage and census. Or try two colors for two related surnames. Or use different colors for variations of the same surname.

A variation of color coding can be used to show concentration of surnames in neighboring counties. As explained in a key to the system you create, you could use a light color to shade in or outline counties that had fewer than five households of a given surname in a census year. Counties with six to fifteen households of the same surname could be shaded with another color; counties with the heaviest concentration, a third color. This kind of coding can help you study the area and figure out where to look for ancestors in the records.

Another idea also uses the outline maps. Write in each county the names of people of your research surname whom you have identified in that county. As you study the family, you see their location and the nearest counties where additional records may be. You also see others who may form a cluster of relatives to study as you seek information on your focus ancestor.

A variation of this technique deals primarily with federal land states and other areas with grid systems for measuring and describing land holdings. First, identify in land or other records the legal descriptions (section, township, range) of property owned by the focus ancestor and plot the location(s) on a county map that shows the grid numbers. Identify other landowners who could be relatives and plot their land from the legal descriptions. Identify other landowners in the vicinity of known ancestors. Proximity alone does not prove relationship, but often extended family members lived near each other. Studying neighbors can often aid in a search for adult siblings or a wife's parents.

Notes

Metes and Bounds: A method of surveying and measuring land using natural landmarks (trees, creeks), artificial landmarks (fence posts, rock piles), and adjacent lands (neighbors' property lines).

With metes and bounds legal descriptions and special care in drawing, it is sometimes possible to estimate the location of ancestral land and of neighbors. Deed records and some wills give these legal descriptions. Copies of survey notes and plat maps can often make this task easier.

With computer technology, you can make your own grids of sections, townships, and ranges. Print out sheets and number them as needed to re-create an ancestral neighborhood. These mini maps can aid in your analysis of research data and help you plan by suggesting ideas or candidates for further study. (See Figures 7 and 8 on pages 96 and 97.) The automated tract book records of the Eastern States Office of the Bureau of Land Management, available online at <http://www.glorecords.blm.gov>, on CD-ROM, and at the Springfield, Virginia, office, are great sources to help identify patentees in ancestral neighborhoods. The thirteen states that are part of the Eastern States Office are Alabama, Arkansas, Florida, Illinois, Indiana, Iowa, Louisiana, Michigan, Minnesota, Mississippi, Missouri, Ohio, and Wisconsin.

5. Mapping Out a Research Plan

Poirot had a good opinion of [Inspector] Japp's abilities, though deploring his lamentable lack of method.
—*Captain Hastings*[4]

Before a search gets underway, it is advisable to map out or design a research plan. Sometimes, this is done so automatically that we are not aware of going through any particular process. For example, is the focus ancestor new to your research? Perhaps you find a parent giving consent for an underage daughter to marry, and that is the first evidence you have of this ancestor. Since weddings usually took place in the bride's county of residence, the marriage record gives you a county in which to begin a search. Often, when we identify a new ancestor, we go immediately to the nearest census record to see what we can find out. This is part of a plan.

The first plan of attack may be to find whatever you can on the person through broad survey sources before zeroing in on more specific information. This survey of such record groups as census, deed, cemetery, probate, marriage, and tax records gives you an overview of the records and perhaps of the family as well. With some survey work done, you can begin a chronology on the new ancestor and study it to determine where you want to focus a more intense search. You cannot become too specific until you have something to go on, such as name, time, or place.

If we divide the plan into general steps, it can apply to most searches.

Technique

1. Write down what you already know. (In other words, write down what is documented.)

2. Write down the research question, and do the necessary mapping according to the steps discussed above.

3. Identify sources that survey the appropriate research landscape, such as censuses, broad or statewide indexes, or compiled biographical sketches (used cautiously). These can be especially useful if you are trying to discover a state or county in which your focus ancestor may have lived. Many of these sources can also provide background information for people of the same surname or same family. Make a written list of those you want to try.

4. Identify sources that may contain the kind of information about your ancestor that you are seeking. Plan to try first the sources most likely to contain direct statements of your information, such as (1) a marriage record to give a marriage date or the bride's maiden name or (2) a will to identify a parent and children. Make a written list.

5. List any known activities or events in which the focus ancestor participated and the records they may have generated, such as (1) a military service record and/or pension application for someone in the Civil War, (2) religious records for someone active in a religious congregation, or (3) school or college records, yearbooks, and histories.

6. Write down a logical order in which to consult the sources you think will help.

7. As you research, analyze what you find, and consider what you do not find, in order to plan your next step. Part of this process is updating what you know about the person.

8. If you have not found a direct answer to your research question, identify sources or techniques that may give you what you need in an indirect way.

9. Repeat these steps as often as necessary.

The discussion that follows addresses steps three through eight individually.

PLANNING METHODICALLY

You become methodical—at last!
—*Hercule Poirot*[5]

Step 3: The Survey Approach to Records

As genealogists begin a new search, the first technique we often try is a survey approach. One great survey tool is census records. The federal and state censuses provide a broad view of the population of the pertinent geographic area. If we are lucky, the family we seek was enumerated, and we gain a sense of the household to which our focus person belonged. We become familiar with names, birth order, changes in the family between censuses, extended family, and all kinds of other information that will help us understand the family and our search for them.

Our job, of course, is to be skeptical and seek confirmation. Is this the right family? Does the entry make sense according to what we already know? After all, the censuses provide us with some fairly direct answers, some statements that contain grains of truth if we can identify them, some information from which to draw clues only, and some downright errors. Yet, they are contemporary documents, usually closer in time to the enumerated family than we are, looking at the records seventy-five to two hundred years after their creation.

Good old index. You can't beat it.
—*Sherlock Holmes*[6]

Surveys can take place also in broad indexes. If your initial search is to find anything and everything you can about a particular person, you would want to try every index available. Statewide marriage, vital record, or militia record indexes are available for a number of states. Some have compiled alphabetical records of voter registrations, taxpayers, and Civil War veterans. Records of land grants, land patents, and, in Georgia, land lotteries provide indexlike surveys. For many counties, enterprising genealogists have collected and indexed cemetery tombstone inscriptions, newspaper abstracts, and early county records. City directories are, in effect, indexes to residents. Availability varies from county to county and state to state, but hundreds of such sources exist.

At the federal level, land patents for some states have already been mentioned as large databases, searchable by name. Federal military service and/or pension indexes have been published in book form for most periods of American history, and a number of the microfilmed records are alphabetical. Thousands of federal government documents are collected and indexed in the *American State Papers* and *The Territorial Papers*. Many books have been published and indexed to help identify immigrants, including the mammoth *Passenger and Immigration Lists Index*, by P. William Filby (Detroit: Gale Research, 1981–). More and more of these kinds of records are being made available via the Internet. Many are abstracted and indexed in genealogy periodicals.

Other survey tools, such as collections of biographical sketches, encompass a comparatively small portion of the community but can provide details, usually from a member of the family. Published county and family histories, surname and society newsletters, electronic databases, and Internet networks often display family groups with vital statistics. Although often submitted by family members, they are not usually compiled by contemporaries of our sought-after ancestor but people of our time, removed sometimes by several generations. Unless the submitters provide proof of accuracy, we must not rush to accept as gospel truth what they tell us. Tempting as it is to jump for joy at "finding" several generations of ancestors in these kinds of sources, we must seek confirmation and documentation. Otherwise, we are likely to perpetuate discrepancies or inaccuracies or, even worse, spend a great deal of time working on someone else's ancestors. Without study, we may never know which information is accurate and which is not.

Once you find an ancestor in indexes, you have places and sources to investigate for more specific information. The next step would be to pursue those investigations. Books on sources in particular states, sources in general, and sources for specific topics (military, land, etc.) are available in genealogy research libraries and bookstores.

Step 4: Sources of Direct Information

Sherlock Holmes once said, "It is simpler to deal direct."[7] In genealogical research, this is certainly true. In one sense, it is much easier to answer a genealogical question with a direct statement of fact found in one reliable source than to search through many sources to piece together an answer. This kind of direct statement is available for many research questions but not for all.

Secondly, it is usually best to go directly to the original source and get whatever information it contains, even if the first survey is of abstracted or transcribed records. Unfortunately, some researchers never check out the original source. Instead, they spend their time trying to find the same information in published family histories and in networks of people who share information. The problem is that many family histories and networks have well-meaning authors and individuals who (1) share information they got from someone else and (2) do not know where the information originated or how accurate it may be. **Ultimately, the validity and accuracy of our work may be determined by our use of the original sources.**

Important

Of course, in any given case, how do you know which original source will end up being the one that has your information? Because we cannot know in advance, we use as many as we can. Sometimes, the original sources themselves are not available. In these cases, we use a copy of the original because it is the closest we can get to it. Examples of such copies are the wills, deeds, and marriage licenses in county and town record books. We like to think of them as the originals although technically they are not. They are usually the available records most contemporary with the ancestor, and we are grateful they have been preserved. Luckily, some courthouses do maintain files of original marriage licenses, probate, and other court documents.

It is the researcher's task to identify sources available for a given time and place that may contain a direct statement of the sought-after information. For example, if you are looking for a statement of a parent-child relationship, look for wills, deeds of gift, estate settlements, guardianship records, census records that state relationships, original family Bibles, baptism registers, vital registrations, marriage records, military pension applications, naturalization papers, court records, newspaper obituaries, and any other source for your ancestor's time and place that could contain your information.

Identifying "original" sources

Part of planning, therefore, is identifying what sources of this nature exist for your target location for your ancestor's time period. These ideas may help:

Idea Generator

- Read books and articles on genealogy research in the target state (or country) or books that have state-by-state coverage, such as those already mentioned in this chapter. Large genealogy libraries often have such books. If you do not have a research library nearby, write or call a public library in your target area to see what the librarians in their genealogy department recommend. Look in *Books in Print* to see what titles are current.
- If the Internet is available to you, visit computerized library catalogs to find out about books on research or histories and biographies pertaining to your focus location. Try interlibrary loan for those you would like to read, or purchase one from a bookstore or the publisher.
- Perhaps a Web site from your target state or county will identify sources specific to the area.
- Read bibliographies and footnotes in histories or biographies about the focus area.
- County and state histories, if well done, will mention essential sources or indicate sources used in the preparation of those works.
- Look for articles in history or genealogy journals that pertain to research in your county or state or deal with a subject from your area. Read their bibliographies and footnotes for ideas.
- Join a genealogical or historical society in the target location and read their publications.
- Talk to other researchers who have worked there.
- Ask the state archives or state historical society in your focus location for lists of materials they have for your county or town.

Locating sources to use

Another step is figuring out how to get your hands on such records. These ideas may work for you:

- Genealogy research libraries often have microfilm or microfiche collections of federal, county, and town records.
- Some local historical museums or university libraries have an archives section with materials pertaining to that town or county, sometimes in-

Sources

To find a Family History Center near you, see these Internet sites:

1. ‹http://www.lds.org› (select "Family History Resources," then "Family History—How Do I Begin?")
2. ‹http://www.family search.org› (select "Browse Categories," then "Libraries")

Also check your telephone directory under Church of Jesus Christ of Latter-day Saints.

cluding church records, tombstone transcriptions, or local newspapers.

- Genealogy libraries usually love gifts and may be willing to order certain items you need if someone—you or the local genealogical society—is willing to pay for them.
- Interlibrary loan may be an option, depending on where you are, where the records are, and what is available for loan. Most genealogical materials are not available on interlibrary loan, but trying does no harm. You may be pleasantly surprised. Some state libraries and historical societies lend microfilm within their own state. Newspapers are widely available on interlibrary loan through your local public library.
- Membership in the American Genealogical Lending Library [(800) 760-2455] gives you access to many microfilm and microfiche sources, and rental is relatively inexpensive.
- The Family History Library in Salt Lake City and its branches worldwide—Family History Centers—give you access to thousands of local, state, and federal records on microfilm and microfiche, and rental is relatively inexpensive.
- If you need a vacation (who doesn't?), plan a research trip to ancestral counties and the corresponding state archives or historical society.
- More and more Web sites have transcriptions and abstracts of records available for searching; some even have graphic images of the records themselves. If you find an abstract with promising information, try to get a copy of the original record.
- More and more genealogical CD-ROMs are available for purchase. In this field at this time, limited numbers of compact discs offer actual record images. Some offer indexes, but try to get those with complete coverage of the target state rather than those containing "selected" counties or records.
- If you have a specific reference, such as for a marriage record or probate file, write to the county courthouse (or other repository that owns the record) for a photocopy. With a phone call to the repository you can learn what the cost may be. A number of counties have typed transcriptions of their earliest records available for the public to see, and they keep their originals in storage or on microfilm. Specify in your request that you want a copy of the original, if at all possible. Perhaps you would feel more comfortable requesting both the original and the transcript.
- Consult books such as Emily Croom's *The Genealogist's Companion & Sourcebook* (Cincinnati: Betterway Books, 1994) to find out where certain sources may be available.

Step 5: Sources Based on Ancestral Activities

This step is based simply on what you already know about your ancestor, in other words, a chronology of the person's life. For example, if you know or think he or she owned land, then look for sources based on that ownership: deeds, tax lists, deeds of trust, deeds of gift, a will, estate settlement papers, and the like. If the ancestor was a member of an organization—civic, professional, social, religious, or fraternal—try to find membership and participation records. Such sources may give you not only information about the ancestor but names of friends and associates whose records could lead you to more information.

Step 6: A Logical Order of Research

I have an idea; let me think. Why don't you start with Leonard's Aunt Tillie?
—*Samuel Clemens* [8]

Each research plan is unique to its search. Thus, the order of research will be different for each situation. The questions and sources that make up the plan obviously cannot be tackled all at the same place at the same time.

If you need to borrow materials on interlibrary loan or rent microfilm from a lending library, it makes sense to place those orders early in your search, because it may take several weeks to get these items. Meanwhile, you could write the letters on your list, find the background histories and biographies, make the necessary phone calls, and research whatever is available to you at a local public or university library.

Another option on the "do" list may be sending queries to genealogical periodicals, family association newsletters, and newspaper columns. Many searchers post queries on the Internet looking for (1) anyone working the same surname or (2) facts about the specific ancestor. The caution with queries is to accept as fact only those replies with documented answers. Undocumented "answers" are simply clues for further searching.

In this step of planning, you may also consider a different meaning of *order*. When you form your research question (what you want to find out about your focus ancestor), think about whether it can be divided into components. For example, if you want to identify the parents of a female ancestor, you may need to break this goal down into several smaller tasks: first determining when and where she first married; second, identifying a maiden surname or several possible names; third, researching to create a list of potential relatives (siblings and/ or parents); fourth, concentrating on the best candidates and narrowing the choices to try to reach an answer. Then think about these new questions and how you might approach them. They too may be broken into more questions. These more specific questions may determine the order of your research.

Step 7: Analyze and Plan

Technique

Well, Watson, what do you make of it?
—*Sherlock Holmes* [9]

Part of the research process is thinking about what you are finding. After research comes further analysis and further planning. This important step will be discussed in more detail in chapters six and nine through eleven. However, it involves at least four elements:

1. Most genealogists go through an analysis process during every day of research. Genealogists who find new information want to take it home and admire it, show it to anybody willing to look, celebrate over it, and, whenever possible, record it on a family group sheet or chronology. The urge is akin to a child getting a new toy and wanting to take it home and play with it immediately. This exultation is the first step in analysis: If the researcher believes in the information enough to perform this ritual, the brain has already considered the source and the detail enough to assign it, at least for the moment, a passing grade in credibility.

2. An essential next step is the conscious study of newly discovered material, in which the researcher looks at each piece of data individually. In a deed record, for example, you would consider with a critical eye the names and residences of the grantee and grantor, the place and date of the instrument, the place and date of its filing with the court, the witnesses, the person drawing up the document (if given), the legal description of the land, adjoining neighbors, the considerations of the sale or transaction, the type of document, whether the people involved were able to sign their own names or needed to make their mark, whether one of the parties was represented by an attorney, and any other details given. Any piece of raw data within the document may be important evidence. Any piece of raw data may be reliable or unreliable, may be firsthand knowledge or hearsay, or may be copied correctly or incorrectly into the record.

   An analysis of the total document or a decision on what it may mean within the total research picture may have to wait for more information, or it may need reflection or mulling over. As Hercule Poirot once told a young detective, "For the moment, that is the best I can do for you, *mon cher*. Reflect upon it."[10]

3. After looking closely at each piece of data, the researcher passes judgment on its quality and validity. If it is considered valid and useful as it stands, it can be entered into the chronology of the focus ancestor, and it becomes a piece of the puzzle that fits. Or it becomes part of a growing database of facts and clues, along with its documentation. (See chapter four.)

4. The researcher then reviews the focus research question. Has it been answered? If so, what is the next question to answer? If the new material adds to the evidence but does not complete a satisfactory answer, what is the next source to try? If the new material creates a contradiction in evidence, what source(s) may help resolve the conflict?

Step 8: Finding Answers Indirectly

I have done that, Mr. Holmes. No replies.
—*Dr. Watson*[11]

At some point in your search, you will try many of the standard sources without finding a direct answer to your focus question, whether it is a date, place, name, or relationship. It happens to every genealogist in every line. Maybe you have found clues to your answer but not a satisfactory level of proof. Maybe you have found no clues at all. Regardless, an answer may still be possible. You may be able to find a direct answer after all, just not in the place or through the sources that you might expect. You may be able to find enough pieces of strong evidence that you can reach a conclusion or a solution.

The answer may lie not in different sources but in new approaches and techniques. Often, no additional sources are readily available to search. However, you may have to look again at sources you have already used, but from a different point of view or in more depth. Continue your research in original records or the nearest you can find to the original. Then correlate what you find in census, land, marriage, probate, tax, court, church, military, and other records. Look for patterns and connections.

Research Tip

Every case is different, so each will proceed in its own way. However, many of the same principles and techniques work for different cases. It is a matter of trying combinations of ideas until something shows promise. Chapters three, seven, and nine through eleven contain examples of genealogy studies for which direct answers were not being found. Questions such as the ones below helped in planning other ways to find answers. Consider such questions as these as you plan your next strategy:

1. Have you listed everything you know about the focus ancestor? Have you updated your chronology on this ancestor? Have you done further research on any of the events or facts on the "known" list? Have you continued research in any of the sources that gave you the known events? Have you documented fully the known information so that you know it is correct for the right person? Are there any discrepancies in what is known? (If there are, these would be avenues for new research.) Have you found any information in reliable records that conflicts with what you believe to be true?

2. Have you looked critically at data you have already collected? Where are the clues? Even documents that do not give direct answers may have valuable leads. Look separately at every tidbit—every name, date, place, and other detail—in every record. Is it new? Is it a clue?

3. Have you found no clues? The lack of evidence may itself be a clue. Maybe you have the wrong time period or the wrong place. Maybe the ancestor was elsewhere.

4. Are you using the known to move toward the unknown? Are you trying to skip back in time too soon without researching the in-between years?

5. Are you researching thoroughly in land, court, and tax records for the known time and place? In this way, you can look for evidence of the focus ancestor's presence in a place. That presence may be evidenced when the ancestor is named as an adjoining landowner, witnesses a document, serves on a jury, or is taken to task for serving spirits on the Sabbath.

6. Have you read and studied all existing census records for your focus ancestor and other known or supposed relatives of that person? Have you recorded and studied census neighbors of your focus ancestor?

7. Have you researched your focus ancestor's known siblings and/or children thoroughly?

8. If searching for a woman's identity, have you researched her husband and children thoroughly? If searching for a man's identity, have you researched his wife and children thoroughly?

9. Have you researched people of the same surname in the same area as your focus ancestor? Who are the other people involved as friends, neighbors, and associates with your known ancestral family? Studying them is often critical to your search.

10. Have you studied the in-laws, if they are known?

11. Could the ancestor have changed names or used an alias? Could a woman have remarried or reverted to using her maiden name?

12. Have you tried every source available for the places in which you know the ancestor lived?

13. Have you tried records in surrounding counties? In a neighboring state?

14. Have you read regional histories to learn about patterns of migration? Could the sought-after ancestor have moved back to an earlier residence, into newly opened territory, or to another location to find land or work?

15. Have you tried state and federal records, especially if the county or town records have been lost or severely damaged? Consult books and articles about state and federal archives' holdings.

16. Have you requested photocopies of records you have seen in abstracts?

17. Have you looked into any family traditions that could change the direction of your search?

18. Have you consulted others in the family who are also researching, even distant cousins?

19. Have you tried looking at the problem from a different perspective?

20. Have you tried finding anything you can?

Find out anything you can; we don't know what'll be useful.
—*Samuel Clemens*[12]

Printed Source

To learn how other genealogists have applied questions such as these to tough research questions, read case studies in the major genealogical journals, such as the *National Genealogical Society Quarterly* (called the *NGSQ*), the *New York Genealogical and Biographical Record* (called *The Record*), *The American Genealogist* (called *TAG*), *The New England Historical and Genealogical Register* (called *The Register*), and *The Virginia Genealogist*. The following are only a handful of the dozens of case studies that appear in these journals and give genealogists good ideas:

Lenzen, Connie. "Proving a Maternal Line: The Case of Frances B. Whitney." *National Genealogical Society Quarterly* 82 (March 1994): 17–31.

McClure, Paul. "Mary (Harrison?) (Jones) Hawkins of Bath County, Kentucky: Non-Conformity and Survival in a Frontier Community." *The American Genealogist* 72 (July 1997): 369–379.

Mills, Elizabeth Shown. "The Search for Margaret Ball: Building Steps over a Brick-wall Research Problem." *National Genealogical Society Quarterly* 77 (March 1989): 43–65.

Rising, Marsha Hoffman. "Problematic Parents and Potential Offspring: The Example of Nathan Brown." *National Genealogical Society Quarterly* 79 (June 1991): 85–99.

Sullivan, Steven Edward. "Abigail[3] Snow, Probable Wife of Daniel[3] Small of Truro and Provincetown, Massachusetts." *The American Genealogist* 71 (July 1996): 137–144.

In addition, case studies can be found in some genealogy books, including the following:

Carmack, Sharon DeBartolo. *A Genealogist's Guide to Discovering Your Female Ancestors.* Cincinnati: Betterway Books, 1998.

Cerny, Johni, and Arlene Eakle. *Ancestry's Guide to Research: Case Studies in American Genealogy.* Salt Lake City: Ancestry, 1985.

Jacobus, Donald Lines. *Genealogy as Pastime and Profession.* 2nd ed. revised. Baltimore: Genealogical Publishing Co., 1968.

Stratton, Eugene A. *Applied Genealogy.* [Salt Lake City]: Ancestry, 1988.

Better yet, maybe we can figure out who the real murderer is. I'm not sure how we're going to do either one of those things, though.

—*Samuel Clemens*[13]

The genealogical application of Clemens's quandary is this: Maybe we *can* figure out who the real ancestor is, but we're not sure how. **Often the key to success involves one or more of the following:**

Research Tip

1. Narrow the focus to more specific questions, perhaps closer in time to you.

2. Grit your teeth and read page by page through land records (county, state, federal), censuses, court records, tax records, and the like for the known time and place. Besides possibly showing evidence of the presence of the ancestor, these records may also establish and add to your knowledge of potential relatives and neighbors.

3. Develop a list of names of the people associated with your ancestor with a goal of working on them. (See chapter three.)

4. Consider hiring a competent researcher on location to look at records to which you may not have access.

5. Share your research problem with another competent researcher. Two or more minds thinking about a problem can often generate more ideas than one thinking alone.

TALKING ABOUT THE PROBLEM

Tell me your problem.

—*Hercule Poirot*[14]

Sometimes, research ideas and plans come to us more readily when we talk about the problem aloud. My cats were wonderful listeners. And, yes, we genealogists often talk to ourselves. If this makes you uncomfortable, try talking with another genealogist before cornering a nongenealogist spouse, friend, or relative. It's often easier that way.

In the conversation, spell out your goal: What are you trying to find and how will it help your overall project? Summarize what you already know and why you believe it is correct information. Maybe explain what you suspect is true but cannot yet prove: Why do you believe it is true? Where did you find it? Maybe your consultants can suggest a different goal or direction. Go over the questions you have asked yourself so far in planning. Ask your listeners, Does this make sense? Do you think I'm on the right track?

If they have other suggestions or have tried something that worked for them in a similar situation, they'll tell you. If you think you will want their opinion again, consider their suggestions graciously and thoughtfully. If you give them all the reasons why you cannot do what they suggest or why "it won't work," they may not be so willing to consult the next time.

I am immensely obliged to you. You have presented me with an idea. How strange it is the way ideas arrive into one's head.

—*Hercule Poirot* [15]

Once you have reviewed what you know, what you want to find, and ways you want to approach the search for an answer, write out a plan. It can be as comprehensive as you choose to make it, but it needs to guide you through the next research effort. After one really good day of researching, you may need to revise the plan in light of what you have found. On the other hand, the plan may last you a period of time as you gather bits and pieces, as in the example below.

EXAMPLE OF A WRITTEN PLAN

Case Study

Research problem: Proving the parents of Caleb Bennett
What is known about Caleb Bennett?

1. Born about 1812–1815, Georgia (from 1850 census, Natchitoches Parish, LA, p. 15, family 240, household of *Calep* and Ellen Bennett, age 38 and 23, respectively; 1860 census, Natchitoches Parish, p. 486, household of *Coley* and Ellen Bennett, age 45 and 32).

2. Married 18 August 1843 in Talbot County, GA, to Harriet E. Hutson [*sic*] (Talbot County Marriage Book A:200, FHL film 0249366).

3. First child Arthur/Arta Bennett, born about 1844–1845, GA. Although the 1860 census (cited above) lists all the children born in LA, the 1850 census (cited above) lists this child born in GA; the second child, Arnold, born in AL, 1845–46; and the third, Ruthe Ann, born in LA, 1848–49.

4. Moved to Louisiana by 1848–49, coming through Alabama (figured from birth dates and birthplaces of children in 1850 and 1860 censuses, cited above).

5. In 1850 census, as *Calep*, living next to Edmund and Mary Bennett, both born in GA, ages 64 and 53, respectively. With Edmund and Mary: William,

Martha, Lucinda, Arta, Bryant, ranging in age from 17 to 7 (1850 census, Natchitoches Parish, LA, p. 15, family 239). First clue to possible parentage of Caleb.

6. Died September 1864, Natchitoches Parish, LA; widow [Harriett] Ellender Hudson (consistently Hudson in this and Natchitoches deed records seen so far); Bryan [*sic*] Bennett appointed undertutor to minors, 3 Jan 1867 [see Edmund Bennett household, 1850]; living minor children: Andrew, Allen, Armstrong, Adam, Matilda Ann, Pamelia Ann; daughter Ruth Ann had married John Bennett, named as brother-in-law of the minors at family meeting; Arthur Bennett present at family meeting [Was this Caleb's Arthur or Edmund's Arthur?]. (Natchitoches Parish, LA, Succession file #1463, first dated 17 Dec 1866, Courthouse, Natchitoches; marriage of Ruth Ann Bennett and John Bennett, 25 Jan 1866, Natchitoches Parish Marriage Book 3:28, Courthouse, Natchitoches).

7. At his death, owned land, 215.78 [*sic*] acres, Natchitoches Parish: W1/2 of SW1/4 S30 + NW1/4 of NW1/4 S31 both in T6 R5, two tracts totaling 109.09 acres, + SW1/4 of NW1/4 and N1/2 of SW1/4, both in S31 T6 R5, totaling 105.87 acres. These tracts add up to 214.96 acres. (Succession file #1463, cited above)

Hypothesis and challenge: Edmund Bennett may be Caleb's father. Look for proof. Keep eyes and mind open to other possibilities.

Research plan—first phase:

1. Check 1840, 1830, 1820 censuses to see if Edmund Bennett's household includes a person of Caleb's age; Georgia is the obvious place to try first.

    Technique

    a. In 1840 census, Talbot County, GA, p. 228, Edmond [*sic*] Bennett household shows no male of Caleb's age (25–28); no other Bennett household in the county. Caleb not indexed under his own name as head of a household.

    b. In 1830 census, Talbot County, GA, p. 343, Edmund Bennett household shows no male of Caleb's age (15–18). However, in same county, p. 325, Jeremiah Bennett household shows three males 15–20.

    c. In 1820 census, Walton County, GA, p. 522, Edmond [*sic*] Bennett household shows 2 girls under 10 and 1 male under 10. Caleb would be 5–8. This is positive evidence.

2. Look for records for Edmund and Mary in known counties. Can records be found of Edmund and Caleb acting together in any way? Results:

    a. No succession record found for Edmund or Mary in Natchitoches Parish (searched at courthouse).

    b. Neither was found in 1860 census; no cemetery record found yet (Natchitoches Genealogical and Historical Association Library, Old Courthouse, cemetery files).

    c. Louisiana land records are inconclusive, could be this Edmund and/or another of same name. Needs more research and study.

    d. Georgia land lottery of 1820 shows Edmund Bennett of Walton County had 2 winning draws, in S. Emmett Lucas, Jr., comp., *The Third or 1820 Land Lottery of Georgia* (Easley, SC: Southern Historical Press, 1986), 24. Needs more research and study.

e. Edmund and Calep [sic] Bennett, signers of petition from citizens of Marion County, GA (next to Talbot County), to governor of Georgia, not dated, but based on Gov. William Schley's term, petition written between Nov. 1835 and 1837, in Donna B. Thaxton, ed., *Georgia Indian Depredation Claims* (Americus, GA: Thaxton Co., 1988), 589–590, document #207. Ongoing study of other signers for possible connections with Bennetts.

f. Walton County, GA, tax digest, 1819 (FHL film 0159188) shows Edmond [sic] Bennett in Capt. Sentell's district, with no slaves and no owned land; Jeremiah *Barnett* also in county (see research notes). Edmund and Jeremiah not shown after 1819. Check Jackson County tax digests. (Jeremiah of interest because of census record above, 1830.)

g. Search is ongoing in land and court records.

3. Get Louisiana land entry files for Edmund and Caleb and study. Results: received, plotted on grid for study. Is this the elder Edmund, a relative by the same name, or someone else?

4. From General Land Office automated records on CD-ROM, identify neighbors of Caleb and Edmund. In progress.

5. Study Edmund's known children, Caleb's children, and descendants for clues: naming patterns, tombstones, censuses, marriages, etc.

6. Try to identify Edmund's children, other than William, Martha, Lucinda, Arta, and Bryant in his household in 1850 census. Results: (a) No other Bennett marriages found in Talbot County, GA, before Edmund moved to Louisiana. (b) Marriages for these five not yet found. (c) Search is ongoing.

7. Study Talbot County, GA, records for Edmund and Caleb, especially acting together: land, court, etc. Tax digests not available before 1850: not in FHL catalog, not on microfilm list in Robert Scott Davis, Jr., comp., *Research in Georgia* (Greenville, SC: Southern Historical Press, 1981), 178.

8. Don't forget Alabama as a potential research field because of the child reportedly born there, but try the known Georgia and Louisiana, first.

The plot thickens.
—*Sherlock Holmes*[16]

Part II: Questioning As a Tool of Planning

CATEGORIZING SEARCH QUESTIONS

Put your questions in categorical order and I will answer them.
—*Lady Detective Loveday Brooke*[17]

The lists of questions in this section can help plan research for basic genealogical problems: birth, marriage, and death dates and places and finding parents' names. If you use each group of questions as a checklist, adding to it as necessary, you can see what you have done and what remains to be done. As several questions are answered, others will logically form the next step.

Part of planning is thinking about different facets of an ancestor's life that may lead you to documents and records. Below are six categories of such activities and phases of life. If you think about these categories in relation to your focus ancestor, you can generate additional questions specific to your search.

Idea Generator

1. **Family records and traditions:** family Bibles, letters, diaries, journals, memoirs, scrapbooks, photo albums, driver's licenses, membership cards and certificates, passports, other family keepsakes, oral traditions and family stories.

2. **Activities in the ancestor's life** that could have generated records: religious and fraternal membership, education, employment, political office or voting, occupation, biographical sketch in a county or professional book, newspaper articles, obituary, military service, pension, immigration, naturalization, the need for a passport, bankruptcy, cemetery burial.

3. **Public records** available during that ancestor's lifetime: federal and state censuses, tax rolls, voter registrations, vital registrations, court and probate records, school records, military records, deeds and land patents, contemporary maps and plats, petitions, town records, other federal, state, or territorial records.

4. **Historical events** that could have affected the ancestor's life and records: war, Indian treaties, the Homestead Act, opening of new lands, promotions for settlement in new areas, economic depression, epidemics, storms.

5. **The ancestor's siblings** and their lives, records, and descendants. (See chapter three.)

6. **The ancestor's neighbors and associates** who could have generated records in which the ancestor is mentioned or involved. These people could also be relatives. (See chapter three.)

A REFERENCE SECTION

He that questioneth much shall learn much.

—*Francis Bacon*[18]

In beginning a particular search, genealogists try different approaches, or a combination of several. Many rush out to find whatever they can before focusing on a specific issue. This approach can be useful if the researchers have little on which to base a focused search. However, it is easy to amass material without making significant progress if the search goes very long without a specific focus.

Other researchers operate by checking off sources as they work through lists of dozens of types of records. The lists are beneficial in reminding searchers of what records may exist, but obviously not everything on such a list will be pertinent or available for the time and place of the focus ancestor.

Still others plan by asking themselves questions to generate ideas for the search. For example: What am I looking for? What is the most direct way of trying to find it? If that does not provide an answer, what is another way of addressing the question? What is a different way of asking the question? Planning through questioning is one way to stimulate the imagination for the search.

The groups of questions listed below are suggestions for those who want to try this approach. The answers may help you determine specific sources to try. Ask any questions about your search that come to mind. Some of the questions suggested below will be pertinent to your search and some will not. In any given situation, some sources will be available and some will not. The kinds of sources that may be helpful can differ depending on whether the family lived in an urban or rural area. The point is to begin to identify sources that may help you plan a particular search.

Some of the questions below are applicable to eighteenth- and early-nineteenth-century ancestors as well as more recent ones. Of course, those for earlier ancestors will differ in specifics (Social Security, World War I, etc.) from a twentieth-century search. Any set of questions will depend on time and place and the circumstances of the family. Regardless of the time period involved, the researcher needs to think about these questions. The focus is the same: to identify ancestral events and the records they may have generated.

Each section below focuses on finding one kind of genealogical answer: birth date or place, marriage data, death date or place, and parents. Some of the questions are repetitious because they can be asked in more than one kind of search. Use this part of the chapter for reference as needed.

Notes

Looking for a Birthplace

For example, consider a typical genealogical problem: Where was Great-Grandpa born? Say you have a firm birth date of 1888 from family Bible, cemetery, and death records, but no specific birthplace, other than the United States. The three sources just mentioned are sometimes sources of birthplace information. What others may give you a *direct answer* about his birthplace? What others may *suggest* a birthplace? Ask yourself such questions as these and write down the ones that seem pertinent to your problem. The first set deals with general sources that often contain birthplace information or clues.

General sources

1. Is there a family tradition about his birthplace? Which descendants have you not yet asked?
2. Are there living family members who knew Great-Grandpa? Would they know his birthplace?
3. Do his federal census entries agree on a state where he was born? Do they give several birthplaces?
4. When did his state(s) of residence begin registering births?
5. Did he file a delayed (or probate) birth certificate?
6. Are state censuses available for his state(s) of residence? Do they give his birthplace?
7. Are there family letters or diaries that may refer to his birthplace?
8. Did Great-Grandpa ever have a passport? Does the family still have it?
9. Did a newspaper or fraternal obituary name his birthplace?
10. Do you have Great-Grandpa's parents' names? Where were they in the

1880 and 1900 federal censuses? (Remember, this great-grandpa was born between the censuses, in 1888.)

11. Can you find evidence that the family was in the same place in 1888 as they were for the 1880 or 1900 federal census? (Tax rolls, city directories, etc.)

12. Is there a published biographical sketch of him, a sibling, or one of his children that could help?

13. Did his marriage record give any birthplace information? (Some do.)

Activities and events that create sources

A second line of questioning is to ask about Great-Grandpa's activities. If you can identify events such as military service or membership in an organization, you may find documents that contain your missing information. Even if you do not find a direct statement of the birthplace, you may find clues to use in determining an answer. Participation in any of the following may have generated documents that give or suggest his birthplace.

1. Was Great-Grandpa in World War I? Do you have a copy of his discharge paper? Is it on file in his county courthouse? If you do not have his military record, contact the National Personnel Records Center in St. Louis to determine whether the record exists. Most were lost by fire in 1973.

2. Did he apply for a military pension? (If so, you will want a copy of the application.) Earlier ancestors may also have service or pension records.

3. Did he register for the World War I draft? (You will want a copy of the draft registration card. These have been microfilmed, but copies may also be requested from the East Point, Georgia, branch of the National Archives.)

4. Did he have a Social Security number? (If so, you will want a copy of the Social Security application.)

5. Did he ever attend a college? College records may have birth or residential information.

6. Was he a member of a religious congregation? Some church records show birthplace.

7. Was he a member of a labor union or professional organization?

8. Did he belong to a fraternal organization, such as the Masons?

9. Did he belong to an organization such as Rotary International?

10. Did he have an employer whose records may still exist?

11. Did he have an insurance policy that might give a clue?

12. Was he ever a resident of an institution that may have asked for that information as part of his records or admission to the facility (nursing home, soldiers' home, convalescent home, prison, mental hospital, etc.)?

Sources for a broader search

A third direction of questioning is to broaden your approach and look for clues by studying other family members or Great-Grandpa's friends. This step is especially important when the other two approaches have not yielded information, but it can be conducted concurrently with them. (See chapter three.)

1. Did Great-Grandpa have siblings whose death certificates might show

where they were born? Studying these might narrow the choices for Great-Grandpa's birthplace.

2. Do descendants of his siblings have family Bibles or obituaries with birthplace or family residence information?

3. Do they have a family tradition of birthplaces for Great-Grandpa's generation?

4. Do Great-Grandpa's children have birth or death certificates that would give clues to his birthplace? Depending on the dates, these may be available only through the family.

5. Where did Great-Grandpa and Great-Grandma marry? Could he have been born there or nearby?

6. Where were Great-Grandpa's close friends or military buddies born? If you can identify birthplaces for them, they may lead you to Great-Grandpa's place of origin.

7. Would a query in a genealogical journal or Internet site help locate someone else researching the same family?

8. Would a computer database give a clue? Remember, until this information can be checked and documented, it must remain a clue and not an answer.

9. In the census years near Great-Grandpa's birth or coming of age, where were other people by his surname living? (Indexes can help, especially if Great-Grandpa had a less common surname.)

Finding anything you can

A fourth option, especially if the first three have not given you an answer, is to study anything you can find on Great-Grandpa in places where you know or think he lived. Other records sometimes give clues. Try such questions as these:

1. Did Great-Grandpa own land? When and how did he get it? Do these records give a previous residence? Sometimes they do.

2. Did Great-Grandpa own land in any prior residence?

3. Was Great-Grandpa ever a party to a lawsuit? Could this provide a clue?

4. Are there land, tax, or probate records for Great-Grandpa's father or grandfather, if they are identified? Create a chronology for them. Where were they when Great-Grandpa was born?

5. Is there a chance that Great-Grandpa was not born in the United States after all?

If the target question is Great-Grandma's birthplace, a similar approach would be in order. However, females generally do not appear in the public records as frequently as most males. Family sources would still be very important because Great-Grandma did not register for the draft, may not have served in the military, may not have worked outside the home, may not have had a Social Security number, and may not have owned land in her own name. In this case, local history sources, newspapers, organizations, religious and educational records and the like may reveal information about Great-Grandma.

Looking for a Birth Date

If the research dilemma is a birth date, the questions would be similar to those for birthplace. In addition, because certain activities required that an ancestor be of a certain age, the researcher would want to ask about tax records, voting records, or jury service to help narrow the possibilities. These sources would apply to few women before 1920.

1. When is the first appearance of the focus person on a tax roll? (Before the Civil War, this applies mostly to free men and widows.)
2. Can evidence be found of the person serving on a jury? (Suggests a person of "lawful age.")
3. Can the focus ancestor be found witnessing a record (deed, will, etc.)? For that time and place, was there a "lawful age" requirement for witnesses? If so, what was it?
4. Are school or college records available to suggest the person's age at a given time?
5. What records created at the person's death may suggest birth information? Do they agree?
6. Does the family have any early voter registration cards or receipts? Does the county have voter registration records?
7. When was the person married? When was the first child born? Back up twenty to twenty-five years for a rough estimate of a parent's birth date.

Even if the ancestor was not born in the United States, the searcher can ask questions to begin the search. In addition to the items suggested above, the queries would include the ancestor's immigration and naturalization.

Looking for Death Date or Death Place

If the target information is death date or death place, questions similar to the birth questions would be in order. Additional questions relating to death dates could include the following:

1. Is there a tombstone, cemetery record, funeral program, obituary, death certificate, family Bible, or other standard source of death information available for this person?
2. When was the last appearance of the person on the county tax rolls (may signify moving, death, exemption, or other reason for not appearing)?
3. What was the last evidence of the person serving on a jury (in other words, evidence of the person being alive)?
4. What was the last evidence of the person conducting any kind of business in the community?
5. What was the last evidence of the person witnessing a record (deed, will, etc.)?
6. What was the last evidence of the person in family letters or photographs?
7. If the person lived in an urban area, are city directories or telephone directories available to search? When was the last appearance of the person in a directory? Did the last appearance suggest death or moving?

Looking for Marriage Date or Place

What if the missing information is marriage date or place? The possibilities again would include both public and family sources. Preliminary questions could include the following:

1. Is there an official county or town marriage record?
2. Is there a religious marriage record?
3. Is there a family Bible that contains a marriage entry for them? Ask cousins and distant cousins.
4. Do family papers or scrapbooks contain memorabilia of the wedding?
5. Is there a newspaper notice or clipping of the marriage?
6. Is there a family tradition about the wedding, the ages of bride and groom when they married, where they married, or something that happened at the wedding?
7. Does the family still own any items they received as wedding gifts? Could these help narrow down a period or place?
8. Do obituaries of them or their children mention their marriage?
9. Do published biographical sketches of the couple or their children mention their marriage?
10. If either belonged to a religious, social, or fraternal organization, would a publication of the organization mention their marriage? (Some do.)
11. If they married before 1900, does the 1900 or 1910 federal census reveal how many years they had been married?
12. Does the 1850, 1860, 1870, or 1880 (or 1890, for the lucky few) federal census indicate that they married within the census year?
13. Do state censuses exist for their residence? What is the first one in which the couple appears? Do the state censuses give marriage information?
14. Does a tombstone give the marriage date? Occasionally, one does.

If no direct statement of their marriage can be found, the researcher has to consider other approaches. Look for any other information that can narrow down a range of dates or places.

1. When and where was their first child born? The marriage date might be estimated from that information.
2. When and where was the husband born? the wife?
3. For their time and region, what was the normal age range for men or women to marry?
4. Is there evidence that either had been married before? Can a record be found?
5. Is there evidence that either married again later? Can a record be found?
6. Is there evidence of them as a married couple in a deed record? a probate record? a court record? What is the earliest such evidence?
7. Do you have the wife's maiden name? Do you know her parents' names? Is there a probate record or deed record for her parent(s) that indicates she was already married?
8. Is there a deed of gift from a parent to suggest coming of age or marriage?
9. Is there a prenuptial agreement in the county deed records?

Looking for Parents

All genealogists are eager to reach back and find the previous generation. Ultimately, each search leads to this inquiry. As in any other part of the search, the questioning and planning here depend on what is already known. The first questions must be "What do I *know* about the parents?" and "What *clues* do I have to their identity?" Then consider such questions as these:

1. Have you identified your focus ancestor's siblings and any stepsiblings, their birth dates and places, their marriage dates and places? Do you have birth and death certificates for them? Identification and location of an ancestor's siblings is important in trying to identify the parents.
2. Have you studied the siblings in depth?
3. If siblings are not identified, do you know where the family lived at any time when the children were growing up?
4. Do you know the name of either parent?
5. Do you have family traditions or clues from research about their identity or their origin, about their death dates or places?
6. Do you have a "suspect" parent or couple already identified through research?
7. Do you know or suspect the birthplaces of the parents from census or other records?
8. What is the time frame for their birth dates? Can you estimate from the birth dates of their known children? (Average about twenty to twenty-four years before the first child for the mother, about twenty-two to twenty-five years before the first child for the father.)
9. Do you know anything else about the parents, such as siblings, occupation, religious affiliation?
10. Have you studied the history and people of the ancestor's place(s) of residence?

Once you establish the known facts or the possibilities, you plan from there to identify the sources that could help in the search. Sometimes the parents emerge as a couple. In other cases, you find one parent and study that one to help find the other. There are some basic questions to address first.

Looking for a male ancestor's parents

Consider a search for a male ancestor's parents. First, list in a chronological profile what you already know and what you believe are possibilities. Clearly distinguish between known, probable, and possible facts. What questions then emerge to begin planning for the search?

1. Have you found the known ancestor in a census (1850 and after) as a child living with adults who may be his parents?
2. If applicable, have you found him in all censuses (state or federal) available after 1850?
3. Did he serve in the military? Did he receive a pension? Perhaps the answer lies in his service record or pension application.
4. Did he register for the World War I draft before he married? (If so, you

will want to see the microfilm records or get a copy of the registration card from the East Point, Georgia, branch of the National Archives.)

5. Does anyone living near him as a young adult have the same surname? Consider census, tax, court, and land records to help identify possibilities.

6. Do neighbors (found in census records) have the same birthplace or birthplace patterns within their family that your ancestor has in his? Could these neighbors be relatives, such as married sisters or cousins?

7. Does anyone in his county or in adjacent counties have the same surname?

8. Do probate records in his or neighboring counties identify groups of heirs of his surname?

9. Does any probate record identify him or someone with the same name as an heir or orphan?

10. Do you know a prior county of residence or a birthplace for him? Can you identify "suspect" parents in that county?

11. Are there deed, mortgage, or deed of trust records for him and others of his surname in his county? These documents sometimes contain valuable parent-child facts or clues.

12. As you address these and other questions, read chapters three and nine through eleven.

Looking for a female ancestor's parents

What about the search for a female ancestor's parents? If you have her maiden name, the questions will be much the same as those for the male ancestor's parents; you will be identifying people of that surname with whom your ancestor had contact. If you do not know her maiden name, that may be the first thing to try to uncover. After listing the known facts and the possibilities about the parents, consider the following:

1. Can you find a birth, baptism, marriage, or death record for this female ancestor (to identify maiden name and/or parents' names)?

2. As a bride, was she of age or underage? Underage brides often needed parental consent to marry; this permission often is part of the record.

3. Was she perhaps married previously? (That marriage record may help identify her maiden name.)

4. Do any of her marriage records contain the names of sureties or witnesses? (Sometimes they are relatives.)

5. Can you tell from census or other records whether she had children by a previous marriage? (Studying their records may lead to her parents.)

6. Have you identified any siblings for this female ancestor? (Studying them may lead to her parents.)

7. Did she live in Louisiana? (Parish records often include the female's maiden name.)

8. Are there deed records and/or court records that show or suggest an inheritance of property? For example, did she or her husband or her children appear in a group of people selling land? The groups were often joint heirs.

9. In census records, especially 1880 and after, can you identify neighbors

with the same or similar birthplace patterns or naming patterns? (Married siblings sometimes lived near each other, as did parents and their married children.)

10. Was there a couple or individual of the right age to be her parent(s) living near when she was young and married? (If so, study them.)

11. In census records of 1850 and after, was someone of a different surname living with her and her family? In the 1840 census, was an older military pensioner named in the household? Could this surname be a clue to her maiden name? Could this be her sibling, cousin, parent, or other relative? (Just because you have never heard of the other person does not mean they are not related.)

12. Was there a prenuptial agreement between her and her husband? (It may give maiden name and possible clues about her parents.)

13. Could she have named a child after one of her parents or grandparents? Could one of her children have named a child after one of her parents?

14. Could probate records (wills, settlements, guardianships, annual returns, etc.) in the county, through a page-by-page search, reveal her as an heir of a parent?

15. Could her husband have had business or disagreements with any of her relatives? Study the husband and his associates thoroughly. Study witnesses to his transactions.

16. Read chapters three, ten, and eleven.

Each search is unique, but many successes have come through working on questions such as these. Make a list of those which you think may be pertinent to your search. You may add or subtract questions as you proceed. Think about an order in which to address the questions. Before the research actually begins, we need to consider another aspect of planning, cluster genealogy, in chapter three.

Now, it seems to me that you're in a good position to find out things I need to know. You might even be able to make the opportunity to speak with certain key people: . . . their friends and business associates, possibly even the victim's relatives.

—*Samuel Clemens*[19]

THREE

Broadening the Scope: Cluster Genealogy

[T]he lives of all of us are very subtly and intricately interwoven.

—*Miss Phipps*[1]

Notes

Endnotes for this chapter begin on page 252.

Cluster genealogy is the idea that ancestors did not live in a vacuum but in a cluster of relatives, neighbors, friends, and associates. Studying the history of one person naturally puts the researcher in contact with members of this group, as witnesses to each other's documents, as neighbors, as in-laws, as fraternal brothers and sisters, as business partners or clients, and so forth. Our ancestors often migrated in family groups, as church congregations, or as a group of neighbors. They often lived very close to other family members. They worshipped with, went to war with, bought land from, and were buried near friends and relatives. Although we may not know the names of this group when we begin researching a focus ancestor, we must train ourselves to look for its members.

Some researchers call this the "whole family" approach or the "big picture" approach. Regardless of name, the principle is the same: We cannot have long-term success if we limit ourselves to a one-name–one-person approach.

When research begins on a focus ancestor, the genealogist may know nothing more than the ancestor's name, with perhaps a date and place of marriage or an entry on a census record. If applicable, after 1850, the next effort is often to find that person in the context of a family in other census records. Then we move to other basic sources—such as vital records, wills and probate files, family Bibles, church records, and newspaper obituaries—to find names, dates, places, and relationships in the life of the target ancestor. We branch out into land records, military and pension files, naturalization documents, and other sources that sometimes identify the spouse, children, birth and death information, or parents.

We compile at least two family group sheets from this information: one with the focus ancestor as a parent in a family, the other with the ancestor as a child.

These two nuclear families are the beginning of, and an important part of, the ancestor's cluster. Sometimes these charts are all we need to move back in time to the parent and grandparent generations.

When we cannot find direct statements of the events, names, dates, places, and relationships we need for our focus ancestor, we search for clues and evidence wherever we can find them to get the answers indirectly. The cluster is often the path toward these clues. Some clusters provide more help than others, and some are easier to identify than others. However, one thing is certain. A researcher has a much greater chance of success when studying the cluster than when clinging to one name as the sole subject of the research. The progress report in chapter seven and the case studies in chapters ten and eleven are examples of the use of cluster genealogy to find answers.

WHY THE CLUSTER?

[I]t would help me solve the case if I can talk to the people he was close to: his family, his close friends, maybe his business partners, if he had any.

—*Samuel Clemens*[2]

Why is the cluster approach necessary? For those who have never tried this approach or have not yet needed it to build pedigree charts, some convincing is often in order. Mostly, we use the cluster approach because we want solutions. As in mystery stories, the family and close associates may hold the key to the answer. True, some of the people you will research with this approach may not be related to you. However, if you stick stubbornly to a one-name-only approach, you may end up claiming as ancestors people not related to you.

Consider these reasons for the cluster approach:

1. In family papers and oral traditions, each child may remember or record different facts about a parent; we put the facts together to get a more complete picture.

2. For some ancestors, answers are simply not found in documents they themselves created. If Major Grace sells his land to Stark Brown, he may not mention that he inherited his land from his father. However, when Stark Brown sells the same land to Pleasant Luster, the deed may name Major's father as the original patentee of the land.

3. Some ancestors left few records themselves; the only way to learn about them is through records that others created. One Mississippi man "disappeared" for a few years from his researcher; then, in someone else's diary, she found that he had gone to California during the gold rush. Ancestors who owned no land, for instance, will not usually appear in the deed books, except maybe as witnesses to others' transactions. Why were they asked to be a witness? Maybe the seller was a brother-in-law, a cousin, or the nearest neighbor. Yet the other person's transaction places the ances-

Technique

tor in that place at that time, alive. That one piece of information is sometimes very important.

4. When several people by the same name lived in the same county at the same time, their nuclear families and close associates are sometimes the keys to sorting them out. We want to find the right elusive ancestor, not just anybody by the same name.

WHO IS THE CLUSTER?

> Who's *they?* Was it family, businesspeople, old friends? . . . [T]his could be important.
>
> —*Samuel Clemens*[3]

When you run into that old brick wall in your search, what are your options? Give up on that line and go to one likely to have more information readily available? Get on the Internet with query after query: "I need the parents, grandparents, wife's maiden name, birth date and birthplace, and names of in-laws of Donald Doe of Whatever County, Iowa. I've looked everywhere, and all I can find is that he came to Iowa as a young man just after the Civil War. Will share information"?

A query such as this says several things: (1) The descendant may have little or nothing of substance to share in return, (2) the descendant probably has *not* looked everywhere, and (3) the descendant may not have a clue of what to try next. That is not an uncommon predicament for researchers at some point along the way. What about the option of researching for the next of kin?

The would-be researcher in the query needs to list everything known about the ancestor and make a research plan. This time, it is cluster time. The disclaimer is that some searches do come to a real dead end before you are ready, but the good news is that many tough searches can be solved. The successful ones often involve the cluster. The cluster includes the next of kin, extended family, neighbors, friends, associates, and other people of the same surname.

NEXT OF KIN

> And who is Great-Uncle Joseph? . . . What did he die of?[4]
> There are some sons, aren't there? . . . What was the row about?[5]
> Who's the next of kin?[6]
>
> —*Lord Peter Wimsey*

The English sleuth Lord Peter Wimsey had a number of occasions to ask pertinent questions about family members. As genealogists, so do we. We usually get the first glimpse of a new ancestor in the context of a nuclear family. This new person could be (1) a spouse of an ancestor already known, found through a marriage, census, land, cemetery, or probate record, (2) a parent of a known ancestor, identified through a census, land, birth, or death record, (3) a sibling of someone once thought to be an ancestor, or (4) a child in a census record who matches name, age, and birthplace criteria to qualify.

In life, and sometimes in genealogy, the nuclear family becomes the first part of the cluster surrounding an individual. It is often through studying this nuclear family and its private and public records that we solidify a new ancestor's identity and at least some vital statistics about the person. Especially in the case of a "new" parent, the proof of relationship may come through studying the children of the nuclear family. For example, we may study a grandmother and her siblings to discover their parents. Even when the parent is not known or the identity is circumstantial, the researcher may need to collect death certificates for all the siblings to establish a parent's name before conducting other research. If death certificates are not available or if they indicate the parents were "unknown" to the informants, the first effort at discovery is through the known nuclear family.

EXTENDED FAMILY

It's lucky that Miss Marple's cousin's sister's aunt's brother-in-law or whatever it was lives near here.
—*Giles Reed*[7]

Families have often intermarried so much that we are kin to almost an entire community either by blood or by marriage. Some spouses know they are also cousins of second, third, or fourth degree. Other spouses, through genealogy, discover they are more distant relations. When we genealogists have difficulty proving names, dates, places, and relationships within the ancestral nuclear family, we often turn to the extended family. We try to contact third, fourth, and fifth cousins who may have family records. We study first, second, or third cousins or in-laws in public records for clues about our own ancestor.

Just as today, in both city neighborhoods and in rural areas, ancestral cousins often lived near each other and interacted in each other's lives. It was often siblings, aunts and uncles, or cousins who drew an ancestor to a new location. Many families have examples of grandparents who moved to Indiana or Oregon because a sister and her husband were already there. One ancestor, who moved from Virginia to west Tennessee in the 1840s, became the drawing card for three of his brothers to go to the same county. He seems to have gone to Tennessee at the recommendation, if not the invitation, of an aunt. Of course, nearly every family has some tradition of brothers migrating together to a new home, whether overseas or over the mountains. We need to study the entire group. Sometimes the study of the original migrating generation, not just one ancestor, is necessary to find their former residence.

Technique

Uncle Henry's Mother's Sister-in-Law

Consider a hypothetical but completely feasible example: that of your Great-Uncle Henry's mother's sister-in-law. Everybody in the family had heard of her, but few remained who remembered her personally. Your parents' generation of the family said she knew a lot about family history. (Whose? They did not know.) All they knew was that she was their Uncle Henry's mother's sister-in-law. (Here we slip into their generation's designation of him as Uncle Henry.) They remembered she was named Kate, and she was no blood relation to Uncle Henry.

You accidentally discovered in your research that she was Uncle Henry's mother's sister-in-law because his mother's first husband was Kate's brother. You decided not to worry about researching someone who was this unrelated. Uncle Henry was no blood relation to you either. He was simply married to your great-aunt, your grandfather's sister, whom everybody called Aunt Sis. How could someone so unrelated as Uncle Henry's mother's sister-in-law help you find Great-Grandma's maiden name? In genealogy, the expression is "She's not mine, so I don't need her."

You dropped Kate. Then, you accidentally learned that Kate and her brother, James, orphaned at a young age, were raised by your great-grandma. Their foster sister and Great-Grandma's daughter, Aunt Sis, married Uncle Henry. Maybe Kate knew about *your* family history if she had been raised with your grandfather and his siblings. But how could you learn what she knew? So you dropped her again.

During your research on Great-Grandma, quite unintentionally you learned that Kate was her niece. (It makes sense that an aunt would raise her orphaned niece and nephew.) Tenaciously, you kept looking for Great-Grandma's maiden name and could not find it anywhere. Then a relative dropped a tidbit about Kate leaving Grandpa some property when she died. You found the tidbit interesting but considered it not pertinent to the bigger research question of Great-Grandma's maiden name.

You then began to realize that you were learning things about Kate, even when you were not looking for them. It almost seemed as if this woman wanted to be found. Why couldn't that happen with Great-Grandma? Then, inadvertently, one day you ran across Kate's name in the probate records. You were not finding what you had gone to the courthouse for, so why not take a look?

You learned that Kate had a very short, simple will, but she had a large probate file. Because Kate never married and neither she nor her brother had any children, her heirs were her cousins, including Grandpa and Aunt Sis. To establish who was to get what from her sizeable estate, her executors had to demonstrate the relationship of her first cousins or their heirs. Her probate file, therefore, contained several generations of family relationships, including Great-Grandma's parents! Great-Grandma's parents were the common ancestors of Kate, her brother, Grandpa, Aunt Sis, and others of that generation.

Aunt Sis and Kate surely knew they were first cousins, but no one handed down the information to your generation or the part of your parents' generation

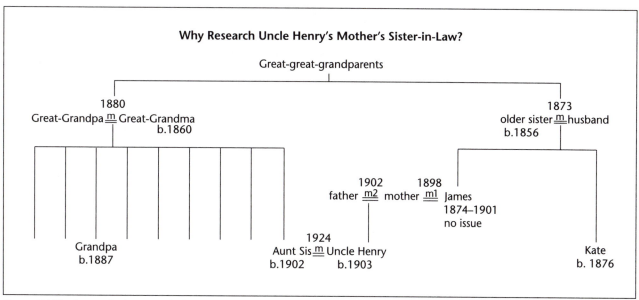

Why Research Uncle Henry's Mother's Sister-in-Law?

Great-great-grandparents

1880
Great-Grandpa _m_ Great-Grandma
b.1860

1873
older sister _m_ husband
b.1856

1902   1898
father _m2_ mother _m1_ James
1874–1901
no issue

Grandpa
b.1887

1924
Aunt Sis _m_ Uncle Henry
b.1902   b.1903

Kate
b. 1876

Figure 3 Why Research the Extended Family Cluster?

you were able to interview. You were the one who discovered it anew. Although no one knew the story when you began your research, Kate had become the pivotal figure in proving Great-Grandma's maiden name.

The study of the extended family cluster, especially Kate, was the key to moving back to the generation before Great-Grandma. And the relative's "memory" that Kate knew a lot about family history was perhaps a child's notion of what went on after Kate died. Members of your parents' generation were young children when Kate died and may have overheard their elders discussing the probate proceedings. This remnant of a childhood event became translated into "Kate knew a lot about family history."

Brick Wall Buster

NEIGHBORS, FRIENDS, AND ASSOCIATES

Talk to the neighbors. . . . Let them talk to *you*. And from their conversation always, somewhere, you will find a clue. . . . Always somewhere there will be a word that sheds light.

—*Hercule Poirot*[8]

In some genealogical searches, it is possible to talk to neighbors, friends, and associates of an ancestor. Talking to one and then another may lead to a third who is living away but no farther than the telephone or E-mail. In some ancestral neighborhoods, a number of relatives lived within a few blocks or a few farms of each other. The researcher who studies that kind of neighborhood is also studying extended family.

Why do you need to talk to neighbors, friends, or associates?
• To gain information about ancestors that is not in books and documents
• To identify the ancestors' house

- To get names of family members
- To hear stories about the family
- To learn more about the family as people

Neighbors, friends, and associates sometimes remember better than relatives do. Neighbors occasionally remember things that relatives living away could not know. Even neighbors who were children when the ancestor was alive remember events, have photos, or know other people to contact.

> Many other persons, neighbors, gave evidence to the same effect.
> —"I" [the storyteller][9]

In another sense, talking to the neighbors, friends, and associates can mean getting what you can from their documents and records. Records created by one person usually mention or involve others: in diaries and letters, deeds, estate settlements, or court cases. By studying the circle of acquaintances and their records, genealogists can sometimes get clues about their own ancestor. Among a group of people buried in the same cemetery, for example, may be several tombstones that mention a birthplace. If your ancestor was a neighbor or friend of those people, you may want to investigate that birthplace as a possible place of origin for your own ancestor.

Reminder

Often, we need the unrelated cluster because we have not been able to identify enough relatives. Sometimes, the "unrelated" are related after all. Sometimes, the unrelated cluster holds answers that relatives do not. These neighbors, friends, and associates can be pastors and fellow church members, employees or employers, clients or patients, buddies from childhood or military service, local tradesmen and retailers with whom an ancestor dealt, and any other person with whom the ancestor had contact.

PEOPLE WITH THE SAME SURNAME

> [W]ould you make out a list of them for me, so that I can look them up. I think it's going to be important.
> —Brent Carradine, research worker[10]

Surname indexes are great tools for genealogy. The statewide census, marriage, or other indexes, printed on paper or CD-ROM, help us see a broad picture of the surname: how widespread it was in the state, what spelling variations existed at the time, where in the state people by the surname lived. The indexes suggest where to look not only for one ancestor but also for other possible relatives. Researchers find it helpful to photocopy the appropriate surname page of an index for study, planning, and future reference.

Unrelated people with the same surname often lived in the same county, even less-populous rural counties. Sometimes, of course, they could have been distant cousins without knowing it. They may have known of a distant relationship but did not leave word for us. Regardless, it does not hurt to check them out. We cannot know until we study them. They can be identified in census indexes, indexes to local land and marriage records, and the like.

When we begin research, we may have no idea who makes up this cluster, but it is often possible to reconstruct considerable portions of it. The process may not give instant gratification because it may take some time, but it often works for those who are patient and persevere.

RECONSTRUCTING THE CLUSTER

> I have been very busy. . . . Assembling elephants, if that means anything to you.
> —*Ariadne Oliver*[11]

The sleuths knew this technique well. The Agatha Christie novel *Elephants Can Remember* was built on this concept. In the story, a woman wanted to unravel an event that had happened some years before. She was convinced the cluster approach was the best procedure to follow: finding people who might remember the event. Hercule Poirot questioned whether anyone would remember anything about it. She explained: "I think they might. . . . I was really thinking of elephants. . . . Elephants remember. What I've got to do is—I've got to get in touch with some elephants. . . . Not elephants, as elephants, but the way people up to a point would resemble elephants. There are some people who *do* remember. . . . I mean, there's always things you *do* remember."[12] In that case, they did, and she and Poirot solved the mystery.

Genealogists need to assemble their own elephants. Depending on the research dilemma, these can be next of kin, extended family members, neighbors, friends, associates, and sometimes people in the vicinity with the same surname.

Family and Extended Family

Start family group sheets for the following:

- The focus ancestor as child, as parent, and as grandparent (with a group sheet on each grandchild)
- Each identified sibling of the focus ancestor
- Each identified niece and nephew of the focus ancestor
- Each identified aunt, uncle, and cousin of the focus ancestor, and any other relative who has been identified
- The focus ancestor's spouse as a child (in other words, a chart for the in-laws) and the spouse's siblings, nieces, and nephews

All these relatives are part of the cluster. Have you found all these people in as many censuses as possible? Whenever your focus ancestor bought or sold land, witnessed a will, or appeared in court, were other relatives involved? Check your family group sheets for identities. Were the witnesses to the ancestor's own transactions relatives? Have you studied the records of these relatives, especially if they lived in the same county with your focus person? Even if they lived in different counties, they could be involved in each other's activities.

What if these are the people you are trying to identify? These relatives can become apparent through census, marriage, land, probate, court, tax, church, and vital records as well as family papers. If the family repeated the same given names in several families each generation, sorting them out may be part of the process. If these relatives have not become apparent through research in these standard sources, you have basically three options:

- Look in every other kind of source available for that time and place. For ideas, consult the Family History Library catalog (available at Family History Centers or online at <http://www.familysearch.org>), the state archives or state historical society catalog of available county records, or books on research in that state.
- Reconstruct the cluster of neighbors and other associates and work on them to try to identify the family cluster.
- Begin looking in a different place. The hardest person to find is the one who was not there. How do you know where to look? Get clues from the records of the family members you have identified. Where appropriate, consult collections such as *The Territorial Papers*. Read chapter eleven.

Neighbors

The ideas suggested below may require careful page-by-page reading of the records in order to reconstruct the ancestral neighborhood. Keep in mind that ancestors often lived near other family members. **Neighbors may turn out to be relatives.**

Tip

The thing to do now is to talk to more neighbours. . . . There must be [more]. *Somebody* has always seen something. It is an axiom.

—*Hercule Poirot*[13]

---

1. Have you looked for the ancestor in every available census during that lifetime? Have you read the entries for the close neighbors, at least ten to twenty households on each side of your ancestor in each census?
2. Have you read the entire enumeration district where the ancestor lived from 1880 forward? Have you read the whole ward, district, precinct or other jurisdiction in censuses prior to 1880? Have you identified those whose entries match your ancestor's in an important way: surname, occupation, birthplace, naming patterns, or parents' birthplaces? Prepare to study them.
3. If the tax rolls identify where taxpayers lived, determine who lived near the ancestor or on the same watercourse.
4. If the ancestor lived in a federal land state (see page 94), have you checked the tract books for the ancestor's township and range or the adjoining ones for other patentees in the same time period? Did those patentees actually live on the land?

5. Have you compared the ancestor's purchases and sales of land with other transactions in the area to determine who the neighbors were at certain times?

6. Have you read deeds and tax records to determine adjoining landowners? Have you found your ancestor mentioned as an adjacent landowner in someone else's deed?

7. Are there plat, insurance, or other maps that show neighbors?

8. Are there city directories from the pertinent time period that show residential addresses so that you can reconstruct the neighborhood?

9. For your ancestor's location, are there sources such as *Cavaliers and Pioneers: Abstracts of Virginia Land Patents and Grants, 1623–1800*?[14] The thorough indexes in these books may help determine others who lived on the same watercourse as your ancestor.

Printed Source

Friends and Associates

The point is not necessarily to study every possible member of the cluster from every phase of the ancestor's life. The point is to study those whose association with the ancestor may help answer your particular questions. Of course, sometimes that means looking at any associates you can identify. Each search is different, so consider what is appropriate to your ancestor's situation.

> The vital point is that an ordinary elderly man is dead and that somebody wanted him dead. . . . [I]f we do not know who the man is—then we have the more difficult task of hunting among those in the surrounding circle for a man who has a reason to kill.
>
> —*Hercule Poirot*[15]

The genealogical application of Poirot's comment is particularly appropriate in cluster genealogy: We have an ordinary unidentified ancestor whom somebody knew; we don't know the ancestor's name—so we have the task of hunting among those in the surrounding cluster for a person who knew or was an associate of the ancestor. Part of this cluster is a known ancestor. The following questions may help in getting from the known ancestor to the unknown one.

1. If your known focus ancestor was part of an organization or religious group, have you identified other members of the same group? Was the known ancestor a godparent or sponsor of another church member?

2. Have you identified an employer or co-workers for the known ancestor?

3. Did your known ancestor have a business partner or employees?

4. Who was in the known ancestor's class at school or college?

5. Who served in the same military unit, especially in the Civil War? Who were the company and regimental officers?

6. Do personal or business papers exist at an archives or museum that once belonged to a lawyer, doctor, merchant, or family from your known ancestor's "neighborhood"?

7. Who witnessed the known ancestor's land transactions, will, or marriage license? Whose deeds, wills, or marriages did the ancestor witness? Who were the other witnesses?

8. Did the known ancestor serve as executor or administrator of an estate? Guardian to any children? Whose?

9. Was the known ancestor a plaintiff or defendant in a court case? Who was the other party? Did the ancestor serve as a witness in a court case? For whom?

10. Who were the buyers or sellers with whom the known ancestor had land transactions?

11. Does any affidavit or similar document exist in the known ancestor's land entry files or military service or pension application file? Who was the affiant?

12. Did the known ancestor sign a petition or memorial that survived at the state or federal level of government? (Some can be found in *The Territorial Papers* and in state archives.) Who were the other signers?

People of the Same Surname

If there were other families by the same surname in the same county or same neighborhood as your focus ancestor, consider these options:

1. List them as you find them and note the context in which you find them.

2. Did they interact with your ancestor at all? In an official capacity (such as justice of the peace or sheriff) or in a more personal way (witness on a marriage license)?

3. From census records, determine their birthplaces or their migration patterns through the birthplaces of their children. Are there any similarities in birthplaces or naming patterns between their families and your ancestor's family? If so, pay attention. They might be related after all.

4. Could they or your own ancestor be using the name as a translation or anglicized version of a foreign surname?

CLUSTER GENEALOGY IN PROGRESS

[L]et's look at the evidence.
—*Samuel Clemens*[16]

The written research plan in chapter two presented the problem of identifying the parents of Caleb Bennett. The prime candidate for his father is Edmund Bennett. Why? Edmund's family was listed immediately above Caleb's family in the 1850 census, both had Georgia origins, and both had a documented presence in Talbot County, Georgia, and Natchitoches Parish, Louisiana. Because no direct statement of relationship has yet been found, the determination of relationship may depend on the accumulation of circumstantial evidence. One part of this accumulation is an attempt to identify Edmund's children, in the hope of connecting them with Caleb as well.

Case Study

The example that follows is part of this search. The hypothesis is that one of Edmund's daughters was one Ruth Ann Bennett. The facts found so far, on the whole, support this conclusion. Although the census ages and land records have posed some questions that require further consideration, no seriously con-

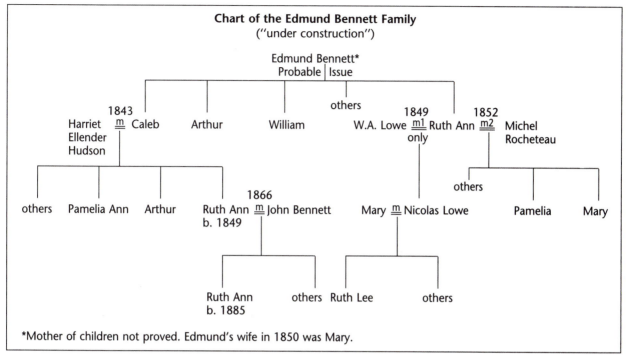

Figure 4 Chart of the Edmund Bennett Family

flicting facts have surfaced. The evidence is presented below as an illustration of studying naming patterns, proximity, and interaction of the cluster to try to determine relationships. (See Figure 4.)

The first five documents prove the identities of Caleb Bennett's daughter and granddaughter named Ruth Ann. These are included here to illustrate the naming pattern in these families. Items six through fifteen continue the illustration of the naming pattern with the other and older Ruth Ann, who was likely a daughter of Edmund Bennett, based on the evidence shown. Besides the naming pattern, this evidence includes interaction between her husband and an Arthur Bennett, believed to be her brother, and the proximity of their land.

1. In 1850, Caleb Bennett's household included a one-year-old child named "Ruthe" Ann.[17]
2. In 1860, this child was listed as ten years old, with the initials L.A.[18] (See #11 below.)
3. Ruth Ann Bennett married John Bennett, 25 January 1866.[19]
4. In January 1867, at the family meeting after Caleb's death, one person present was John Bennett, "brother-in-law to [the] minors," meaning Caleb's younger children.[20]
5. Caleb's daughter Ruth Ann had a daughter Ruth Ann as shown (1) in the 1900 census, where she appeared as 14 with a November 1885 birth date, and (2) in her marriage record of 1902.[21]
6. The Natchitoches Parish records show the marriage of a Miss Rutha Ann Bennett to William Augustus Lowe on 8 October 1849.[22]
7. The 1850 census shows W.A. Low (28), Ruthie (17), and infant Nicolas.[23]
    The age of this Ruthie is the same given for Edmund Bennett's son William,

who is also shown as 17 in the 1850 census. William was listed as head of household twice in 1860, once as 26 and once as 27.[24] He has not been found conclusively in censuses or other records after 1860. Ruthie is listed as 52 in 1870 and as 37 in 1880, neither of which makes sense.[25] She has not been found in 1860 or 1900. However, Caleb Bennett's family and descendants include some twins. It is at least possible that William and Ruthie were twins. It is also quite possible that either William's or Ruthie's age in 1850 was incorrect. This does not seem to be a major stumbling block.

8. The 1840 census of Edmund Bennett's household does include a girl five to ten years of age (birth between 1830 and 1835) which would accommodate the seventeen-year-old Ruthie (Bennett) Lowe of the marriage record and 1850 census. So far, there is no other candidate for this slot in the family. (Edmund Bennett's household of 1830 includes another girl, still unidentified, who was born between 1825 and 1830, who was still in the household in 1840 but was not in the 1850 Bennett household.)[26]

9. Parish records show that Ruth Ann Lowe married Michel "Rocherneau" on 7 April 1852. Listed as "Kitty Ann" once in the text, she is "Ruthy" in the margin of the record book. The wedding took place in the parish at the house of "Edward" Bennett, who was called "Edmund" later in the same document.[27] (The researchers have seen no Edward Bennett in other parish records at this time.) The groom's name was probably Rocheteau, as there were others in the parish. However, the name is spelled many ways in contemporary records.

10. This couple has not been found in 1860. In 1870, Mitchel Rocheteau and Ruth A. were in neighboring Grant Parish with children Nicolas (20), Pamelia, Zelia, Emily, Louis, and Mary.[28] Of note, Caleb had a daughter Pamelia and Edmund's wife was Mary; there was a neighbor named Zelia. Apparently Zelia Rocheteau was listed as Ophelia in 1880.

11. In 1880, Mitchel Roston and wife "Luthian" were in Grant Parish with their children. With two of the Ruth Anns being "L.A." and "Luthian" in census records, one wonders about the families' pronunciation of the name or the regional accent that may have resulted in the census takers hearing an *L* instead of an *R*.

12. In 1900, Nicolas Lowe, son of Ruth Ann (Bennett) Lowe, and his wife, Mary, had a daughter reported as Ruth Lee, age 4, born December 1895.[29] (See number 7 above for the infant Nicolas.)

13. Federal land entry files illustrate the proximity of this Rocheteau family and two other Bennetts. Michael Rosto of Rapides Parish (also Roshtoe in the same record) patented land in Natchitoches Parish (receipt dated 4 January 1860), adjoining land of an Edmund Bennett (receipt dated September 1860), both in S65-T7N-R6W. One corner of Roshtoe's tract touched a corner of a tract patented by Arthur Bennett in the same section (receipt dated 20 December 1859).[30] When Arthur got his land, Michael signed with his mark the corroborating affidavit. When Michael got his

land, Arthur signed the corroborating affidavit. Edmund's file contains no corroborating affidavit, only the patentee's affidavit, which he signed with his mark. (The 1850 census entry indicates that the elder Edmund could not read and write; the 1870 census indicates that Rocheteau could not read and write.)

14. Caleb Bennett had an Arta/Arthur in his 1850 and 1860 households (ages 6 and 15, respectively). Edmund Bennett had an "Arta" (age looks like 16 with 10 superimposed) in his 1850 household. In 1860, one Arthur Bennett, possibly Edmund's Arthur, was in Natchitoches Parish, age 23, with $200 worth of real estate.[31] Neither Roshtoe nor Edmund Bennett has been found in the 1860 census. At least one of the Arthurs, presumably Caleb's, was present at the family meeting after Caleb's death.

15. Edmund Bennett, who was 64 in the 1850 census, was not found in the 1860 census and was presumed deceased. This patent under the name of Edmund Bennett was made in September 1860, after the 1860 census. Would a 74-year-old man be patenting and cultivating land under the act for "actual settlement and cultivation"? This patent and two others in neighboring Winn Parish have raised the question of whether there was a son named Edmund Bennett. This part of the study needs more in-depth research.

In conclusion, with the evidence gathered so far, it appears likely that the Ruth Ann Bennett who first married William Augustus Lowe and then married Michel Rocheteau was a daughter of Edmund Bennett of Natchitoches Parish. Because she married before 1850, she did not appear in a list of names within his household. Studying her and her husband and their interaction with other Bennetts has led to this conclusion.

How about other close family? Any domineering mother-in-law, or worthless brothers, or jealous sisters? . . . [T]his could be important.

—*Samuel Clemens*[32]

FOUR

Documenting Research

Where did you get it?
—*Sherlock Holmes*[1]

A
ll genealogists accumulate paper. If we are organized, we develop a paper trail on any given ancestor. If we are smart, that paper trail tells us exactly where we found each piece of information and how the bits and pieces fit together. When we establish a name, relationship, date, or place in the life of an ancestor, the proof should be reflected in that paper trail. Therefore, creating the paper trail involves collecting information on the sources from which that information comes.

This documenting of our research is more than deciding whether to put a comma or period after the title of a book. It has important implications in our analysis and the quality of our results. **Documenting your work may sound difficult, but it's not. It may sound bothersome, but it's not. It may sound optional, but it's not. It is absolutely essential.**

Who Documents Their Work?

Legitimate researchers in any endeavor keep track of things: the evidence they have and where they got it. Each discipline has certain standards and forms to follow in the process. Archaeologists record the depth at which each artifact is found and in which pit. Before taking important items out of the ground, they often photograph or map each pit floor where those items rest. Then they bag or box everything together that comes from one level in the pit so these items can be studied in the context of where they were found.

In genealogy, we must keep track of our artifacts as well—our land records, wills, and censuses—and record where they rest before we put our copies of them into our notebooks or folders. This means that genealogists who want to join a lineage society or share what they find with any other person or leave a legacy of family history for children and grandchildren—all of us—need to document what we find. Only then can we study what we have found in its proper context.

Important

Notes

Endotes for this chapter are on page 253.

WHAT DOES IT MEAN TO DOCUMENT YOUR WORK?

I don't want to know where you got this material, do I?

—*Agent Pickering*[2]

The genealogical answer to this question should be "I hope you *do* want to know where I got this material. I've made a genuine research effort, and I have nothing to hide. My sources are legitimate. My information is real. My conclusions are based on the best facts I could find. So help yourself to my documentation."

On the most basic level, documenting means citing your sources in detail as you research. Sources are the books, documents, interviews, letters, Web sites, tombstones, or other places from which you get any information. On the next level, documenting means backing up your conclusions with specific evidence from these sources. Then, documenting means systematically matching each piece of evidence with its source in the form of footnotes (or endnotes) as you fill out charts or write up your project.

Why Do We Need to Document Our Work?

- To show where we have found, or have not found, our information
- To help us find our sources to look at them again
- To let other researchers know enough about the sources so they can find them
- To credit others from whom we quote directly
- To substantiate and support our conclusions with legitimate evidence
- To give our work credibility and validity

When and Where Do We Cite Our Sources?

In short, we cite our sources often and everywhere. To be more specific, you should cite your sources

- On notes as you research, any time you add information to your own database, whether in the library, courthouse, cemetery, interviews, or wherever you get information.
- On charts and forms where you record your results, such as family group sheets, chronologies, and pedigree charts.
- On any set of information that you share with anybody else for them to read and use. That includes any set of information that you share on the Internet, in an article, or in a book.

HOW DO WE CITE OUR SOURCES?

One thing at a time—let us be methodical.

—*Hercule Poirot*[3]

Your citations need to tell you, or anyone else who is interested, exactly where you found each particular piece of information. As Poirot suggests,

Reminder

an important part of *method* is being methodical. In documenting, we have to train ourselves to write down the specifics first, before we take notes. Of course, we get in a hurry because we suspect that the book before us is about to reward us with significant revelations about an elusive ancestor for whom we have searched high and low. However, if we do not get the details of the source first, we are likely to forget to do it at all. At the very least, record the citation details at the top of your page of notes. If you are also organized enough to keep a research log or calendar, write the citation details there as well. Some researchers use the calendar, number each source, and code the page of notes to the source. I personally want the citation details on the notes, regardless of where else they appear.

In practice, most of us cite our sources with different degrees of formality. First, if you are taking notes at a research facility, the form you use in recording your sources does not really matter, as long as you get all the necessary information. This can include notes about the appearance of the source: blurry film, pages dark or stained with age, a certain name hard to make out, pages unnumbered, pages not numbered consecutively, ink smeared on a given word, a page torn and words missing, a skip in a numbering sequence, etc.

Second, if you are updating a source list for study, for a progress report, or for recording on a family group sheet, you probably need to adhere to a somewhat consistent style so that you or those with whom you share it can tell readily what you have used. Consistency and thoroughness also tend to give someone else an impression of the care with which you have done your work. This step also represents the second level of documentation: backing up each conclusion (each event, name, date, place, or relationship) with specific evidence from the sources you used.

Third, if you decide to arrange your research into a formal presentation, whether published or not, you will need to use a consistent form at least similar to that recognized by major publications and style manuals. This step represents the third level of documentation: systematically matching each piece of evidence with its source in the form of footnotes (or endnotes) as you fill out charts or write up your project.

In recording your sources, you will need to answer Sherlock Holmes's question, "Where did you get it?" In which census? In which book? In whose will? In whose family Bible? On the back of a photograph and in Grandpa's handwriting? This is the beginning of the process. You will need enough to write a footnote or bibliography entry. For published materials, this means author, title, publication information, and what part of it you used. Obviously, many genealogical sources do not have authors, titles, or publication information, but they do have identifying characteristics of source, date, and location. What you need is whatever it takes to identify the source so that you, or someone else, can find it again. Although not always used in footnotes and bibliographies, this identification can also include the place you used it, its call number in that facility, and the date of your research.

CONSIDERING SPECIFICS

Be exact, my friend.
—Hercule Poirot[4]

Footnotes (or endnotes) and bibliographies, the two common types of citations, usually have slightly different forms. A footnote and a bibliography entry for the same source generally contain the same basic information but differ in slight ways because they serve different functions. When gathering your citation details, you need to get enough information for both kinds of citations.

Footnotes

Genealogists often benefit from reading the footnotes in articles, books, and case studies. Not only do footnotes give the specific sources to validate the information presented, but they also give the rest of us ideas for our own research. One friend found in a book an interesting footnote about a county where her ancestors lived. She looked up the article cited in the footnote and found in it another footnote that mentioned one of her ancestral surnames in that county. This led her to certain county records where she found more family information.

The parts of a footnote are usually separated by commas. This is standard form for published books:

Author, *Title in italics* (Place of publication: Publisher, date of publication), page number from which your information came.

For example:

David Ludlum, *Early American Winters, 1604-1820* (Boston: American Meteorological Society, 1966), 65.

Even in the kinds of special sources genealogists use, commas usually separate the various elements. For example, a citation of a census record could look like this:

U.S. Census of 1860, New County, Tennessee, Newburg District, National Archives microfilm M653, roll 1263, p. 196, family 187, household of Newman Newberry.

This citation tells exactly where the information is and gives the researcher and the reader enough information to find the same record again.

Bibliography

Whereas the footnote matches the specific information with its source, the bibliography is a general list of sources cited, sometimes with recommendations for further reading or reference. Genealogists may find a bibliography at the end of a full-length family history rather than a case study or article. In a short work, with good footnotes, a reader probably does not need a separate bibliography.

In standard form, the parts of each bibliography entry are usually separated by periods. Often, the order is the same as in the footnote; however, the punctuation differs and the most specific items are omitted. An entry for a book would be:

Author. *Title in italics*. Place of publication: Publisher, date of publication.

The footnotes in the examples above could be altered for bibliographic entries in this way:

Ludlum, David. *Early American Winters, 1604-1820*. Boston: American Meteorological Society, 1966.

U.S. Census of 1860. Population Schedule. National Archives microfilm M653. Roll 1263, New County, Tennessee.

Style Manuals

Good manuals of style, such as *The Chicago Manual of Style*, 14th ed. (Chicago: The University of Chicago Press, 1993), hereafter cited as CMS, give examples of standard form for footnotes and bibliography entries that cite published books and articles, newspapers, letters, interviews, and some unpublished documents. Genealogists use these recommendations. In addition, two works have dealt with some of the specialized kinds of sources genealogists use:

- Richard S. Lackey, *Cite Your Sources: A Manual for Documenting Family Histories and Genealogical Records* (Jackson: University Press of Mississippi, 1980).
- Elizabeth Shown Mills, *Evidence! Citation & Analysis for the Family Historian* (Baltimore: Genealogical Publishing Company, 1997).

Citing Genealogical Sources

The style used for footnotes varies from researcher to researcher although certain standard ingredients are usually included. The examples below identify the ancestor(s) in the record, the exact source of the record, and the form in which the record was used. Records may be available to us in many forms, such as microfilm, record books or document files in a courthouse, photographs of tombstones, published books of abstracts, documents in family papers, images or abstracts in an electronic format, or documents in a collection in an archives. By recording the form of the record we actually used, we or another researcher can find the same record again and can begin to evaluate the reliability of the record.

Below are a few examples of genealogical footnotes not usually discussed in style manuals such as CMS. A much broader reference section appears in appendix B, beginning on page 219 of this book. The appendix illustrates footnote and bibliography styles for books, articles, electronic sources, newspapers, letters, interviews, and a variety of unpublished documents. The examples given there are based on standard style manuals and the way various researchers have treated sources that genealogists use. If you have a particular type of source to cite, check the appendix for ideas on form.

Some genealogists begin footnotes with the name of the person who created the record or the name of the ancestor involved in the record. Examples would include the following:

[1]Huckleberry Greenapple, deed of gift, 1835, Old County, Virginia, Deed Book 8:300, FHL microfilm 000001.

[2]Elderberry Greenapple to Cora Thorne, original marriage license, file 007, New County, Texas, County Clerk's Office, Courthouse, Newtown.

[3]Charity Ball tombstone, Pearly Gate Cemetery, Oldville, Old County, Kentucky, photographed by researcher, 1976.

Other genealogists prefer to write footnotes stating the type of record first. Examples could read as follows:

[4]Will of Peter Piper, dated 4 July 1776, Old County, Virginia, Deed and Will Book 3:27, County Clerk's Office, Courthouse, Oldville.

[5]New Parish, Louisiana, Marriage Book 4:44, Green Cash to Petina Brown, 4 April 1844, Parish Clerk's Office, Courthouse, Newburg.

[6]New County, Georgia, Superior Court Minute Book A, 1 January 1824 (pages not numbered), lists both Logan Berry and Pleasant Hays on jury no. 2, microfilm at Georgia Department of Archives and History, Atlanta.

The specific form you choose is not dictated by a universal standard. The key is to record all the necessary information as you research, choose the form that makes sense to you, and use it consistently. This means that you use the same form for all census records, the same form for all deed records, probably the same form for all courthouse records of whatever kind, the same form for all tombstone data, and so forth.

You can always keep a set of index cards or a master list to remind yourself of the form you prefer. It will not take long to get used to your system if you use it regularly. We all have to train ourselves to get enough information when we use the source the first time, and even the most experienced among us sometimes forget something and have to go back to the source in order to complete the citation.

Tip

SOURCES IN THE FAMILY

I wonder if you could tell me what evidence you have that impels you to think so?

—*Eleanor Roosevelt*[5]

Many families have interesting gems of information tucked away in boxes and drawers. They can contain important evidence for the genealogist and, therefore, sometimes need to be cited as sources.

Style books basically do not cover these kinds of sources, and Mills and Lackey deal with very few of them. It is not feasible for any book to cover all conceivable examples. Therefore, you will need to develop your own citations for most of these items. This is perfectly acceptable as long as you include the necessary details to let you or someone else know exactly what source gave you the information, where it can be found or where it was when you used it, any necessary comment on its reliability or usefulness, or any other specifics that would help someone else decide that it was a legitimate source.

The following account illustrates some kinds of records families may have, their use in genealogy, and citations to document their use. The story is true and the documents are real. They help answer one specific research question. For illustration purposes, the citations follow one pattern: type of document, name and date on document, source of document, and description of document where pertinent. The endnotes follow the story. Although this example does not include photographs and other family sources, they could be cited using the same pattern.

Case Study

A True Story

Although Mama[1] always told her children she had no middle name, in 1974 she proudly told her friends that her new granddaughter had been named for her, with her middle name, Elizabeth. Her daughters were suspicious that age was playing with her mind. She had no middle name until the granddaughter was born, and suddenly she had the same one. When confronted with this puzzle, she became very indignant. Not until after her death did her daughters try to answer the question as they sorted through family papers. Was Elizabeth really her middle name?

The daughters knew that many documents and papers created after her marriage reflected the prevailing sentiment of many of her generation. She and most of her friends were glad to be Mrs. Jeffrey Giles or Mrs. William Blackstock rather than Mrs. Rebecca Giles or Mrs. Twila Blackstock. It was proper and comfortable. Their personal stationery was printed with their husbands' names, and they addressed letters to each other in the same way. When governments issued Social Security cards, passports, and drivers' licenses, these ladies used their given names. In such instances, when Mama needed a middle initial, she always used *M* from her maiden name. In order to study the middle-name question, therefore, her daughters had to find premarriage documents.

First, her daughters found her 1939 driver's license, which gave no middle name or initial at all.[2] Likewise, without any middle name or initial was a letter from the University of Texas registrar to the Board of Civil Service Examiners in Washington, DC, certifying that she had graduated with highest honors on 8 June 1936.[3] An official university transcript from the same registrar's office indicates that Mama's college records were in the name of Miss Fletcher Metcalfe.[4] (*Miss* was always added because her given name was a traditionally male name although a family name for both males and females.) Not surprisingly, the same was true for a church "encampment record card" dated 1 August 1931,[5] when she was sixteen, exactly forty-three years before the birth of her granddaughter, Sarah Elizabeth. Also, only the given name and maiden name were printed on Mama's parchmentlike high school graduation invitation, announcing commencement exercises on 20 May 1932.[6] These documents and numerous contemporary letters in the family's possession all indicated that Mama apparently did not use any middle name officially or unofficially after her midteen years. The daughters would have to look for something of an earlier period.

They found her fifth-grade through eleventh-grade report cards that, likewise, gave no middle name.[7] The document that should have helped, if anything would, was a carbon copy of an affidavit of her father, sworn before the local notary public, that he was the father of Miss Fletcher Metcalfe of Marfa, Texas, who was born in Georgetown, Texas, on 16 May 1915, the daughter of himself and his wife, Mrs. Fletcher McKennon Metcalfe.[8] Of course, the purpose of this document was to establish an official record of birth date, birthplace, and parentage, not to establish or refute a middle name.

The daughters sorted through more papers than they ever knew existed. The next items were books of various kinds. That is where they found three pieces of evidence that their mother, at one time, had a middle name. The first clue appeared on a school booklet, dated for the 1927–1928 school year, with its cover inscribed as the property of Fletcher E. Metcalfe.[9] Comparison with family handwriting samples suggested that the hand responsible for this inscription was probably that of the teacher, who would have had a reason greater than creative imagination to use the initial.

The second reference came from a little Bible, presented to "Fletcher by Mother and Daddy, Xmas 1925."[10] Written in pencil after the first name was "Elizabeth Metcalfe." The penciled script appears to be that of a child and was no doubt added at some time after the gift was given. Regardless of who wrote in the middle name, she (for the children in that family were two girls) obviously considered it reasonable and appropriate. Even if the younger sister wrote it, the older sister had not erased it. Its motive did not seem to be a stunt to irritate big sister but an attempt to complete the inscription.

The third evidence appeared in Mama's photograph album-memory book, also a Christmas gift in 1925.[11] About midway through the book, photographs gave way temporarily to other memorabilia, including greeting cards, party napkins, concert programs, and gift tags. The four gifts tags saved from Christmas, 1927, included one from Mama's cousin, Josephine Metcalfe, inscribed "For Fletcher Elizabeth." At the top of the tag, Mama identified the gift, "flowers for my coat." Since this cousin was nine at the time and the handwriting on the tag appears to be that of an adult, it is reasonable that the tag was written by one of her parents. An aunt or uncle would not arbitrarily assign a middle name to a niece on a gift tag. Here, then, were three independently created pieces of evidence giving a strong indication that the middle name had indeed been bestowed.

To get a contemporary perspective, Mama's younger sister was asked about the middle name question. She recalled hearing a story at various times during childhood.[12] Apparently, the baby was originally named Fletcher Elizabeth, after her mother, or maybe simply Elizabeth. Shortly thereafter, a family friend called at the home to exclaim over "little Lizzie." The new parents decided on the spot that their daughter would not be called Lizzie and dropped any idea of using it as her primary name. The sparse evidence of its existence suggests that Fletcher herself chose not to use it.

The daughters then learned that the old Mood family Bible, in the family of Mama's maternal grandmother, had an entry in the handwriting of that grandmother, stating that Fletcher Elizabeth Metcalfe was born 16 May 1915.[13] The entry itself is not dated, but at least the grandmother believed the name enough to record it in the official family record. Mama must have been right after all. Mothers usually are.

Endnotes for "A True Story"

[1]The family of "Mama" has given permission for this story to be shared here.

[2]Operator's license, stamped "duplicate," issued 13 September 1939, to Fletcher Metcalfe by the Texas Department of Public Safety, Drivers License Division, Austin, Texas, copy in the author's possession.

[3]Letter from E. J. Mathews, registrar of the University of Texas, Austin, to the Board of U.S. Civil Service Examiners, Washington, DC, 20 October 1936, copy in the author's possession; the letter is on university letterhead stationery and embossed with the university seal.

[4]Official transcript of Miss Fletcher Metcalfe, University of Texas, Austin, 3 January 1936, prepared by the office of the registrar, E.J. Mathews, with the university seal, copy in the author's possession.

[5]Encampment Record Card of Fletcher Metcalfe, dated 1 August 1931, from the Paisano Baptist Assembly, between Marfa and Alpine, Texas, copy in the author's possession. The card identifies this young lady as a Methodist and is a record of activities she attended during the weeklong camp meeting.

[6]Graduation invitation of Marfa (Texas) High School, May, 1932, printed in the name of Fletcher Metcalfe, copy in the author's possession. Printed in Art Deco style on parchmentlike paper, the original invitation is enclosed in its own parchmentlike envelope and then in a mailing envelope.

[7]Report cards of Fletcher Metcalfe, 1925–1928, Marfa, Texas, Grammar School, and 1928–1932, Marfa, Texas, High School, privately held in Metcalfe family papers, Houston, Texas. The white cards are 5″ × 7¼″, preprinted with subject names, filled out in a teacher's handwriting, and signed monthly on the back by a parent.

[8]Affidavit of H.O. Metcalfe, notarized by Thalia Crenshaw, Marfa, Texas, 16 July 1936, a carbon copy but with the notary's seal, copy in the author's possession. Its purpose was to establish his daughter's birth date since, "for cause unknown to the affiant," her birth was not recorded at the time; according to family tradition, the "cause unknown" was that the doctor was drunk at the delivery.

[9]*The News Outline: An Elementary Current Events Lesson, Weekly* (Columbus, OH: The News Outline, weekly), issues from October 1927 through June 1928, booklet in Metcalfe family papers, privately held, Houston, Texas, copy of cover in the author's possession. The booklet is about 6″ × 9″, with card stock cover and held together with brads; inside are the weekly news items and various student assignments, including a census of classmates.

[10]*Holy Bible*, American Standard Version (New York: Thomas Nelson & Sons, 1901), inscribed in ink by one of the parents, probably the father, this judgment being made by a comparison of handwriting in family letters; copy of inscription page in the author's possession.

[11]*My Memory Book*, album and scrapbook of Fletcher Metcalfe, album privately held with Metcalfe family papers, Houston, Texas, copy of pertinent page in this author's possession. The album of black cover and black pages is 7″ × 11¼″ and filled with autographs, photographs, and memorabilia dating from 1923 to about 1934; the inside cover is inscribed as a gift to her from Miss Gertrude McDaniel of San Antonio, Texas, Christmas, 1925.

[12]Mary Katherine Earney, Georgetown, Texas, telephone conversation with the author, Bellaire, Texas, 20 May 1999.

[13]Birth registry for Fletcher Elizabeth Metcalfe, Dr. Francis Asbury Mood family Bible, *Holy Bible, . . . with a perpetual genealogical Family Register*, new edition (Nashville: Southern Methodist Publishing House, 1859), 28 of the registry, in the Special Collections of the A. Frank Smith, Jr., Library Center, Southwestern University, Georgetown, Texas. Dr. Mood and his children kept the Bible current for many years, and it eventually passed to his grandson, Dr. Robert G. Mood of Wichita, Kansas. At his death in 1994, at age 95, his son Rob Mood of Houston, Texas, gave the Bible to its present caretakers at the university where Dr. Mood served as founding president. The grandmother who made Mama's entry in the Bible was a daughter of Dr. Mood; her handwriting was quite distinctive and is identified in a number of family papers and by family members who knew her.

Are you—are you sure of this piece of intelligence?

—*Detective Gregson*[6]

To Bib or Not To Bib

A short account, such as "A True Story," does not call for any second, shortened citation from any of these sources and has no need for a bibliography. The endnotes give the necessary details; anything more would serve little purpose. Many formal articles do not include a bibliography.

If the items in the middle-name story needed to be listed individually in a bibliography, we could simply use the necessary elements from each endnote and separate them by periods rather than commas. If the date is essential to the bibliography, it is usually combined with another element. Descriptions of the items would not appear in the bibliography.

The following are examples of bibliography form:

1. Using the form: Name. Document and date. Collection. Location.

> Metcalfe, Fletcher. Official college transcript, University of Texas, Austin, 1936. Metcalfe family papers. Privately held, Houston, Texas. Copy held by author.

> Metcalfe, Fletcher. Operator's License, Texas Department of Public

Safety, Drivers License Division, Austin, 1939. Metcalfe family papers. Privately held, Houston, Texas. Copy held by author.

Metcalfe, H.O. Affidavit, carbon copy. Thalia Crenshaw, notary public, Marfa, Texas, 16 July 1936. Metcalfe family papers. Privately held, Houston, Texas. Copy held by author.

Mood, Dr. Francis Asbury. Mood Family Register. *Holy Bible.* New edition. Nashville: Southern Methodist Publishing House, 1859. Special Collections. A. Frank Smith Jr. Library Center. Southwestern University. Georgetown, Texas.

The News Outline: An Elementary Current Events Lesson, Weekly. Columbus, OH: The News Outline, weekly, October 1927 through June 1928. Metcalfe family papers. Privately held, Houston, Texas.

2. General bibliography entry that would cover the entire collection of family papers.

Metcalfe, Fletcher. Personal documents. Metcalfe family papers. Privately held, Houston, Texas.

Mood, Dr. Francis Asbury. Mood Family Register. *Holy Bible.* . . . [same as above]

A FINAL WORD

This chapter and appendix B work together. One of their purposes is to make citing sources less of a mystery than some think it is. Another purpose is to encourage researchers to do their best at documenting in order to give their own work validity and credibility.

Do your durnedest—"Angels could do no more."
—*Inspector George L. Patton*[7]

FIVE

Gathering Information: Research

> Give me research. After all, the truth of anything at all doesn't lie in someone's account of it. It lies in all the small facts of the time. An advertisement in a paper. The sale of a house. The price of a ring. . . . Truth isn't in [historical] accounts but in account books. . . . The real history is written in forms not meant as history. In Wardrobe accounts, in Privy Purse expenses, in personal letters, in estate books.
>
> —*Brent Carradine, research worker*[1]

R esearch takes place in a great variety of records and documents contemporary with the ancestors we seek. However, this chapter is not intended as a presentation of sources; they are a focus of many books, including *The Genealogist's Companion & Sourcebook*. This chapter considers the process of research and strategies for research in certain types of sources.

Many authors of genealogy books, articles, and lectures advise people to start any new search with a survey of secondary literature (published family histories and charts submitted to electronic databases) to see what other people have already done on the same family. The chief reason given for the advice is that researchers need not spend time repeating what has already been researched. The reason given has merit, and those who want to take that step first may benefit from it. However, **my own experience and conversations with other researchers have lead me to disagree with the secondary effort as the first step.** Why?

1. I have rarely found any published material, readily available in database or paper form, that included my family in the eighteenth, nineteenth, or twentieth centuries, the time period in which most genealogy projects begin and focus. A number of other genealogists have shared similar experiences.

2. The few things I have found in such an effort were undocumented and, by the time I found them, I knew that a significant number of the details were inaccurate because I had been researching them for myself.

3. Researchers starting a first genealogy project or beginning work in a new

Notes

Endnotes for this chapter begin on page 253.

Warning

lineage need some background with which to judge what they find in computer databases or printed works, especially if the name is a common one. How can researchers new to a surname or new to a particular ancestor judge the validity of what is already published without having some knowledge or background with which to judge it? The only thing they can really evaluate is mistakes in logic, such as a grandmother having her first child after her reported grandson was born. They could not, however, identify an error that places a man's death in 1757, even though his will was probated in 1735, unless that will is mentioned. (Such errors seldom come from a submitter or compiler who has actually done research and has read the will and probate record.)

4. In genealogy seminars and classes, people continually report, "I am so excited; I just found nine generations of my family on the XX database," and "I found all my grandfather's ancestors on the Internet." Such people rarely use what they find as clues or try to get in touch with the submitter. They swallow the information as part of their completed genealogy and do not do the research necessary to check it out. Instead, they turn to another part of the family that was not on the database to begin their research. Miss Marple would probably say to these folks, "[Y]ou've fallen into the trap again—the trap of believing *what is said to you*."[2] When she is not around to say it, the rest of us must find a way.

Two clarifications are in order. First, much good can come from working with other researchers, one on one, however they are found. The parties (giving and receiving) can help each other find and document information. A relatively recent genealogy that includes the author's address may be a source for surveying certain generations and getting in touch with the author for ideas or comparing notes as research progresses.

Second, many high-quality genealogies and case studies have appeared and still appear in genealogical journals. Reading the journal of a society in your research area can sometimes acquaint you with ancestors and their other researchers. Several types of indexes can help you find such journals and articles. These are several standard examples.

Printed Source

The Genealogist's Companion & Sourcebook discusses such indexes at more length in its chapter eight.

- The *Periodical Source Index* (PERSI), published by the Allen County Public Library in Ft. Wayne, Indiana, and also available on CD-ROM, indexes more than two thousand North American historical and genealogical periodicals published since the early 1800s. This is not an every-name index, but ancestors who have been the subjects of journal articles may well be indexed. PERSI can also lead researchers to hundreds of valuable abstracts of records in the indexed periodicals.
- The *Genealogical Periodical Annual Index* (GPAI), published by Heritage Books of Bowie, Maryland, indexes close to three hundred periodicals whose publishers subscribe to the service.
- Although indexed in PERSI, the *National Genealogical Society Quarterly* is also available on CD-ROM from Brøderbund. The CD-ROM includes volumes one through eighty-five, through 1997, and can be searched by name. One feature of this high-quality journal is well-researched and well-documented case studies on specific families.

- In university and large public libraries, the *America: History and Life* index is a good source of articles outside the traditional genealogical journals.

Warning

The fact remains that undocumented family histories, articles, and charts by people no longer available to the researcher fall into that "database" category that can be hazardous to one's genealogical health. Thus, it is advisable to have some background on the family before going to the published materials, whether paper or online. If you do find that someone has published something on one of your ancestral names, you need enough background to know it is *your* ancestor in the right place at the right time with the correct family members. How can you know without at least some preliminary research?

Where do we go from here, then?
  —*Investigator Jill Keller*[3]

For genealogists who decide to investigate someone else's compilations or truly want to solve genealogical questions themselves, there is research into records and documents. Those who do it find it intriguing, enlightening, stimulating, rewarding, and sometimes challenging. And we invite others to join us in the endeavor. If you are relatively new to genealogy, please read appendix A at the back of this book for information on research and sources.

A readily available place for most searches to begin, after doing the necessary preliminary gathering within the family, is in the broad-based federal census records, beginning with 1920 (or 1930 if you are reading this after that census's release in 2002) and working back in time as far as possible for the known families. These records are widely accessible on microfilm, have many printed indexes, and give the researcher background in the makeup of the focus family over a period of years. Strategies for census research will be discussed later in this chapter.

GENERAL PRINCIPLES OF RESEARCH

One thing, *mes amis*, must be clearly understood. To solve any problem, one must have the *facts*. For that one needs the dog, the dog who is a retriever, who brings the pieces one by one and lays them at—[the feet of the master].
  —*Hercule Poirot*[4]

We genealogists are the retrievers, gathering the pieces one by one, largely for ourselves rather than someone else. Thus, the retrieving process itself deserves as much of our attention as do the sources themselves. Most endeavors, whether archaeology or cooking, have a set of principles that describe and govern their

Notes

process. Genealogy is no different. **The following are basic principles of genealogical research.** Each one will be considered individually.

1. Research is a diligent and careful inquiry or investigation to discover and interpret facts or revise theories in light of new facts.
2. Research basically has two components: methods and sources.
3. Appropriate research methods are as vital to success as legitimate sources.
4. Research takes place in the context of a specific time and place for a specific person or group of people.
5. Research cannot be rushed.
6. Research must be specifically documented in order to be considered valid.
7. Research progresses from the known to the unknown.
8. Research is a continual cycle of planning, looking, and analyzing, with each new effort building on the results of the previous one.
9. Reliable sources are the foundation of good research.

A Diligent Inquiry

[A]fter a long and very deliberate scrutiny, I saw nothing to excite particular suspicion.

—*C. Auguste Dupin*[5]

Research is a diligent and careful inquiry or investigation to discover and interpret facts or revise theories in light of new facts. The definition implies that the researcher is patient, alert, industrious, cautious, persistent, attentive to detail, and thorough. It also indicates that the researcher thinks during the process. At least, we can strive for these qualities. *Inquiry* to answer research questions implies exploration of such aids as indexes and maps; it also means exploration of new sources and new techniques. It proposes the examination of many kinds of records and examination of the facts to see where they lead.

Discover suggests the use of original, or nearly original, records to uncover facts once known to the family but lost during intervening generations. *Interpret* means that once we recover the facts, we examine and analyze them to determine how they fit together, what they mean, what hypotheses we can form from them, or what conclusions we may reach based on the evidence.

The definition of *research* does not mean that we do away with intuition and gut feelings in deciding where to look, which records to search, or what a legitimate hypothesis may be. It does mean that our conclusions must be based on the facts. However, genealogists must not look at the facts the way one man did; he was described to Lord Peter Wimsey as one who "only sees the facts which fit in with the theory."[6] Neither can we be like the woman who told Hercule Poirot why she was certain of the identity of the criminal (or the ancestor?): "[W]hy am I sure? I tell you I *know* it! I am funny about those things. I made up my mind at once, and I stick to it."[7]

Two Components: Methods and Sources

As Sherlock Holmes so aptly and so repeatedly put it, being a successful detective is simply a matter of applying iron logic to observed facts.

—*President Franklin Roosevelt*[8]

Research basically has two components: methods and sources. In Roosevelt's statement about Holmes, the iron logic is his method to work out a solution, based on facts gathered previously either by observation or from his informants. A genealogical application would be this: Being a successful detective in genealogy is a matter of applying iron logic to facts gathered through research. The process involves both methods (what we do and how we do it) and sources (where we get our information).

Appropriate Methods and Sources

I'll tell you how I want this investigation run. I want a log kept. Every question, every answer, every phone call, whatever we hear, from whomever we hear it—I want it all written down. I want a complete record of everything we do.

—*Chief Investigator Ron Fairbanks*[9]

Appropriate research methods are as vital to success as legitimate sources. Some people gather extraordinary information from marvelous sources and do not document a word. Others expect, and therefore look for, only direct statements of what they need and never find their information. Often, researchers focus on checking off sources and forget about trying different techniques in researching or new ideas for organizing their material.

Important

On the other side of the coin, some people have elaborate systems of organization, with highly developed research logs and written plans, but they have never read tax rolls or court minutes. They may have elegantly crafted pedigree charts they developed from undocumented information, without ever consulting records that the ancestors themselves helped create. As Samuel Clemens once put it, "[They] talk like they've solved the case, but I think they're going in the face of the facts."[10] Successful genealogy requires both appropriate methods and legitimate sources.

Appropriate methods are procedures that fit into the definition of "good genealogy," such as documenting your work, using records that are as near as possible in time to the original, and considering the reliability of the source before accepting its information as fact. Appropriate methods would also include procedures that fit the particular project under study. You would not, for example, spend an exhaustive amount of time searching in Irish records for an ancestral name until you knew that the family had actually originated there. What if they had anglicized their name from a German or Scandinavian name when they immigrated to the United States and the new name simply sounded Irish? Wouldn't it be smarter to start with what you know and work backward in time to identify the immigrants and determine their origin or their original surname before trying to work beyond them?

We would not want said of us what one sleuth said of a case he observed: "The measures adopted were not only the best of their kind, but carried out to absolute perfection. . . . The measures, then, were good in their kind, and well executed; their defect lay in their being inapplicable to the case."[11]

Likewise, legitimate sources are records and documents of many kinds that give us information. Especially valuable and desirable are those as near as possible in time to the original and whose reliability can be judged or estimated. Many of the records we use were created at the federal or county level of government as our ancestors interacted with census takers, the military establishment, tax collectors, notaries public, probate court judges, and county clerks. Some of the records were affirmed and signed as being accurate. Others were entered as the official record of the transaction. We hope our ancestors told the truth and the clerks recorded it accurately. Because we do not always know the truth when we see it, we use another appropriate research procedure: looking for corroborating evidence. Consider the old saying "Whatever is worth doing at all, is worth doing well."[12]

In the Context of Time and Place

Be specific.
—*Cathryn Crawford*[13]

Research takes place in the context of a specific time and place as we look for a specific person or group. For example, we read the 1866 Mississippi state census for Pontotoc County for three brothers and their families. Or we request a certain land entry case file created in 1853 at the Springfield, Missouri, land office for land in Section 27, Township 28 North, Range 32 West for a widowed ancestor.

Reminder

If genealogy ever became so automated that we could enter our own names, click a search button on the Internet, and pull up ourselves and all our ancestors, documented and ready to frame and hang on the wall, it would no longer be fun. There would be no challenge, no puzzle, no sense of fulfillment, no feeling of connection with the past. We could, however, find a parking place at the library on Saturdays.

Unfortunately, some people believe that magic click on the computer is possible now—that they can type in their name or someone else's and voila! That's all they need—a name. Librarians and genealogy teachers constantly ask firsttimers, "Where was your ancestor living in 1920?" This question becomes an early lesson in the concept that genealogical research must take place in the context of a specific time and place.

We have to know *when* and *where* in order to find appropriate records. There may be a dozen or more Huckleberry Greenapples in the country, some related and some no kin at all. We can distinguish them only by placing them in a given place at a given time. Even then, we may have to work with other facts about them to sort out the two who may have been in the same place at the same time.

In addition, part of our research, and part of what makes genealogy interesting, concerns what was going on in the time and place of the ancestor under scrutiny. Geography and history (social, political, economic, military, even meteorological) helped shape the experiences of our ancestors and do much to shape our research. We need a basic knowledge of geography and history in order to understand what we find or do not find in our research.

A story to illustrate the point is an experience a librarian had with a patron at a research facility. A woman came, wanting to find her grandfather in the 1900 census. Since she had never used the census before, the librarian helped her. They found the grandfather in the Soundex and moved to the census itself. When they found the entry, the librarian thought the woman would be excited, but she was downcast. The librarian asked why she was not pleased and said, "This is the grandfather you came to find." And the woman replied, "Yes, but what I need is his Social Security number and it's not here."

(Social Security did not exist in 1900. The Social Security Act of 1935 went into effect in 1936.)

Research Cannot Be Rushed

Start . . . at the beginning. Do not hurry yourself.
—*Hercule Poirot*[14]

Research cannot be rushed. Consider some of the reasons:
1. "You are not quite in possession of the facts yet."—Sherlock Holmes.[15]

    Genealogy is not a hobby for those who expect instant gratification. It takes time to gather the facts we need to build a case. It takes time to get material on interlibrary loan. It takes time to study what we accumulate. It takes time to be sure we are in possession of the "right" facts.
2. "Count me in, Holmes. I have nothing to do for a day or two."—Dr. Watson.[16]

    Genealogy is not something you can do on a Saturday afternoon while your spouse waits in the car and you run into the library to get your family tree. Besides, that would be no fun at all. Even the excitement of getting your family tree would not be permanent until you studied it, gave it time to soak in, and began to appreciate all the intricacies and details of the lives of your forebears. How many people really take the time to do that unless they are researching it for themselves?
3. "You go too fast, my friend."— Hercule Poirot.[17]

    When we try to move too fast, we make mistakes of omission. We forget to write down page numbers or note witnesses on a marriage license. We forget to write down enough information for good documentation, or we read something quickly without taking notes at all. We also make mistakes of commission. We copy something wrong. We get home in a rush, stack the day's research with the mail, and cannot find either the next day. We all get in a hurry sometimes and regret it later.

If a confession is admissible, I admit that when I am in a hurry, one thing I forget to do is write down what is *not* in a document, e.g., nothing reported in the "value of real estate" column of the census, or no adjoining neighbors mentioned in a deed record.

4. "I have just made a discovery of the highest importance, and one which would have been overlooked had I not made a careful examination of the walls."—Sherlock Holmes.[18]

When we are too eager to move on, we may neglect to make a careful examination of the source at hand and may miss a vital piece of evidence. Thus, we may fail to observe and analyze the record carefully enough.

5. "I am afraid it is a little early for us to be feeling self-congratulatory." —Eleanor Roosevelt.[19]

When we find a great piece of evidence, we naturally want to celebrate. However, when we try to rush the research, we run the risk of considering that tidbit a fact before completing the research on it. Then, we are tempted to draw conclusions prematurely.

6. "I need a break to let the ideas ferment a little."—Samuel Clemens.[20]

Especially when we accumulate great amounts of material in a short time or have long drought periods, we need thinking time. We need time to let ideas gel. We need to mull over what something means, or where we should look next.

7. "[Poirot] considered it a point of honour to persevere until he finally succeeded."—Captain Hastings[21]

Given the fact that real life often gets in the way of research, genealogists can spend years working on certain ancestors. Besides, some cases simply take more effort than others. When Plan A does not work, we have to develop Plan B to try a different way of getting our answers. Then, we occasionally spend hours reading microfilm without finding a single clue. However, we persevere because we are determined to find an answer and, like Poirot, we want success—the best possible answer.

Specific Documentation

Pray be precise as to details.
 —*Sherlock Holmes* [22]

Important

Research must be specifically documented in order to be considered valid. Chapter four and appendix B discuss the topic of documenting information found during research. Examples of documentation are also found later in this chapter and in chapters three, seven, and nine through eleven. **This process of documenting should be considered an integral part of the research, not something tacked on later when we want to write up what we have found.** If it is not already second nature to us, we must condition ourselves to record the source information as we research. If we write down the publication information or document identification before looking at any of the data, we have half the job done. The other half is getting the specific page numbers and dates as we turn from page to page, gathering data. Even those of us who have been researching many years sometimes miss a page number and have to go back and look again.

- "I make it a rule to take nothing that is told to me as true, unless it is *checked*."—Miss Marple.[23]

  Miss Marple would agree that this rule applies to what we read on the Internet, in electronic databases, in books and articles, and even in census records and courthouse documents. Each piece of information needs to be checked, corroborated with other evidence whenever possible, or at least analyzed to see that it makes sense in light of all that is found. And each source that is checked needs to be written down; the documentation becomes part of the proof.

- "I agree. But we can't assume anything."—Chief Investigator Ron Fairbanks.[24]

  In genealogy, this statement is especially true. In order to prove a lineage or some other piece of the puzzle, we need to *know*, not *assume*. We can hypothesize, infer, propose, or suspect on the basis of the evidence, but we cannot simply assume something is fact. We need to check it out and record where we found the data that turns our belief into fact.

From the Known to the Unknown

Where shall I begin?
  —*Brent Carradine, research worker*[25]

Research progresses from the known to the unknown. We cannot research the unknown without clues on which to base our looking. It is a waste of time and effort to hunt for a surname all over the country without some specific limitation of given name, time, and/or place. That is why, in planning a search, we list what we know to be true about the focus ancestor or that person's children. Then we divide the puzzle into smaller pieces to research in order to build a bigger base of information, a foundation for the larger search. When we have enough, we can research intelligently and with a greater chance for success. The unknown gradually becomes known.

Cycle of Planning, Looking, Analyzing

I'll be the mastermind of the entire operation.
  —*Samuel Clemens*[26]

Research is a continual cycle of planning, looking, and analyzing, with each new effort building on the results of the previous one. When someone asked Samuel Clemens what role he would play after assigning jobs to everyone else, he answered that he would be the mastermind. This is the role we genealogists play in our own research. We are responsible for the planning, the research, and the analysis, over and over again. Someone has to keep the big picture in mind, has to stay focused on the ultimate goal, and has to map out the way to get there.

- "I've checked up as well as I could on the family history—nothing much there."— Superintendent Garroway.[27]

  We would like to ask the superintendent what he checked, how thoroughly he analyzed what he found, and how carefully he thought about the big picture, for family history was a key to solving the mystery. Hercule Poirot did the thinking, connected the pieces, and saw in the big picture what the superintendent had missed.

- "I should prefer to have clearer proofs before I speak."—Sherlock Holmes.[28]

  Proving a case takes time and requires an accumulation of evidence. Sherlock Holmes usually did not divulge his suspicions until he was certain that each piece of evidence fell into place. We genealogists must do the same: think about what we find, what else we need, how or where we might find it, and what it all means to the overall picture.

- "There doesn't seem to be any shortage of leads, but there's no single area of suspicion strong enough to tell me I ought to concentrate on it alone." —Samuel Clemens[29]

  Clemens, as the mastermind, and we, as genealogists, have to look at all the evidence. If no particular combination of clues points strongly toward a conclusion or a direction of research, we have to choose one or two to follow—Plan A. If this choice does not bring us closer to an answer, we may have to rethink and formulate Plan B, and so on until one "area of suspicion" becomes strong enough to be the center of research.

Use of Reliable Sources

Data! Data! Data! I can't make bricks without clay.
—*Sherlock Holmes*[30]

Just as clay is the basis of bricks, so sources are the foundation of research. To make really good bricks, you need really good clay. To produce credible research, we need reliable sources. Records and documents contemporary with an event, or as close as possible to the event, usually have a greater chance of being reliable and accurate than records and documents created years later, especially by someone without firsthand knowledge of the event. Undocumented accounts by "genealogists" relying on what others have said or written may contain truth, but how can we know? **We must be very cautious with "facts" in these accounts and try to corroborate the contents with information from other, more legitimate sources.**

Warning

How can we judge reliability? Ask yourself questions about the records you use. You may not be able to answer all the questions. However, on the basis of what you can answer, you may be able to determine whether you can accept the information. In reality, we consider two aspects of reliability. One is the document, record, or family story itself. However, each source contains any number of individual pieces of evidence that we must consider as well. A relatively reliable document, such as a deed recorded in a county deed book, can contain copying errors or names misspelled so badly that they are different names. An official death certificate can be correct in its report of the death but inaccurate about the age, birth information, or parentage of the deceased.

Although these questions are written for thinking about an entire record, we must ask them also in relation to individual pieces of evidence.

1. Is this record or document contemporary with the event it describes? If it is not contemporary, who made the record, when, and why?
2. Who probably furnished the information? Was the informant in a position to know and give correct facts? Was the informant a participant in the original event? Was the informant using secondhand information? Would the informant have benefited from giving incorrect or incomplete answers? Did the informant give the facts under oath and affirm their accuracy?
3. Is this the original record or a first-generation copy, as is a will copied into a county will book? Is it a published abstract of the original or near original record? If not the nearest to the original version available, can you get a photocopy of a version closer to the original?
4. Does the document itself have problems that may affect its readability: smears, tears, missing words, faded ink, scribbled handwriting, very dark microfilm that is difficult to read, etc.?
5. Does the record itself contain obvious errors or discrepancies in fact? Were these probably errors of the clerk or errors of the informants? An example is a death certificate in which the age at death and the birth date do not fit properly together.
6. Is the information (names, dates, places, relationships) in the record logical and reasonable? Does it make sense in the context of time, place, and the people being researched?
7. Does more than one reliable source give the same information?
8. What other facts or evidence support the information in this record?
9. Have you found any reliable evidence that contradicts the information or gives conflicting information?

A WORD ABOUT SOURCES

There is often a great deal to be said in favor of looking for a clue in the place where you know it isn't. You see things you would never have noticed otherwise.

—*Dr. Gideon Fell*[31]

Genealogists have available numerous kinds of sources, both public and private (family), as illustrated throughout this book. We find valuable information in both categories, sometimes when we least expect it. Since we cannot know in advance which records our ancestors created or caused to be created, we need to take advantage of whatever records are accessible for their time and place. Sometimes we learn things we would not have learned otherwise.

Record books in courthouses usually are copies of the original records, especially deeds, wills, and estate records. Sometimes, the clerk's office also maintains files of the original wills and probate records; original deeds were family papers, not usually kept at the courthouse. In some court minute books, researchers find original signatures of ancestors, added to the record as the clerks reported the transactions of the court. Although many of the courthouse records are not the originals, they are the official records and the nearest to the original that is available. Thus, they are valuable sources for research, and many are accessible on microfilm. We must use any document carefully, for sometimes even official records contain mistakes.

Occasionally, the most readily available version of an older record is a published abstract (on paper, on CD-ROM, and on the Internet), which is very useful. When we find an ancestral record in such a source, we should get a copy of the version nearest to the original to be absolutely sure of the facts it reports. Consider the following example.

A book containing abstracted county records for Harrison County, Ohio, gives the following entry: "EBENEZER GRAY, Green township, date of will, Feb. 4, 1850; date of probate, Feb. 16, 1861; wife, Margaret; children, William, Jonathan, John-P., Samuel-R., Benoni, Rezin. Phebe; exec., Jonathan Gray."[32] However, the microfilmed will records of Harrison County (1852–1878) at the library at Cadiz, the county seat, show in the will and codicil the additional names of daughters Ann (who married Robert Crouch), Mary (who married Daniel Welch), and Margaret (who married John Taggart); the codicil of 1854 also stated that daughters Anna and Mary were then deceased, both leaving children.[33]

With so many opportunities to get records that ancestors helped create, researchers have little excuse not to use them. Genealogists can learn about available sources by consulting books and articles on sources in general, books and articles on researching in the ancestral state, pamphlets from research facilities, and articles on various genealogical Web sites. Reading high-quality genealogical journals, such as the *National Genealogical Society Quarterly*, *The Virginia Genealogist*, the *New England Historical and Genealogical Register*, the *New York Genealogical and Biographical Record*, and *The American Genealogist* can give you additional ideas about sources and the problems they can help solve.

Printed Source

SUGGESTIONS FOR EFFECTIVE RESEARCH: A REVIEW

Are you a looker-upper?
—*Investigator Alan Grant*[34]

Sometimes it is helpful to review what we have heard before. If you are new to research or would like a brief refresher course, please read the research section in appendix A.

1. When planning to visit an unfamiliar library, archives, courthouse, or other research facility, call first to check the hours of operation, as well as any days they are closed. It is very disconcerting to arrive from out of town for a day's research at 9 A.M. on Thursday and find that the courthouse always closes at noon on Thursdays or that they are closed that day for remodeling.

2. Take with you enough reference material on the family you are researching that you can double-check whatever question or identity arises during the day.

3. Read whatever introductions are provided in the sources you use, including this book.

4. As you take notes, if you use any abbreviations or shorthand of your own creation, define them at the top of the page so you or someone else can decipher your notes at a later date. For example, in researching my Robertson ancestors, I used numerous deed indexes and tax lists. In taking notes, I got really tired of writing down the whole name for each person. Yet it was necessary to record on the same page the several spelling variations of the surname, primarily Robertson, Robinson, and Roberson. After a short time, I began using an abbreviated form—*Robt^n* and *Robin^n* and *Rober^n*—to distinguish the way each name appeared in the record. Even this process got old in a hurry. I then changed to a marginal note before each entry: *t* for Robertson, *n* for Robinson, and *r* for Roberson, with a key at the top of every page to explain the system. This shorthand really streamlined the process, saved time, and improved my attitude about finishing each volume.

5. Take breaks occasionally to eat a snack or walk around. You cannot think or research at your best when you are too tired or too hungry or have concentrated too long without a short break. (Do as I say, not as I do.)

6. Remember that each source can contain multiple pieces of evidence.

7. Observe and think at the same time.

OBSERVE, ANALYZE, AND EVALUATE AS YOU RESEARCH

So the neighbours' conversation was no use to you, eh? I found one most illuminating sentence. Do you remember that after talking of living abroad, Mrs. Bland remarked that she liked living in Crowdean *because she had a sister here. But Mrs. Bland was not supposed to have a sister.* She had inherited a large fortune a year ago from a Canadian great-uncle because she was the only surviving member of his family.

—*Hercule Poirot*[35]

Are we overlooking something important in our research? Are we observing all that we can? This aspect of research includes not only seeing what is on the page or hearing what we are told but also thinking about it and writing our impressions and questions as we proceed.

1. "[T]he analyst . . . makes, in silence, a host of observations and inferences. So perhaps do his companions. And the difference in the extent of the information obtained lies not so much in the validity of the inference as in the quality of the observation. The necessary knowledge is that of *what* to observe."—Edgar Allan Poe[36]

   In genealogy, *what* to observe is not only (a) the names, dates, places, and relationships mentioned but also (b) little details that could seem unimportant or inconsequential and (c) what is missing.

2. "I fancy that I have investigated every nook and corner of the premises in which it is possible that the paper can be concealed."—Monsieur G——, Prefect of the Paris police.[37]

   Monsieur G——was not going to find the paper because he was looking in the wrong way. He had a preconceived notion of what he was looking for, and that was all he expected to find. So, his notion of its appearance drove his search. The problem was that the paper was not concealed. It was in plain view, although disguised. If we go into genealogical research with preconceived ideas, we too may miss something important that is right before our eyes. The preconceived notions can range from a one-way-only spelling of a surname to assumptions about a birthplace or a maiden name.

3. "Noticed anything peculiar about the room?"—Sherlock Holmes.[38]

   Have you noticed anything peculiar about what you are researching? What about a tombstone? Is it newer than it "should be"? If so, did it replace an older one? If not, who initiated the effort, and what is the source of the dates? We need to ask ourselves such questions, even subconsciously, about every record we research. Documents do not always have a "peculiar" characteristic, but we need to develop the skill of observation just in case.

4. "[I was] built noticin'—improved by practice."—Lord Peter Wimsey[39]

   Some people come by it naturally; the rest of us have to develop it. Each time we have to reorder rented microfilm to check a date or a name, we learn the hard way. Each time we have to make a special trip to the research facility to get the rest of information we did not think we needed the first time, we learn from experience. Maybe we too will improve by practice.

5. "I confess that I have been as blind as a mole, but it is better to learn wisdom late than never to learn it at all."—Sherlock Holmes.[40]

   "For a week, almost, we've overlooked a fact that could have a major impact. *I've* overlooked it. . . . I didn't see the possible significance of the fact when it came to my attention."—Eleanor Roosevelt.[41]

   None of us is perfect, but we keep trying.

6. "You should keep your eyes open, Bowes."—Reggie Fortune[42]

Observe and Analyze: An Example

Genealogists train themselves to look for all kinds of specifics when researching. Each specific is a piece of evidence. As you research, ask yourself a number of questions about what you find. You may not be able to answer the questions, but it helps to ask them. The example below concerns cemetery research, but the process is similar when using other kinds of sources.

The gravestone inscriptions, abstracted some years before, had been placed in the file of cemetery abstracts at the library of the Natchitoches Genealogical and Historical Association in the old courthouse in Natchitoches, Louisiana. After photocopying the abstract at the library and learning from the volunteers which of three Russell cemeteries in the parish was the appropriate one, the researchers visited the Russell Cemetery on Bayou Derbanne, southwest of Montrose in Natchitoches Parish. The following notes were made during that visit.[43]

Russell and Pine Island cemeteries

1. The reason for going to the cemetery was to find the tombstones of Ruth Ann and John Bennett and other members of their family. Ruth Ann's and John's stones are in the middle row. Ruthie Ann Bennett: Feb. 14, 1849–Dec. 20, 1923. John Bennett: Sept. 7, 1844–Aug. 22, 1916. The stones are contemporary with their death dates. John's stone is also inscribed "We will meet again." Ruthie Ann's says "Rest mother, rest in quiet sleep, While friends in sorrow o'er thee weep." No other information or artwork is on the stones. Photographed both stones. They are the same shape but not identical. John's is also larger. They are next to each other but separated by enough space that at least two unmarked graves could lie between them.

2. Of their 11 known children, 4 are buried in this cemetery: Sivility Bennett Russell: Oct. 4, 1874–Nov. 12, 1952; Adam Bennett: Feb. 14, 1888–May 27, 1975; P[earlie] or P[arilee] Bennett Butler: Feb. 28, 1878–March 6, 1901; Briant Bennett: May 4, 1880–Sept. 2, 1965. The 1910 census indicated that one of their children died between 1900 and 1910; this must have been P. Bennett Butler, who died in 1901. The censuses of 1900 and 1910 indicated that Ruth Ann had had more children, but no record of any of them was found at the cemetery. Perhaps unmarked graves? Perhaps a different location?

3. A puzzling discovery concerned their daughter Ruth Ann. She appeared in the 1900 census as a 14-year-old daughter, Ruth A., with birth date as Nov. 1885; her marriage record to Ezra Carter in 1902 is registered in Natchitoches Parish; Ruthie A. and Ezra are listed as husband and wife in the 1910 census. Ezra is buried at the cemetery (Dec. 28, 1877–May 8, 1964). Next to him is buried "Ellen D. Carter: Nov. 20, 1885–Feb. 9, 1965." What happened to his wife, Ruthie A.? Did he have a second wife with the same birth month and year? Back to the records!

4. Checked all other Bennetts against the abstract and corrected it. Checked entire abstract and noted new stones since the abstract was done. Will send corrections and additions to the library for their file. A rusty metal cross marking one grave was listed "unmarked" on the abstract. It actually had information scratched on the back: "Lavini Karry, wife of Vol__ Karry d Jan. 4 1928 b 1883." A number of stones were marked "mother," "father," or "sister." A Garlington stone and two Bennett stones gave marriage dates; these two Bennett stones also listed the children's names! Apparently some Bennetts still live in the area. Potential contacts.

5. One funeral home marker near one Leroy Bryant Bennett grave (1986): Blanchard-St. Denis funeral home in Natchitoches. No church near cemetery. No indication found of who maintains the cemetery and where any additional records may be.

6. Later in the day, found Ruthie Ann (Mrs. John) Bennett's mother's stone at Pine Island Cemetery just out of Simpson: an old stone, "Harriet E. Hudson, wife of Caleb Bennett, born July 12, 1828, died Sept. 20, 1890." Photographed stone. Burial place of Caleb Bennett unknown. Copied other Bennetts there.

7. At Pine Island, found a very recent stone for Ann Cato, wife of Samuel D. Williamson. Gives their marriage date and children, in agreement with what we already have. Gives Ann's dates as 1829–1862. How do they know? Who had the stone made? The 1829 date is suggested by the 1860 census, but differs with the 1850. Tradition says Ann died when they arrived at the site of present Simpson. Her husband was in the Confederate army; must check service dates. Was he in the service in 1862? Would they have moved from Alabama to Louisiana during that year of the war? Would he have stayed single 5 more years before remarrying (in 1867), with 4 young children? Needs study.

The best time to write down questions and editorial remarks in your notes is when you think of them. The best time to write down what you see or do not see is at the time of research. These remarks and descriptive notes can be filed with research notes for reference in planning the next step.

WORKING WITH DATES

I sometimes wonder how things would have gone if I'd noticed at the time just that one essential detail that I never appreciated until so many years afterwards.

—*The Storyteller*[44]

One of the essential details in research is working with dates. The context of dates is important as we re-create chronologies for our ancestors and study their lives and associates. Especially pertinent to our efforts are dates we find in official record books at county courthouses, in federal (and some state) land entry files, in census records (see later section in this chapter), and in the colonial period dealing with the Old Style and New Style calendars.

Dates in Official Record Books

Wills, deeds, marriage licenses, and other documents recorded in town or county records have at least two dates: the date of the instrument and the date it was recorded in the official record. Sometimes these dates are years apart. Researchers must be alert to these delays in recording and look for ancestors' activities in record books created even after the ancestors died or moved away.

An example of this phenomenon appears in the deed records of Putnam County, Georgia. Robert H. Sledge sold William Arnold a tract of land on 15 November 1827, but the deed was not recorded until 18 January 1839.[45] The documents were copied into the record book that was in use at the time (1839), not the record book with other instruments made the same year (1827). A more extreme example occurred in Irwin County, Georgia, where a deed of William Rice to D.H. Smith was dated 1840 but recorded in 1893.[46]

Dates in Federal Land Entry Files

Another kind of record that may contain different dates is the land case files of the General Land Office. For most of the eastern federal land states, the information from the tract books is available on CD-ROM and online at <http://www.glorecords.blm.gov> in the section "Search Land Patents." A recording date is given with each record. You may well find a large number of patents from a given land office that have the same date. However, inside the case file, available from the National Archives, may be a document with an earlier date. One file, recorded on 1 June 1860, contained the certificate and receipt, both dated 16 April 1859. If the patentee sold the land in March of 1860, it could appear at first glance that he had sold the land before he bought it.

Likewise, in Jasper County, Missouri, one Lorenzo J. Speegle went before the probate court on 16 October 1852 to apply for letters of administration on the estate of Priscilla Speegle.[47] This same Priscilla, then, patented land in 1853. Well, yes and no. The Speegle patent from the Springfield land office was indeed recorded 15 April 1853, six months after Mrs. Speegle died, and that is the date used as the official patent date. However, the case file contains the preliminary certificate and receipt for the $100 she paid, dated 2 January 1852.[48] This is an illustration of the need for doing chronologies on ancestors and the need for getting the full land case files and probate records in order to sort out the events.

Use of Old Style and New Style Calendars

Although much of the western world switched from the old Julian calendar to the new Gregorian calendar between 1582 and 1700, Great Britain and her colonies did not adopt the new calendar until September 1752. (For a review of the calendar switch, see appendix A.) **Thus, genealogists working with colonial ancestors find the old calendar in use in colonial records.**

Reminder

One example comes from Cumberland County, Virginia, where in October 1749, Daniel Johnson wrote his will. In the document, as recorded in the county will book, the date was actually written in Roman numerals: "MDCCxlix." The record illustrated the official use of the old Julian calendar, for the will was probated in court four months later, in February *1749*.[49] Since the new year began on March 25 under the old calendar, when Daniel Johnson's will was presented in court, the new year, 1750, was still a month away. We could write the date 1749/50 to indicate that the year was still 1749 under the old system but 1750 for those already using the new system. Or we could write O.S. after the year 1749 to indicate the use of the Old Style calendar.

Another instance of the use of the Old Style calendar appears in the Bible record of Archer Allen, son of Samuel Allen of Cumberland County, Virginia.[50] This record reports the births of Samuel Allen's children, including Martha Field Allen on 25 August 1746 and Obedience Allen on 1 March 1747. Under our calendar, such a record would suggest that Obedience was born about six months after her sister, and if this ever really happened in those days, the baby would have been too premature to live. However, such was not the case here, as the family was using the old calendar. Six months after Martha's birth was 1 March 1746. Under the Julian calendar, the new year did not begin until March 25. Thus, Obedience was born barely within the calendar year 1747, about three weeks before 1748 began. The time between the two births, 25 August 1746 and 1 March 1747, therefore, was almost nineteen months.

Under the Gregorian calendar, when we speak of the fifth month, we mean May. Under the Julian calendar, the fifth month was July. This meant, of course, that September, October, November, and December were the seventh, eighth, ninth, and tenth, just as their names indicate; the names derive from the Latin words for the numbers seven, eight, nine, and ten. The Quakers preferred using the numerals themselves instead of the names of the months with their pagan origins.

Use and Analysis of Dates

Researchers must be alert to the use and language of dates. For example, in studying records available on Cora Greenapple to determine her correct birth year, a genealogist found that census records suggested a birth range of 1814–1817. Family records and other records were clearly in agreement that she was born on December 25; the year was the question. Four additional pieces of evidence were found.

- Cora's tombstone, erected by her son, Elderberry Greenapple, in the Pearly Gate Cemetery gave the dates 25 December 1816 to 27 April 1908. (A receipt for payment was found in his papers, and the researcher photographed the tombstone.)
- A handwritten note in Elderberry's family Bible said "Mother died April 27, 1908, age 92."
- Cora's death certificate, filled out by her daughter, Barbery Thorne, gave her birthdate as 25 December 1815 and her age at death as ninety-two years, four months, and two days.
- The local newspaper obituary, reported as coming from Cora's daughter, Mayberry Bush, said Cora died on 27 April 1908 in her ninety-third year.

First, consider the death certificate. Do the age at death and birth date agree? Back up four months and two days from the death date of April 27 and the resulting birthday of December 25 is consistent with all other known sources. Then back up ninety-two years from what year? If she died in April 1908 and had turned ninety-two on her previous birthday, the researcher must subtract 92 from 1907, the year of her last birthday. This gives a birth year of 1815.

Second, consider the newspaper obituary. The phrase "in her ninety-third year" was common language in the nineteenth and early twentieth centuries and is found on tombstones as well as in print. The meaning is clear: she already had turned ninety-two (1907) and would have had her ninety-third birthday during the year in which she died (1908). Thus, she was in her ninety-third year when she died. Subtraction again gives a birth year of 1815 (1908 minus 93).

Third, consider the handwritten note from her son, acknowledging her age as ninety-two when she died. From the evidence involving at least three of the siblings, it appears they agreed that their mother was ninety-two when she died.

Fourth, what about the tombstone? The researcher can only suppose that when Elderberry ordered the tombstone, he must have done a quick subtraction in his mind: 1908 minus age 92 is 1816. And the stonecutter made the stone accordingly. When his sisters saw it, they probably gave him a piece of their minds and perhaps a lesson in dates, although we cannot know for sure.

The known evidence, all coming from Cora's children, points to 1815 as the correct birth year, and at least two of her seven census records agree. The two existing census reports prior to 1850 would support either birth year. The census of 1900, when Cora was living with her son Elderberry, reports her birth as December 1816. The other two censuses indicated 1814 and 1817, which no other evidence supports. Unless the researcher finds any strongly conflicting evidence, we can say Cora Greenapple was born probably in 1815.

Selected Bibliography for Further Reference: Calendar Change and Dates

Berry, Ellen T., and David A. Berry. *Our Quaker Ancestors: Finding Them in Quaker Records*. Baltimore: Genealogical Publishing Co., 1987.

Croom, Emily. *Unpuzzling Your Past*. 3rd ed. Cincinnati: Betterway Books, 1995.

Dollarhide, William. "It's About Time: Calendars and Genealogical Dates." *Genealogy Bulletin* 15 (March/April 1999):1, 6–13.

Jacobus, Donald Lines. *Genealogy as Pastime and Profession*. 2nd ed. revised. Baltimore: Genealogical Publishing Co., 1968.

Remington, Gordon L. "Quaker Preparation for the 1752 Calendar Change." *National Genealogical Society Journal* 87 (June 1999):146–150.

Rubicam, Milton. *Pitfalls in Genealogical Research*. Salt Lake City: Ancestry, 1987.

Printed Source

USING PUBLIC RECORDS

And now, . . . what would you advise me to do?

—*Monsieur G ——, Prefect of the Paris police*[51]

Sources for research abound. The balance of this chapter outlines strategies for using four major groups of sources—census, probate, land, and tax—that pertain to a broad base of ancestors. These record groups also play an important role in the case studies presented in chapters nine through eleven. Because we all need to use these records whenever they pertain to an ancestral family, discussing them here is one way of encouraging everyone to use them.

Court, military, and immigration records and newspapers form other large record groups of great value to the genealogist. Research into these groups and all the others involves certain specific strategies because each type of record is different. However, the general principles of research and strategies of observation and analysis already discussed apply in general to all the others. It is beyond the scope of this book to discuss every group or source.

STRATEGIES FOR USING CENSUS RECORDS

I've had a little experience with this sort of thing, you know, and it suggests that the best way of solving a mystery is to accumulate all the information you can—after which you have to try to organize it so that it leads you somewhere.

—*Eleanor Roosevelt* [52]

Many genealogists begin research of any new family by reading census records. In this effort, we often do what Eleanor Roosevelt mentioned: accumulate all we can from census records and try to organize it in a meaningful way so that we can plan other research.

Federal and state censuses form an important group of sources for genealogists. In order to get the most from these records, researchers must read them thoroughly, carefully, and knowingly. The strategy for reading census records will have to match the needs of each individual case. However, genealogists recognize that certain strategies generally work to their advantage. Those relatively new to census research are urged to read the census section in appendix A in addition to this one.

Use Indexes Creatively

1. When reading the printed indexes for your focus ancestor, note other people by the same surname in the county and/or surrounding counties. If only a few entries for an ancestral surname appear in the index, note all of them.

2. Look in the index, including Soundex, for spelling variations of your ancestral names. To guess at variations, try saying the names with regional or ethnic inflections, as the ancestors or their neighbors might have said them.

3. Remember that some discrepancies resulted from the indexing process: an indexer not familiar with the surnames in the county or the enumerator's handwriting. Occasionally, the typist created errors: Smith indexed as Smiht, or Simpson as Smipson. Once Edmund Bennett was entered as *Bennett,E dmund* with the space in the wrong place; in the computer sorting, his name was indexed apart from the other Bennetts.

4. Make a running list of the variations you find or think you may find for your ancestral names. Note how the differences may change the Soundex coding for the name, as in these examples:

| Thompson | T512 | Rodgers | R326 | Walter | W436 |
| Thomson | T525 | Rogers | R262 | Watters | W362 |

5. Remember that the Soundex for 1880 covers only those households with children ten and under, and even households meeting this criteria were sometimes missed by the enumerator or by the indexers.

6. Remember that for 1910, Soundex and Miracode exist for only twenty-one states; for 1930, twelve states.

Soundex
Soundex Coding

1	b, p, f, v
2	c, s, k, g, j, q, x, z
3	d, t
4	l
5	m, n
6	r

Begin code with first letter of name. With remaining letters, strike vowels and *y, w, h*. Code remaining letters to form three-digit code. Double letters or two consecutive letters with the same code count only once. If you run out of key letters, add zeros. If you have too many key letters, use only the first three.

Examples:	Carter	King	Meyer	Robberson
	C 636	K 520	M 600	R 162

States with Soundex or Miracode for 1910
Alabama, Arkansas, California, Florida, Georgia, Illinois, Kansas, Kentucky, Louisiana, Michigan, Mississippi, Missouri, North Carolina, Ohio, Oklahoma, Pennsylvania, South Carolina, Tennessee, Texas, Virginia, West Virginia.

States with Soundex for 1930
Alabama, Arkansas, Florida, Georgia, Kentucky (7 counties), Louisiana, Mississippi, North Carolina, South Carolina, Tennessee, Virginia, West Virginia (7 counties).

---

7. In using the Soundex or Miracode, write down all information that you will need to find the family in the census: state, county, enumeration district (e.d.), sheet number (in Miracode, the family number), and line number.

8. Any time you do not find your ancestral names in an index or Soundex, read the entire county where you think they were living. If you don't find them there, you could try the surrounding counties before you declare them missing, moved, or deceased. Also try finding all married siblings of the nuclear family and all siblings of the parents.

9. For residents of large cities for which there is no index or when the family has no listing in the index, try the microfiche 1910 Cross Index to City Streets (National Archives publication M1283). It may help find families for which you have a street address. Discussions of this index and the enumeration district descriptions appear in *The Genealogist's Companion & Sourcebook*, chapter two.

   If you are looking for a 1920 city family and with no Soundex entry, you might (1) use their 1910 address to identify in the cross index its enumeration district number, then (2) check the description of that 1910 district in the enumeration district descriptions (National Archives microfilm T1224), and (3) check the 1920 enumeration district descriptions (also T1224) to find a district that matches or approximates the location of the 1910 district.

10. Armed with the index and Soundex entries, read the actual censuses. The index is not a substitute for the real document.

Important

Spelling Variations

If the informant who talked to the census taker was illiterate and could not spell the family name, or did not spell it, the enumerator had to spell it the way it sounded. **Variant surname spellings may be minor but may still require the researcher to look in several parts of the index.** Depending on regional speech patterns, the census taker may have heard sounds that are not part of the usual spelling of the name or heard an entirely different name: Osborn as Orsborn, Walter as Waters, Morris as Morse.

Map Study

Once you find the county of residence for your ancestral family, locate it on a map and make note of surrounding counties for the appropriate time period. My favorite source for this kind of information is *Map Guide to the U.S. Federal Censuses, 1790–1920*, by William Thorndale and William Dollarhide, a volume that belongs in every genealogist's personal library. These maps can also help determine whether the county boundaries changed between censuses, even though the family may have remained in the same place.

If you find your ancestors or their known relatives in the central county, why not read the families of the same surname(s) indexed in the parent and surrounding counties as well? Brothers, cousins, or parents often lived near each other but in separate counties. This process may help you establish migration patterns, naming patterns, and collateral relatives to study as part of the ancestral cluster.

Reading the Census Thoroughly

> I suppose I risk looking like Sherlock Holmes if I ask for a magnifying glass, but if someone has one—
> —*Eleanor Roosevelt*[53]

Thorough and accurate reading is easier when you can see the words, numbers, and marks clearly. Thus, a valuable tool of genealogy research is the magnifying glass. Thoroughness and accuracy also depend on your reading of the census taker's handwriting. Notice the style the individual uses to form letters and numbers; double-check your reading of both when recording data.

Record everything in the family's entry, keeping spelling and ages as they appear there. Remember:

- These pieces of information can suggest ideas for other sources to search.
- People in the household with different surnames may be related.

Obviously, some entries are more accurate than others. Many researchers experience the amazement of finding a census record that must be the right family although much of the information is amiss. An 1870 example appears in chapter eleven on page 166.

Read several pages on each side of your family's entry to look for other relatives or cluster members. Have you identified married daughters or families of the same surname who may not be indexed? If you are looking for associates of your ancestor, look for families with the same birthplace patterns, with similar naming patterns, or with the same occupation, such as stonemasons in a community of farmers.

Why do we read additional pages or the whole enumeration district? One of my favorite examples is an 1880 Louisiana household whose entry began at the bottom of one page with parents and two daughters. The other five children, who should have been at the top of the following page, were indeed at the top of a page, ten pages later, apparently separated in the original copying process or in the binding of the volume. The first portion of the family included only the children over ten and therefore was not Soundexed. If the others, ages two to ten, were Soundexed, I did not find them.

The microfilmed copy of this district's census gave no family or dwelling numbers; everyone was strung together. Husbands and wives were usually identified, and some other relationships were recorded. The five younger children of the family had no stated relationships and were not attached to any other family. Since the family did not appear in the Soundex, I was reading the entire parish (county) where I believed them to be. They were enumerated next to two other households of the same surname, neither of which was in the Soundex.

Finding these households unexpectedly as a cluster opened up new problems in the research on this particular family. The discovery reminded me of the comment of President Franklin Roosevelt to Joe Kennedy in *The Hyde Park Murder*: "Well, where is all this getting us, old chap? It seems to me that every fact you and my missus come up with only leads us deeper into the mystery. When do we begin to come out?"[54]

When, indeed? When we have enough evidence to make a good case. The evidence in this 1880 census cluster effectively negated one of the working hypotheses on this family. As researchers, we must take into account even contrary evidence, although not always welcome, when re-creating the family group.

Read Every Available Census

Your reasoning is certainly plausible.
—*Dr. Watson*[55]

Research Tip

The 1880 example above illustrates the benefit of another census strategy: **Read every census available for each ancestor. We never know what we may learn in the next one.**

Some census takers give genealogists very nice surprises. We cannot afford to miss these gems. For example, censuses that went beyond the instructions (or whose enumerator interpreted them differently) and identified a specific town or county of birth for each inhabitant include parts of Chatham County, Georgia (1860); Caldwell County, Kentucky (1850); Edgar County, Illinois (1850); and Baker, Cobb, and Muscogee Counties, Georgia (1850). The 1850 censuses of Houston and Anderson counties in Texas reported the county of birth for each child born in Texas. One marshal in Caddo Parish, Louisiana, in 1850 recorded the year of marriage for each couple and labeled twins. His counterpart in Saline County, Arkansas, that year also gave the year of marriage for each couple and labeled adults as married, single, or widowed. Part of the Chatham County, Georgia, census of 1860 also gave ages of many children, not just infants, in years and months, aiding researchers in more closely estimating birth dates.

Countless census entries contain helpful notes that explain relationships, label heirs of a deceased parent, or otherwise provide us with valuable evidence. The marshal recording the 1830 census of St. Joseph County, Michigan, in the entry of Abiel Fellows added a jewel of a note. It is repeated here with its original spelling intact:[56]

> This man is sixty five [years] of age   has nineteen living children ten of which is under his care   was a soldier in the Revolution   is a man of Sober Habits of unusual enterprise and great strenght of mind   has never received any thing from our government for his Early and Youthful strugle for Independence   is it to late to hope??

Document Your Censuses

Write down in your extracts of census entries whatever identifying information is on the page, as well as the film and roll number: enumeration district number, sheet or page number, local post office or political division, date of enumeration, family and dwelling numbers, and line numbers, especially if the film is difficult to read. The name of the town, community, ward, or precinct, although not always given, may help locate the family's neighborhood within the county and provide clues for further study.

Usually Work Backward in Time

Generally, we work from the most recent census backward in time. However, when you identify siblings of your ancestor, you often need to work forward again to find them with their own families and develop a family group sheet for each. This process helps sort out relatives with the same names and identify persons who may still be living and may communicate with you about the family.

If your family or their neighborhood was missed and if the error was in the copying process only, you may be able to find your family in the original enumeration at the state archives or state historical society. Thorndale and Dollarhide's *Map Guide to the U.S. Federal Censuses 1790–1920* identifies "lost" counties for each state in each census.

Who Was the Informant?

We do not know exactly who gave the information to the census taker. Thus, we cannot say, "*He* gave his birthplace as Kansas in 1880, but in 1900, *he* said he was born in Colorado." In addition, until we have studied further, we have to consider both states as possible birthplaces. As students of the family, we must remain neutral on the questions of name, age, birthplace and other data until we have other evidence to help determine which answers are the most accurate.

CENSUS DAY 1790–1930

1790: August 2, first Monday	1830–1900: June 1
1800: August 4, first Monday	1910: April 15
1810: August 6, first Monday	1920: January 1
1820: August 7, first Monday	1930: April 1

Census Day

Remember what the instructions to the marshals said about census day: Each person whose regular place of abode was in that household on that day was to be included with the household in the census. The actual date of the enumeration did not matter. For the 1830–1900 censuses, census day was June 1. All and only living members of the household as of June 1 were to be included, even if one died or another was born between June 1 and the enumerator's visit later in the summer. The age given was to be the age attained on the most recent birthday. Thus, a reported age of seven in 1850 should mean that the child had turned seven between 1 June 1849 and 1 June 1850. Unless we have a specific date from other sources, we have to estimate the birth as 1842–1843 because we do not know which year is correct.

However, we do not know whether the family actually followed the rule. A child who had turned twelve the week before the census taker's visit may have been reported as twelve, being the age at the most recent birthday, even if it was July 17. Likewise, a family member who died after June 1 is sometimes listed with the family and sometimes crossed out or notated "deceased" on the page. Those who actually died between 1 June 1849 and 1 June 1850, for instance, were supposed to be listed in the mortality schedule although omissions did occur.

Ages for infants, and sometimes for older children, were normally expressed in months: $9/12$ for nine months of age. It is helpful and interesting to find other designations, such as $1/365$ (one day old) or $21/30$ (twenty-one days old). If the family was following the census day rule, these designations can narrow the birth date to a range of two or three days, depending on how they were figuring it (full twenty-four-hour periods, calendar days, counting census day as a day or stopping the day before, etc.). Although we do not know whether the family observed the rule, we can still narrow down the date of birth. For example, for the one-day-old child in 1860, in a family enumerated on July 20, we could estimate the birth at May 30–31 (with June 1 as census day) or July 18–19 (if they counted from the census taker's actual visit).

Filing and Census Check

File your findings where you can find them easily and often. I like to keep a census section for each ancestral state in each surname notebook. It is helpful to file the census forms in chronological order. If you have multiple pages for some years of the census, it is also helpful to have a separate divider for each of those years.

A helpful tool to complement and file with the census extractions is the census check form from *The Unpuzzling Your Past Workbook*. It allows you to record documentation and summarize findings for each census for any given person, as a child and as an adult. In addition, this summary tells you, at a glance, which census records for that person you have found, which you have looked for and not found, and which you still need to read.

Analyze and Evaluate Each Piece of Data

Makes plenty of sense to me. Keep on talking.
  —*Samuel Clemens*[57]

Study and analyze your findings. Record tentative birth dates and places on working family group sheets and chronologies, with documentation. Identify individuals or families whose census records you need to read next. To analyze and evaluate each piece of data (age, sex, birthplace, ability to read and write, etc.) ask yourself such questions as these:

- Does this piece of information alone make sense for this person?
- Is it consistent with data from other censuses or other sources? Are reported ages consistent from one census to the next? What range of birth years do the ages suggest?
- Is it inconsistent with data from any other census or source? In what ways?
- Are there any surprises in the newly gathered material? For example, are there indications that the family moved within the county between censuses? Are different birthplaces or different occupations reported? Is someone in addition to the nuclear family living in the household?
- If the entry does not give relationships, what are the logical possibilities in this household? Which later censuses or other records confirm any of the relationships?
- Were any known relatives reported living nearby?
- What clues did I get from reading entries of the neighbors?
- What conclusions, if any, can I draw from each piece of data or the entry as a whole? Which parts of the entry appear correct and which seem questionable?
- What do I need to do next? For example, if real estate value is reported, do I have information on the purchase, sale, and location of that land?
- Do I have all the censuses for this family? How do they compare with each other?

Figure 5 is a chart for one of two Frierson families in the 1840–1860 censuses, created from the research of Texas genealogist Gay E. Carter. Such a chart is a helpful way to get an overall picture of the family and to evaluate census entries. Of course, the names appear only in the 1850 and 1860 entries, but matching the ages with the 1840 census entry helps account for the family members. An estimated range of birth dates, figured from the censuses, is listed last.

Chart of the Charles C. Frierson Family of Maury County, Tennessee, and Lafayette County, Mississippi, 1840–1860
(Key: M = male, F = female, < = less than, c = *circa*, about)

1840 Age [58]	Name	1850 Age [59]	1860 Age [60]	Estimate of Birth date
M30–40	Charles C. Frierson	39	49	c 1810–1811°
F20–30	Millard N. (Mildred)/Melane	38	48	c 1811–1812°
F5–10	Mary Elizabeth Frierson	18	25	c 1831–1835
F5–10	Sally W. Frierson	17	24	c 1832–1836
M5–10	Ed L. Frierson	16	[married]	c 1833–1834°
M<5	James G. Frierson	13	22	c 1836–1838
F<5	Adaline A. Frierson	10	19	c 1839–1841*
—	Edwin Dickey Frierson	8	17	c 1841–1843
—	Eugenia C. Frierson	6	15	c 1843–1845
—	Emma S.P. Frierson	3	13	c 1846–1847
—	Martha Frierson	1	11	c 1848–1849
—	Ida Frierson	—	9	c 1850–1851
—	Robert Frierson	—	7	c 1852–1853

° All these birth years allow for the possibility of a full year range for each age reported. With the census year running from 1 June 1839 to 1 June 1840, for instance, and the census question asking for the age of the person as of the most recent birthday, we have to allow for the birthday, in the case of Charles, occuring in the latter half of 1810 or the first half of 1811. Apply the same process for the rest of the family.

* From the censuses alone, we cannot know whether another little girl was the one in the 1840 census as the female under five and died before the 1850 census, with this Adaline being born after census day in 1840 or in 1841, as the 1860 census suggests. However, Adaline's tombstone records her birth date as 11 March 1840 and places her as the youngest member of the 1840 household. [61]

Figure 5 Census Study of the Charles C. Frierson Family

Although the makeup of the Charles C. Frierson family remained constant over the three census records, the family of his brother, Edward Livingston Frierson, changed from census to census. Consider their entries in Figure 6. Comparison of these entries led the researcher to cemetery research.

Chart of the Edward L. Frierson Family of Maury County, Tennessee, and Lafayette County, Mississippi, 1840–1860
(Key: M = male, F = female, < = less than, c = *circa*, about.)

1840 Age [62]	Name	1850 Age [63]	1860 Age [64]	Tombstone Data[65]
M40–50	Edward L. Frierson	52	62	
F30–40	Sarah E. Frierson	49	60	
F15–20	Mary J. Frierson	—	—	1823–1844 (January)
F10–15	Eugenia W. Frierson	—	—	1827–1844 (February)
F5–10	Salina A[melia] Frierson	19	—	1830–1852 (July)
F<5	Janett/Jennette W. Frierson	15	—	1835–1858 (June)
M<5	Charles C. Frierson	12	22	
—	Sarah D. Frierson	7	17	
—	Gaston L. Frierson	3	—	1846–1857 (August)

Figure 6 Census Study of the Edward L. Frierson Family

STRATEGIES FOR USING PROBATE RECORDS

It was very cold and I was hungry; but excitement would not let me eat. I was getting my first zest for this new game I was playing, and I was losing my shrinking horror of spying into affairs that were not my own.

—*Nurse Detective Hilda Adams*[66]

Important

Probate records form a large body of many different kinds of documents, held in the offices of different county officials, depending on the state: the probate court, county court, orphans' court, surrogate court, chancery court, or others. (In Louisiana, the probate records are called *succession* records.) **Usually we think of probate records as the kind generated after someone dies, but they can also pertain to issues of lunacy, adoption, bastardy, apprentices, and orphans.** If you look for microfilm of these records, usually finding aids and library catalogs call them, first, probate records regardless of the name of the court of jurisdiction.

Kinds of Death-Related Records

The death-related records in probate books and files can be quite varied, but usually fall into these categories:

1. Wills, which help identify heirs, locate land, and narrow the possibilities for a date of death.
2. Codicils to wills (additions or changes made after the will was written), which can identify further heirs, changes within the family, and changes in the instructions of the will itself.
3. Inventory and appraisal of testate or intestate estates. Even if the ancestor had no will, you will often find an inventory of the estate and an appraisal of its value. Even if these do not prove relationships, they give an interesting picture of lifestyle and are part of the family history. For those tracing slave genealogy, these can be particularly important when the slaves are named, because the records sometimes help track ages and family groups. Even the values placed on slaves can help determine who were the adults and who were the children or the elderly.
4. Record of an estate sale, including the sale of land or slaves. If slaves are named in such a sale, the record becomes a clue to where to look for them next or tells you how they came into the new master's household.
5. Guardianship appointments and reports if there were minor children.
6. Administrator (intestate estates) and executor (testate estates) bonds.
7. Bills from the estate's creditors and receipts for payment.
8. Annual returns reporting the business of the estate before its final settlement, usually a record of income and expenses, but with the potential for much genealogical evidence. Those tracing slave genealogy can sometimes learn whether a slave ancestor was hired out, what occupation or trade

the person pursued, who employers were, and other information that can help track that ancestor.

9. Court proceedings generated over the division of the estate or provisions of the will.

10. In Louisiana, notes from any family meeting held on behalf of the minor heirs.

11. Final division of the estate, often with names of heirs and daughters' husbands and what each heir received.

Suggestions for Use

1. Read and/or photocopy all the probate documents you can find for a focus ancestor. Be aware that in a courthouse or on microfilm there may be more than one index.

2. If you know the identities of the ancestor's siblings, look up their probate records as well. Brothers often acted as executors for siblings. Combining the probate records for several brothers can help produce a more complete picture of the family group.

3. Some of the records will be copied into will or probate books, but ask about the original files. They may contain items not copied into the books.

4. When studying your notes and photocopies, put them in chronological order to give you a clearer picture of the chain of events.

5. Look at each document as a separate entity. Consider each tidbit it contains: names, dates, transactions, etc. Analyze what it says or means in the study of the whole. (See chapters seven and nine through eleven.)

6. Look for any direct statements the record makes: a death date, a relationship, the widow's new husband, a daughter's husband, names of heirs, the death of an heir before final distribution, etc.

7. Look for evidence that can help establish proof: activities of the deceased that can narrow the possibilities for a death date; indications of the death or remarriage of the widow or of one or more heirs; changes in guardian or executor; business of the estate that will show continuation of the family business, the education of the children, the hiring out of slaves, the minister who preached the funeral sermon (may help identify church records), etc.

8. When tracing slave genealogies and focusing on a white family in a probate record, get any information given in each record in the file, even if the slaves are not named. (See chapter ten.)

STRATEGIES FOR USING LAND RECORDS

You should never neglect a chance, however small it may seem.
—*Detective Gregson*[67]

Land records are among the most valuable sources in genealogy research. They can be found at the county (or town), state, and federal levels of government, depending on the kind of record. Although not all ancestors owned land, a significant number did, especially in the nineteenth century. Besides, deed record books often contain more than purchases and sales of land.

Did My Ancestors Own Land?

A number of records will help you determine whether your ancestors owned land. The 1850, 1860, and 1870 censuses had columns for reporting the value of real estate a person owned. The 1900 and 1910 censuses asked whether the head of household owned or rented the residence or farm, and in 1920 and 1930, the question asked whether the home was owned or rented. Some state censuses ask the same questions. In addition, deed record indexes, tax rolls, probate records, and General Land Office records at both state and federal levels of government are the usual sources of this information. Other important sources include published documents in the *American State Papers* and *The Territorial Papers*, family tradition, and family papers.

Locating the Ancestral Land

In the census records, the local community or district listed at the top of the page or the local post office can give a general idea of where the family lived. Deed records, land patents, some tax rolls and probate records, some contemporary maps or atlases and, in Georgia, land lottery records can help determine the location.

FEDERAL LAND AND STATE LAND STATES

Federal Land States: All states west of the Mississippi River except Hawaii and Texas, and including Louisiana and Minnesota, which are split by the river.

These states east of the Mississippi River: Alabama, Florida, Illinois, Indiana, Michigan, Mississippi, Ohio, and Wisconsin.

Federal Land States under the Eastern States Office of the Bureau of Land Management: Alabama, Arkansas, Florida, Illinios, Indiana, Iowa, Louisiana, Michigan, Minnesota, Mississippi, Missouri, Ohio, and Wisconsin.

State Land States: These states west of the Mississippi River: Hawaii and Texas.

The original thirteen states: Connecticut, Delaware, Georgia, Maryland, Massachussets, New Hampshire, New Jersey, New York, North Carolina, Pennsylvania, Rhode Island, South Carolina, and Virginia.

States derived from the original thirteen: Kentucky, Maine, Tennessee, Vermont, and West Virginia.

If the ancestor lived in one of the thirty federal land states, the land case files, tract books, subsequent deed records, and applicable probate records usually give the specific location of the land within a section, township, and range. These are relatively easy to locate on maps of the county or township. The federal land patent was the first transfer of ownership, from the government to an individual. Subsequent sales between individuals are recorded in deed records in county courthouses.

If the ancestor's land was in a state land state that used (or uses) a metes and bounds system of legal descriptions, plotting exact locations requires more effort. By studying neighbors, county maps, survey notes and plat maps, legal descriptions, and watercourses or other landmarks, diligent researchers can closely identify the ancestral land. With the legal descriptions from deed or probate records, researchers can plot on paper, fairly accurately, the relative shape and location of tracts. Those legal descriptions that used notches on trees, rock piles, or stakes in the prairie for corners of property are more difficult to re-create on maps today unless specific and accurate directions and distances (metes and bounds) of property lines were given in documents pertaining to the land.

Figure 7, on page 96, is a diagram of a standard township in the rectangular survey system, used predominantly in federal land states. If you have legal descriptions of ancestral land, plot that land on such a diagram, being aware of the section numbers that adjoin the land in neighboring townships and/or ranges. Relatives sometimes lived in different sections, townships, or ranges and still were near each other.

Likewise, for federal land states, Figure 8 illustrates the system of numbering townships north and south of a base line and ranges east and west of a meridian. Try to get county maps that show the township and range numbers that belong within the county. Such maps help you plot your ancestral land and that of other relatives and ancestral associates. An example is shown in Figure 15, page 194.

Locating land on a map or diagramming it on paper can help the researcher in several kinds of searches.

1. Mapping can help determine the proximity of families with the same surname in an attempt to identify other same-surname relatives.

2. Studying adjoining landowners, even of different surnames, may help identify (a) heirs of someone who owned a larger, unified tract at an earlier date or (b) possible in-laws.

3. Studying the acquisition of ancestral land from grants and purchases can help determine what a man acquired on his own and what he may have inherited. This process can help in trying to identify parents. It may also help in the identification of the wife's parents if the land appears to have come into possession by inheritance rather than purchase, but not from the husband's parents.

4. Mapping to help identify neighbors can be useful in a search for a wife's maiden name and parents.

5. Studying all documents of purchase and sale for land owned in a particular name can help determine whether you are dealing with one person or several different people with the same name.

6. Studying a neighborhood by plotting land ownership can help in reconstructing a genealogical cluster.

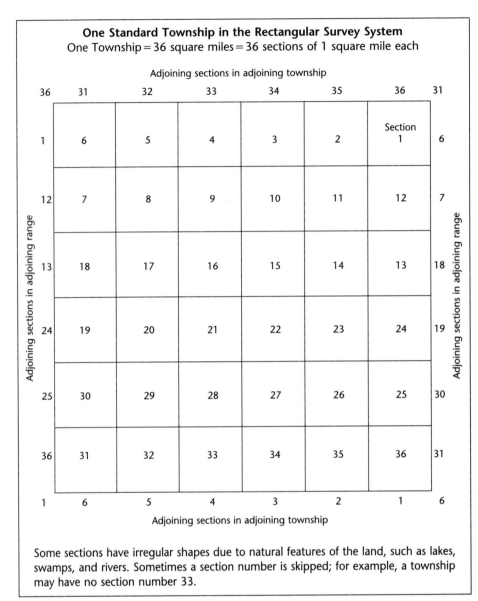

One Standard Township in the Rectangular Survey System
One Township = 36 square miles = 36 sections of 1 square mile each

Figure 7 One Standard Township in the Rectangular Survey System

Suggestions for Land Record Research

1. Look in the county or town (in parts of New England or independent cities in Virginia) deed index for your ancestor(s) and others of the same surname, even for deeds recorded after your ancestor died or moved away.

2. Read all the deeds mentioned in the index under the ancestral surname, of both grantees and grantors.

3. Read in the deed volume several pages on either side of ancestral deeds to see if the same ancestor was mentioned in or was witness to other deeds made about the same time. This kind of activity places the ancestor in a given place at a given time and is especially useful when it occurred between censuses. It can help establish death or moving dates.

4. It can be helpful to read the entire volumes recorded during your ancestor's

Numbering Townships and Ranges From Base Line and Meridian

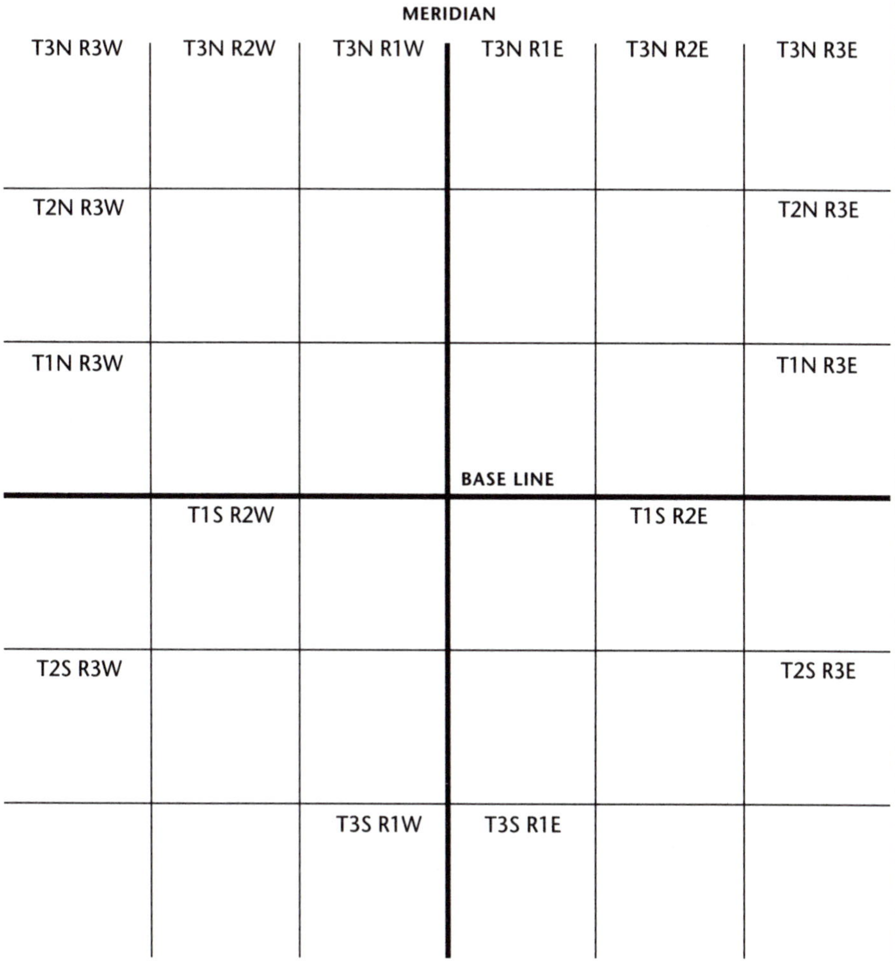

MERIDIAN

T3N R3W	T3N R2W	T3N R1W	T3N R1E	T3N R2E	T3N R3E
T2N R3W					T2N R3E
T1N R3W					T1N R3E
	T1S R2W		BASE LINE	T1S R2E	
T2S R3W					T2S R3E
		T3S R1W	T3S R1E		

Like longitude, ranges are numbered east or west of a meridian. Like latitude, townships are numbered north or south of a base line. Townships and ranges can have very high numbers, meaning that they are some miles away from their base line or meridian.

Figure 8 Rectangular Survey System

time in the county to look for your ancestor and other family members as witnesses, adjoining neighbors, or even as notaries, justices, lawyers, creditors, sheriffs, or clerks. These add to the knowledge of ancestral activity and place people in a given place at a given time.

5. Record all names, dates, places, relationships, legal descriptions, and terms of the deeds. With experience in reading in a given location, you can determine what was standard legalese and what may have been unique in your ancestor's deeds. Get photocopies when you feel the document is too long to abstract in the time you have or if the document has a large amount of detail, such as in a deed of trust.

6. Note the adjoining neighbors mentioned in and the witnesses to your ancestor's land documents. These people may or may not be related. They do become part of the cluster of associates if you need to reconstruct that

list in order to work on a tough genealogical problem.

7. In the record books, look for other transactions to which the ancestor may have been a party or participant. Some deed books also contain other kinds of transactions, such as wills and probate records, deeds of gift, mortgages, deeds of trust, marriage contracts, polling (voting) lists, powers of attorney, bills of sale for slaves, contracts, and other business dealings. One deed book from the 1840s even contained house plans for four homes, along with the contracts for building them.

8. To aid in your study, if the ancestor owned multiple tracts of land, make a record of each tract—its purchase and its sale—to try to account for the disposition of each property. Note whether there was a purchase without a sale, or vice versa. A purchase without a subsequent sale could indicate land that passed to heirs or land given to a child. (Look for a deed of gift.) A sale without a purchase could indicate land the husband or wife inherited.

9. Get copies of any state land grant or patent and federal land patent, especially homestead files. The file may not contain additional information, but documents in the file sometimes help identify other relatives, in-laws, former residences, and even naturalization information. Besides, these files complete your record and account for the acquisition of land the ancestor may have sold later.

10. Correlate information from land, marriage, census, probate, and other records for the neighborhood to determine how various families were interrelated, especially your own family and those related to them.

Selected Books for Further Reference: Land Research

Many resources deal with land records and land research. Below are selected helpful ones.

Printed Source

American State Papers: Documents Legislative and Executive of the Congress of the United States. 38 vols. Washington: Gales and Seaton, 1832–1861. Class 8: *Public Lands.* Class 9: *Claims.*

Barsi, James C. *The Basic Researcher's Guide to Homesteads & Other Federal Land Records.* Colorado Springs, CO: Nuthatch Grove Press, 1994.

Bockstruck, Lloyd DeWitt. *Revolutionary War Bounty Land Grants Awarded by State Governments.* Baltimore: Genealogical Publishing Co., 1996.

Carter, Clarence E., comp., ed. *The Territorial Papers of the United States.* 28 vols. Washington, DC: Government Printing Office, 1934–1975. There are several additional sets of similar papers available on microfilm.

Eichholz, Alice, ed. *Ancestry's Red Book: American State, County & Town Sources.* Rev. ed. Salt Lake City: Ancestry, 1992.

Greenwood, Val D. *The Researcher's Guide to American Genealogy.* 2nd. ed. Baltimore: Genealogical Publishing Co., 1990.

Hawkins, Kenneth, comp. *Research in the Land Entry Files of the General Land Office: Record Group 49.* Washington, DC: National Archives and Records Administration, 1997. General Information Leaflet Number 67.

Hone, E. Wade. *Land & Property Research in the United States.* Salt Lake City: Ancestry, 1997.

McMullin, Phillip W., comp. *Grassroots of America: A Computerized Index to the American State Papers Land Grants and Claims (1789–1837)*. Salt Lake City: Gendex Corp., 1972.

STRATEGIES FOR USING TAX RECORDS

He was excited.... Excited and happy, like a dog which has followed a cold trail for a long time, and suddenly finds it a hot one.
—*Nurse Detective Hilda Adams about Inspector Patton*[68]

Research in tax records has produced this reaction of excitement for many genealogists and has resulted in many "hot trails." A number of states and towns have preserved tax records that date to their early years; others have not been so diligent. Nevertheless, the genealogist needs to use them whenever they exist. They are particularly valuable for research in Georgia, Kentucky, North Carolina, Virginia, and early West Virginia when it was part of Virginia. The surviving records are usually found in county courthouses or in state archives. Many have been microfilmed and are available from the Family History Library.

Tax records are kin to land records because residents paid taxes on land they owned, as well as on slaves, horses, cattle, oxen, personal property, and luxury items such as clocks and carriages. In some cases, specific items were taxed in a given year, such as certain items of furniture, mirrors, and window curtains in Virginia in 1815. Sometimes, as in Virginia, the land tax records and personal property tax records are separate. People who owned no land could still have paid poll taxes (head taxes) on themselves, slaves, or sons of taxable age. Widows were not normally taxed except on their land and slaves, although men of taxable age in their households were taxed.

Notes

Following the existing tax rolls for a given ancestor over a period of years can give the researcher quite a bit of information. Yet, each state had its own laws, forms, and lists of taxable property. Free men could begin being taxed when they became sixteen or eighteen or twenty-one, depending on the state and the time period. Slaves were often classified in the tax rolls in age groups, such as those under twelve, twelve to sixteen, over sixteen, or sixteen to fifty-five. These categories also varied from place to place and year to year. Usually the tax laws designated an age after which a person was exempt from certain taxes.

Information Sometimes Found in Tax Records

What kind of information, in general, may be shown in these records? Below are some of the standard column headings, but these vary from state to state, even year to year.

1. Name of the person charged with the tax, usually the head of household
2. Names of free men of color being taxed
3. Number, and sometimes names, of taxable free white males in the household

4. Number of acres of land owned, sometimes with location information—adjoining neighbors, watercourse, distance from the courthouse, or district number
5. Name of original grantee of land
6. Number of slaves in the household each year, sometimes with their names
7. Rent received on rented property
8. Number of horses, oxen, or cattle owned
9. Value of land, slaves, or other taxable property
10. Amount of tax paid

What other information might the genealogist glean from studying *some* tax rolls?

1. Relationships, either expressed, deduced, or suggested
2. Suggestions of birth order among sons in a family, depending on when they first were named or became a head of household
3. Suggestions of death year or moving, when someone no longer was listed, when an estate was listed, when someone was named as guardian of the children or administrator of an estate, or when someone is taxed for the property formerly belonging to another person
4. Occupations, expressed or implied by paying license fee
5. Suggestions of family groups of slaves, when, over the years, the same slaves were named in a household; sometimes, slaves' ages
6. Changes in a person's net worth or lifestyle, expressed in changes in the number of slaves, livestock, and luxury items
7. Preliminary identification of neighbors, by studying adjoining landowners and watercourses, or when the tax collector dated each entry and it appears that he visited the households in person

Illustration Tracing a Female Ancestor Through Tax Rolls

Case Study

Texas researcher John Dorroh found a gold mine in the microfilmed personal property tax rolls. Dorroh had traced his ancestor, William Norton, from Missouri back to Nelson County, Kentucky, where he was listed for the first time in the 1811 tax roll. An Alexander Norton was listed in the Nelson County roll in 1816 next to William Norton. Dorroh had learned from the 1880 census entries of William Norton's children about his supposed Virginia birth. Two other puzzle pieces appeared, but no proof had surfaced to tie them to the ancestor, William Norton:

- The 1776 census of Prince George's County, Maryland, listed the family of William Norton Jr. (age 36): Mary Norton (33) and children Walter Mudd (12), John Mudd (8), and Amelia Norton (3).[69]
- A Mary Gibbs seems to have married a John Mudd although no marriage record has been found.[70]

The challenge was to find the childhood family and parents of the ancestor, William Norton, of the Nelson County, Kentucky, tax roll of 1811. The personal property tax rolls for Loudoun County, Virginia, provided rather conclusive evidence.[71] Since the microfilm rolls begin with 1782, Dorroh read them coming forward in time, with the results capsuled in Figure 9. He did not find listings for Nortons or Mudds in the 1782–1786 rolls. (Tithable ages varied but were usually expressed as "over sixteen" in the pertinent years.)

Studying these tax records in reverse chronological order, the genealogist can suggest the following:

1. William Norton moved to Nelson County, Kentucky, about 1809–1810. (He married there in 1810 and was there for the 1811 tax roll.)[72]

Tax Year	Person charged with the tax	Tithable white men in the household	Notes
	Norton Family Evidence in Loudoun County, Virginia, Tax Rolls		
1787	Mary Norton	one white male 16–21	
1788	Mary Norton	John Norton [sic], 16–21	Last appearance of Mary Norton
	Thomas Gregg, potter	self, Levy & Josiah Gregg	
	Walter Mudd	self	
1789	Walter Mudd	self & John Northcut	
	Thomas Gregg Sr.	self, John Mudd, Levy Gregg	
1790	Walter Mudd	self, Walter Law, John Northcut	
	Thomas Gregg, potter	self, Levy Gregg, John Mudd	
1791	Walter Mudd	self, John Mudd	
	Thomas Gregg, potter	self, Levy Gregg	
1792	Walter Mudd	self	
	Thomas Gregg, potter	self, Levi Gregg, John Mudd	
	(In mid-1792, one Thomas Gregg Sr. died in Loudoun County, leaving a will that named his wife, Mary, two daughters, and seven sons, including Levi, Josiah, Thomas.[73])		
1793	Thomas Gregg, potter	self, Josiah Gregg	It appears that Mary Norton had
	Mary Gregg	John Mudd	been married to Thos. Gregg Sr.
	Levy Gregg	self, Walter Mudd	
1794	Thomas Grigg [sic]	self, Josiah Gregg	
	Mary Gregg	John Mudd	
	Walter Mudd	self	
1795	Mary Gregg	"sons John and Alexander"	
	Thomas Gregg, Josiah Gregg, and other Greggs named as separate households		
1797	Mary Grigg [sic]	"sons J. Mudd and A. Norton"	Important wording!
1798	all in one household:		
	John Mudd, Alexander Norton, William Norton, John Keith		First naming of William
1799	Mary Gregg	"sons Alexander and William"	
	John Mudd	self	
	A number of Gregg households were taxed, including three Thomas Greggs, separated by the appellations "son of John," "Sr.," and "S.H." The new Thomas Gregg Sr. had a son named Thomas in his household.		
1800	John Mudd	self	
1801, 1802	Mary Gregg	"sons Alexander and William"	
1803	Alexander Norton	self	
1805–1807	Alexander and William Norton paying taxes on themselves		
1808	no taxes collected, no tax roll		
1809	Alexander and William Norton paying taxes on themselves		
1810–1812	Alexander Norton	self	

Figure 9 The Search for William Norton's Parents

2. Alexander and William Norton lived in the same household between 1805 and 1809.

3. It is not clear where William Norton was in 1803 and 1804.

4. The rolls of 1799, 1801, and 1802 clearly identified Alexander and William Norton as Mary Gregg's sons. The use of their surname in 1798 was the link between the entries for 1797 and 1799. John Mudd was head of his own household by 1799, at about age thirty-one, figured from the 1776 census mentioned above.

5. The 1802 list was Mary Gregg's last appearance on the tax rolls. This would not necessarily suggest anything: she may have died or she may have continued living with her sons. Other sources would have to be consulted to make any determination. At least, it is clear she lived until early 1802 in order to appear on that year's list.

6. Mary Gregg probably was in the 1798 household with her sons.

7. William Norton was listed for the first time in 1798, a suggestion that he was then at least sixteen years of age. This would suggest that he was born by 1782. That date is not inconsistent with the makeup of the family and Mary's age of about thirty-nine in 1782, figured from the 1776 census mentioned above.

8. The most important entry was 1797, which offers the strongest evidence that Mary Gregg was the mother of John Mudd and of Alexander and William Norton. (See number 4 above.)

9. The naming of sons John and Alexander in 1795 was clarified by the 1797 use of their surnames. By this time, the Gregg brothers were each heads of their own households. It makes sense that Mary Gregg, their widowed stepmother, would have had her own sons living with her.

10. The 1795 entry was the first presence of Alexander Norton as a tithable white male over the age of sixteen. This appearance on the tax roll suggests that he was born by 1779 (1795 minus 16), not inconsistent with Mary's age of about thirty-six in 1779 and the presence of the young Amelia Norton in the 1776 family.

11. John Mudd's presence in Mary Gregg's household in 1793 and 1794 is consistent with his presence there in later years. His age would have been about twenty-five in 1793, and many young men of that age were still in the household of a parent, especially a widowed mother.

12. The 1793 and 1794 presence of Thomas Gregg, potter, and Josiah Gregg in the same household supports the idea that these were the sons of Thomas Gregg Sr. as named in his will. Thomas, the potter, dropped the occupational designation in 1794, possibly due to the death of his father and the lack of need for separation in the records. The presence of Walter Mudd in Levy Gregg's household in 1793 is evidence of the intermingling of the two families.

13. Although Mary is a very common name among women of this period, the 1792 will of Thomas Gregg Sr. naming his wife, Mary, supports the appearance of the Mary Gregg on the tax rolls.

14. John Mudd's presence in the household of Thomas Gregg, potter, in 1792 is further evidence of the intermingling of the two families.

15. In light of the 1792 will of Thomas Gregg Sr. it appears that Thomas Gregg, the potter, may have used the occupational designation to distinguish himself from his apparent father.

16. In 1791, the two Mudd brothers were in one household, as were two Greggs, Thomas (the potter) and Levy. Where were Thomas Gregg Sr. and Mary Gregg? Mary would have been about forty-eight. The couple, apparently still together, could have been in either household: Walter Mudd or Thomas Gregg, potter. Was the elder Thomas also a potter? The young men, one set or the other, could actually have been living with the older couple in their home. The age or possible infirmity of Thomas Gregg Sr. may have made him exempt from the poll tax.

17. The presence of Walter Mudd as an adult in 1788 is consistent with the reported age of twelve in the 1776 census twelve years before.

18. In about 1788, Mary Norton seems to have married Thomas Gregg Sr., her son John Mudd going to the new household with her (1789 and 1790).

19. The John Norton in 1788 in Mary Norton's household appears to be the John Mudd who was age eight in the 1776 census and in 1788 would have been about twenty and still in the household of his mother. The unnamed male age sixteen to twenty-one in 1787 may also be John Mudd, since Walter Mudd would have been about twenty-three, based on the age reported in the 1776 census.

20. It appears that Mary Mudd married second William Norton Jr. and third, Thomas Gregg Sr. The researcher is still working on the in-between years of 1776–1787 to determine where Mary and children and Mr. Norton were. It appears that Mr. Norton died by 1787, or Mary would not have been listed on the tax roll. He did not appear on the Loudoun County tax rolls at all before Mary appeared in 1787.

MISTAKES WE MAKE IN RESEARCH

The blundering fool! Just to think of his having such an incomparable bit of good luck, and not taking advantage of it.

—*Sherlock Holmes*[74]

In researching any source or record group, we sometimes do things we should not do or fail to do things we should do. The following list of common research mistakes is intended as preventive medicine.

1. Assuming that a family not in an index is not in the record; failing to look for them in the actual record

2. Skipping a census that is known to exist; neglecting major record groups such as probate, land, or tax records

3. Forgetting to write down complete citation data for any record; forgetting to write down both enumeration district number *and* page number for 1880 and later censuses

4. Not looking for variant spellings of names in indexes; assuming that a name with a different spelling is not the right family or person
5. Not planning and organizing well; wasting time and duplicating previous efforts
6. Making only a partial extract of the information given in any record
7. Collecting only one nuclear family; neglecting other potential or known relatives
8. Not taking advantage of family sources, especially interviewing older relatives
9. Making assumptions about the family before gathering enough data
10. Drawing conclusions about the family before gathering enough data
11. Not filing notes (from all sources) for a family in a way that facilitates study; not filing all the census forms together for each family
12. Not analyzing and evaluating each piece of evidence, each record, *and* the total picture

---

Never trust to general impressions, my boy, but concentrate yourself upon details.

—*Sherlock Holmes*[75]

SIX

Examining Evidence: The Gray Cells in Action

Get your facts first and then you can distort them as much as you please.

—*Mark Twain (the real Samuel Clemens)*[1]

P erhaps Samuel Clemens observed genealogists as well as newspaper reporters, politicians, interviewers, and the others who were the objects of his humor. Nevertheless, his statement acts as a reminder to researchers: What we do with our facts is as important as where we get them.

Standards of genealogical evidence and proof have been the subject of numerous chapters and articles by many researchers. Some of these writers take a very legalistic point of view; others, a scientific point of view. Some speak or write as if they are trying to make genealogy a legalistic science and fit our thinking and our evidence into neatly labeled boxes.

With these labels, some draw very minute distinctions between various kinds of evidence, the ways they relate to each other, and the ways they affect the conclusions we reach as we study them. Some of those who write about this subject do not agree with the others who write about it. They seem to be trying to sort out genealogical procedures, sources, and thought processes and establish a definitive or authoritative set of standards by which we can measure our proofs.

While they engage in this endeavor, we engage in our own endeavor: researching, studying, and trying to draw conclusions about our lineages. Even as we read the different articles, some of us wonder whether we are "doing it right" or "calling it the right thing." Let's leave the distinctions in vocabulary to others and continue to use our best judgment on what our evidence means in the context of our own lineages.

Notes

Endnotes for this chapter begin on page 256.

EVIDENCE

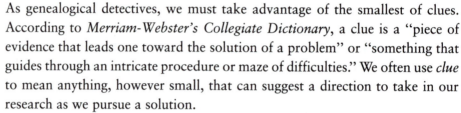

I believe in evidence.

—*Mr. Reggie Fortune*[2]

Printed Source

Several specialized dictionaries have been helpful: Paul Drake's *What Did They Mean By That?* (Bowie, MD: Heritage Books, 2 vols., 1994 and 1998); Barbara Jean Evans's *A to Zax* (1978; 3rd ed. by Alexandria, VA: Hearthside Press, 1995); and Henry Campbell Black's *Black's Law Dictionary* (St. Paul, MN: West Publishing Co., 1979, 5th ed.)

As genealogical detectives, we must take advantage of the smallest of clues. According to *Merriam-Webster's Collegiate Dictionary*, a clue is a "piece of evidence that leads one toward the solution of a problem" or "something that guides through an intricate procedure or maze of difficulties." We often use *clue* to mean anything, however small, that can suggest a direction to take in our research as we pursue a solution.

Since the early days of my genealogical experience, dictionaries and common sense have helped me understand what I find in courthouse records. One of these dictionary compilers has offered a logical definition of evidence that we can use. Evidence is any "single fact, word, memento, monument, and state of being that in any way, no matter how slight, tends to prove some matter of lineage."[3] This definition would include clues. (Mementos would be papers and personal belongings that family and friends preserved. Monuments would include tombstones and houses. An example of state of being would be finding a person alive in a given place at a given time, not finding a family where they were "supposed to be," or finding that someone had died.)

In sleuth terminology, a lead is the same as a clue. As genealogical sleuths, then, we can use the word *evidence* as the umbrella word for all the details that help us make research decisions and move toward conclusions. Even when we find direct statements of genealogical facts, it is reassuring to know that other evidence supports these statements. Thus, we often seek corroborating evidence. If we placed these three words—*evidence, clue,* and *lead*—on a scale to determine their relative weight or value in solving a case, *clue* and *lead* might, at first, seem to weigh less, and we might consider them less useful. However, we still regard them as evidence and follow through to study them. They could turn out to mean nothing or they could be extremely valuable.

An example would be the reported fact in the 1850 census that a middle child of a family was born in Georgia when all the others, older and younger, were born in Mississippi. What may seem to be evidence of little value, perhaps even an error, becomes a more substantial set of evidence when the researcher discovers that all five of this person's census records reported the same birthplace. In addition, the siblings' other census records reported their births consistently as Mississippi. The genealogist would want to know why, where, and what were the overall implications in the family history. As one sleuth said, "[I]t's certainly just one interesting little fact that might be a pointer."[4]

This example also indicates that each source or each record we consult may contain many pieces of evidence: dates, names, places, events, relationships, and other information. Even if a member of the family was missing from one census, the absence is evidence. We cannot always tell what a piece of evidence means, alone and of itself. We must consult other sources and gather other evidence before we can make a determination.

THE SMALLEST CHINK OF LIGHT

If a problem exists, a solution must exist. It's only a question of finding a path in. Sometimes it can be by the smallest chink of light.
—*Father Anselm*[5]

As other sections of this book demonstrate, evidence can include such small things as a name on a Christmas gift tag in a scrapbook, a symbol on a tombstone, a name on a schoolbook, an age in a census record, a person's appellation on a tax roll, a date on a legal document, or a slave's name in an estate inventory. Part of being an effective genealogist is paying attention to the little details.

The Little Things

1. "It has long been an axiom of mine that the little things are infinitely the most important."—Sherlock Holmes[6]
2. "Just an odd lead I thought might be worth following. I could be one hundred per cent wrong."—Captain Kennelly[7]

    For example, a genealogist sometimes finds an ancestral family member with a very unusual name, such as Semiramis Lucetta Artemesis McClendon, who lived in Georgia in the mid-nineteenth century. If another female in the same area had the same initials or one of the names, the researcher would have every reason to follow the lead and study the second person. Many ancestors were named for relatives; others, for friends, neighbors, or prominent personalities; the rest, because the parents liked the name. We do not know whether a name similarity will lead to a great discovery until we do the research. It may or it may not.

3. "The solving of almost every crime mystery depends on something which seems, at the first glance, to bear *no relation whatever* to the original crime."—Dexter Drake[8]

    A genealogical translation of this statement could be this: The solving of a genealogical mystery may depend on a fact which seems, at first, to have nothing to do with the question being studied. An example of this scenario is described in chapter nine. For whatever reason, an ancestor's military discharge paper and his pension application gave differing age information. This discrepancy ultimately brought about the creation of the document that solved the genealogical mystery: the identity of his parents.

4. "Why, here it is! . . . This is a different initial."—Dr. Watson[9]

    A small, seemingly insignificant difference can alert the sleuth or the genealogist to new possibilities for research or to new meaning for existing evidence.

5. "Yes, it was bad English but good American."—Sherlock Holmes[10]

In this case, the spelling of the word *plow* (American) instead of *plough* (English) in an advertisement helped solve the case. A small, perhaps unimportant difference, once noticed, became the key. Another example is in the next sleuth's observation.

6. "This large and subtle . . . crime was built on the plain fact that a gentleman's evening dress is the same as a waiter's. . . . [T]he whole of this tale turns on a black coat."—Father Brown[11]

In genealogy small details can make a large difference in solving a lineage. The key is observing carefully and thoroughly and thinking about the evidence in ways that can lead to these recognitions.

Lest We Make Mistakes

Important

What we do with evidence once we have it is as important as where we get it. However, when we look at larger chunks of evidence, **sometimes the small, trifling details get lost in the shuffle.** Lest we make mistakes, let the sleuths instruct us.

1. "Beware! Peril to the detective who says: 'It is so small—it does not matter. It will not agree. I will forget it.' That way lies confusion! Everything matters."—Hercule Poirot[12]

2. "It is one of my most painful memories that for a month I examined that newspaper cutting frequently and that I failed entirely to grasp the significance of the reverse side. We all have a mental blind spot. That was mine."—Nurse Detective Hilda Adams.[13]

Where are our mental blind spots? Failing to grasp the significance of a witness on a document? Not being thorough enough in abstracting the records because we cannot see any immediate connection to our focus ancestor? Forgetting to read the reverse page in the census or deed book and thereby missing a big lead to the identity of the wife's parents? Having a favorite theory that prevents us from being objective?

3. "It is odd how the cleverest people slip up over details."—Hercule Poirot[14]

EVIDENCE AT WORK

[J]ust by applying a little common sense, I believe I really did solve a problem that had baffled cleverer heads than mine.
—*Miss Marple* [15]

Evidence can function in different ways as we think about what it means. When Miss Marple said she applied common sense and solved the problem, she meant she used common sense to consider the evidence and solved the problem. Let the sleuths explain in their own words several functions of evidence.

1. "There is nothing like first-hand evidence."—Sherlock Holmes[16]

We generally consider an eyewitness to an event more likely to remember the details accurately than someone hearing about it second- or third-hand, especially if the firsthand account comes fairly soon after the event. The closer we can get to an original document or original account, the more likely we are to get accurate information. This may or may not be in the form of direct statements of fact. The information may be pieces of evidence that help establish facts indirectly. However, when differences occur, we usually give firsthand accounts more weight in analysis than later versions of the event.

2. "On the floor lies a dead man. . . . Nobody knows who he is (or again so they say). In his pocket is a card bearing the name of Mr. R.H. Curry, Seven Denvers Street, Metropolis Insurance Company. But there is no Metropolis Insurance Company, there is no Denvers Street and there seems to be no such person as Mr. Curry. That is negative evidence, but it *is* evidence."—Hercule Poirot.[17]

In Poirot's case, the business card contained at least three main pieces of evidence: two names and an address. Further research showed all of them to be false. Thus, Poirot knew he would have to seek identity in another way.

In genealogy also, further research can suggest or prove that an earlier piece of evidence is not true. The process of elimination works on this same principle: finding additional evidence that lets you cross a possibility off the list. In this way, you narrow the remaining possibilities in search of an answer, as Sherlock Holmes describes below.

3. "That process [of thought] . . . starts upon the supposition that when you have eliminated all which is impossible, then whatever remains, however improbable, must be the truth. It may well be that several explanations remain, in which case one tries test after test until one or other of them has a convincing amount of support."—Sherlock Holmes[18]

4. "Circumstantial evidence is a very tricky thing. It may seem to point very straight to one thing, but if you shift your own point of view a little, you may find it pointing in an equally uncompromising manner to something entirely different."—Sherlock Holmes[19]

Such is the case when we do not yet have enough evidence to make a firm conclusion one way or another. We may have evidence that implies Great-Grandma was a daughter of one couple who were near her neighbors in the 1870 and 1880 censuses. On the other hand, we may have different evidence that implies she had no close relatives living in the county at that time. Logically, in the way the two pieces of evidence were proposed, they cannot both be correct. We cannot draw a conclusion without gathering more evidence. We must study both implications, keep open an option that neither is correct, and consider the possibility that one or both may be partially correct.

One angle of study could be to try to prove both implications correct, or both implications incorrect. Shifting the point of view in this way can lead the researcher to look at the research possibilities and the evidence creatively and think about the question more thoroughly. The researcher would need to ask "What needs to be true for the first theory to be correct and the second one, incorrect?" and vice versa. If the evidence is particularly sketchy, it is probably better not to focus on a theory at all until more research is done. A blank slate may be better than one with part of a picture drawn on it.

5. "Everything's important in this case."—Inspector George L. Patton[20]

Until evidence is shown to be irrelevant or invalid for the case, it remains a factor, important enough to consider or research further.

THE LITTLE CELLS OF GRAY

To "see things with your own eyes" as they say, is not always to see the truth. One must see with the eyes of the mind; one must employ the little cells of gray!

—*Hercule Poirot*[21]

Chapter two proposed that the thinking process has at least four stages. First, observation and thinking go hand in hand, happening simultaneously, during research. Second, observation and thinking are part of an ongoing cycle of activity—plan, research, and analyze—until we answer the questions we have outlined.

Third, we study the accumulation of evidence, making a judgment on the quality and validity of each piece in the context of the whole. If the piece of evidence passes scrutiny, it becomes part of the body of evidence we use to prove or support a larger genealogical fact. If it does not pass scrutiny, we have to decide whether it is irrelevant to the question at hand, conflicts with it, or needs to be held in reserve for further consideration. Conflicting facts usually lead us back to the research cycle. Fourth, the accepted genealogical facts combine to form the broader picture of a lineage, and we consider whether we have indeed proved our focus question and what to research next.

We can call the thinking process analysis, but we can also call it examination, review, scrutiny, reflection, even dissection. Naming the process does not matter as much as doing it: taking our research apart, reducing it to its basic elements—each piece of raw data—and putting it back together as proven facts and answered questions. For the sleuths, part of the process is creating the best atmosphere for thinking.

The Atmosphere for Thinking

1. "If it is any point requiring reflection, we shall examine it to better purpose in the dark."—C. Auguste Dupin.[22]

Dupin's point is well taken. Reflection or thinking requires concentration, without distractions. Many adults find they can do this better without the noises of television or a room full of people. One friend did her best thinking at the kitchen sink because the family left her alone when she was washing dishes. Dupin preferred the dark.

2. "The mind is confused? Is it not so? Take time, *mon ami*. You are agitated; you are excited—it is but natural. Presently, when we are calmer, we will

arrange the facts, neatly, each in his proper place. We will examine—and reject. Those of importance we will put on one side; those of no importance, poof! blow them away!"—Hercule Poirot[23]

Just as an overactive mind sometimes prevents us from falling asleep at night, agitation and confusion hinder clear thinking. Likewise, fatigue, hunger, and hurry are not conducive to contemplation.

3. "I knew that seclusion and solitude were very necessary for my friend in those hours of intense mental concentration during which he weighed every particle of evidence, constructed alternative theories, balanced one against the other, and made up his mind as to which points were essential and which immaterial."—Dr. Watson about Sherlock Holmes[24]

4. "Well, I gave my mind a thorough rest by plunging into a chemical analysis. One of our greatest statesmen has said that a change of work is the best rest. So it is."—Dr. Watson[25]

After strenuous exercise, physical or mental, a change of pace is beneficial for most of us. We generally work and think to greater advantage when we are refreshed.

Thinking About the Evidence

As we study our evidence, at any stage of the project, we think about it in different ways. Below are some general considerations from sleuths, from whose ideas we can benefit.

1. "We have to build a file and keep cross-checking it. Somewhere it ought to show an anomaly."—Chief Inspector Ron Fairbanks[26]

When we are well organized and our search is well planned, we gather quite a bit of material. The files must be readily available for study so that we, too, can cross-check our findings. Since I am mostly a visual learner, I like to make charts, maps, chronologies, and lists to help in comparing, thinking, and questioning. Anytime we take evidence out of its original form in our notes and either isolate it or combine it with other evidence, we see it in new light or from a new perspective. We are more able to see what is different, peculiar, or out of the norm as well as what is similar.

2. "In some cases we've seen too many clues, in this one too few."—Eleanor Roosevelt[27]

This phenomenon happens in genealogy. In the cases with many clues, we can generally sort them into groups to focus on several at a time. By a process of elimination, we can sometimes reach a manageable number of significant pieces of evidence for more in-depth study. When we have too few, we have several choices: (a) lay the case aside and go to another focus ancestor for a while, (b) expand our research into record groups we have not tried, (c) revise our planning and strategy, (d) read articles about other searches for ideas, or (e) take a nap and come back to it later.

3. "I could make what I wanted of those two statements, Mary's and hers, although I was pretty much puzzled."—Nurse Detective Hilda Adams[28]

Genealogists often find conflicting statements, and often family tradition contradicts itself. Our task is to increase our evidence until we can evaluate the conflicting pieces. If we have no further ways to check family stories, as opposed to family versions of genealogical facts, we can preserve each one and attribute it to the person who told it. It may still enliven our family history.

4. "I have a fancy for having it analysed again, that is all."—Hercule Poirot[29]

There's nothing wrong with reconsidering a conclusion or a piece of evidence. New evidence or a new day may call into question an analysis we thought we had finished and advise us to reevaluate it. When writing progress reports (chapter seven) or planning research, we often reach intense levels of thought and should take advantage of these new opportunities to examine our evidence and our strategy. You may see no need for changes; you may see new possibilities.

5. "Who's the most logical suspect?"—Samuel Clemens[30]

Often genealogists have several candidates for a key position on the pedigree chart or family group sheet. Based on the evidence we gather, we may be able to narrow the possibilities to the candidate who is the most logical and reasonable choice.

6. "All my instincts are one way, and all the facts are the other."—Sherlock Holmes[31]

"Do not fear. Speak your mind. You should always pay attention to your instincts."—Hercule Poirot[32]

Such a situation is illustrated in chapter eleven with a matter of an ancestor's birthplace. Instincts can be powerful tools in the thought process. We cannot make final conclusions on the basis of instinct, but it can help us decide how to direct our research.

7. "I'd be careful if I was you."—Sergeant Williams[33]

Caution and thoroughness go hand in hand, in research as well as in analysis. We need to look at the evidence in ways that avoid mistakes in judgment and from different points of view, as shown in the sections below.

Lest We Err

1. "[H]e erred continually by the very intensity of his investigations. He impaired his vision by holding the object too close. He might see, perhaps, one or two points with unusual clearness, but in so doing he necessarily lost sight of the matter as a whole."—C. Auguste Dupin[34]

We genealogists impair our observation and analysis of evidence when we focus too narrowly on a preconceived idea (as in the case Dupin observed) or neglect part of the evidence. If we impair our observations and our thinking, we likely impair our conclusions.

2. "She jumped at conclusions from insufficient data. That's the worst of circumstantial evidence."—Perry Mason[35]

"Circumstantial evidence" is a piece of evidence that implies a conclusion but, alone, does not prove it. A common genealogical example is finding a male ancestor as head of household in a census record and assuming the older couple "next door" by the same surname are his parents. Often they are, but there is no guarantee. If we do not attempt to prove the relationship, we are jumping to conclusions from insufficient data. One friend appropriately calls that jump a "giant leap of faith." Probably all of us have been guilty at one time or another. We must continually ask ourselves, How do I know?

3. "I had come to an entirely erroneous conclusion which shows, my dear Watson, how dangerous it always is to reason from insufficient data."—Sherlock Holmes[36]

4. "I have made a point of being always ready to disbelieve as well as believe anything that is told to me."—Miss Marple[37]

5. "We must take things as they are, not as we would prefer them to be."—Mr. Chitterwick[38]

6. "How often must I tell you that clues come from *within*? In the little gray cells of the brain lies the solution of every mystery."—Hercule Poirot[39]

   The clues come from sources, but the little gray cells let us recognize evidence when we see it, give us the ability to study it, lead us to reasonable conclusions, or send us back to the drawing board for another plan of research. Poirot was right: In the little gray cells lies the solution.

7. "Still you are right in one thing. It is always wiser to suspect everybody until you can prove logically, and to your own satisfaction, that they are innocent."—Hercule Poirot[40]

   In genealogy, this is true. If we are using a process of elimination, we must "suspect" everybody until we can prove logically and reasonably that each can be checked off. In a broader sense, it is wiser to keep an open mind until we can prove a conclusion, logically and convincingly, based on the evidence.

8. "You are talking without method or order . . . Let me beg of you to let me have the facts."—Hercule Poirot.[41]

   Present your case to yourself first. In order to do that, you need method and order. For this, you need an updated chronology of the ancestor's life or a chronological list of what is *known* to this point. Also you need a separate list of any other evidence. Then you are prepared to think about it, one event at a time or one piece of evidence at a time, but also as a whole set of evidence.

9. "The whole thing was obvious! So obvious that the only thing which prevented me from seeing the solution was the trifling fact that it was *completely impossible*."—Dirk Gently.[42]

   In genealogy, the solution may seem impossible when we do not keep an open mind. Sometimes it seems impossible because we do not have enough evidence to make it obvious. Sometimes the answer is very different from other situations we have encountered; after all, some ancestors were real characters with very independent spirits.

10. "You have an excellent heart, my friend—but your gray cells are in a deplorable condition."—Hercule Poirot.[43]

    Fortunately, the more we exercise the gray cells the better they function. When in doubt, talk over your evidence with another thinking person.

Point of View and Perspective

Thinking can often be more effective if we change points of view when we are studying our evidence. As in a debating society, try taking one side and arguing for it. Then switch and argue the opposite side of the question. Then be an objective judge: Which side made the stronger case?

1. "If it's possible to have a suicide arranged to look like a murder, why not a murder that looks like a suicide?"—Nurse Detective Hilda Adams[44]
2. "Let's take a different angle on this [case]. Suppose there wasn't any reason to blame the cook for it, and you had to figure out the whole thing from scratch. What would you be looking at?"—Samuel Clemens[45]
3. "Not too fast! Let's take the other side for a minute."—Inspector George L. Patton[46]
4. "I read it all in another light, you see."—Lady Detective Loveday Brooke[47]
5. "I just wondered if it might have been the wrong murder."—Miss Marple[48]
6. "You will see that I have shifted the question from the mode of egress to that of ingress."—C. Auguste Dupin[49]
7. "[I]t's always interesting when one doesn't see. If you don't see what a thing means, you must be looking at it wrong way round, unless of course you haven't got full information."—Miss Marple[50]

Thinking With Someone Else

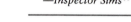

Why, certainly, M. Poirot. Two heads are better than one.

—*Inspector Sims*[51]

Tip

Perhaps you have discovered, as many others have, the value of thinking out loud. **Explaining your research and analysis aloud to yourself, or the cat, has a way of keeping you on the subject,** of not letting your mind wander or fall asleep. Use such an opportunity to try proving your case to yourself. One friend starts these conversations with, "OK, self, listen up."

If being counsel, jury, and judge at the same time is not to your liking, find another person willing to listen and play devil's advocate, gently, with your ideas. When we discuss our "cases" with well-chosen others, they can often provide insights that we have not seen. In their objectivity, like the sleuths in this chapter, they can help direct our thoughts in ways we have not considered. Whether or not we have another suitable person handy, the sleuths have a number of legitimate points for us to consider. Think about what they have to say and apply whatever fits to your own case. Notice that much of their help comes in the form of further questions to help us think. As you study, answer their questions in light of your own case. Try answering aloud.

1. "I think perhaps you've misplaced your emphasis . . . What in your judgment . . . is the most significant single fact about the [case]?"—Justice Friedrich[52]
2. "Let us make our deductions together. What points strike up specially as being difficult?"—Hercule Poirot[53]

3. "And what does that suggest?"—Eleanor Roosevelt[54]
4. "How can you tell?"—Sherlock Holmes[55]
5. "And so far you have no idea?"—Hercule Poirot[56]
6. "Do the names suggest anything? . . . Are there any names you can't identify at all?"—Investigators Jill Keller and Gabe Haddad[57]
7. "How I miss my friend Hastings. He had such an imagination. . . . It is true that he always imagined wrong—but that in itself was a guide." —Hercule Poirot[58]

HYPOTHESES AND THEORIES

I've got my facts pretty clear. All I want now is to know what they all mean.

—*Inspector Stanley Hopkins*[59]

As soon as we begin gathering evidence, we begin to look for patterns or ways various pieces of information may fit together. We immediately want to know what it all means. It is natural to think about possible scenarios, theories, and hypotheses to explain sets of facts. We have to do this sometimes in order to plan what to do next because this kind of thinking can guide our research. When a Plan A scenario does not work out, we go to a Plan B scenario. The key is to keep an open mind to a variety of possibilities as we research and not lock into a favorite theory too soon.

Caution: Don't Theorize Too Soon

1. "I didn't want to form a hypothesis too early for fear it would color the entire course of the investigation."—Kinsey Millhone[60]
2. "I have no data yet. It is a capital mistake to theorize before one has data. Insensibly one begins to twist facts to suit theories, instead of theories to suit facts."—Sherlock Holmes[61]
3. "In any investigations, my Bunter, it is most damnably dangerous to have a theory."—Lord Peter Wimsey[62]
4. "Cool off, cool off, you're beginning to be partisan. That's no way to conduct an investigation."—Inspector Alan Grant[63]

Thinking About Theories

As we think about our material and what it means, it is, again, advantageous to explain the case to another genealogist or to the juries in our heads. In doing so, we must consider what these distinguished sleuths have to say.

1. "I have nothing to say against your theory—but it does not go far enough. There are certain things it does not take into account."—Hercule Poirot[64]
2. "How does all that fit into your theory?"—Sherlock Holmes[65]
3. "What have I always told you? Everything must be taken into account. If the fact will not fit the theory—let the theory go."—Hercule Poirot[66]

Is There an Alternative Explanation?

1. "We all learn by experience, and your lesson this time is that you should never lose sight of the alternative."—Sherlock Holmes[67]

2. "I begin to see. Yes, dimly I begin to see . . . the possibilities, shall we say, of an alternative explanation."—Hercule Poirot[68]

3. "It seems to me such a very odd thing—such an inexplicable one unless—of course—Dear me, I think I must be *very* stupid."—Miss Marple[69]

4. "[W]e can't leave out any logical suspect."—Samuel Clemens[70]

5. "I don't mean to deny that the evidence is in some ways very strongly in favour of your theory. I only wish to point out that there are other theories possible."—Sherlock Holmes[71]

6. "I don't uphold that theory. I only mention it."—Inspector George L. Patton[72]

7. "Personally, I don't think you've touched this story. You've got your case, but you have enough left over to make another."—Nurse Detective Hilda Adams[73]

In the nurse's opinion, an alternative was clearly likely. The inspector had proposed a conclusion that covered the facts of one event, and his conclusion did not cover all the evidence. The nurse believed that their mystery was broader than one event and that, only by answering all of the questions, including the "leftovers," could they reach a legitimate conclusion. In genealogy, the same caution applies. If we have too many leftovers, we probably need to look for an alternate or more complete solution.

SEEKING THE TRUTH (PROOF)

There is another way to truth: by the minute examination of facts.
—*John Masefield, poet*[74]

Reminder

Genealogists often ask, "How many sources are considered enough to prove something?" The only appropriate answer, as I see it, is "as many as it takes." **Proof may, but does not always, come in one direct statement.** If it does not, we must search for as much evidence as it takes to convince the genealogy jury in our heads that we have indeed made the case and proved the point.

Occasionally someone asks, "Why do you want more than one source to give you a birth or death date? What difference does it make? I get a birth date; I go on to something else."

Many genealogists would answer as I do: We need to be as accurate as we can. Otherwise, why bother? As a researcher, I want to know that I have the most correct answer that I can determine, an answer that makes sense in the overall picture of the ancestor's life and makes sense in the context of the evidence I can gather. Maybe I inherited this bias because my dad was an engineer—a very precise person with a mind and an eye for minute detail.

Those of us who prefer "as accurate as possible" over "guess and go on" may not move fast through the generations and may never get back to Charlemagne. However, we probably end up *knowing* more about the ancestors we do accumulate and maybe feeling a closer tie with our past. We *know* because we have researched the available original records, contemporary with the ancestors; we have documented each piece of the puzzle; and we have thought about each piece to make sure it fits.

In order to achieve "as accurate as possible" lineages, we must be as accurate as possible with the individual details that make up each lineage. These details include birth, marriage, and death dates and places; the identity of parents and siblings; and whatever we accumulate trying to establish these facts. Research is obviously the way we get our material, but thinking about the material we gather is an equally important part of the process.

Sorting the Evidence

1. "It is of the highest importance in the art of detection to be able to recognize, out of a number of facts, which are incidental and which vital. Otherwise your energy and attention must be dissipated instead of being concentrated."—Sherlock Holmes[75]

2. "The principal difficulty in your case lay in the fact of there being too much evidence. What was vital was overlaid and hidden by what was irrelevant. Of all the facts which were presented to us we had to pick just those which we deemed to be essential, and then piece them together in their order, so as to reconstruct this very remarkable chain of events."—Sherlock Holmes[76]

3. Hercule Poirot gave this answer in response to the question "How do you decide what is important and what isn't?"

   Voyons! One fact leads to another—so we continue. Does the next fit in with that? *A merville!* Good! We can proceed. This next little fact—no! Ah, that is curious! There is something missing—a link in the chain that is not there. We examine. We search. And that little curious fact, that possibly paltry little detail that will not tally, we put it here! [It fits.] It is significant! It is tremendous![77]

4. "The good old missing link."—Chief Investigator Ron Fairbanks[78]

5. "Yes, it fits. It would certainly explain the thing that has puzzled us from the beginning in this affair."—Inspector Alan Grant[79]

6. "I now proceeded, using my familiar method of logical analysis, to narrow down the possible solutions."—Sherlock Holmes[80]

Lest We Make Mistakes

1. "My case is, as I have told you, almost complete, but we must not err on the side of overconfidence. Simple as the case seems now, there may be something deeper underlying it."—Sherlock Holmes[81]

   Often there is something else: a more complete alternative explanation, an important piece of evidence (maybe a missing link) that has not yet turned up, a piece of evidence that *almost* fits, or some little doubt that nags at the gray cells. The simplicity may mask a more involved scenario, something for which we do not yet have a full explanation and therefore cannot see. A direct or simple solution may have no hidden traps, but the possibility is something to think about.

2. "The evidence you have suggests something of the kind but fails as yet to prove it."—Eleanor Roosevelt[82]

    When Mrs. Roosevelt is not there to think with us, we must be cautious in our judgments and try objectively to prove our conclusion to ourselves first and then to another thinking person.

3. "Never judge a man until you have all the facts."—Samuel Clemens[83]

    We cannot make a conclusion until we have enough facts to make a reasonable and convincing argument, one that also seems clear and reasonable to someone else.

4. "Don't worry, Mr. Clemens, I don't draw conclusions without I have all the facts."—Detective Richard LeJeune[84]

5. "Why is that possibility more likely than the others?"—J. Edgar Hoover[85]
    Asking ourselves this question will help us check our conclusions.

Judging the Evidence

The sleuths have shared many of their ideas about their cases and their methods with us. As we think about our genealogy research, we can benefit by applying their ideas to our own cases. According to the old proverb, if the shoe fits, wear it.

1. "I'm saying that it is all very simple if one only looks at it in the proper way."—Miss Marple[86]

2. "What possible explanation can there be for his omission to make capital out of the fact that the boys were missing? . . . There is only one explanation. . . . And that is that the boys weren't missing."—Inspector Alan Grant[87]

3. "Can't solve a case on facts we don't have."—Captain Kennelly[88]

    We evaluate what we know before, during, and after research in order to determine whether we have enough facts to reach a solution. *Facts* is the key word: Our conclusions must be based on good, quality evidence and the pieces must fit together.

4. "Just the facts, ma'am. Just the facts."—Sergeant Joe Friday.[89]

    Hearsay, family stories, undocumented details, and community legends may give us a direction for worthwhile questioning, and each may contain some useful truth. Still, it is specific and reliable facts from other sources that create convincing proof.

5. "Once again I could not get the theory to fit the facts."—Sherlock Holmes[90]

    As we study the evidence, we often try out different theories in an effort to find the one that works best with the facts. If no conclusion becomes obvious, we may need to gather more facts or arrange the facts differently.

6. "[A] man should never torture clues to make them point in the direction he thinks they should go."—Perry Mason[91]

7. "Before I tell you what, who, I suspect, let me tell you why I suspect it.

Otherwise it's *very* hard to believe."—Chief Investigator Ron Fairbanks[92]

8. "It's the height of absurdity . . . That is why historians surprise me. They seem to have no talent for the likeliness of any situation."—Inspector Alan Grant.[93]

   Genealogists must consider the same likeliness in finding genealogical answers. Is the conclusion likely in the time, place, and other circumstances of the ancestor's life? Is a person marrying too young or much later than the norm? Is a child born when the mother is older than about forty-five? Do gaps of years between children suggest the existence of two wives? Is the proposed conclusion likely, logical, and reasonable from what is known of the ancestor's life? Is the evidence strong and convincing? Is there any conflicting evidence? Would other researchers, looking at the same set of evidence, be likely to agree with the proposed conclusion?

9. "I was just thinking of what is likely."—Miss Marple[94]

Reaching Conclusions

When we believe we have found the correct conclusion for a set of evidence, we need to consider the following three points as a double check.

1. "Everything makes sense. Everything."—Hercule Poirot[95]

   Does the conclusion make sense according to the evidence? Does the evidence make sense when put together to form this conclusion? When the best conclusion is reached, everything falls into place.

2. "Does your explanation cover every point?"—Sherlock Holmes[96]

   Is any evidence left dangling or unanswered?

3. "I have found no evidence to justify any other conclusion."—Reggie Fortune[97]

   No other conclusion is possible with the same set of evidence. No other evidence conflicts, or no contradictory evidence is strong enough to offer a different, reasonable conclusion.

RESEARCH AND ANALYSIS: THE QUESTION OF REV. WILLIAM HARRISON'S DEATH DATE

My whole examination served to turn my conjecture into a certainty.
—*Sherlock Holmes*[98]

In the minds of some researchers, settling the question of a birth or death date may not seem as important as establishing the spouse or parents of the same ancestor. However, if we are not cautious or thorough in the smaller details, are we likely to be less cautious or thorough in the larger questions? The example below considers one of the smaller details, a death year. It illustrates the use of probate and tax records to settle an issue and reports the researcher's thought process.

Case Study

At the front door of Blandford Church in Petersburg, Virginia, is the tombstone of an early Anglican priest of that congregation, Rev. William Harrison.[99] The tombstone reads:

> To the sacred memory of
> Rev. William Harrison
> who departed this life
> 20th November 1814
> aged 84 years
> In tender regard of whom
> his widow
> hath caused this monument to be erected

It is an old tombstone beside that of his wife, who was responsible for his stone. She died 2 July 1829, according to her stone, erected by her children. Thus, Rev. Harrison's tombstone seems to have been made within about fifteen years after his death.

Conflicting Date

The second piece of information the researcher found was Harrison's will, written 29 May 1812 and presented in court for probate on *3 January 1814*.[100] This probate date was a piece of evidence in conflict with the death date on the tombstone. Since, of course, a will cannot be probated before the testator dies, it appeared that Harrison died in 1813, not 1814 as the tombstone indicated.

The court record is the official record, but even official records can contain errors just as tombstones can. The researcher resolved this conflict (1) by checking dates within the will book to be certain that the 1814 probate date was logical and/or correct and (2) by finding other contemporary but independently created records that could provide or suggest a death date.

Resolving the Conflict

Another look at the will book showed that the five pages before the will were dated September through November 1813. The will was the first item of business recorded in 1814. The following pages were recorded from February 1814 forward. Another piece of evidence appeared in the appraisal of Harrison's estate, which was ordered by the court in *March 1814* and presented in court on 29 June 1815.[101] Thus, it appeared that January 1814 was the correct probate date.

At least three contemporary but independently created records added to the evidence in the will book. First, since Harrison's tombstone bears a Masonic emblem, the researcher wrote to the Grand Lodge in Richmond, Virginia, for information. The librarian furnished several pieces of data, including the fact that the Blandford Lodge Number Three at Petersburg listed Harrison on their 1813 list of deaths.[102]

The second set of evidence sought was in the Petersburg City land tax rolls. The rolls for 1801–1814 revealed that Harrison owned ten town lots that he rented out for an annual income of about $400 until 1812, when his rent income jumped to over $700.[103] Other than giving the tax year, most of the rolls were not dated. However, the 1801 list was dated October 2; the 1803 list, September 7; and the 1807 list, September 16. These dates marked the completion of the lists, after the taxes were actually paid. Nevertheless, if these were representative of the customary procedures, the lists would have been completed by early fall, with taxes paid earlier in the year. The 1813 list shows the same taxable property for Rev. William Harrison as the previous lists. The 1814 roll lists the same property in the name of the **"Estate of William Harrison," filed alphabetically under *E* for *estate*.** The dating of the rolls indicates that Harrison was still alive for tax time in 1813 and had died before tax time, certainly before early fall, of 1814.

Tip

The third group of records examined was the personal property tax rolls for Petersburg, 1800–1815.[104] Most of the lists were completed and dated between the end of May and the first of October. Those for 1810–1812 were dated the end of May; the 1813 list was dated June 1. In 1813, Rev. William Harrison paid tax on one white male over sixteen (unnamed), three horses, five slaves, and one two-wheel carriage. The 1814 list, like the land tax roll, was not dated but Harrison's estate (also listed under *E*) was taxed for the same property as Rev. Harrison had been the previous year and an additional horse. The 1815 tax roll was dated June 31. The dating of these rolls supports the land tax rolls in indicating that Harrison was alive at tax time in 1813 and had died before midyear 1814.

The evidence in these tax and probate records, considered together, indicate that Harrison died after midyear of 1813. This is consistent with, or does not conflict with, the November 20 date on the tombstone.

The men preparing the tax rolls, the man reporting the Masonic lodge roster, and the clerk recording the several probate proceedings had no reason to falsify, individually or collectively, the indications of Harrison's death. Mrs. Harrison or the stonecutter probably would not have used inaccurate information knowingly but apparently one of them simply made a mistake. In this case, therefore, the various pieces of evidence from records fairly contemporary with the death and not connected with each other outweigh the lone tombstone date and do so in a clear and convincing manner. With no hesitation, we could say Harrison died probably in 1813. However, the strong and convincing evidence discussed and the lack of any other evidence to the contrary leave little or no doubt that Rev. William Harrison of Petersburg, Virginia, died in 1813.

I have employed my gray cells to some advantage.

—*Hercule Poirot*[105]

SEVEN

Arranging Ideas: Progress Reports

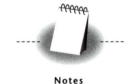

Notes

Endnotes for this chapter begin on page 259.

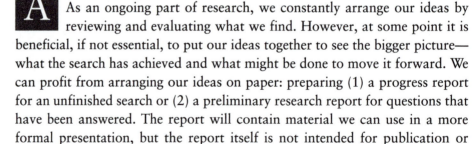

Technique

Said Inspector Japp, "Morning, Poirot. . . . I've done some good work! And you?" "Me, I have arranged my ideas," replied Poirot placidly.[1]

Arranging ideas is as essential in genealogy as it is in detective work. As an ongoing part of research, we constantly arrange our ideas by reviewing and evaluating what we find. However, at some point it is beneficial, if not essential, to put our ideas together to see the bigger picture—what the search has achieved and what might be done to move it forward. We can profit from arranging our ideas on paper: preparing (1) a progress report for an unfinished search or (2) a preliminary research report for questions that have been answered. The report will contain material we can use in a more formal presentation, but the report itself is not intended for publication or general distribution.

Preparing a report can be extremely valuable also in preparation for writing up a completed search to share with others. Your aspiration may be publication, a Christmas gift for family, or a donation to the local genealogy library. What form it will ultimately take is not the issue here. The key here is assembling the pieces of the puzzle in one place, on paper and with documentation, to see whether they indeed fit together.

Putting your findings into a report lets you look at the project in a new light, ask additional questions, tighten up loose ends, and evaluate progress.

It may help you see new significance in certain details. It may allow you to see patterns of behavior or events that you had not seen before. It can help you draw conclusions. It should help you solidify the details of your documentation.

PRELIMINARY HEARING

Let us hear how you arrived at this most gratifying result.
—*Sherlock Holmes*[2]

It is often recommended that performers, as they near a big recital or concert, practice while imagining their audience seated in the room listening and watching. This process has helped musicians, dancers, and actors reduce performance anxiety and polish their work in a way that can lead to a higher quality performance. Calling the family or friends together for a preview or dress rehearsal can achieve the same results.

As genealogists, we can benefit from the same pre-presentation exercise. The goal is to prove the case to ourselves. Anyone who reads the report or discusses it in depth with us makes up the dress rehearsal audience. The process may even include playing devil's advocate, taking apart each section to look for flaws or omissions. The experience can be worthwhile for several reasons:

1. It gives us the opportunity to fine-tune details.
2. It allows us to dust off old notes and data before renewing the search.
3. It lets us critique our own work for accuracy and logical conclusions.

Fine-Tuning Details

A report is an opportunity to focus on details to a degree that compares with the demands of a formal presentation. Each search is unique, with its own problems and triumphs. Each progresses in its own way, not exactly like another. Each requires special thought and attention at times when it flounders or when it makes extraordinary strides in a short time. Even when we feel it is as complete as we can make it, someone else may suggest valid ways to improve it. The dress rehearsal process is a way of reviewing what has been accomplished and thinking about what still might be done to make a better or stronger case.

Never, never will the grey cells function unless you stimulate them.
—*Hercule Poirot*[3]

Arranging your ideas in a written report will, or should, stimulate your own gray cells to ask questions about the details of your research. For example: Is this actually the earliest evidence I have found for the family's presence in this county? How do I know the elder woman was the father's sister? Did the 1850 census really say she was born in Illinois? How do I know she was the firstborn child? Have I ever tried to figure out a birth year for all these siblings? When Uncle John said he found on the Internet that Great-Great-Grandmother's maiden name was Castlebury, did I ever find a county record to confirm that? How could the wife named in the will be the mother of the first three children? Why did I think he had married four times? Where did the children go after both parents died? Unless we take the opportunity to present the case to ourselves in some way, we may neglect this fine-tuning.

Dusting Off a Search

Few genealogists can devote all their time solely to one search until it is "completed." Most of us have to work, cook, mow, coach, or drive carpools in between the hours given to genealogy. After months or years of off-and-on research, ideas get fuzzy or lost. They need dusting off and restimulating in order to move forward. Keeping some kind of running commentary is one way to review the search and plan for the next trip to the library.

The written report also lets you do your analysis and keep it for future reference. The time may come when you look at a research conclusion and say, Why did I assign him *that* birth year? Your progress report should refresh your memory. And you have every right to change your conclusion by updating the report based on new information.

Critiquing

We must critique our own work for accuracy and logic. If we genealogists perpetuate inaccuracies or pass along discrepancies without ever recognizing them, we do a disservice to ourselves, our families, and the rest of the genealogical community. Without accuracy, what we do is worthless. Little good comes from working a jigsaw puzzle where the pieces *almost* fit together. In such a puzzle, it is a funny-looking cat that has a church spire where its tail should be just because the colors match. Little good it does our genealogy if we claim the wrong ancestor or miss a whole generation. It is a funny-looking family where the names match but the mother is thirty years old, the son is twenty-three, and the father is seven. If we never study our work in its totality, we may never notice a problem in the details. Without critical care and thought, we may inadvertently set traps for ourselves.

If he can be wrong about a big, known fact like a coronation, then he's not to be trusted as a reporter.

—*Brent Carradine, research worker*[4]

Warning

The genealogical application of Carradine's observation is this: **If the genealogist is wrong about major facts, historical or genealogical, can we trust the rest of the presentation?**

We may not be the only ones who study a particular family. Others may have written or may yet write on the same crowd. We do not want to be the ones who make major errors. If anything, we have a greater opportunity now than ever before to do quality research, correct errors of past carelessness or oversight, and share valid conclusions with more people. This reality gives us a greater responsibility to be as thorough and as accurate as possible.

LISTENING TO WHAT WE SAY

Do you think historians really *listen* to what they are saying?
—*Investigator Alan Grant*[5]

The genealogical equivalent of Grant's concern is this: Do genealogists really pay attention to what they are saying? Once we've been researching a particular question over time, we get used to looking at our notes and charts. They become comfortable, like old shoes. When we stir ourselves to put these notes into a report form, we give ourselves a different perspective. We see with different eyes, and we notice things we have not noticed before. This is usually advantageous. The process allows us to be more objective and maybe less defensive about our own work.

Putting a case in writing, like a recital preview, can have the added benefit of getting someone else's feedback and suggestions. If it is difficult to find someone to examine and think through the details with you, write the report for yourself. Read it aloud, to yourself or the cat. Imagine a sleuth, such as Miss Marple or Hercule Poirot, standing near to nudge at appropriate times, as if to suggest that we ask a different question, find an additional fact, or double-check a point.

I have to double-check everything, and then see it all with my own eyes, before I dare believe it.
—*Samuel Clemens*[6]

Have you ever heard other genealogists talking to themselves in the library? "Why can't I find him where he's supposed to be?" "Oh, no! It's not the right wife!" "Wait a minute; this says Henry Middleton, not Middlebury! What's going on?" "What is she doing *here*?" "I can't *believe* this!" "Yes!! Yes!! You old goat. I caught up with you at last!" These folks may give the rest of us a chuckle, but at least they are thinking.

How do you do your best thinking? On paper or aloud? Alone or with someone else? Nurse detective Hilda Adams answered, "I went up to my room and stood in front of the mirror, which is where I do most of my thinking. I talk things over with myself."[7]

If we want all this thinking to stick around, we must write it down. Making notes to ourselves on individual pages of research data is beneficial, but putting them all together in report form is even better. This way, we see them as a whole.

Our thinking and evaluating may bring us to good conclusions, but setting them down in an organized manner is our double check of the whole. Have we connected all appropriate pieces of the puzzle? Have we left out some vital link? Poirot's statement below brings the point home.

> It is one thing to know that a man is guilty, it is quite another matter to prove him so.
>
> —*Hercule Poirot* [8]

Important

The genealogical application of Poirot's point, in this context, could be this: **It is one thing to find four generations of ancestors, but it is quite another matter to be sure you have the facts right and can prove the lineage.** Arranging your ideas and your evaluations into a report pulls your facts together to help you know whether you have a "solid case" yet.

Unfortunately, some people do not want to bother with the in-between steps of study. They want a finished product too quickly. As a case in point, a distant cousin once congratulated himself on being accepted into a particular lineage society that he had always wanted to join. He had hired someone to compile the necessary lineage and papers. When I questioned whether his membership ancestor was really the right one, he answered, "I've got my papers. That's what counts. I don't care if it's right or not." Nor would he share the documentation by which his researcher had supposedly proved his membership ancestor. I found his attitude appalling but have learned over the years that he is not alone. Thus, all of us who wish to share our findings with others need to consider what Sherlock Holmes said of his brother:

> I said that [my brother Mycroft] was my superior in observation and deduction. If the art of the detective began and ended in reasoning from an armchair, my brother would be the greatest criminal agent that ever lived. But he has no ambition and no energy. He will not even go out of his way to verify his own solutions, and would rather be considered wrong than take the trouble to prove himself right. [9]

COMMITTING YOUR WORK TO PAPER

> Your best way is to make a clean breast of the facts.
>
> —*Detective Gregson* [10]

Let us assume that all who read this chapter want to follow appropriate and desirable steps of planning and preparation before they rush off to publish everything in their research notebooks. Good research and constant evaluation come first. At some point, a progress report becomes not only appropriate but necessary.

Regardless of how you approach the report, its purpose is to help you analyze the search. The goal is to prove your conclusions to yourself and to any others who will read or hear what you have to say. Its procedure is to make a clean breast of the facts, a full disclosure of what you have found and where. The report is for you and a chosen few. It is not meant for general distribution or publication.

Anyone who attempts to write knows that the hardest part is getting started. That is why, in a progress report of the kind we are talking about here, we are not overly concerned with form and style: where to put commas and semicolons, whether to spell out state names or use the standard postal abbreviations. This is a preliminary report, not a final product. For the moment, do your best with style, grammar, and spelling. Try to write so that your meaning is clear. Try to think thoroughly. However, do not let these aspects of committing your progress to paper worry you to the extent that you decide not to do it at all. Checking and editing details of style for consistency, clarity, and accuracy will come later when you prepare a formal presentation. Here, we are concerned about getting the facts of the case on paper.

What Is Your Ultimate Goal?

Consider your ultimate goal for your research material. Your choice may affect the way you organize your written report.

(1) You may wish ultimately to write a biography of your focus ancestor, starting with his or her birth and parentage. If you have kept a chronological profile of the ancestor during the search, you already have the beginnings of a biography. The profile can also be the basis of a written report. If you have not kept a chronological profile, make one now. It compiles everything you have found about the focus person. You may want to do this on index cards (one per event or fact) or a sheet of paper for each year or decade. Working with a word processing program allows flexibility in organization. Listing your documentation along with the events in the ancestor's life will supply a record of your sources. It may be helpful to include some sources that did not yield information as you expected they would. These might include specific wills, cemeteries, or censuses.

(2) Your goal may be to compile family documents, letters, recipes, and photographs and simply tie them together with narrative. Chances are you would place the documents and letters in chronological order. Your narrative, then, would probably be biographical; some presentations of this type are more anecdotal than factual. By all means, use the same care and thought that you would give to a broader research project, documenting the facts and attributing the stories you include. We all have seen such collections that make many claims, some of which we know to be incorrect. It becomes obvious the compiler did not bother to check the details. To avoid this kind of pitfall, plan from the beginning for a creditable product. Writing a progress report is still an appropriate and desirable step in producing credibility.

(3) You may want to write a multigenerational family history. Perhaps your format of choice is to begin with the focus ancestor's biography and work through the generations coming forward in time, as a story of descendancy from that earliest ancestor. If so, each generation and each member of it needs an in-depth look. You are, in effect, creating several biographies that happen

to overlap because the generations overlap. Have you ever considered taking this approach and concentrating on the female ancestors?

(4) As the reverse of (3), you may choose to start with a generation that came between you and the focus person and work backward in time, one generation at a time. Proceed in the same way, with biographical summaries of each generation.

(5) Quite possibly, your search is ongoing, and you want to write an account to help evaluate your overall progress. Think about approaching your report in different ways. It may be useful to write your report more or less in the order the research took place. Although most of us are not disciplined enough to do this consistently, it is advisable to keep a running commentary of this kind from the very beginning of the search. This approach to a report allows you to include what you chose to do, why you thought it would be helpful or what you expected to achieve by doing it, and the results.

Another approach to the report is topical, based on the events identified in the chronological profile: birth date and place, childhood, marriage date and place, occupation, land ownership, military service, and so forth. If you are doing lengthy research for friends or clients, you should keep them informed on the status of the research by sharing a copy of written progress reports.

Organizing a Progress Report

How you organize your report is up to you. What makes sense to you? What helps you think? To make your report less intimidating for you or others, consider dividing it into sections. Give each section its own introduction, presentation, summary, and conclusions.

Idea Generator

To create your report, use your research material and add such items as these:

1. A list of what you knew about the person or problem before research began.
2. Evaluation of sources, including those that yielded good information and those that did not.
3. Any pertinent sources you have not yet tried and how they may help.
4. Ideas for further research to make a stronger case or more complete case.
5. Analysis of evidence.
6. Your theories on what may be true, probable, or possible. Include facts that support your theories and any that contradict them. You may find yourself listing pros and cons on a particular decision: why these may be his parents and why they may not. Other compilers or researchers may have different theories about your ancestors. Evaluate theirs against what you have found. Evaluate yours critically and objectively.
7. Any additional material from your research that needs to be used to support an argument.
8. Any additional questions that come to mind during this fine-tuning of your research.
9. Techniques you used when you could not find direct statements of information.
10. Conclusions you reached after studying the evidence.

Whatever form your report takes, it is essential that you include your documentation as you go. It does not matter whether it is in the form of footnotes, notes at the end of the report, or notes within the text at each cited fact. What matters is that you demonstrate that your evidence and conclusions are supported by legitimate sources. You may want to use two columns, with your discussion and facts in the left column and your documentation of that material in the right column. This form takes more space than paragraphs with notes, but it has the advantage of showing the data and the notes at the same time. This is the format I often use for my chronological profiles and sometimes for progress reports. For other reports, I prefer paragraphs and footnotes. It is a matter of choice.

Word processing programs are great time-savers in creating these reports. They permit easy changing and rearranging of text. I find it helpful to write this way, but I like to print out the report for study so that I can see the whole.

A progress report or preliminary research report is different from the reports you can print from a genealogy software database. Genealogy software can create charts of your generations with individual notes you have previously entered, sometimes with adequate footnotes. Family group sheets, pedigrees, and other charts may well form part of your progress report, but they do not substitute for it.

Once you have written your progress report, share it with someone else and ask for feedback. Does your data support your conclusions? Do your conclusions make sense in light of the data? Is your thinking logical and appropriate to the time period?

The remainder of the chapter is a sample progress report. Figure 10, on page 130, shows the family members discussed in it.

He took his mind away from personal histories and began to think police-fashion. It was time he tidied up his case. Put it shipshape for presenting. . . . [I]t would clear his own mind. It would be down in black and white where he could see it.

—*narrative on Investigator Alan Grant*[11]

PROGRESS REPORT ON A STUDY OF WILLIAM COLEMAN SR.

Identification: William Coleman Sr. was a son of Thomas Coleman Sr. and a grandson of Daniel (d. c. 1770) and Patience (d. 1771) Coleman, all of Cumberland County, Virginia.

Introduction: In putting together a biographical sketch of William Coleman Sr. it became necessary to investigate several questions for which no definitive or direct answers had been found:

(1) When did William Sr. die?
(2) When was William Sr. born?
(3) What was the birth order of William Sr. and his siblings?
(4) Who was the mother of William Sr.?

Case Study

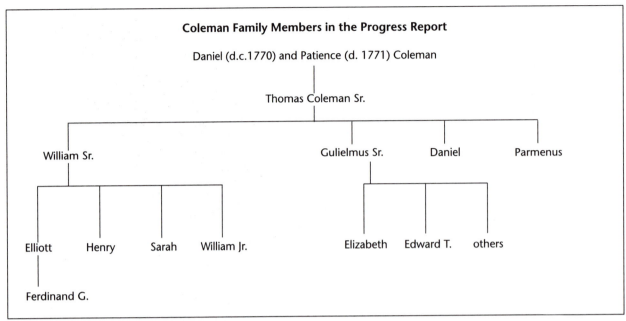

Figure 10 Coleman Family Members in the Progress Report

Research Question #1: When Did William Coleman Sr. Die?

William Coleman wrote his will on 23 May 1810. He divided his 400-acre plantation equally between his son William and his grandson Ferdinand, son of his son Elliott Coleman, whom he appointed as one of three executors. His will was probated in Cumberland County, Virginia, in the May term of court, 1811.[12] In the accounting of expenses and receipts of the estate for 1811, one entry was dated 10 May 1811, for cash the estate received for selling 3 pints of brandy.[13] This item alone suggests William Sr. had died by May 10. He had met with the tax collector on 19 April 1811.[14] We can assume therefore that William Sr. died between April 19 and May 10.

[Note: Court records need to be checked for earliest date of probate proceedings, since a specific date was not given in the will book when the will was recorded. A 1785 state law indicated that no will could be probated until the person had been deceased for at least fourteen days.[15] If we can find the first probate date, we can back up fifteen days and compare it with what we already know. This might help narrow the death date a little more.]

Research Question #2: When Was William Coleman Sr. Born?

No direct evidence of the senior William's birth has been found. No public vital records were kept during his life. No family Bible, tombstone, or church records have been located. For this family, letters and papers apparently do not exist from the early nineteenth century. Those known to exist from the mid-nineteenth century do not mention him. No indirect statement concerning his age or birth has been identified in any sources consulted.

Printed Source

William Waller Hening's *Statutes at Large, Laws of Virginia* is available in many university and genealogy libraries that have Virginia materials.

Therefore, to establish a range of possible birth years, we considered public records in which he appeared, one grandson, his known children, and his siblings.

Study of grandson

The grandson Ferdinand G. Coleman, named in the senior William's will, appeared in the 1850 and 1860 censuses in Cumberland County, Virginia, with reported ages of 56 and 65, respectively.[16] These suggest his birth occurred between mid-1793 and mid-1795. (With the official census day of June 1 for 1850 and 1860, the reported age was to be correct as of June 1 in each year. This means that his birthday would have fallen between May 31 of the census year and the previous June 1.)

The 1820 census gives Ferdinand's age as 16–26, suggesting a birth range of 1794–1804, and the census of 1830 reports his age as 30–40, suggesting birth between 1790 and 1800.[17] An August 7 census day in 1820 implies that, if he was 26, he would have turned 26 in the year before 7 August 1820. Thus, he would have been born between 7 August 1793 and 6 August 1794. Since age is given as a range of ages in 1820, Ferdinand would not have been born earlier than August 1793. If they are relatively correct, the compiled census records suggest a birth between about August 1793 and May 1795. (The 1840 census is inconsistent with these, repeating the 30–40 age.[18])

Ferdinand's first appearance on the county's personal property tax roll in 1815 indicates that he was over 16 by the time the roll was made.[19] This adds nothing of substance to the estimation of his birth because it simply means he was born before early 1799. Ferdinand appeared for the first time on the land tax roll in 1812 with 345 acres, the bulk of which seems to have been the inheritance from William Coleman Sr.[20] He may well have been only about 18 at this time. These add nothing of substance to the estimation of his birth. He could inherit and own land before the age of 21 but could not sell it.[21]

A concurrent study of Ferdinand's siblings suggests that he was probably the first or second child in birth order. Backing up an estimated 25 years per generation (for Ferdinand and his father) would give one estimate of his grandfather William Coleman's birth at about 1744.

Study of sons Elliott and Henry

The senior William's son Elliott Coleman received his marriage bond on 23 November 1789.[22] The bond shows no indication of the groom being underage, and his age, therefore, would be at least 21, the legal age for marrying without parental consent.[23] This suggests a birth no later than November 1768. Elliott is named in the 1787 personal property tax list, prepared in March, as a white male over 21, in the household of William Coleman (Sr.).[24] This suggests a birth date for Elliott no later than March 1766.

The 1782 and 1783 tax rolls for the William Coleman Sr. household indicate only one tithable male over 21, presumably William Sr. himself. For the next three years, this William paid tax on two tithable males over 21, before naming himself and Elliott as the two tithable males in 1787. If these reports are accu-

Notes

Hening's *Statutes at Large.* states that a person under 21 who owned land could have the guardian execute a deed to sell it; this indicates that persons under 21 could own land but could not, on their own, sell it.

rate, Elliott may have been the second tithable male in the earlier years since he was still at home in 1787. However, the same 1787 tax roll also shows Elliott's brother Henry Coleman in the nearby household of Samuel Allen as a white male over 21. The 1787 tax roll was the first to name both Elliott and Henry. We do not know when Henry left home or which brother was the older and therefore the first to be taxed.

Comparison with the 1782 and 1783 household suggests that, if both Elliott and Henry were living at home, neither brother was 21 by the time those rolls were made. This could place both births, or at least one of them, between early 1762 (1783 minus 21) and March 1766. Since these two brothers seem to be the eldest children, their ages are more helpful in estimating their father's birth date. The range of 1762 to early 1766 for at least one of the brothers suggests the father's birth in the vicinity of 1737 to 1741 (1762 minus 25 and 1766 minus 25). (The fact that William Sr., in his will, named Elliott as one executor of his estate, and the only family member so named, may indicate that Elliott was the elder son.)

Remaining children: Sarah and William Jr.

The other two known children of William Coleman Sr., as named in his will, were Sarah, who married Wyatt Coleman (a cousin?), and William Jr., whose wife was Parmelia.[25] At this time, Sarah's birth date cannot be estimated. It is clear from the elder William's will that both Sarah and William Jr. had married these spouses before April 1810, the date of the will, and that William Jr.'s son Spilsby (or Spelsby) was born by this time, because he was named as a legatee.

William Jr. was named a taxable male over 16 in the elder William's household at the time of the 1804 personal property tax assessment.[26] This would suggest birth before 1788. Presumably, he was born considerably before 1788. The polling (voting) list for 1805 shows William Coleman Jr. and thus suggests his birth by April 1784.[27] These records do not affect the calculation of his father's birth date.

However, the senior William's entries on the tax roll show only one white male over 16 from 1789 to 1803. [Note: Could this indeed be William Jr.? Court minutes and/or tax laws need to be consulted. Was William Sr. by this time old enough to be exempt from the personal poll tax? Was he infirm or for some other reason exempt? Can evidence be found for William Jr. living elsewhere during these years?]

Grandfather's will

Another document supporting William Coleman Sr.'s birth by 1741 or early 1742 is the will of his grandfather, Daniel Coleman of Cumberland County, written in August 1763.[28] William Coleman, "son of my son Thomas," was given Daniel's 300-acre property at the death of Daniel's wife, Patience. One William Coleman was also named as an executor of the estate. Presumably, this William was age 21 or older in order to be an executor. He probably is the same William who was the legatee, the son of Thomas. Why? The elder Daniel had no known son named William. The other grandson named William, son of Daniel Jr., was not named in the 1763 will and, according to one compiler, was only about 11 years old at its writing.[29] No other adult William Coleman has been found in the county or in the immediate family at that time.

Estimate of birth range

These documents suggest that William Coleman Sr. was born before early 1742. A legitimate estimate of his birth date would be "about 1737–1741."

Research Question #3: What Was William Coleman's Birth Order?

William Coleman Sr. had a brother named Gulielmus Coleman (Sr.), as named in the will of their grandmother Patience Coleman.[30] Gulielmus was already 21 by early 1782, when he appeared on the personal property tax roll in Cumberland County.[31] Thus, his birth occurred before early 1761. His appearance on the 1820 census adds nothing to the search for a birth date, as he is listed as over 45 (thus, born before 1775).[32] He died before the 1830 census.

Estimating a birth date for Gulielmus (Sr.) meant studying his children.

Study of brother Gulielmus and his children

The children of Gulielmus Coleman Sr. are documented in his widow's will (1823) and an 1807 deed of trust he made to William Guthrey:[33] Elizabeth Guthrey (named as a daughter only in her mother's will), Edward Turner Coleman, Gulielmus Coleman (Jr.), Sarah Coleman (married Thomas Coleman), Eleanor W. Coleman (married John R. Apperson), Benjamin Coleman, James C. Coleman, and John S. Coleman. [Note: Was Elizabeth married before 1807 and thus not named in the 1807 deed of trust? Was the William Guthrey, to whom the deed of trust was made, Elizabeth's husband and thus son-in-law of Gulielmus Coleman? It may be so; see her entry in *American Guthrie and Allied Families*.][34]

If the Guthrie work just cited is accurate, Gulielmus's daughter Elizabeth was born in 1783. This could push her father's birth back to about 1758 (1783 minus 25) or sooner. Since she seems to have been the first to leave the nest, she may have been the oldest daughter but not necessarily the oldest child. Thus, the births of the sons had to be considered. So far, the estimate of the father's birth is 1758 to 1760.

Gulielmus Sr. sold to his son Edward Turner Coleman a slave, Jim, in September 1807.[35] This purchase, recorded in the county deed book, may or may not suggest that Edward was already 21. In Virginia at that time, it was possible for those under 21 to own slaves, for those 18 and older could write wills bequeathing slaves to others.[36] Thus, this record does not really help estimate Edward's birth.

Edward first appeared on the polling (voting) list in Cumberland County in April 1809.[37] Voting indicates that he was already 21 and was born by April 1788.[38] He also appeared on the land tax rolls for the first time in early 1810.[39] (Question: Why did he appear for the first time on the personal property tax rolls in 1810 as a white male over 16 and not earlier?) He married on or after

17 March 1809, when he got his marriage bond.[40] Young men were often older than the minimum 21, frequently 23 to 25 years of age, when they married. If Edward fit the typical pattern (21–25), he could have been born about 1784–1787, no later than March 1788.

These documents suggest that Edward may be the second child, after his sister Elizabeth, mentioned above. A legitimate estimate of his birth range would be "about 1784–1787." Thus, the father's birth remains estimated at 1758 to 1760.

A similar and concurrent study of the other children of Gulielmus Sr. indicates that they were younger than the ones just mentioned. The estimates of their births, therefore, do not affect the estimates for their father and grandfather.

Remaining brothers, Daniel and Parmenus

Gulielmus Sr. and William Coleman Sr. had two brothers, Daniel and Parmenus, as named in the will of their grandmother Patience Coleman.[41] Both were born before 1763, as suggested by their appearance on the 1784 personal property tax rolls for Cumberland County.[42] That year, they were listed one after the other and just below Thomas Coleman, their father. This hints that they were still living at home or on their father's land. Daniel was again listed just below Thomas in 1785. One Daniel Coleman was on the 1782 list; he may or may not be this Daniel. The last listing on the tax roll for a Daniel was in 1796. Thomas's son Daniel did not appear on the land tax rolls of Cumberland County.

Parmenus was married to a Martha (Patsy), who was administratrix of his estate in March 1831.[43] They have not been found in any Cumberland County census, although Parmenus, under variant spellings, was listed in various personal property tax rolls between 1784 and 1797.[44] He never appeared on the land tax roll for the county. [Note: Can Daniel and Parmenus be found in surrounding counties in census or other records?]

The four brothers, William (Sr.), Gulielmus (Sr.), Daniel, and Parmenus, are the only known children of Thomas Coleman, son of Daniel (d. c. 1770) and Patience Coleman (d. 1771), as previously cited. From the wills and census, tax, marriage, and deed records already cited, their birth dates can be suggested as (1) William Sr., about 1737–1741, (2) Gulielmus Sr., about 1758–1760, (3) Daniel, before 1763, and (4) Parmenus, before 1763. The order of their listing in their grandmother's will—William, Daniel, Gulielmus, and Parmenus—may or may not suggest their birth order.

Grandmother's will

The will of their grandmother Patience Coleman indicates that in 1771 William was clearly an adult and the other three brothers were probably under 18. Patience left instructions in her will that her grandson William (Sr.), son of her son Thomas, was to receive the Negro Hannah and her child, Peter, for whom he would pay the estate £60. From this money, he was to pay various bequests and divide the remainder among five of her children. Among the designated bequests were 20 shillings each to William's three named brothers, "to be applied toward their schooling." This provision clearly implies that (1) William was grown and had income and the means to pay £60, a considerable sum, and (2) the other three had not come of age (21) and were probably still under 18. No record has yet shown that any of these became a doctor, lawyer, teacher, or minister through schooling, and 20 shillings would not go far toward higher education. Possibly they were still young enough to attend a "common school" or go to a tutor in the neighborhood. Arithmetic, therefore, indicates that these three were born after 1750 (1771 minus 21) and probably after 1753 (1771 minus 18).

Thus, the birth gap between William Sr. and his three brothers seemed to be at least twelve years (1741 to 1753) and perhaps as much as sixteen to twenty (1737 to 1753 or after, for not all the younger brothers were born in 1753). Other children may have at one time filled the gap, but none has been identified.

In light of Patience Coleman's will, the list of brothers, not necessarily in birth order, might be revised to read: (1) William, 1737–1741, (2) Gulielmus, 1753–1760, (3) Daniel, 1753–1762, (4) Parmenus, 1753–1762.

Research Question #4: Who Was the Mother of William Coleman Sr.?

The implications of Patience Coleman's will in 1771 force the question, Did the brothers have the same mother?

In 1769, William Coleman (Sr.) bought from his father, Thomas Coleman Sr. [sic], 170 acres that may have belonged to William's grandfather Daniel Coleman Sr. and on which William was then living.[45] Recorded with the deed was the attachment by which Thomas's wife, Elizabeth, relinquished her dower right to the property. This is the only specific mention found to date of a wife of Thomas. Another possible indication of her presence is on the 1788 personal property tax roll. There an Elizabeth Coleman appeared with three horses, two slaves over the age of 16, and a white male over 16: Daniel Coleman.[46] (The other three brothers were listed on their own that year.) Then, for three more years, either Elizabeth or Daniel (but not both) was listed with the same property. Elizabeth's last appearance on the tax list was 1791.

No indication of Elizabeth's age is given in documents identified so far, and no marriage record has been found. Because of the large gap between the suggested birth dates of William Sr. and the other brothers, it seems likely that Elizabeth could have been the mother of the three younger boys and that William Sr. was the son of an earlier wife, whose name is unknown.

If William Sr. was born in the middle of the estimated range, 1739, and one of the younger brothers was born in 1753, a fourteen-year gap still exists, and the other two sons were born later. This would imply a childbearing period of nearly twenty years. That in itself may not be unreasonable, but it poses other questions: Were seven or eight other children born into the family during the time gap and did not survive? Did other children survive of whom no record has been found? Since their father in 1769 (deed record above) called himself Thomas Coleman Sr., it is possible that he had another son, a nephew, or a young cousin, Thomas Jr., who died after 1769 without appearing in the county records studied so far. This possibility needs study.

At this time, with the information so far uncovered, a mother for William cannot be named and no name, other than the Elizabeth in the 1769 deed, has surfaced for consideration.

Summary and Conclusions

From the research to date, the following answers have emerged to the four research questions pertaining to William Coleman Sr. of Cumberland County, Virginia.

(1) William's will and probate file, with his last appearance on the tax roll, suggest his death between April 19 and May 10 of 1811.

(2) Pertinent documents for William himself, his children, and one grandson suggest William Sr. was born probably between 1737 and 1741.

(3) Study of William Sr. and his known siblings suggests that William was considerably older than his three brothers, whose birth order cannot yet be stated conclusively. Their birth dates can be narrowed as follows: (a) Gulielmus, about 1753–1760, (b) Daniel, 1753–1762, and (c) Parmenus, 1753–1762.

(4) The gap between the ages of William Sr. and his three known brothers suggests that he may have been the child of a first wife and his brothers, the children of a second wife, possibly the Elizabeth who has been identified as the father's wife in 1769.

I'm afraid I always like to prove a thing for myself.

—*Miss Marple*[47]

EIGHT

Reporting: Case Solved

I want to write it the way it happened. You know; . . . how we stuck
to things that actually happened and not what someone reported
afterwards about it, . . . and that sort of thing.

—*Brent Carradine, research worker*[1]

Carradine's plan has genealogical relevance: Like Carradine, some genealogists want to share their solved cases with others by writing about
their research, the way it happened. They want to tell of the challenges
and show that success can come from original research, from doing their own
research and not relying on what other people have reported.

Those who solve their tough cases quite naturally want to "show and tell." The
celebratory part of that sharing is certainly understandable. However, how many
nongenealogist friends, neighbors, or family members have you found who will
sit with you and listen to your tale of triumph? We can see in their faces the feeling
that one sleuth expressed: "All this listening makes my ears ache."[2]

Notes

Endnotes for this chapter
are on page 261.

WRITING ABOUT THE SUCCESSFUL PROJECT

Smart—very smart!

—*Sherlock Holmes*[3]

Other genealogists are more likely to comprehend what your success means to
you. One way of sharing the achievement is through a written account of the
research effort. The purpose is not just to say, "I did it! I did it! I found them!"
Rather, the greater objectives are (1) to describe, and therefore preserve an
account of, the particular methods and sources that led to the answers in case
they can be helpful to others, (2) to examine the overall project to assess the
ways the experience has made you a better researcher, and (3) to preserve the
story of the search for future generations of the family.

First, articles and studies of this nature are one way genealogists learn from
each other. After all, who does not want new ideas when confronted with a

tough research situation? When genealogists get together, the conversation always eventually gets around to "I've looked everywhere and I can't find them. I don't know what to do next." Someone else usually answers with "Well, when I was looking for my mother's people, I had to. . . ." Like a one-on-one conversation, a written account of the successful project shares it with other genealogists who may benefit from the researcher's experience.

Second, looking at the finished product lets the researcher review the project as a kind of evaluation. In what ways am I now a better genealogist? What mistakes did I make along the way, and how can I learn from them? What might I have done differently to improve the process? What aspects of the project worked best? How can I build on this success? What procedures from this research can I apply to other projects?

Chapter seven discussed the creation of progress reports so that you, as researcher, can think aloud, so to speak, and preserve your thought process in key phases of your research. Likewise, writing about an answered question lets you, as strategist, check the overall project and tighten any loose ends that still exist. The English philosopher Francis Bacon knew well the benefit that writing brings to an author, whether man or woman.

> Reading maketh a full man, conference a ready man, and writing an exact man.
> —*Francis Bacon*[4]

Third, preserving the story for the family is fitting and sensible. We all hope that down the line, sometime, another family member will be interested in what we have learned about the preceding generations. Committing the research process to paper in a form akin to a case study shows that you have done legitimate research, explains your thinking about the research as it moved along, and illustrates how you achieved positive results.

Reminder

Future generations can benefit from your work by being able to point to documented facts about the ancestors and by having a foundation from which to judge new information that may come to light. They can avoid the trap of perpetuating exaggerations, errors, and contradictions, even unknowingly, when they have a reference work that demonstrates its own accuracy. Besides, you could be preserving a record of some sources that may one day disappear or become inaccessible. What if you record and document information from a set of court cases or church baptism records that are later lost in a fire and were never microfilmed? At least your family would have their valuable information. And perhaps most important, you have the opportunity to teach by example, showing future generations that good genealogy can be done and how.

If you decide to produce a family history book, it may be a collection of descendancy charts with notes on the individuals. It may be a biographical and historical narrative, or a combination of features. Regardless, it will likely be different from the kind of research study or case study that details your quest for answers. It will surely be different from your progress reports. The three types of compositions have different purposes and formats.

CASE STUDIES

I assure you, Holmes, that I marvel at the means by which you obtain your results in this case.

—*Dr. Watson*[5]

Everyone runs into "brick wall" problems. Fortunately, many of these cases can be solved with appropriate methods and the right sources, but finding what works often takes a while, maybe years. We may have to work through Plans A, B, and C before finding the one clue that jumps off the page to give us hope. We may be into Plan E before finding the mother lode of information. We may not find the mother lode at all but enough significant evidence to be able to say with confidence, "This is the way it must have happened, and this is why I believe it."

The major genealogical journals, such as the *National Genealogical Society Quarterly* and *The American Genealogist*, publish case studies in each issue. These articles are interesting and informative and belong on the reading list of all genealogists, especially those working on challenging situations. Each case study generally examines a specific question and the pursuit of its answer, which was usually found by applying a distinct or unique technique discussed in the study.

Many genealogists could benefit from reading such success stories, even those achieved with conventional techniques. Wouldn't it be helpful if more local society journals and quarterlies included such examples, even short and informal ones, from their own members? Many editors of society publications call for articles and pedigree charts from members to help fill pages. It could be beneficial to include case studies or research experiences in that plea. You never know who may get new insight and ideas from that effort. One local publication that sometimes contains such informal but informative articles is the *COGS Quarterly* of the Clarke-Oconee Genealogical Society headquartered in Athens, Georgia. Articles do not have to be scholarly to be appealing and helpful to readers.

INTRODUCING CHAPTERS NINE, TEN, AND ELEVEN

By Jove, Watson, I've got it!
  —*Sherlock Holmes*[6]

Chapters nine, ten, and eleven present three success stories. The researchers hope readers will gain from learning how someone else handled "brick wall" questions. However, the benefits are not only on the side of the reader. Researchers gain by pulling their own projects together, as in the progress reports in chapter seven. The difference is that the completed research study has an answer to its major question, and the researcher is ready to move on to the next one.

These particular studies are included because they address the ultimate genealogical challenge of identifying the parent generation. All three began with a

Brick Wall Buster

few family traditions and very little else. The research techniques used were not new or unique, but they were successful in these cases.

During the quest for answers, these genealogists also dealt with other research issues of identifying location, discovering vital statistics, reconstructing a cluster of ancestral associates, and sorting out people of the same name. These searches were set in the United States in the nineteenth century and involved the use of census, land, and tax records. For one case, the breakthrough came in military records; two depended heavily on probate records for their solutions. Each project benefited from some research in person in the ancestral location, where information was discovered that is not available on microfilm.

The three studies progressed in their own way, for each case was unique. They are presented here as they took place and report the work and findings of the researchers themselves. Although getting plenty of lessons in patience and persistence in the process, all these researchers were determined to find answers. All three cases were brought to successful conclusions and opened new avenues for continued research beyond the brick wall.

The researchers in chapter nine developed a commendable practice during their project. Whenever they discovered something really important or had a particularly successful day of research, they declared a "steak night" and treated themselves to a steak dinner. It does you good to pat yourself on the back when you deserve it. It has a way of recharging enthusiasm and motivation. Maybe, it is best to treat yourself between a day's research and an evening's analysis, for Hercule Poirot was right: "[T]o think, the stomach and the brain must be in harmony."[7]

Technique

All three projects illustrate the steps and procedures discussed in earlier chapters of this book:

1. Focusing on one research question, sometimes dividing it into smaller units and addressing them one at a time
2. Planning strategy at the beginning and at various milestones along the way
3. Reconstructing the cluster of ancestral relatives, friends, and neighbors and studying people of the same surname
4. Documenting each piece of evidence
5. Relying on records and documents contemporary with the ancestors being studied
6. Keeping up with what was known
7. Analyzing what was found in order to plan the next step
8. Thinking and rethinking to evaluate the big picture

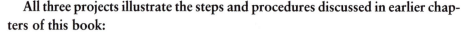

You know my methods. Apply them.
—*Sherlock Holmes*[8]

NINE

Finding the Parent Generation: The Search for Isaac Heldreth's Parents

[N]othing is known of his antecedents.
—*Hercule Poirot*[1]

Nothing is known. Every genealogical search reaches this point, sooner or later. We may as well not dread these words unless we choose to give up and surrender. Perhaps it is the void that attracts and challenges us since we know that at one time, there was no void at all. Who were those ancestors who once filled that place in the family?

This report illustrates one search for a male ancestor's parents, about whom nothing was known and no family tradition existed. It involved the century between 1826 and 1928, a period of remarkable mobility. Before it was resolved, the search spread over five states as it traced the movement of the family. The researchers were Michigan native Garrett Graham and his wife, Dory, who spent her early years in Illinois, Ohio, and Michigan.

Dory Graham's maiden name was Heldreth. Her grandfather was William Owen Heldreth, born 12 December 1877, at Perry Springs Station, Pike County, Illinois. His younger brother, Frank (born 31 March 1888 near Griggsville, Pike County, Illinois; died 12 July 1975), compiled a booklet of descendants of their parents, Isaac Newton Heldreth and Harriett Emily Winegar.[2] The major challenge for the Grahams was to identify Isaac Heldreth's parents. A second issue was to establish a correct birth year for Isaac.

Case Study

Notes

Endnotes for this chapter begin on page 261.

WHAT WAS KNOWN WHEN THE SEARCH BEGAN

Let me get the facts quite clear.
   —*Miss Marple*[3]

In the family history booklet, Frank Heldreth reported that his father, Isaac, was born in Virginia, 26 August 1839. He died 11 December 1928 in Davenport, Iowa. He married Harriett Emily Winegar at Chambersburg, Pike County, Illinois, 4 July 1867. She was a daughter of John and Freelove D. (Sutliff) Winegar, born in 1807 and 1812, respectively, and buried at Chambersburg, Illinois. Other than his birth in Virginia, the only residences known for Isaac were towns in Pike County, Illinois, where his ten children were born, and Davenport, Iowa, where he died.[4]

Frank Heldreth had preserved his father's Union army discharge paper from the Civil War. The paper stated Isaac's birthplace as Virginia, his enlistment date as 28 July 1862, and his unit as Company B, First Regiment of Missouri Engineers. On the date of the discharge, 30 May 1865, Isaac was reported as twenty-one years of age.[5] This report of age suggested an 1843 birth year, assuming the August 26 date was correct. It contradicted the 1839 date the family believed to be correct.

According to Frank Heldreth, "Nothing is known of the parentage of Isaac Newton Heldreth except they were Scotch Irish."[6] The Grahams also knew nothing of his siblings. Such knowledge would have greatly aided their search. As meticulous as Frank Heldreth was in many things, according to the Grahams, it is a wonder that he did not include these siblings in his booklet. At the end of the search, the Grahams received from a cousin, William Heldreth Harms, a copy of a letter written by Frank Heldreth to all his cousins, 6 March 1967, naming his father's siblings as his father had reported them to him. At least Frank's list confirmed what the Grahams had already discovered in their research.

SETTING THE STAGE

Of *course* there's an explanation . . . but what is it?
   —*Investigator Alan Grant*[7]

At the time this search began, the generation of Isaac's children had passed away. The researchers knew of no remaining relatives who could remember Isaac personally. They did collect information on his ten children in preparation for working from the known generation to the unknown one. They also obtained Isaac's death certificate, which gave his birth as 26 August 1839 in Virginia and his death as 11 December 1928 in Davenport, Iowa. The informant was his youngest son, Frank S. Heldreth, who also lived in Davenport at the time. He was the same man who compiled the family history, and he supplied the same birth and death dates in both documents.[8]

In this preliminary research and from firsthand experience with the surname, the researchers also expected to find the name spelled in a variety of ways. The most common was probably *Hildreth*. This particular family used *Heldreth*. In at least one record, it was *Heldrett*. Others appeared in the course of the research.

The researchers decided to focus first on another Pike County, Illinois, family, the Grays, who were the in-laws of Dory Graham's grandfather, William Owen Heldreth. This choice was partly due to a special interest in the Gray ancestors and partly to the dearth of information on Isaac. How can you study someone when you have so few clues to suggest where to look, beyond Pike County? They decided to wait to search for Isaac and his parents, but they remained alert to possible clues. They did what inspector George L. Patton instructed nurse detective Hilda Adams to do, "Just as usual. Keep your eyes open, that's all."[9]

WITH EYES AND MIND OPEN

> Indeed, I would probably have abandoned the idea altogether if I had not made a rather curious discovery shortly after luncheon.
> —*Nurse Detective Hilda Adams*[10]

During a trip to Ohio and Michigan to research the Grays, the Grahams were driving through Preston County, West Virginia, and saw a billboard advertising The Heldreth Motel. Although the name is usually spelled Hildreth, here it was Heldreth, the same spelling that Isaac's family used. Maybe Isaac Heldreth had had connections in this area of West Virginia. Then the light dawned: Isaac's birthplace was said to be Virginia, but West Virginia was, of course, part of Virginia at the time of his birth. Were there still Heldreth families here? The Grahams detoured to the motel in Kingwood long enough to ask questions, visit the public library, and find lots of Heldreth names in the telephone directory. They felt they now had a general area in which to begin their search for the young Isaac: northeastern West Virginia.

After their trip, they surveyed West Virginia materials at Clayton Library, Center for Genealogical Research in Houston, Texas, and found a number of tidbits about Heldreths in that state. Continuing their work on the Grays, the Grahams began reading the entire 1870 census for Pike County, Illinois. (At that time and for years afterward, no index was available.) This effort became one of those times when information shows up on the doorstep and knocks. Here they found the names of Isaac Heldreth (age thirty) and family and, several pages away, his known in-laws, John and Freelove Winegar. Two households from the Winegars lived a Nancy Hildreth (age sixty-nine), with two apparent sons, William (twenty-seven, born in Virginia) and Nicholas (twenty-three, born in Kentucky).[11]

Checking this family against material they had recently accumulated on Heldreths, the Grahams found a reference to a marriage in 1826 in Harrison County, West Virginia, between Uriah Heldreth and Nancy Nutter.[12] Could the Nancy in the 1870 census be the same Nancy who married Uriah Heldreth in

1826? The couple had married in the right time frame to be Isaac's parents. The census listed a Virginia birthplace for Nancy, William, and Isaac. Could this possibly be Isaac's mother?

In addition, this census supported Isaac's 1839 birth (age thirty), as did the 1900, 1910, and 1920 censuses, showing ages sixty, seventy, and eighty respectively.[13] This situation was getting serious and called for research focusing on Isaac.

LOOKING FOR SOLID EVIDENCE

A lot of it makes sense. Have you got any solid evidence?
—*Samuel Clemens*[14]

Warning

Most genealogists would recognize immediately that Nancy Hildreth at sixty-nine could indeed have sons of the ages given in the census: twenty-three, twenty-seven, and thirty. In addition, Nancy and two of these potential sons reported Virginia births. Many would have declared Nancy as Isaac's mother on the spot, but **the Grahams knew the pitfalls that could result from giant leaps of faith in research.** They wanted more than one circumstantial clue; they wanted solid evidence.

Since Nancy Hildreth's apparent son, Nicholas, was born about 1846–1847 in Kentucky, the Grahams decided to look back to the 1850 Kentucky census to try to find Nancy and Nicholas and other family members. In Greenup County, they found Uriah and Nancy Hildreth (ages forty-eight and forty-nine, respectively) enumerated with fifteen other Hildreths, ranging in age from two to twenty-six. Three were likely the wife and two young children of one of the Hildreth sons, Vincent. William and Nicholas, the two young men with Nancy in the 1870 census, were listed among the 1850 siblings at ages eight and four respectively.[15]

As fate would have it, there was no Isaac in this 1850 household. So far as the Grahams knew, he was ten years old at the time of this census, but the child Susan E. Hildreth in the household was listed as ten. Was this not Isaac's family after all? With so many folks in the household, was one simply overlooked in telling the census taker about the family? Was a name perhaps listed incorrectly? Did the census taker omit a name in the copying process?

Notes

What did the Grahams know about Isaac Heldreth at this point?

1. The family believed he was born on 26 August 1839 in Virginia, as shown on the death certificate.
2. The censuses of 1870, 1900, 1910, and 1920 supported this birth year.
3. His military discharge paper indicated an 1843 birth.
4. He had not yet been found in the 1850 or 1860 censuses.
5. He enlisted in Missouri in 1862 for Union army service in the Civil War.
6. He married Harriett Emily Winegar in Pike County, Illinois, in 1867.
7. In 1870 and 1900, he and his family lived in Pike County, Illinois.

8. In 1910, he and his family lived in Colchester, McDonough County, Illinois.
9. In 1920, he and family members lived in Davenport, Iowa.
10. He died in Davenport, Iowa, in 1928.

What evidence did they have about a possible parent for Isaac?
1. In 1870, a Nancy Hildreth lived very near Isaac's in-laws and in the same county as Isaac.
2. Like Isaac, Nancy and one other family member were reportedly born in Virginia.
3. Nancy was of the right age to be Isaac's mother.
4. The search had turned up no other heads of household in Pike County or its six adjacent counties named Heldreth or Hildreth except Nancy and Isaac. (When the index to the 1870 Illinois census was published on CD-ROM in 1998, it was checked for this surname. Nancy and Isaac again were the only Hildreth heads of household reported in Pike County and the only two Hildreth heads of household in the state reporting Virginia as their birthplace.[16])

What problems existed with the evidence?
1. In 1870, Nancy's household included an apparent son born about 1842–1843, and at least one document suggested Isaac's birth year as the same.
2. In 1850, Isaac would have been seven to ten and was not listed in the Uriah and Nancy Hildreth family.

ON LOCATION

We can but try.
—*Dr. Watson*[17]

Later, the Grahams made a trip specifically to West Virginia, especially the Wood County and Harrison County courthouses, cemeteries, and libraries. Although they found no mention of Isaac, they researched Heldreth families of Isaac's time period and before, including Uriah, and verified the marriage record for Uriah Heldreth and Nancy Nutter in 1826.[18]

Through land records, they were able to estimate that Uriah had moved his family to Kentucky between September 1842 and December 1844.[19] In fact, the censuses of 1850, 1860 (found later), and 1870 all reported Nancy and Uriah's son William with a Virginia birthplace. A tombstone found later for this William Hildreth indicates his birth in April 1844 and suggests that the family was in Virginia then and thus may have moved to Kentucky between April and December of that year.[20]

While on location, the Grahams also gathered information on Nutters in the area. They would need this research if the Nancy Heldreth in Pike County,

Illinois, was indeed Isaac's mother. Besides, studying the Nutters could potentially lead to more information about the Heldreths.

In Harrison County, they found the will of Frazier Heldreth, dated 11 May 1831. He named a daughter, Anny Piggott, sons William and Joseph, and son Uriah, to whom he left his land.[21] (Uriah and Nancy had a son named Frazier, as evidenced later in the 1850 and 1860 censuses.) The Grahams learned enough about the senior Frazier to connect him through deeds and wills to his immigrant ancestor, Thomas Hildreth, who came to Massachusetts by 1635. The problem still was linking Isaac to Uriah and Nancy.

While in West Virginia, the Grahams expanded their information on Frazier and Uriah Heldreth through census records. In 1830, Harrison County was home to four Heldreth families, enumerated as *Eldridge*: David, Frazier, Joseph, and William. Although Uriah had married in 1826, he was not listed as a head of household in the 1830 census. However, the household of Frazier "Eldridge" included Frazier and a woman of the age to be his wife; a couple aged twenty to thirty, of age to be Uriah and Nancy; and four children under ten, who could easily account for the four eldest children in Uriah's 1850 census: Vincent, David, Jonathan, and Ann.[22]

The 1840 census showed Uriah as head of household in Wood County, Virginia. The entry contained enough family members of the right ages to account for everyone in the family at the time, based on the 1850 census. If Isaac's 1839 birthdate was correct, he too fit within the household.[23]

WHAT IS THE CLUE?

There's a clue here . . . I know I've seen it. It'll come to me presently.
—*Lord Peter Wimsey*[24]

Having found that Uriah and Nancy Heldreth were in Kentucky in 1850, the Grahams tried to find them in the 1860 census in Kentucky and Illinois, with no success. Then they discovered that Uriah had died in Greenup County, Kentucky, on 28 September 1852.[25]

Family tradition claimed that Isaac had run away from home in Virginia at an early age, some said sixteen, and enlisted in the Civil War in Missouri. Obviously, the story had some details awry. If Isaac was born in 1839 as the family believed he was, he would have been twenty-one, not ten or sixteen, when the war began and thus twenty-two when he enlisted in Missouri. Had he run away from home before his eleventh birthday? If he actually left at the tender age of ten, it was not to join the army.

Isaac's military discharge paper indicated that he enlisted in Missouri. Because the researchers had not found the names of Isaac or the widowed Nancy in the 1860 census in Kentucky or Illinois, they decided to look in Missouri. In the Daviess County enumeration, they found the entry of Nancy Hildreth (age sixty, born in Virginia), with six of the children who had been with her and

Uriah in 1850, including William and Nicholas, and Isaac, age twenty.[26] In addition, Isaac's age (twenty) in this census was again consistent with the 1839 birth date, not the one suggested in his military discharge paper.

The researchers then requested a copy of his military service record from the National Archives.[27] It confirmed his Missouri enlistment at St. Joseph on 28 July 1862 but indicated his first unit was Company D, 25th Regiment of Missouri Volunteers. His signature showed that he spelled his name Heldreth. The service record showed that he had also served as a private in Company A (as a cook) and Company B (as a teamster) of the First Missouri Engineers, United States. He was mustered out at Louisville, Kentucky, with enough money to return to St. Joseph, Missouri. The file indicated that he had received a $25 bounty upon enlistment and was still due $75. The papers gave his physical description, health history, and other details about his service but no additional clues about his age, parents, or family. Further research into his units revealed a Winegar man in one of them. Perhaps Isaac met his wife through this buddy.

Evidence now pointed more strongly to Uriah and Nancy as Isaac's parents. Although the Grahams had found no evidence to the contrary, they felt there was not yet enough evidence to consider the issue settled. They needed to find something more that would link the couple to Isaac.

THE MISSING LINK

Oh, my friend, have I not said to you all along that I have no proofs. . . . I, Hercule Poirot, know, but I lack the last link in my chain.

—*Hercule Poirot*[28]

The 1880 census of Illinois reported Nancy (age seventy-nine) and her unmarried son, William (age thirty-six), in Chambersburg, Pike County. Only five households away was listed Isaac (age forty-one) and his family. Nancy was enumerated next to another Heldreth sibling, Sarah, with her husband, John Todd.[29]

Of course, the Grahams did not expect county records in Illinois, Missouri, Iowa, and Kentucky to give evidence of Uriah and Isaac acting together, such as witnesses, plaintiffs, or parties to a deed, since Uriah died in 1852 in Kentucky when Isaac was only thirteen years old. However, various kinds of county records sometimes contain evidence of a father-son or mother-son or brother-sibling relationship that becomes the key to such a search. This is what these researchers had hoped to find. However, no such evidence was showing up in Illinois, Missouri, Iowa, and Kentucky county records.

Although concerned by the lack of conclusive evidence, these researchers refused to give up. Going back over their findings, **Dory Graham realized that they had received copies of Isaac's military service record but had never asked for a pension record.** Not knowing whether he had ever had a Civil War pension, she wrote to the National Archives. She received a bundle, indeed containing

Brick Wall Buster

147

a number of pension-related papers. These listed all Isaac's residences since the war. The 1890 "Declaration for Invalid Pension" affirmed that Isaac was badly crippled and needed a pension because he could not work, possibly due to the arm injury reported on the application.[30] At that time, Isaac was living in Beardstown, Cass County, Illinois. (*Invalid* in the government pensions meant that a person was infirm, injured, or otherwise disabled; it did not mean that the pension application was rejected or not valid.)

Apparently, the pension board also had questions about Isaac's age, which he now reported differently from what was on his discharge paper. In a 1926 "Declaration for Pension," he declared his birth as 26 August 1839.[31] Earlier, on 4 October 1909, he had signed an affidavit that he was born in Harrison County, West Virginia [sic], on 26 August 1839, as his parents had always told him.[32] According to the affidavit, although there was no public record of his birth, his mother had kept a family record until her death about twenty-three years before (about 1886). The record had passed to a sister, now dead, and he had no idea if that record still existed. He was now seventy years old and believed that he was twenty-three when he enlisted. (In fact, he seems to have enlisted only a month before his twenty-third birthday.) At the time of the 1909 affidavit, Isaac was living in Colchester, McDonough County, Illinois.

After the 4 October 1909 meeting with the pension board, a question remained about his age, and he again went before a notary public on 15 October 1909. As a "very respectable and credible person," in the words of the notary, Isaac swore that he lived with his parents in Greenupburg, Greenup County, Kentucky in 1850.[33] His father died, and he lived with his mother in St. Joseph, Buchanan County, Missouri, in 1860 and until he enlisted in 1862.[34] He affirmed that his father was Uriah Heldreth and his mother was Nancy Heldreth. (See Figure 11.)

Here we have our material!
—*Sherlock Holmes*[35]

There it was, the record waiting to be found. It answered both focus questions: Isaac's birth date and the names of his parents. The pension application of 1926 and the affidavit of 1909 furnished the same birth date, which was also consistent with family information and with the ages stated in five of the six censuses in which he was found. The names of his parents on the 1909 affidavit were consistent with the implications in the various census records and the cluster of relatives living in Isaac's vicinity from at least 1870 to 1900.

The Grahams wondered whether they should have thought to ask for a pension record closer to the beginning of the search. They decided they might not have gathered all the other data that supported Isaac's depositions if they already had the answer of his parentage. They decided that in any future case, they would request service and pension record searches at the same time, but they were not sorry they had conducted this particular research as they had.

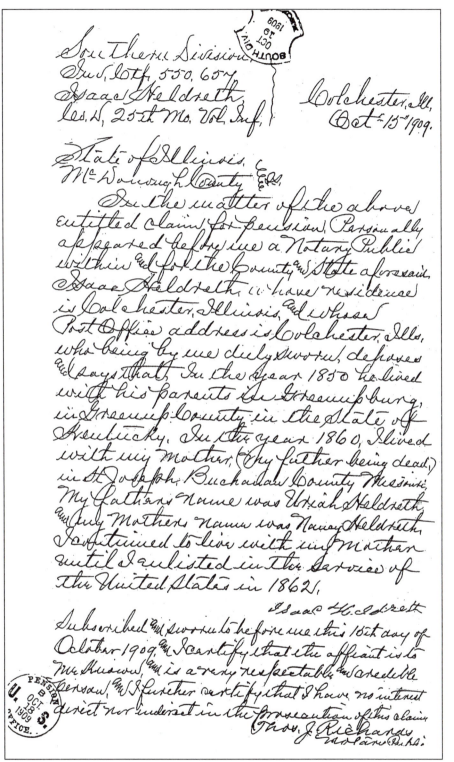

Figure 11 Isaac Heldreth's Affidavit of 15 October 1909

TEN

Finding Slave Ancestors: The Search for the Family of Archie Davis Sr.

Notes

Endnotes for this chapter begin on page 263.

Technique

I was afraid that I would not be able to do what was required of me. It seemed so very difficult, almost impossible at first. . . . Oh, well, it's just perseverance, isn't it, that leads to things?
—*Miss Marple*[1]

U sually in genealogy, the farther back we reach, the more challenging are the searches. Identifying and proving early ancestors must often be done with careful thought and creative research. This is certainly true when tracing those African-American ancestors who were slaves before the Civil War. After 1865, genealogists find these ancestors in the same kinds of records as other Americans, but before 1865, they were not named in census records and had almost no opportunity to create their own records. Therefore, **finding them and their forebears depends on finding records created by their masters.** Often, the greatest challenge is identifying those masters.

That identification process was a major effort within this study. The researcher was Franklin Smith, formerly of Claiborne County, Mississippi, and now of Texas. Skills developed through experience, along with determination and perseverance, have led to the discovery of a number of pre–Civil War ancestors. As in many of our searches, some luck and some useful oral tradition were also mixed into this case. The focus of the research was Archie Davis Sr. of Claiborne County, Mississippi. However, this study is a prime example of the value of cluster genealogy.

Tracing black ancestors is a diverse proposition because the ancestral population was quite diverse. Ancestors come in many varieties, from different ethnic, geographic, and economic situations. For example, in 1860, of the 31.44 million residents of the United States, only about 20 percent lived in urban areas; the rest were on farms and in small towns.[2] However, somebody's ancestors made up that 20 percent, and research to find them can be somewhat different from research to find rural ancestors.

Like the total population, the pre–Civil War black population was also diverse. In 1860, blacks in the United States numbered about 4.44 million, 14 percent of the total inhabitants. Census figures show that about 11 percent of these were legally free. Census figures also indicate that of the 3.95 million slaves, about 9 percent lived in towns and cities.[3] Research for ancestors in these situations can vary from other searches.

Another small percentage of slaves lived on the few huge plantations that had a hundred or more slaves.[4] The largest plantations were big businesses and kept business records that included accounts of slave births and deaths, family groups, illnesses, purchases, and sales. Some of these records survive in archives collections and are a gold mine for researchers.

Although it is estimated that about "half of all slaves worked on plantations"[5] of varying sizes, the majority of slaves lived in relatively small situations, from a farm with one or two slaves to a small plantation with about twenty to twenty-five. The family in this study was part of this more typical pattern. Research to find them, therefore, took a path similar to that commonly necessary to find black ancestors.

What Was Known When the Search Began

Let us have the facts.
—*Investigator Alan Grant*[6]

1. Archie Davis Sr. was Franklin Smith's great-great-grandfather: his mother's mother's father's father (Franklin[5] Smith, Sylvia[4] Boines Smith, Hattie[3] Davis Boines, Henderson[2] Davis, Archie[1] Davis Sr.).
2. He owned about 100 acres near the Willows community in Claiborne County, Mississippi.
3. Smith's mother often spoke of and knew some of Archie Davis's children, particularly Archie Jr., Henderson, and Harriet. Shortly after her marriage in 1936, she lived on land then owned or managed by Archie Davis Jr. She also inherited a portrait of Archie Davis Sr. and remembered that he died when she was a small child. Nothing more was known of this ancestor.
4. Smith was of the opinion that Archie Davis Sr. was born a slave.

Notes

The number after the name represents the generation. Franklin[5] Smith is the fifth generation from Archie[1] Davis Sr.

EARLY RESEARCH

[L]et us get down to what is practical.
—*Sherlock Holmes*[7]

The first research effort was a study of Archie Davis Sr. in the 1870–1900 census records. The 1910 and 1920 censuses were not yet open when research began, but they were consulted later. Aware that the 1870 census was the first to name all black citizens after the Civil War, the researcher chose to begin with it. Since he did not find Archie in the available Mississippi index for 1870, he moved forward to the 1880 census.

The Soundex furnished the basic information for the Archie Davis family in 1880 because the family's part of the microfilmed page was very faded and difficult to read.[8] Archie was reported as forty years of age, which suggested a birth date of 1839–1840. He and his wife, Martha (age thirty-six), had seven children, ranging in age from sixteen-year-old daughter Amanda to two-year-old son Archie Davis Jr. In the family was also eighty-year-old Nellie Davis, designated as mother to the head of household. Her identity was a most fortunate discovery.

The research progressed to the 1900 census. Archie was listed as fifty-eight, with a stated birth year of 1842. Archie's wife, Martha, was not enumerated in this census, and Archie was listed as a widower. However, four additional children had been born into the family between 1880 and 1900. The youngest of these, son Shelly Davis, was reportedly born in September 1888.[9] It appeared, therefore, that Martha had died between September 1888 and June 1900. Archie's mother, Nellie Davis, was also mentioned for the last time in the 1880 census.

By 1910, "Arch" Davis Sr. was sixty-eight, still farming, and head of a household that included his son Elias, daughter-in-law Virginia, and young grandson Fred. His son Archie Jr. with his wife and mother-in-law, lived very near, as they were enumerated next to the senior Archie in the census.[10] Both Elias and Archie Jr. were listed as thirty years old in this census, although the 1900 census, supported by that of 1880, gave the younger Archie's birth as April 1878. He would have been thirty-one or thirty-two by the 1910 census, depending on which side of the April 15 census day his birthday occurred. Likewise, the 1900 census reported that Elias was born in April 1881, making him three years younger than Archie Jr. All things considered, it was not unusual for families such as this one to estimate age and birth date if they had no written record.

The 1920 census taker found "Arch" Davis Sr. still head of a household that now included Arch Jr.; his wife, Alice; his mother-in-law, Dina Clark; and a widow, Ann Blackstone, age seventy, whose relationship was reported as sister. Whose sister? Probably Archie's or Dina's, but an answer has not yet been determined. Yes, the stated relationship was supposed to be to the head of household, but the researcher has found no other evidence of Archie having a sister named Ann. Archie Sr. had aged more during the previous decade than between the other censuses, as his age was given as eighty-one.[11] Combined information from the four censuses places his birth between mid-1838 and mid-1842.

Reminder

The official census day in 1900 was June 1; all information given to the census taker was to be correct as of that day. If Martha Davis was alive on June 1, she was to be included in the census. Since she was not included and her husband was listed as widower, it is assumed she died before 1 June 1900, perhaps years before.

FOCUS ON MOTHER

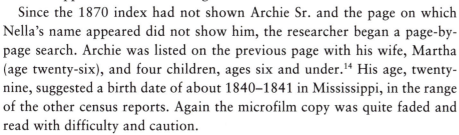

We must proceed logically—however absurd it may seem.
—*Hercule Poirot*[12]

Research Tip

The researcher knew that before striking out to search for any of Archie Sr.'s ancestors, **he needed more background material and more information on a family cluster.** Thus, the next focus was Archie's mother, Nellie Davis. Was she in the 1870 census? *Nella* Davis was enumerated in the Grand Gulf precinct of Claiborne County as an eighty-year-old [*sic*] black female.[13] In her household were Harriet Woods (forty-one, black), Jane Green (thirty-five, black), Betsy Woods (thirteen, black), and Matthew Green (ten months, black), all born in Mississippi. Both the 1870 and 1880 censuses gave Nellie Davis's birthplace as Mississippi, and Archie Sr. reported his mother's birthplace as Mississippi in the censuses of 1880 through 1920. Thus, the search would probably remain in Mississippi for at least another generation.

Since the 1870 index had not shown Archie Sr. and the page on which Nella's name appeared did not show him, the researcher began a page-by-page search. Archie was listed on the previous page with his wife, Martha (age twenty-six), and four children, ages six and under.[14] His age, twenty-nine, suggested a birth date of about 1840–1841 in Mississippi, in the range of the other census reports. Again the microfilm copy was quite faded and read with difficulty and caution.

Analysis of the census reports suggested that Harriet and Jane in Nellie Davis's household in 1870 were probably Archie's sisters since they were in the household of his mother. Based on the 1870 census, the only one in which they were identified, Harriet's birth occurred about 1828–1829 and Jane's about 1834–1835. One concern was that Nellie was shown as eighty years of age in both 1870 and 1880. Considering Archie's age of forty in 1880, it seemed likely that Nellie was closer to eighty in 1880, having had her son Archie at about forty years of age, rather than eighty in 1870, which would have placed Archie's birth when his mother was near fifty.

WHAT WAS KNOWN AT THIS POINT ABOUT THE FAMILY OF ARCHIE DAVIS SR.?

1. Archie Sr. was born in Mississippi probably between 1838 and 1842.
2. His mother was Nellie Davis, born in Mississippi about 1800.
3. He had two probable sisters, Harriet (born 1828–1829) and Jane (born 1834–1835).
4. He and his wife, Martha, had eleven identified children, as listed in census records: Amanda, Robin (son), Henderson, Mary Ann, George? (son), Harriet, Archie Jr., Elias, John, Lenora, and Shelly (son).

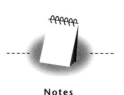

Notes

5. His wife, Martha, died between 1888 and 1900.

6. Archie died after 1920.

7. At least from 1870 forward, the family lived in Claiborne County, Mississippi.

FOCUS ON WIFE

Any coincidence is always worth noticing. You can throw it away later if it *is* only coincidence.

—*Miss Marple*[15]

Cluster genealogy plays an important role in tracing tough lineages. Since nineteenth-century families often lived among a cluster of relatives, Smith knew it would be important to look at the neighbors in the census records, especially in 1870, the first census after emancipation. In that year's enumeration, listed next to Archie Davis Sr. was Jesse Humphreys, his wife, Caroline, and four children. Only two households away, listed next to Nellie Davis was James Humphreys, his wife, Eliza, and their family.[16] Were they related to the Davises? Were they connected to Archie or his wife, Martha?

What about Archie's wife, Martha? Because Archie Sr. and Martha had their first child between mid-1863 and September 1865, according to the 1870–1900 censuses, the question of a marriage record arose. Did they legalize and record their relationship after the war as many former slaves did? No record was found in the compiled index to Mississippi "Marriage Records Prior to 1926" on microfilm (produced by the Works Progress Administration from records then at the state board of health), in the Claiborne County marriages, or in the records of the Mississippi office of the Bureau of Refugees, Freedmen, and Abandoned Lands, which sometimes recorded marriages of former slaves.

Nothing was known, therefore, of Martha Davis other than what was in the censuses. When the research began, none of Archie and Martha's children was still living. Therefore, no family members who had known Martha were available to interview. A few of the grandchildren were still living, but with addresses unknown, they could not be contacted.

FAMILY ORAL TRADITION PLAYS A ROLE

I need somebody to go quiz the family.

—*Samuel Clemens*[17]

A visit with Smith's mother and aunt uncovered a clue. While going through old photographs that had belonged to Smith's great-aunt, they found a picture of an elderly lady seated in a chair. The two ladies identified her as Aunt Cindy Haywood and said her husband had fought in the war. In the South, "the war" often meant the Civil War, as it did here, even after World War II. Also in the South, close friends of the family are occasionally called "aunt" or "cousin" even if they are not related, but sometimes a relationship exists that is not always explained to the younger generations. In this case, Smith's mother and aunt were not sure of the Haywood relationship to the family but thought Aunt Cindy was related to their grandfather, Henderson Davis, a son of Archie Davis Sr. They recalled that she lived with Henderson's sister Harriet, a daughter of Archie Davis Sr., until her death.[18]

Smith contacted the oldest living grandchild of Harriet Davis's family, who remembered that Cindy Haywood was Harriet's aunt.[19] The marriage records for Claiborne County showed that Jordan Haywood had married Lucinda Humphreys in 1870.[20] There was now more reason to believe that the Humphreys neighbors in the 1870 census had some connection to Archie and Nellie Davis. Smith's family believed that Lucinda, not her husband, was their relative.

Since Jordan Haywood and Lucinda Humphreys were married after the 1870 census, would Lucinda's name appear in the census in a household with possible parents? Looking up all Humphreys households in the Grand Gulf District of Claiborne County, both black and white, Smith found a Lucinda Humphreys, a twenty-two-year-old black female, listed in the household of a black couple, Willoughby Humphreys and his wife, Mary.[21] Willoughby was said to be fifty-five and born in Mississippi; Mary was listed as fifty-six and born in Missouri.

Since the oral tradition was that Lucinda Haywood was an aunt of Archie and Martha Davis's children (namely, Henderson and Harriet), it was logical that she was a sister of either Archie or Martha. Archie's mother was already identified as Nellie, not Mary. Thus, it was plausible and probable that Lucinda (Humphreys) Haywood was Martha's sister, and Willoughby Humphreys was Martha's father. (Research continues on the question of whether Willoughby had more than one wife and, therefore, who might be Martha's mother.) Perhaps the James Humphreys, age fifty-five, living next to Nellie Davis in 1870 was Martha's uncle, and the Jesse Humphreys, age forty, next to Archie and Martha Davis was Martha's brother or uncle.

That might mean a lot, or it might not.
—*Inspector George L. Patton*[22]

These extended family relationships could be important in identifying slave owners and slave families. **Like many other families, former slave families after the Civil War often remained within a cluster of prewar friends and relatives.** The proximity of the Davis and Humphreys families to each other and the now apparent relationship between them strengthened the cluster. The broad search would need to include both families.

Research Tip

SOME EXAMINATIONS

[L]et us enter into some examinations for ourselves, before we make up an opinion . . .

—*C. Auguste Dupin* [23]

With this background, the research could focus on Archie Davis Sr. as part of a family cluster, in the hope of finding ancestors. His mother, Nellie Davis, would certainly be a key to any discovery; maybe the Humphreys connection would be too. This effort would take the search into the era when most blacks had no public or official identity other than that created by the whites who owned them. The research process, therefore, would involve tracing several generations of white families through the records they created in order to try to identify their slaves.

Based on the census records, it was estimated that Nellie was born about 1800, reportedly in the young Mississippi Territory, created in 1798. Archie was also born in Mississippi, between 1838 and 1842. The first step in finding Nellie and Archie in records was identifying an owner in Mississippi. Beginning with the known to find the unknown, Smith worked on white families named Davis and Humphreys in the Claiborne County area. He searched probate, deed, and tax records prior to the Civil War and the 1850 and 1860 censuses without establishing any obvious connection between the white Davis families and Archie and Nellie Davis.

At first, the research into Humphreys records seemed to suggest a connection, at least with the black Humphreys. The surname had appeared in the Claiborne County area by the late 1790s. Between 1800 and 1843, when he died, one George Wilson Humphreys acquired large land holdings and many slaves. A thorough search of the probate records of this Humphreys and others of his family revealed the frequent appearance of the name Willoughby among the slaves. However, the records revealed none of the other black Davis or Humphreys family members during the appropriate period of time. **This absence of the Davis and Humphreys cluster was important evidence in itself.** It became apparent that this was not the correct white family and the research had to continue elsewhere.

Important

PLAN B

Well, well, we have made a beginning. I should not expect any fresh developments until next Tuesday.

—*Sherlock Holmes* [24]

Indeed, all tough investigations take time; they cannot be rushed. When Plan A meets a dead end, it is time to go to Plan B. Smith's Plan A had been a same-surname approach. This technique is appropriate, reasonable, and, at times, successful, but here it met a dead end. Plan B would be to investigate the white landowners who (1) lived in the same part of the county as the Davis family cluster in 1870, regardless of surname. Since Smith was looking for slaves, he limited the search to (2) only those 1870 white families with property and (3) those whose 1850 and 1860 census records showed slave ownership. About a dozen Claiborne County landowners qualified as candidates.

Other potential candidates may have died or moved away after the 1860 census or after the Civil War. However, since the black Davis and Humphreys families were in Claiborne County from the end of the war forward, it was reasonable to begin with white families who also remained. If this process did not work, the search could go to Plan C.

[T]here is such a thing as being too profound. Truth is not always in a well.

—*C. Auguste Dupin*[25]

Through a process of elimination and/or lack of available records, the search came to a thirty-three-year-old white farmer named John P. McIntyre. In 1870, he was living within five households of Archie Davis Sr. and two households from Nellie Davis.[26] Since his real estate was valued at $4,000, he fit the profile for a search. In 1880, he was enumerated next to Archie Davis Sr.[27]

In 1880, in the same rural "neighborhood" lived Willoughby Humphreys and James Humphreys, believed to be brothers. (Willoughby Humphreys, now a widower, was also the prime candidate for the father of Martha Davis, wife of Archie Davis Sr.) These families lived near enough to each other that the census taker had enumerated all of them—McIntyre, Davis, and two Humphreys—on the same day, 19 June 1880.[28]

J.P. McIntyre, in 1860, was twenty-two and single, living in the household of Dr. E. Pollard (thirty-one), along with D. McIntyre (nineteen), probably a brother. The slave census schedule showed that J.P. McIntyre owned thirty-four slaves.[29] In 1850, John T. [*sic*] (thirteen), Duncan H. (nine), and Louisa (fourteen) were the three children in the household of A.C. McIntyre, a thirty-eight-year-old white female with thirty-four slaves.[30] She was identified as J.P. McIntyre's mother in the 1880 census of his household and named as Adeline C. in his 1870 household, both previously cited.

The Claiborne County 1840 census and probate records indicated that she was the widow of Duncan H. McIntyre, who had settled in Claiborne County in the 1830s from Franklin County, Mississippi.[31] Duncan H. McIntyre died in 1842. His probate records revealed that he owned two plantations, Caledonia and Beeches, and 102 slaves.[32] Among these slaves appeared a few familiar names, but it was clear they were not part of the Davis-Humphreys cluster.

A WILD POSSIBILITY?

[W]hat else can we do? Don't you see we must either follow one wild possibility or else go home to bed?

—*Valentin, head of Paris police*[33]

The proximity of the McIntyre, Davis, and Humphreys families in postwar censuses was strong evidence, too strong to ignore, and the list of candidates was getting short. Thus, the researcher turned to a more thorough study of McIntyre records. Deed records revealed two McIntyre purchases of land from Josiah B. Sugg in 1838: One grantee was Duncan H. McIntyre; the other, his probable father, Peter McIntyre.[34] Earlier, in 1833, Josiah B. Sugg married Elizabeth McIntyre, daughter of Peter McIntyre and of the generation to be Duncan H. McIntyre's sister.[35] In 1860, John P. McIntyre, son of Duncan H. McIntyre, bought land and slaves from his brother-in-law, W.R. Sugg.[36] A study of the land tax records showed that Josiah B. Sugg and the estate of D[uncan] H. McIntyre owned adjoining land in Claiborne County, all of Sections 16 and 17, respectively, of Township 12, Range 3 East.[37]

Because the connections between Sugg and McIntyre families were strong, the Suggs were targets of the next phase of research. The 1830 census for Claiborne County showed the households of Josiah B. Sugg (twenty to thirty) and Margaret Sugg (twenty to thirty), later found to be Josiah's sister-in-law.[38] Margaret's household included a boy five to ten years old and a male fifteen to twenty. By 1840, W.R. Sugg appeared as a single male, fifteen to twenty, living alone.[39]

The probate records of Claiborne County contain files for two Sugg estates: William and Margaret. William Sugg died in 1824, leaving a minor son, W.R. Sugg, and a widow, Margaret. His brother, Josiah B. Sugg, acted as executor. The estate included eight slaves, listed by gender but without names. An 1829 accounting of his estate mentioned twelve slaves.[40] His widow's census entry in 1830 showed fourteen slaves.[41]

In 1831, the widow Margaret Sugg died. The inventory and appraisal of her estate, dated 25 March 1831, registered sixteen slaves, with names of fifteen.[42] The following January, another inventory of the property of William R. Sugg, returned by his guardian, Josiah B. Sugg, reported the names and ages of the same slaves.[43] Among them were a boy James (twelve or thirteen), a boy Willoby (thirteen or fourteen), a girl Harriet (eight or nine), a girl Caroline (five or six), a girl Jenny/Jane (four or five), and a boy Jess (five or six), and a woman Nelly (twenty-five to twenty-eight) and her infant child Eliza (in the 1831 list) or Elisha (twelve months old in the 1832 list). All of these, except the infant, were associated with the Archie Davis cluster of families. (Neither Archie nor his wife, Martha, was born by this time.)

One of the other women, Celia, was listed as thirty-eight to forty, certainly of the right age to be the mother of Willoby, James, and Jess. The boy Sampson (eight or nine) was another possible son of Celia, especially since James Humphreys later had a son named Sampson.[44] In the 1831 report, Celia had an infant child, who was perhaps the young John (eighteen months) in the 1832 inventory.

The others were a man Moses (twenty-six or twenty-eight), a man Abram (same age as Moses), a woman Till (eighteen to twenty) with a child two or three years old (unnamed), and a girl Mary (four or five). The 1831 list also concluded with a boy named Albert, not named separately in the 1832 inventory. He was probably Till's unnamed child in that 1832 report. The research on this group is ongoing, but early indications are that the men, Moses and Abram, may have been relative newcomers to the plantation. Also, the girl Mary (four or five in 1832) is difficult to place into a suggested family unit. In Figure 13, on page 161, she is named apart from the family groups although she could belong to one of them, or perhaps be a child of Till.

A new inventory was made in 1842 after William R. Sugg's guardian, Duncan H. McIntyre, died and Peter McIntyre was appointed his guardian.[45] (Duncan McIntyre had become guardian when the boy's uncle, Josiah B. Sugg, moved to Louisiana about 1837–1838.[46]) The 1842 inventory named eighteen slaves and reported their ages. This was an important find because, for the first time, and so far the only time, Nelly and Archie (Davis), then a three-year-old boy, were listed in a prewar record together. Figure 12, on page 160, shows this inventory and its transcription.

REVIEWING THE RESULTS IN CLAIBORNE COUNTY

The case he builds up is very strong—very strong.
  —*Hercule Poirot*[47]

The Claiborne County probate, deed, and census records yielded a progression of owners for the Davis-Humphreys families. Below is a summary of the research results.

1. The Davis-Humphreys cluster of families was part of the William Sugg estate when he died in 1824.
2. His widow, Margaret Sugg, owned them until her death in 1831.
3. Their only son, William R. Sugg, owned them, although as a minor he was not actually farming, and they probably were hired out between 1831 and about 1844 when he married. (He married just after his twenty-first birthday.)[48]
4. In 1860, William R. Sugg, apparently in preparation for a move to Louisiana, sold his property to his brother-in-law, John P. McIntyre.[49]
5. Records have not yet shown the exact disposition of the slave families between 1842 and 1865, but apparently they remained in Claiborne County. The 1860 sale of Sugg property to John P. McIntyre probably helps explain why these families were living so close to him in 1870 and 1880.

Notes

159

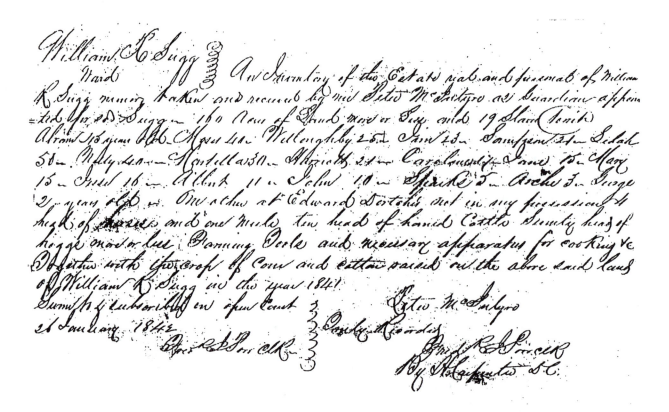

Figure 12A Peter McIntyre's Inventory of William R. Sugg's Estate, 1842

William R. Sugg

       Ward   An inventory of the Estate real and personal of William R Sugg minor taken and recused by me Peter McIntyre as Guardian appointed for sd Sugg~160 Acres of Land more or Less and 19 Slaves to wit Abram 45 years old~Moses 40~Willoughby 25~Jim 23~Sampson 21~Selah 50~Nelly 40~Martella 30~Harriett 21~Caroline 17~Jane 15~Mary 15~Jesse 16~Albert 11~John 10~Sparks 5~Arche 3~George 2 years old~One other at Edward Dortche's not in my possession--4 head of horses and one mule ten head of horned Cattle Seventy head of hoggs more or less Farming Tools and necessary apparatus for cooking &c Together with the crop of corn and cotton raised on the above said land of William R Sugg in the year 1841

Sworn to & subscribed in open Court   Peter McIntyre

26 January 1842   Truly Recorded

      Fred RJ Poor Clk~   Fred RJ Poor Clk

                                        By H Carpenter D.C.

Figure 12B Transcription of Above Document

Figure 13 compares the useful inventory lists with the 1830 and 1840 censuses. The two likely family groups are shown as units; the others in the household are reported but not in any intended family group. In the chart, M is male, F is female, < is less than, numbers are the reported ages.

Slaves Held by the Sugg Family, Claiborne County, Mississippi, 1830–1842					
Name in inventories	1830 Census	1831 Inventory	1832 Inventory	1840 Census	1842 Inventory
Celia/Selah	F24–36	woman	38–40	F36–55	50
Willoby/Willinghty	M10–24	boy	13–14	M10–24	25
James/Jim	M10–24	boy	12–13	M10–24	23
Sampson	M<10	boy	8–9	M10–24	21
Jess	M<10	boy	5–6	M10–24	16
infant, John	—	infant	18 mos.	M<10	10
Nelly	F10–24	woman	25–28	F36–55	40
her infant	—	Eliza	Elisha, 12 mos.	(died, 1832)	—
Harriet	F<10	girl	8–9	F10–24	21
Caroline*	F<10	girl	5–6	F10–24	17
Jenny/Jane	F<10	girl	4–5	F10–24	15
Archie	—	—	—	M<10	3
Others:					
Mary	F<10	girl	4–5	F10–24	15
Till/Martella	F10–24	woman	18–20	F24–36	30
Albert	?	infant	2–3	M<10	11
Abram	—	man	26–28	M36–55	45
Moses	—	man	26–28	M36–55	40
Sparks	—	—	—	M<10	5
George	—	—	—	M<10	2
who?	F<10	—	—	3M<10	—
who?	F10–24	—	—	—	—
* Caroline appears to be the same Caroline who married Jesse Humphreys.					

Figure 13 Comparing Slave Lists in Census and Probate Records

ONE MORE STEP UP THE HILL

Maybe it's an uphill race, but if I give up now, I might as well have never started it.

—*Samuel Clemens* [50]

It is not yet known how and when Nellie Davis came into the Sugg household. The search for her and a possible childhood family for her continues. However, William Sugg may be the key to Willoughby Humphreys's ancestors and, therefore, to those of Martha Humphreys Davis, wife of Archie Davis Sr.

In January 1804, William Sugg, who died in 1824, and his brother Josiah

Bryan Sugg, both of Claiborne County, Mississippi, each received three slaves from their mother, Nancy Bryan Sugg, widow of Josiah Sugg, and their grandmother, Elizabeth Bryan, widow of Britton Bryan.[51] The slaves were from the estate of Britton Bryan. One of those who went to William Sugg was a girl name Selah (the same spelling used for Celia in the 1842 inventory). In addition, the 1804 inventory and appraisal of Britton Bryan's estate listed his slaves and their ages.[52] Selah was reported as about eleven years of age. This report places her birth at about 1793 and is consistent with the age of thirty-eight to forty in Margaret Sugg's 1832 inventory, which suggests birth about 1792–1794. In the 1804 inventory, the slaves were not grouped by families but by ages. Among the women was one named Molly, of the age to be Celia's mother. This possibility is under investigation.

Needless to say, the Davis family research has a new focus in the Bryan estate and family to try to identify Celia's childhood family. Although not yet found in an 1800 census, a Britain Bryant was enumerated in the 1790 census of Edgecombe County, Halifax District of North Carolina.[53] This area will be the next focus for research.

What began as a search for ancestors of Archie Davis Sr. has yielded more evidence for ancestors of his wife, Martha. Research happens that way. As the research continues, this is the generational picture as it stands at this writing: Franklin[7] Smith, Sylvia[6] Boines Smith, Hattie[5] Davis Boines, Henderson[4] Davis, Martha[3] Humphreys Davis, Willoughby[2] Humphreys, Celia[1].

Now go to it! Go out for a breath of fresh air between seven and eight each evening, and—keep your eyes open. I have a hunch that you'll get this thing.

—*Inspector George L. Patton*[54]

ELEVEN

Finding the Parent Generation: The Search for Ann (Robertson) Croom's Parents

I hope you won't think me *very* inquisitive if I ask you to let me know how you progress?
—*Miss Marple*[1]

T he goal of most genealogical searches, including this one, is to move backward to discover and prove the next generation, the parents. This study illustrates (1) working with two known female ancestors to identify a husband and father, (2) searching in the pre–Civil War rural South where many desirable kinds of sources are not always available, (3) bringing together various kinds of evidence, records, and methods, and (4) researching a common surname with a number of interchangeable variations.

As this search progressed, it needed its "dress rehearsal" structuring and fine-tuning. In other words, it needed to be written down as a whole, not as bits and pieces in notebooks. If any imaginary audience was in the room during the process, it was Miss Marple, seated in an armchair, knitting and listening intently, occasionally clearing her throat gently to focus my attention on a particular point.

This search began in 1969 and moved slowly, spliced into life among busy work schedules and tight budgets. Research on other families also frequently interrupted the project, especially when its progress was stymied by the old question, What do I try next? The original question has finally been answered and new questions have entered the picture to carry the search toward the next generation.

Notes

Endnotes for this chapter begin on page 266.

Genealogists have to work within their resources of time and money and with the genealogical sources available. Some of the decisions in this case (what to do when, what to try next, why this or that seemed necessary) perhaps would be different if the search began today, because sources and tools are available now that were not available in 1969 or even 1985. Nonetheless, the search is presented here as it took place.

WHAT WAS KNOWN BEFORE RESEARCH BEGAN

Why don't you start with the main facts.
—*Samuel Clemens*[2]

Notes

1. Albert S. Croom identified his parents as Isaac and Ann Croom in his family Bible record, now in the author's possession, and gave his own birthplace as Pinson, Madison County, Tennessee.

2. Before Albert died in 1954, he told his son, P.B. Croom, that he had many brothers and sisters, named about half of them, and remembered fondly two half sisters, Clarkey and Docia (Theodocia). This list was important in finding the family in the records.

3. Albert did not remember his mother because she died when he was small, and these sisters, especially Clarkey, raised him. After marriage, Theodocia moved to Mississippi and then to Texas.

4. Albert left home after his father died and never returned to his home county or family. However, he kept up with his sister Theodocia (Croom) Hopper and her husband, Dr. Samuel N. Hopper, and in 1903 moved to Texas because of them.[3]

5. P.B. Croom remembered that his father sold an interest in some property near Shreveport before World War I. There had to be a reason why he had an interest in property near Shreveport, for he had never lived there himself.

The initial quest was to prove Albert Croom's paternal line, which was a rather straightforward, or straight *backward*, lineage laid out in wills, land records, and court cases from west Tennessee back to North Carolina and Virginia. The second focus, to find Albert's maternal line, was a much greater challenge.

WHAT WAS KNOWN FROM THE PATERNAL-LINE SEARCH

One must go further—further back, further forward, further sideways, to find out.
—*Hercule Poirot*[4]

In the search for proof of Albert's father, Isaac Croom, several sources provided a background for the search for Ann, Albert's mother: (1) census data with ages and birthplaces, (2) a court case and deed that listed Isaac Croom's surviving children, the younger of whom were Ann's children, (3) county records of Isaac Croom's two marriages, and (4) circumstantial evidence that Ann and her mother had both married men named Isaac Croom, uncle and nephew. This information is summarized below.

Census Summary

First is a family summary of the name, age, and birthplace information from the Madison County, Tennessee, census records, as shown in Figure 14 on page 166. The material for Isaac's household from the four censuses was all gathered at the same time, but without the advantage of indexes. It was apparent that each entry was the right family because of (1) Albert S. Croom's list of brothers and sisters, (2) his speaking fondly of the two half sisters, Clarkey and Docia, who appeared in three of the entries, (3) his own knowledge and belief that Isaac and Ann Croom were his parents and that he himself grew to adulthood in Madison County, (4) the fact that the other Isaac Croom in the county at the time was a younger cousin, Isaac Newton Croom, single and living with his parents in 1850.[5]

Besides, Isaac Newton Croom later had wives with different names, Mary and Rachel, consistently used his middle initial in his records, and became a physician, not a farmer. His residence in 1870 has not been identified, but he was in Henderson County, Tennessee, in 1860 and 1880. His children, from the 1860 and 1880 censuses, were Mary E. (or Mary Ada Ann), Mary J., Isaac N., Virginia (Annie), Lula E., and Thomas L.[6]

The names in the census summary for Isaac Croom's household match the combined censuses for each person. The children listed simply as "(married)" in 1870 and 1880 were already out of the household but have not yet been found with their own households.[7] In 1870, the census taker listed each person by initial only, so the chart gives the initial and the sex of the person as reported.

This 1870 entry for Isaac Croom's household was a mess. When compared with other records found in the course of the search, this entry obviously contained a number of mistakes. Males and females were mixed up, reported ages were more than a little off, and all the birthplaces except Isaac's are now known to be incorrect. One wonders whether the family went fishing that day and a neighbor, new to the neighborhood, gave the census taker the information. Yet, it was the only I[saac] Croom household in the county that year and a number of details did fit. In addition, the details do not fit the younger Isaac Newton Croom's family, although they have not been found in the 1870 census.

The children listed as "(age, married)" in 1880 have been found with their own spouse and children as cited in the footnote for the 1880 column of the chart. The 1880 census noted the birthplace of each person and of each person's father and mother. In this case, the mother of the younger children was reportedly born in Louisiana.

As illustrated in chapter five, this kind of chart gives an overall picture of the family as a reference for names and birth order. It shows the changes in the household over the years. It suggests the children of each wife. It alerts the researcher to discrepancies in data and thus suggests areas for further investigation.

Name	1850 [8] Age/Birthplace	1860 [9] Age/Birthplace	1870 [10] Age/Sex/Birthplace	1880 [11] Age/Birthplace/ Birthplace of Parents
				Summary of Census Data on Isaac Croom Jr. Family, 1850–1880
Isaac Croom	29 NC	37 NC	50 m "I" NC	59 NC NC NC
wife Elizabeth	28 NC	—	—	—
wife Ann	—	24 TN	50 f "A" NC	—
dau Catherine	8 TN	18 TN	(married)	(38, married)
dau Susan	7 TN	17 TN	(married)	(36, married)
son Charles E.	5 TN	15 TN	35 m "C" NC	(34, married)
dau Laura J.	3 TN	13 TN	(married)	(married)
son Napoleon Bonaparte	1 TN	11 TN	24 m "BN" NC	(31, married)
dau Clarkey F(laure?)	—	8 TN	20 m "C" NC	27 TN NC NC
dau Theodocia	—	5 TN	18 m "C" NC	(married)
dau Louisiana	—	9/12 TN	12 f "L" NC	19 TN NC LA
son Thomas	—	—	10 f "T" NC	18 TN NC LA
son Major Lee	—	—	9 m "M" NC	15 TN NC LA
son Rufus L.	—	—	8 m "R" NC	12 TN NC LA
H. (no further info)	—	—	5 m "H" NC	—
son Albert S.	—	—	—	10 TN NC LA
dau Elizabeth	—	—	—	7 TN NC LA

Figure 14 Census Summary for the Isaac Croom Jr. Family

Evidence on Ann Croom

What does this chart suggest about Albert's mother, Ann Croom? First, since the 1880 census showed the youngest child, Elizabeth Croom, at age seven, the mother was probably alive at least to 1872–1873. Albert, shown as ten in 1880, was actually born in 1872, according to his own knowledge and belief, so his sister Elizabeth could have been born earlier or later. Thus, their mother probably died between 1874 and 1880. She did not appear in the 1880 census or mortality schedule.[12] If the family followed the census instructions, they would have reported her death for the mortality schedule if she died between 1 June 1879 and 1 June 1880. However, this schedule is not infallible. Perhaps she died in childbirth after 1873. Perhaps she was a victim of the 1878 yellow fever epidemic in the South and the Mississippi Valley. The truth may never be known.

Second, when the 1870 census was taken, the two younger children, Albert and Elizabeth, were not yet born. Thus, the age of the female, A., given as fifty, had to be questioned if she was to be their mother.

Third, the close match between the 1850 and 1860 entries lends weight to their credibility. There is also close correlation between these entries and the three family members who were still in the household in 1880: Isaac, Clarkey, and Louisiana. Thus, Ann's age in 1860 (twenty-four) may well be closer to truth than what the 1870 census reported.

Fourth, Ann's birthplace was suggested as Tennessee, North Carolina, and Louisiana.

PROOF OF ISAAC CROOM'S SURVIVING CHILDREN

Who's the next of kin?
—*Lord Peter Wimsey*[13]

The second piece of background information was the confirmation of the children of Isaac Croom Jr. found in 1889 and 1891 probate court proceedings after his death.[14] These records helped clarify the 1850 to 1880 census data. In addition, the September 1889 court record reported the two minor children as Albert Sidney, age seventeen, and Lizzie, age fifteen, suggesting birth dates of 1872 and 1874 respectively. The date of Isaac's marriage to Ann (1856, see below) separated the children of the first wife from those of the second.

Thus, the seven known children of the first wife, Elizabeth, were these:
1. Catherine (Kate), who married Sterling M. Watlington
2. Susan E., who married Thomas A. Haynes
3. Charles E.
4. Napoleon Bonaparte, who died before 1891
5. Laura Jane, who married John G. Haynes
6. Clarkey F., who married W.T. Mathis/Mathews
7. Theodocia E., who married Dr. Sam N. Hopper

The seven known children of the second wife, Ann, were these:
1. Louisiana, who married Thomas N. Jones
2. Thomas J., who apparently died between 1880 and 1891 without issue
3. Major Lee ("Major" was a common given name in the Croom family.)
4. Rufus L.
5. probably the boy "H" in the 1870 census, who seems to have died before 1880
6. Albert Sidney
7. Elizabeth C., who later married O.P. Armour

The Willie Croom (no gender indicated) listed as another heir in 1891 perhaps was the male child listed as "H" in the 1870 census, for the name William Henry or William H. was present in the extended family. Isaac had a brother, at least two nephews, and at least one great-nephew with this name. On the other hand, the heir is more likely to be Willie P., the six-year-old girl and only child in the 1880 household of Napoleon Bonaparte Croom.[15] This child is listed as part of the household but at the top of the page after Napoleon and his wife. Perhaps as a result of the copying process, her relationship to the two adults was not given. In the probate proceedings in 1889 and 1891, Napoleon B. himself was not named among the heirs. A publication of cemetery tombstone transcriptions for Madison County shows that he died in 1882.[16]

ISAAC CROOM'S MARRIAGES

Our material is rapidly accumulating.
—*Sherlock Homes*[17]

The third set of background data was Isaac Croom's marriage records. Isaac Croom Jr. [*sic*] first married Elizabeth Sturdevant after 22 July 1840, the date of the license, in Madison County, Tennessee. Although the county marriage book indicates the marriage took place on 13 August 1840, a family Bible gives the actual marriage date as 3 August 1840.[18] The researcher did not find Isaac's second marriage in the Madison County records.

Albert Croom and his mother did not appear in a census record together, but fortunately Isaac and Ann did. This supported Albert's Bible record statement that his parents were Isaac and Ann. The gap between the last two daughters in the 1860 census suggested the period during which Isaac remarried, about 1855 to 1859. Where might he have married if not in his home county? Because of the family tradition of a Shreveport land connection, Caddo Parish, Louisiana, seemed a likely place to search next.

The Caddo Parish marriage records yielded good information. There, in 1856, an Isaac Croom Jr. married Ann Maria Robertson, with Isaac Croom Sr. as the surety on the bond.[19]

The marriage book also showed an Isaac Croom's marriage to Mrs. Elizabeth Robinson, with the bond dated 22 June 1846. The senior Isaac's first wife, Olive (Godwin) Croom, had died on 1 November 1844. An 1890 biographical sketch of their son Calvin Stewart Croom also mentioned Olive's death and Isaac's subsequent marriage to Elizabeth Robertson.[20] Wills and other records of the Croom family in Tennessee and North Carolina had already revealed that the Madison County Isaac Croom was a son of Charles Croom Jr., who had a brother, Isaac Croom. The Caddo Parish marriage records seemed to bring the uncle and nephew together.

PRELIMINARY CENSUS CHECK

I will make a note to do it at once.
—*Chief Inspector Charles Parker*[21]

The marriage records made it imperative to check the Caddo Parish census for 1850. Together, these records revealed the fourth piece of background information: the suggestion that the two Isaac Crooms had married mother and daughter. The 1850 census showed the elder Isaac Croom (age fifty-seven, born in North Carolina). His family included Elizabeth (forty-one, born in Georgia), Ann (fourteen, born in Georgia), James (eight, born in Georgia), and Louisiana (two, born in Louisiana).[22]

The 1846 marriage date of Isaac and Elizabeth, along with the children's birthplaces, suggested that the Croom children, Ann and James, in the Caddo Parish 1850 census were actually Elizabeth's children by her Robinson husband. In addition, the names were intriguing. Elizabeth, Ann, and Louisiana, although common names in the South, also appeared in the Madison County Isaac Croom household over the next three censuses.

The 1860 census for Caddo Parish did not enumerate Isaac and Elizabeth. Even a page-by-page reading did not find them listed. (The indexes for neighboring states did not include them either.) However, in the same household with Isaac Croom's son Calvin S. Croom was a young clerk, T.J. *Robberson* (eighteen, born in Georgia).[23] In all likelihood, this was Elizabeth Robertson Croom's son, James, from the 1850 census. At least, the age and birthplace matched. The surname was close enough, and the initial *J* (for James?) was encouraging. Also, in 1870 and 1880, the Madison County Isaac Croom family included a son named Thomas J. Was he named for an uncle, T. James Robberson?

It was full daylight before I dropped off into an uneasy sleep. My mind was abnormally active and filled with questions.
—*Nurse Detective Hilda Adams*[24]

The mind does rush ahead to all kinds of questions that arise. Who was this T.J. Robberson? Was he Elizabeth Robertson Croom's son? Did the two Isaac Crooms indeed marry mother and daughter? If so, did the Robertsons really come from Georgia? If not, why did Georgia appear on the 1850 census entry? Were these people listed in other census records that could give a background of data with which to work? If this was the right Ann, who was her father and Elizabeth's first husband? What would be the best approach to the research? What should be done next?

REVIEWING THE INITIAL EVIDENCE

There is nothing more deceptive than an obvious fact.
—*Sherlock Holmes*[25]

As Sherlock Holmes suggests, in genealogy and detection, facts may not be as straightforward or as accurate as they first appear. **Any individual statement of "fact" has to be tested and analyzed before it can stand alone.** Such "facts" include the names, dates, places, and relationships that make up genealogical research, and several deceptive facts were already apparent in this search.

By this time, it had become painfully clear that the focus of this search was a very inconsistent surname. Already the research had revealed what appeared to be the same family listed as Robertson, Robinson, and Robberson. Add Robison as another possibility and all the spelling variations, and brace yourself for a real research adventure. Anyone who has worked on these or other interchangeable names knows that, even in the same document,

Important

different versions of the name often appear for the same person. More often than not, the person who appears as Robinson in one record is Robertson or Roberson in the next.

This phenomenon means the researcher must look for ancestors under all the variations, regardless of what the family members called themselves, and must not rule out a candidate just because the surname is different. In the present search, with no idea what the family called itself or what the name was supposed to be, the name Robertson is used in discussion for simplicity.

Ann (Robertson) Croom's Birth Date and Birthplace

The first question for analysis was Ann's birth date and birthplace.

1. In 1860 and 1870, Ann Croom, nee Robertson, was enumerated with her husband, Isaac Croom Jr., in Madison County, Tennessee. Her children were listed with Isaac in 1880 with a reporting of the mother's birthplace.

2. Information from the Caddo Parish 1850 census combined with the Madison County 1860 to 1880 censuses suggested four birthplaces for Ann (Georgia, Tennessee, North Carolina, and Louisiana) and two consistent indications of a birth year about 1835–1836.

3. Because the 1870 census entry contained a large number of errors and inconsistencies for the whole family, the North Carolina birthplace for Ann in that census did not seem to be a realistic candidate.

4. Her age of fifty years in 1870 was also suspect in light of the future births of the last two children. Indeed, if Ann was Elizabeth Robertson's daughter and if Elizabeth was born about 1808–1809, Ann was not likely born before her mother reached age sixteen, about 1824–1825. Even that early date would place Ann near fifty when her last child was born. The 1835–1836 suggested birth date for Ann from the 1850 and 1860 censuses made much more sense.

Crime is common. Logic is rare. Therefore it is upon the logic rather than upon the crime that you should dwell.

—*Sherlock Holmes*[26]

What is the genealogical application of this Sherlock Holmes piece of advice? In this particular instance, I think it would be this: "Facts" are plentiful. Logic is rare. Therefore dwell on logic rather than getting bogged down in the mass of data.

Logic suggested that birthplaces would be vital in this search, not only Ann's, but everybody else's. The 1850 census suggested Elizabeth Robertson Croom's birth about 1808–1809 and James's birth about 1841–42, both in Georgia. The 1860 census supported this birth information for James. How much credence could be placed in these two census entries? Think about it.

The 1850 census taker found only five individuals in the senior Isaac Croom's household, and at least three of them were old enough to know the birthplaces and ages for the children. If Georgia was indeed the birthplace and former residence of Elizabeth, Ann, and T. James, at least Ann and her mother would have remembered coming to Louisiana five to eight years before. They would not have been confused or uncertain on that point, and Elizabeth, if she talked to the census taker, would have known where her own children were born.

Because this census was closest in time to those events and the people directly connected with them, its information seems less likely to be garbled in retelling. It is impossible to know for sure who gave the information to the census taker in any given enumeration and how reliable the evidence may be. However, this 1850 entry seemed to be strong, logical, and credible evidence for Georgia as a birthplace; and T.J. Robberson's 1860 census entry supported it.

Ann (Robertson) Croom's Chronological Profile

In review, what was known or suspected about Ann? What was her chronological profile?

Notes

1. Ann (Robertson) Croom was born about 1835–1836, probably in Georgia, maybe in Louisiana.
2. She was probably the daughter of Elizabeth Robertson Croom.
3. If T.J. Robberson was Ann's brother, born about 1841–1842 in Georgia, the family could have come to Louisiana between about 1842 and 1846.
4. Ann Robertson married Isaac Croom Jr. in 1856 in Caddo Parish, Louisiana, and moved to Madison County, Tennessee.
5. She had at least six or seven children and died between about 1874 and 1880, probably in Madison County, Tennessee.

The search to confirm her birthplace and parentage would have to begin in Louisiana and focus on the years 1842–1846, with the hope of moving back in time to Georgia. If, with further evidence, Georgia seemed not to be the correct place of birth, the search could always move elsewhere.

SEARCH FOR BIRTHPLACES

> Then let us go and look. . . . [W]e may as well learn all that is to be learned.
> —*Sherlock Holmes*[27]

In light of these facts and suppositions, several points emerged as focuses for research. One effort was to identify further clues for a birthplace for the three Robertsons: Elizabeth, James or T.J., and Ann. That question would have to be addressed before any in-depth search outside of Louisiana could be conducted. Several new developments affected the quest for birthplace information.

1. Unfortunately, the name of James or T.J. Robberson has not yet appeared conclusively in a census after 1860. However, he seems to have married in Caddo Parish: T.J. Robertson married M.A. Gerrald, 28 December 1865, united by the same Baptist minister, John McCain, who married Ann Robertson and Isaac Croom Jr.[28]

2. On 24 April 1868, the elder Isaac Croom executed a deed of gift to his daughter Louisiana (Croom) Harris, giving her half of all his land and all personal property he might own at his death, with the provision that he be able to use it until his death.[29] As this document mentioned no wife, it probably suggests that Elizabeth Robertson Croom was no longer living and therefore would appear in no more census records. Perhaps she was one of the many victims of the yellow fever epidemic that hit Caddo Parish in October 1867.[30]

Later in the search, Isaac Croom (seventy-seven, born North Carolina) was found in neighboring Panola County, Texas, in the 1870 census with a new wife, as evidenced by a 15 November 1868 marriage record.[31] Since Elizabeth herself would not be found in any more censuses, further clues for her birthplace would have to come from studying her only known child by Isaac, Louisiana (Croom) Harris.

3. Since Ann (Robertson) Croom too apparently died before 1880, the only way to get more evidence on her birthplace was to follow her children's census records for "birthplace of mother." The problem was that Ann's children were young when she died. Anything they knew about her would be what their father or older siblings told them or what they believed from what they heard about her. Of Ann's children, the one most likely to remember her and know something about her was her elder daughter, Louisiana, who was a teenager when Ann died. Finding this daughter in the later censuses could be important.

4. In 1969 when the search began, the 1900, 1910, and 1920 censuses were not yet open to the public. Getting clues from these records had to wait. This part of the search took place in the 1980s and 1990s after the opening of the later census records.

A Positive Clue

Elizabeth Robertson Croom's daughter Louisiana (Croom) Harris was the first target. Her mother's birthplace would have appeared only in censuses of 1880 forward. Of these, Louisiana's name has been found in only the 1880 and 1900 censuses, although she lived until 1911. In both years, she and her husband were still in Caddo Parish. In both entries, her birthplace was correctly reported as Louisiana; her father's, correctly as North Carolina; and her mother's, as Georgia.[32] Perhaps it too was correct.

So. Another appropriate little pebble in the mosaic.
—*Investigator Alan Grant*[33]

Finding the Children of Ann (Robertson) Croom

Finding the census entries of the children of Ann Robertson and Isaac Croom Jr. was the other effort toward identifying a birthplace for Ann and her proposed brother and mother. Of the five surviving children of Ann and Isaac, Rufus has not yet been found in any records after 1891. The focus group had to be the other four: Louisiana Jones, Major L. Croom, Albert S. Croom, and Elizabeth Armour.

First, the names of Louisiana (Croom) Jones and her husband, Thomas N. Jones, appeared only in the 1910 census, in Marshall County, Mississippi. The entry gave the birthplace of Lou's father as Tennessee and that of her mother as Louisiana.[34] Her father's birthplace is well established in Croom research as North Carolina, not Tennessee. Thus, this report of her mother's birthplace deserved to be questioned. This Lou was Ann's eldest child and the one most likely to have remembered her mother, but it is impossible to know whether they ever discussed Ann's birthplace or who reported the family for the census taker. (Furthermore, no death certificate has been found for this Louisiana.)

Second, Major L. Croom was listed in 1900 and 1920. In both, his birthplace was given as Tennessee; his father's, as North Carolina; his mother's, as Louisiana.[35] Major was probably about nine to twelve years old when his mother died. Did he give the information to the census takers in the 1900s? Did he know his mother's history? Did he know only that she came to Tennessee from Louisiana? We cannot know. (No death certificate has yet been found for Major.)

Third, Albert Sidney Croom was enumerated in all three censuses, one in Tennessee and two in Texas. In all three, his birthplace was reported as Tennessee. In the 1900 and 1910 entries, his father's birth supposedly took place in Tennessee; only in 1920 was it given as North Carolina, which other Croom research supports as accurate. The 1900 entry showed his mother's birthplace as Tennessee, but the 1910 and 1920 ones reported it as Louisiana.[36] Albert was no more than eight years old, perhaps as young as three, when his mother died. Did he really know her history? Did his wife give the census information? We will never know. (Albert's death certificate gives his mother's name and birthplace as "unknown."[37])

Fourth, the youngest of Ann's children, Elizabeth C. (Croom) Armour, was named only in the 1900 census and apparently died about 1904–1905, before Mississippi began registering deaths. (Her middle initial stood for an apparent middle name, not her maiden surname, Croom.) Her husband remarried and was listed with his new wife, Minnie, in the 1910 census.[38]

Interestingly, Elizabeth C. (Croom) Armour was likely named for her grandmother, Elizabeth Robertson Croom, and in turn named her fourth child Annie, likely for her mother, Ann Robertson Croom, whom she never really knew. Her third child was a son named Croom Armour. In the 1900 census, Elizabeth (Croom) Armour's parents were given Tennessee and Louisiana birthplaces.

Again, because North Carolina, not Tennessee, is supported by other Croom research to be Isaac's actual birthplace, the researcher can legitimately question the accuracy of the Louisiana birthplace for the mother. This 1900 census reported Elizabeth's birth date as July 1873, consistent with the 1880 census. This date suggests that the mother, Ann (Robertson) Croom, died between July 1873 and 1880. It also implies that this child was younger than seven years old when her mother died.

What do you make of all this?
—*Inspector George L. Patton*[39]

Mixed Results or Deceptive Facts?

What, indeed? What did all of this accomplish? As it turned out, the results did not materially change anything, but the survey had to be done. First, in the seven census reports of Ann's children, six reported her birthplace as Louisiana; one, as Tennessee. It is obvious that Louisiana played a role in Ann's life, and records there were already being searched. Second, of the thirteen census entries to address a birthplace for the three Robertson family members (Elizabeth, Ann, and T. James), six reported it as Louisiana; four, as Georgia; two as Tennessee; one, which has already been eliminated as a serious contender, as North Carolina.

Had other evidence been different, the researcher might have had to admit that perhaps Ann was not Elizabeth's daughter but the child of a different Robertson family in Louisiana. However, certain evidence was too strong to ignore:

1. Both Ann and Elizabeth were Robertsons before they married the two Isaac Crooms.
2. The Tennessee Ann obviously had Louisiana connections, if not a Louisiana birth, for she and her Isaac married there, with the elder Isaac as the surety on the marriage bond.
3. Elizabeth's household in 1850 included an Ann of the "right" age (fourteen) to marry six years later and be twenty-four in the 1860 census as the younger Isaac's wife.
4. Both had daughters named Louisiana. Ann had a daughter Elizabeth and a son T(homas) J. Elizabeth's daughter Louisiana had a daughter named Ann. Part of the search had to be to find proof of their supposed relationship.

This compilation of birthplace data is a good example of the caution genealogists must exercise. Numbers alone do not prove anything. Repetition of a "fact" (Louisiana birthplace) over and over again does not, alone, make it truth. Was this one of those deceptive facts in Sherlock Holmes's warning? Research might or might not prove its validity. Regardless, the search had to focus first on the family's known presence in Louisiana but also had to account for the strong probability of its prior residence in Georgia.

I'll keep poking around for some hard evidence.
—*Detective Richard LeJeune*[40]

The point of trying to discover the family's birthplaces was (1) to learn more about the individuals and (2) to accumulate the kind of information on family members that could help address the bigger question: Who was the Robertson husband and father? A search cannot simply strike out to find one person without having a given name, location, time period, or other information that can focus the effort.

SURVEY RESEARCH IN LOUISIANA

In this business, try direct methods whenever you can. They save time.
—*Inspector George L. Patton*[41]

Notes

Before beginning a direct-methods approach to research in Louisiana, it was necessary to look at Mrs. Elizabeth Robertson Croom. What was now known about her?

1. She was born about 1808–1809, reportedly in Georgia.
2. She and at least two probable children, Ann and T. James, came to Louisiana between about 1842 and 1846.
3. She married Isaac Croom in 1846 in Caddo Parish and lived there until at least 1850.
4. She apparently had one child by her second husband: Louisiana (Croom) Harris.
5. She apparently died between June 1850 and April 1868.

The Louisiana Plan

The goal of Louisiana research was to establish facts about Elizabeth's life and to look for her first husband. The first part of the Louisiana plan was the most direct: to search whatever records were available for the 1842–1846 years to find Robertson men. The second part of the plan was a little less direct but necessary: to search for any records Elizabeth created, her second husband's records, and their Louisiana "neighborhood."

These two efforts were expected to generate a list of first husband candidates and cluster members, people who may have been associated with her first husband. Possibly Elizabeth's first husband could be identified directly. If not, the candidates could be studied one by one. If a candidate or suspect was then found in records after June 1846, when Elizabeth remarried, or was identified with a wife of a name other than Elizabeth, he would be eliminated from the list.

By this process of elimination, the list of Robertson men would potentially narrow to any likely candidate for the first husband. The cluster list of Caddo Parish associates might narrow to suggest relatives or associates of the first husband. Georgia was an enticing ground for research, but an in-depth Louisiana search would have to start first, focusing on records from 1842 forward. Genealogists, like good detectives, must work from the known to the unknown.

I have been working on that problem a little myself. Forgive me, but I believe the correct procedure is to follow a logical process of elimination.
—*Eleanor Roosevelt*[42]

Other Robertsons in the Parish

The first task attempted was to identify other Robertsons in the parish. The 1850 census enumerated eight Robinson/Roberson households and two young, single Robinson men, one born in South Carolina, one in Alabama. Of the eight families, the census reported the heads of household born in North Carolina, Tennessee, Mississippi, Massachusetts, and Scotland, with spouses and children, for the most part, born in the same states plus Alabama and Louisiana. These entries revealed not a hint of any direct Georgia connection.[43] Thus, it appeared that Elizabeth Robertson and her children did not have Robertson relatives in Caddo Parish at that time.

The same process was done for Robertsons in Madison County, Tennessee, on the chance that these precipitated Elizabeth's introduction to the Croom family. The twelve households and individuals in the 1850 census reported North Carolina, South Carolina, Tennessee, Kentucky, Alabama, and Ireland births, with no apparent Georgia or Louisiana link.[44]

A Robertson Husband in Parish Records?

The second effort was to address the question, What records in Caddo Parish might directly identify Elizabeth's Robertson husband? The first and most obvious were death-related records: cemetery and probate records, called succession records in Louisiana. (Louisiana did not register deaths on a statewide basis until 1914, so neither Robertson parent would have had a death certificate.) The available compilations of parish tombstone transcriptions to date have not yielded any evidence of Isaac Croom Sr., Elizabeth Robertson Croom, or a Robertson candidate for Elizabeth's first husband. Nor did a visit to the cemetery at Mooringsport, where some of the Croom family is buried, reveal tombstones for these primary folks.

The index to parish successions contained six Robinson files before 1860. None of the six files contained reference to the three individuals believed to be part of Elizabeth Robertson Croom's family. Four of the deaths occurred after Elizabeth had already married Isaac Croom. The 1845 decedent, Archibald Robinson, left a wife named Mary, who married William B. Wooldridge in 1850, and four children: Susan Jane (wife of Cicero Bates), Robert V., James C., and Mary P.E. Robinson. His brother, Robert Robinson, became administrator of his estate. The earliest succession file, for R.M. Robinson, a doctor, mentioned no heirs and had a suggested death date of about 1842.[45] The T. James Roberson birth information from the censuses suggested that his family may have been in Georgia rather than Louisiana in 1842.

Notes

County court minute books, in many counties, often show jury lists, contracts, information on court cases, and orders of various kinds, including road maintenance, in which ancestors are mentioned. Existing Caddo Parish court minute books, according to the clerk's staff, begin in 1872, so these were not a source available for the Robertson research.

The parish index to civil lawsuits did not reveal any additional Robertsons as parties to lawsuits during the crucial five-year period. To find other individuals mentioned within case files, such as jurymen or witnesses, one needs to read the individual case files created during those years. Some do exist but are not readily accessible because of the time delay (several days) and other difficulties in getting them from the warehouse to the courthouse for use. In addition, such a search is labor intensive and time consuming. It was decided, for the time being, to postpone this direction of study in favor of other avenues that might be more productive and cost effective.

Tax rolls are often an excellent tool for determining a person's presence in a county, or narrowing down a death or removal. The available tax rolls for Caddo Parish begin with 1865 and thus are too late to help directly in the search for Elizabeth Robertson Croom's first husband. These also did not show the presence of her son T. James Robertson. Isaac Croom Sr. did pay taxes from 1865 through 1867 and in 1869, with his son-in-law John H. Harris acting as his agent in 1870 and 1871. No list exists for 1868.[46]

For More Info

See chapter five for strategies for using tax records.

CLUES IN LAND RECORDS?

I hope you can get the proof you need to close the books on Mrs. Robinson; let us know how it comes out, will you?
—*Samuel Clemens*[47]

Because Louisiana is a federal land state, this search had two sets of sources to investigate: federal land patents and parish land records. The federal patents were searched for Robertsons after the records of the Eastern States Office of the Bureau of Land Management became automated. In these records, the date of the final certificate and recording of the patent was usually some months, sometimes more than a year, after the date of the receipt for payment. The final certificate and recording date is the one used in the electronic databases on CD-ROM and the Internet. In a number of cases, the patentee had already sold the land or had died before the recording date.

Research Based on Federal Land Records

Federal land patents and their case files sometimes provide valuable clues to a person's residence, arrival, or removal. In the early 1840s, the federal land office at Natchitoches, Louisiana, southeast of Caddo Parish, handled these purchases for the area. Any Robertson husband would probably have acquired federal land between about 1842, when the son T. James was reportedly born in Georgia, and early 1846, for Elizabeth remarried in late June of that year. During this 1842–1846 window of time, neither Elizabeth Robertson nor any Robertson man received a patent. From the Natchitoches land office during the given years, only four patentees had one of the variant surnames: John, Aaron, William, and Archibald Robinson.[48]

All of these were eliminated as candidates for Elizabeth's first husband with evidence from other records. First, John patented land in the newly formed DeSoto Parish early in 1843 and continued adding adjoining land to his holdings in 1846, 1848, and 1849.[49] This activity beyond 1846 rules him out. In addition, the John Roberson of DeSoto Parish in the 1850 census had a wife named Winney and a birthplace reported as New Jersey.[50] The marriage record shows that John Robinson married Mrs. Winny (Lane) Rhodes in Caddo Parish

For More Info

See chapter five for strategies for using land records.

in 1841.[51] Remember, the variant names are used interchangeably in the records. This John was the only one found in that parish at that time even though his name appeared as Robinson and Roberson.

Second, Aaron Robinson patented his land also in neighboring DeSoto Parish before 1 January 1846.[52] The 1850 census (after the magic date of 1846) enumerated him with his wife, Nancy, both born in Alabama.[53] He also witnessed the marriage licenses for William Robinson and John Robinson in Caddo Parish in 1840 and 1841, before Elizabeth Robertson and her family supposedly came to Louisiana.[54]

Third, William Robinson acquired land in Caddo Parish near the DeSoto Parish line also before 1 January 1846.[55] He and his wife, Mary Blou(n)t, whom he married in Caddo Parish in early 1840, were enumerated in Caddo Parish in the 1840 census.[56] They were selling land adjoining his patented land in 1849.[57] These facts eliminate him as a possible husband for Elizabeth.

The fourth man, Archibald Robinson, lived with his family in adjoining Claiborne Parish at the time of the 1840 census.[58] Although his land patents were recorded in 1843 and 1844, he sold the same land in December 1840.[59] The tracts, in what is now Bossier Parish, adjoined present Shreveport in Caddo Parish. Archibald died in 1845 and his widow, Mary, married William B. Wooldridge in 1850. Archibald's succession file finalizes his elimination as a candidate for Elizabeth Robertson Croom's first husband by naming his family and mentioning his widow's remarriage.[60]

Parish Land Records

Notes

Caddo Parish conveyances (*deeds* to the rest of the country) date from 1837. The index revealed no conveyance in the name of Elizabeth or other Robertsons (or variant) between 1837 and 1850 other than names already eliminated from the hunt. A page-by-page search of the five volumes of conveyances recorded between January 1841 and 1851 revealed no other Robertson as a witness. Nor did it reveal Isaac Croom witnessing transactions for others.

Two deeds executed in 1860, however, did involve Elizabeth's probable son, T.J. Robertson. Isaac Croom's son Calvin S. Croom sold land to Samuel Gerrald, with witnesses T.J. Robertson (Calvin's probable stepbrother) and John D. Bickham (Calvin's brother-in-law). Gerrald immediately sold the same land to John D. Bickham, with C.S. Croom and T.J. Robertson as witnesses.[61] These transactions illustrate the existence of a cluster, friends and relatives associating with each other in business dealings or other activities of life. Ancestors did not live in a vacuum but in a cluster of friends, relatives, neighbors, and associates. Studying the cluster is crucial to making discoveries about an elusive ancestor.

In these 1860 conveyances, Samuel Gerrald was the only unidentified person. Although not a Robertson himself, he had to be studied as a potential relative or associate of the first husband. (Although T.J. Roberson married a Gerrald girl in 1865, no connection has yet been made to this Samuel Gerrald.) The 1850 census enumerates him as Samuel Jarrell, age fifty-three, born in Texas [*sic*], with wife and sons all born in Louisiana and Alabama.[62] His reported Texas birth is highly unlikely since very few Anglo-Americans lived in Texas in 1797. In 1860, his birthplace was given as South Carolina,[63] which makes more sense. These records suggest no direct ties with Georgia.

FIRST PROOF OF RELATIONSHIP

Ah, that is just what I want to know.
—*Sherlock Holmes*[64]

Besides looking at Robertson records, an important part of the plan was to study Isaac Croom's records. In fact, parish conveyance records did confirm what was already a convincing scenario: that the two Isaac Crooms had married mother and daughter. The following conveyances show Ann, Thomas J(ames), and Louisiana as children of Elizabeth Robertson Croom.

1. In 1857, Isaac Croom of Caddo Parish sold a quarter section of land to James Christian of Caddo Parish. On 5 November 1857, Elizabeth C. Croom appeared to relinquish her rights to the land.[65] Of interest is the fact that her middle initial matched that of her apparent Tennessee granddaughter, Elizabeth C. Croom, who married O.P. Armour (see below).

2. As mentioned earlier, on 24 April 1868, Isaac Croom, still of Caddo Parish, gave half his land and all personal property owned at his death to his daughter Louisiana, wife of John H. Harris of Caddo Parish. Then, in November 1868, Isaac married his third wife, Mary N. (Ann?) Jones, in neighboring Panola County, Texas. These events are evidence that Elizabeth C. Robertson Croom died between November 1857 and April 1868.[66] As mentioned earlier, no entry for Isaac and Elizabeth has been found in the 1860 census, so it is not known whether she was alive in 1860.

3. On 23 October 1871, Isaac Croom, now of Panola County, Texas, sold to John H. Harris (his son-in-law) his undivided half interest, held in common with heirs of Elizabeth C. Croom, in 376.5 acres located in five adjacent tracts in Caddo Parish.[67]

4. On 16 December 1871, Thomas J. Robertson of Lafayette County, Arkansas, sold to John H. Harris (his brother-in-law) for $165 cash his undivided interest held in common with other heirs of his deceased mother, Elizabeth C. Croom, and stepfather, Isaac Croom.[68] Yes! The property described was the same 376.5 acres of Caddo Parish land mentioned in (3) above. This record accounts for one of Elizabeth's children and heirs. John H. Harris was married to a second one, the daughter Louisiana, and was buying out the other heirs. The third child and heir, Ann (Robertson) Croom, was yet to be heard from.

5. In January 1909, documents were filed in Caddo Parish to ratify mineral leases that John H. Harris had made with Guffey/Gulf Oil Company. The parties filing were Albert Croom of Mills County, Texas, and M(ajor) L.

Croom of Madison County, Tennessee, two surviving heirs of Mrs. A.M. Croom; Lou Croom Jones, wife of T.N. Jones of Marshall County, Mississippi; and O.P. Armour of Chickasaw County, Mississippi, and his children by his deceased wife, Lizzie Croom: Opra, Bland, Croom, and Annie Minons Armour.[69] These documents represent all of the surviving children of Isaac Croom Jr. and Ann (Robertson) Croom. They still owned their mother's interest in the land.

6. Finally, on 5 April 1909, A(lbert) S. Croom of Mills County, Texas, sold for $250 cash to W.C. Dew (a local banker, according to P.B. Croom), of Mills County, Texas, his undivided interest in all real estate or other property, including oil and gas leases, from the estate of his late mother, Mrs. Ann Robertson Croom and Isaac Croom, his father, in Caddo Parish, Louisiana.[70] Yes!

Now, at last, the family tradition of land near Shreveport was confirmed, along with the children and heirs of Elizabeth Robertson Croom. In addition, Elizabeth's death date had been narrowed to some time between November 1857 and April 1868. No clues to her first husband's identity had turned up.

RESEARCH BASED ON ISAAC CROOM SR.'S LAND RECORDS

Talk to the neighbors. Converse with them. Find out about them. Their backgrounds. But above all, engage in conversation.
—*Hercule Poirot*[71]

The genealogical application of Poirot's advice is exactly what he says. However, in the case of a search in which all primary parties are deceased, the advice can take two directions. One is to talk with descendants of early residents or current residents of the neighborhood where the primary parties lived. This would be fun and preliminary contact has been made, but the effort is more than 130 years after the last presence of Elizabeth and Isaac Croom in the area. The other avenue is to study the people in the neighborhood at the time the primary parties lived there. Since this phase of the search was taking place some 140–150 years after the original events, this seemed the more direct approach. In this search, Poirot's advice was interpreted to mean: Study the neighbors; find out about their backgrounds; engage them (find them) any way you can.

Reminder

Genealogists plan and research, then evaluate and plan the next stage. Since Caddo Parish records were yielding no evidence (or negative evidence) of the Robertson husband, the research had to broaden. In addition to searching for Robertsons directly, the researcher now had to study the second husband, Isaac Croom, and the cluster of his friends, neighbors, and associates. Perhaps one or more of them would prove to be the key. This cluster included primarily neighbors and witnesses to Isaac's documents.

The majority of small rural churches in the South do not have records that extend before the Civil War. The Rev. John McCain, who married the two Robertson siblings, seems to have been pastor of the Bethel Primitive Baptist Church, just south of the community of Albany, which was north of Shreveport in Caddo Parish. Attempts are being made to find church members to learn whether any of the records exist from the Civil War era.[72] The problem is that this church and community seem to have been about nine miles from Isaac's known land, although Isaac and his family were enumerated in the 1850 census as part of the Albany beat.[73]

Research of Isaac Croom Sr.'s Land Records

The first question addressed was whether Elizabeth Robertson had previously owned any of the Croom land through inheritance or whether her interest in it was due only to her marriage to Isaac Croom Sr. The question for study was "How did Isaac Croom get his land?" If Elizabeth had inherited any of it, the search would be closer to identifying a husband, father, or other relative for her. If she did not own it, perhaps a relative of hers did.

When Isaac Croom moved to Caddo Parish in late spring or early summer of 1844, he bought two adjoining quarter-sections of land from two men already in the parish, Joseph Allen and Joseph R. Belton.[74] He and his family must have lived on this land at least until some time in 1852, when he received a federal patent for adjoining land.[75] The following year he gave his son Calvin three-fourths of his original purchase and traded the other fourth to a neighbor, Timothy Mooring, for enough adjacent land to complete his new quarter section.[76] Isaac sold this second farm to James Christian in 1857 and purchased his third farm, partly from James Christian and partly from Thomas Philyaw/Philyan/Philshaw.[77] Isaac added to this property with federal patents in 1859.[78] Based on the legal descriptions in the various conveyance records, the researcher believes this last farm was the one involving the oil and gas leases and Elizabeth's heirs.

Apparently, Elizabeth never owned any part of these three farms on her own. Were these neighbors and landowners possibly her relatives? Did they exhibit any Georgia or Robertson connections?

Study of Landowners in Isaac's Records

First, Joseph Allen, age fifty-two, was listed in the 1850 census in Caddo Parish with wife, Mahala, and sons John C. and Patrick H. Allen, all four with Tennessee births.[79] The younger son's age, fifteen, suggests they came to Louisiana after 1835, and no Georgia connection was indicated. Allen patented by 1843 the land he sold to Isaac Croom.[80] Thus, no individual had owned it prior to his patent.

Second, Joseph R. Belton, age fifty-two, was listed in the 1850 census in Caddo Parish with his wife, D.A., age fifty-one, both reportedly born in Maryland. The entry showed their twenty-year-old daughter, Elizabeth, as a native Georgian.[81] Because of this daughter's birthplace, it was considered necessary to find Belton in Georgia, in a census if possible. In 1830, Joseph R. Belton and wife, of ages consistent with the 1850 census, were enumerated in Thomas

County, Georgia, with three children, including a female under five (a match to the daughter in the 1850 census) and two young boys.[82] They were in Caddo Parish in 1840 but have not been identified in the 1860 census.[83] Although Belton sold his federal land to Croom in July 1844, the patent was not finalized and recorded until 1 September 1846.[84] Nevertheless, no individual had owned the same land prior to Belton. The Maryland births of Belton and his wife tentatively suggest that they were no relation to Elizabeth Robertson Croom, and their sojourn in Georgia may be simply coincidental. The researcher could always return to this family for more in-depth study if necessary.

Third, Timothy Mooring, age forty-nine in 1850, and his wife, Eliza, were both of North Carolina origin, according to the census, and all their children except the five-year-old were reportedly born in Tennessee.[85] One discrepancy exists in the Tennessee birth reported for the ten- and twelve-year-old children. Calvin S. Croom, Isaac's son, married the Mooring daughter Margaret in 1851. His biographical sketch of 1890 stated that the Moorings came to Caddo Parish from Henderson County, Tennessee, in 1837.[86] If so, these two children would have been born in Louisiana, not Tennessee. Nevertheless, the Mooring family did not exhibit any Georgia connection and thus did not seem to be related to Elizabeth Robertson Croom.

Fourth, James Christian appears to be the same one who was in Madison County, Tennessee, in 1850, age fifty-four, with his wife, Pherelize, and three teenagers, one of whom was Thomas H., age fifteen.[87] Two teenagers, Sarah and Thomas, were reportedly born in Tennessee; James, his wife, and eighteen-year-old James M., in North Carolina. The family may have moved to Caddo Parish before February 1855, when one James Christian and Calvin S. Croom, son of Isaac Sr., offered a reward together for stolen property.[88] In November 1857, James Christian bought land from Isaac Croom.[89] In Caddo Parish in 1858, James Christian, Esquire, hosted the wedding of Miss J. E. Jones of Spring Creek, Tennessee, to D.J. Mooring.[90] One of the several Spring Creeks in Tennessee is in Madison County, where James seems to have been in 1850.

James Christian (sixty-four) and his wife, S. (fifty), reported in the 1860 census that they were born in North Carolina and Kentucky, respectively, and married in 1856.[91] In fact, a Caddo Parish marriage record shows James Christian marrying Mrs. Susan Kerley in November 1855.[92] The Thomas Christian, age twenty-four and born in Tennessee, in their 1860 household was likely James's son from the 1850 census. These interactions with the Croom family and apparent connections with both Caddo Parish and Madison County do not, however, exhibit any Georgia connection with Elizabeth Croom.

The family next door to the James Christian family in 1850 was M. Milam and Mary, both twenty-seven, born in Tennessee and North Carolina, respectively.[93] Although no Madison County, Tennessee, marriage record was found for them, this Mary perhaps was James Christian's daughter, as her infant son was named James C. Milam. This M. Milam of 1850 was the younger Isaac Croom's age and lived in the same county. Perhaps he was Isaac's friend and accompanied him to Louisiana for his marriage in 1856; perhaps he had moved from Tennessee to Caddo Parish. Regardless, one Marcis [sic] B. Milam witnessed Isaac's marriage to Ann Robertson, and an M.B. Milam, also called Mark in the record, married Sarah Harris in Caddo Parish in 1859.[94]

Other than these records, Marcis B. Milam has not been found in Caddo Parish records. Milam has not been found in Louisiana, Texas, Arkansas, Missouri, or Tennessee in the 1860 census. Nor has he been found in Louisiana in 1870 or 1880. His witnessing of the junior Isaac Croom's marriage in 1856 made him an important part of the Caddo Parish cluster being studied for possible connections to Elizabeth Robertson Croom, discussed below. However, his connection seems to be with Isaac Croom Jr. rather than with Elizabeth.

The fifth person with whom Isaac dealt in land was Thomas Philyaw (the name varies in the records). The 1850 census reported him as Thomas Phillshaw, age thirty-one, a wheelwright born in South Carolina.[95] His wife, Sarah, twenty-one, was born in Alabama, along with their two young children. The seventy-four-year-old Easter Phillshaw in the household, presumably Thomas's mother, was also born in South Carolina. Living with them was a child, Thomas Vincent, born in Georgia. The conveyance showing Isaac's purchase from Philyaw identifies the vendor's wife as Sarah W. Attaway.[96]

A number of Attaway families lived in Caddo Parish by 1850. The middle-aged generation was born in Georgia, along with their older children. Birthplaces of other children indicated they had been in Alabama since the mid-1820s and in Louisiana only several years. However, one J.C. Attaway witnessed T.J. Robertson's marriage license in 1865 and thus became part of the cluster of friends being studied.[97] He has not yet been positively connected with any of the Attaway families in Caddo Parish. This Philyaw-Attaway family had to be kept in mind as the study progressed since they were Georgia-born neighbors and associates of the Robertson-Crooms.

This focus based on Isaac Croom's land showed that his wife had not owned or inherited any of the land that he bought or sold. Only one of the buyers and sellers with whom he dealt, Philyaw, seemed to be a candidate for any prior Georgia connection with his wife. This development brought the search to the next step: the broader cluster of Croom-Robertson associates.

CLUSTER OF ISAAC CROOM SR.'S ASSOCIATES

Let us approach it from another angle.
—Inspector Dermot Craddock[98]

The first part of the cluster was the men with whom Isaac dealt in land transactions. The rest of the cluster combined witnesses to the marriage licenses of Isaac Croom Sr., T.J. Robertson, and Isaac Croom Jr.; witnesses to the land transactions of Isaac Sr.; and neighbors. All three men married in Caddo Parish, with a combined total of seven witnesses and one known minister. Nineteen other men had witnessed the senior Isaac Croom's conveyance records, and eleven additional individuals had patented land in the 1840s within a section or two of Isaac's first farm. These formed a list of thirty-seven men.

The census records revealed numerous other households in the parish with at least one Georgia-born parent of middle age and some families with children also born in Georgia. Using the whole parish as a cluster for study seemed an inefficient use of time unless the smaller cluster produced no leads. Obviously, some of these Caddo Parish families could become part of the big picture at a later date, when the Georgia search was more focused.

The study of this cluster of thirty-seven men and their families moved forward much as the earlier Caddo Parish searches had. It was still a convincing hypothesis that Elizabeth Robertson Croom had come from Georgia, so the Caddo Parish search had to look for Georgia connections or other evidence of kinship or acquaintance with her.

Because data reported in census records is sometimes inaccurate, the researcher tried to find the subjects in several censuses or other records, including biographical sketches and deed records. Surveys of the 1850, 1860, and 1870 censuses located much of the cluster list and eliminated twenty who appeared to have no direct Georgia ties as shown in birthplaces. Another seven were placed on the back burner, so to speak, since neither they nor anyone else with their surnames have been found in censuses of the parish or surrounding parishes. Nor have they been found in the other parish records being surveyed, but the key here was to identify Georgia connections by identifying birthplaces.

Who were the remaining ten of the Caddo Parish cluster?

1. Three Georgia-born men: Samuel Hollingsworth, Ezekiel Attaway, and Bailey W. George.

2. Three men who had not been found themselves in Caddo Parish census, land, or marriage records as grooms but who had the same surname as others in the parish with Georgia connections and surnames present in Georgia at the same time: David C. Hearne, J.C. Attaway, and James A. Arnold. The first two of these were possibly of a younger generation than Elizabeth Robertson Croom because of the dates of their interaction with one of the Croom men.

3. Samuel D. Bishop, who appeared in a number of records other than census, whose origin was not yet determined, and who had the same surname as others in the parish.

4. Three early, neighboring landowners whose origins were not yet determined: Alfred Bradshaw, Robert P. Baker, and Joshua Howard.

The list would need in-depth study both inside and outside of Caddo Parish to determine any specific connection with Elizabeth Robertson Croom. Looking for them without more specific clues was the same as looking for the unknown Robertson husband ten times over. Besides, as Georgia records were beginning to show, Robertsons were everywhere. Even if all ten of this cluster were found in Georgia, the search still had no Robertson name or location with which to connect them. These did remain on the "watch list" during further research into Louisiana or Georgia records. Looking back, if anything were done differently in the search, this is the place. A survey of broad-based Georgia county records for these ten names may have saved some research time.

One interesting factor became apparent during the Louisiana search. Although in many places, witnesses to deed records are often relatives of the grantor or grantee, the conveyance witnesses in this part of Louisiana did not seem to follow this pattern. Usually one witness was a notary public of the parish. The other one or two witnesses were (1) sometimes the apparent wife of the notary, (2) sometimes an apparent relative of one party, or (3) quite often the same men over and over again.

One such repeat witness was Isaac Croom's son, Calvin S. Croom. As a young adult, he worked as a printer in Shreveport and was apparently well acquainted with several notaries. In fact, he may have named one son for the notary (and fellow North Carolinian) Henry John Gray Battle: William Henry Battle Croom. When Battle or several other notaries drew up conveyance documents for clients, they frequently used Calvin Croom as a witness, perhaps because he was handy and they knew him well. Since the majority of deeds seem to have been drawn up by the notaries, as was standard Louisiana practice, witnesses were apparently collared from nearby businesses or others waiting to see the notary. This observation may explain why most of the conveyance witnesses to Isaac Croom's transactions seemed to have no relationship to his family.

THE FIRST GEORGIA SURVEY: THE 1840 CENSUS

I want to try an experiment.
—*Nurse Detective Hilda Adams*[99]

After the Robertson search in Caddo Parish was underway but before Isaac's cluster was narrowed down to the final ten, the temptation was too great to ignore Georgia completely. About 1974, then, the search broadened to take place, slowly, on both fronts. At the time, the only Georgia statewide source readily available for the right time period was the 1840 census. Naively, a plan developed for a survey of the 1840 census to find out about Robertsons in Georgia.

The plan was to survey all Robertsons (and variants) in 1840 to identify families who could accommodate Elizabeth Robertson, the mother, and Ann Robertson, the daughter. The next step was to eliminate the men who appeared in the 1850 census since Elizabeth had remarried in Louisiana in 1846. Those left would be candidates for more in-depth study into county records. Any found after early 1846 would be eliminated. Surely, a process of elimination would help zero in on a Robertson husband.

The only census index available at the time was the *1840 Index to Georgia Census*, compiled and published in 1969 by Mrs. Barbara Woods and Mrs. Eileen Sheffield and arranged alphabetically by county. Ordinarily, this arrangement would be less user friendly, but for this study, it was a blessing and a great time-saver. Of the ninety-three Georgia counties in 1840, seventy plus the city of Savannah contained 274 households named Robertson, Roberson, Robinson, and Robison. Over a course of years, the search visited all seventy-one of these jurisdictions in the 1840 federal census and recorded each Robertson (or variant) household.

Criteria for the Georgia Census Search

Notes

What criteria did families have to match to fit the profile and remain on the suspect list?

1. The only evidence for Elizabeth's age was from the 1850 census, which would place her 1840 age at about thirty-one. Because ages, especially of women, were not always reported accurately, allowances had to be made to include women in the twenty to thirty age bracket as well as those thirty to forty. Families therefore had to have a female in one of these age brackets.

2. The two known and consistent pieces of evidence on Ann's age would mean she was under five in 1840. However, because the 1850 census suggested she was age four in 1840, the possibility existed that she could be enumerated in the five-to-ten age bracket instead. Candidate families, therefore, had to include at least one girl under five or five to ten years old.

3. Since there was at least one more child, Thomas James, born about 1841–1842, the operating premise was that the Robertson husband was still alive and the family unit was intact in 1840. (If this proved not to be the case, other hypotheses could then be tested.) Thus, households headed by single females or without an adult female would be excluded.

4. Although Ann and T.J. were the only Georgia-born children with Elizabeth in 1850, it was possible that others had been in the family in 1840 and by 1850 had died or married.

One could argue that these criteria did not allow for all possible explanations. However, this researcher chose to follow another searcher's advice:

> I always think myself that it's better to examine the simplest and most commonplace explanations first.
>
> —*Miss Marple*[100]

The Georgia Master Suspect List

After the compilation of the 274 households and evaluation based on the four criteria, 101 households remained on the "master suspect list." The International Genealogical Index (IGI) and Ancestral File at a local Family History Center (of the Church of Jesus Christ of Latter-day Saints) helped eliminate two of the families. Nine others were placed in a category of less-serious contenders due to the overall picture of the household. This brought to ninety the number of candidates to study. At least, these ninety each provided a name and a county in which to search.

These ninety first became the subject of an intensive comparison with the

1850 census. When it could be determined with a high degree of probability that an 1850 household was the same family that had appeared in 1840, taking into account those who may have died or married, they were eliminated from the chase.

The 1840s were years of great mobility in this country, and the South was no exception. In that decade, many Georgians moved to states to the north and west while numbers of others moved to neighboring counties or newer counties elsewhere in the state. A family's presence in one county in 1840 certainly did not guarantee they would be there in 1850. Thus, the search for the "master suspect list" in 1850 had to branch out into other states. This was complicated by the fact that new households were being created all the time. Even Robertsons with less common given names, such as Guilford, Anderson, and Walter, appeared in multiple states. These ancestral Robertsons were like ants: They were everywhere. As soon as it seemed they were cornered, they tunneled to another location and their trail was lost.

Patience, my friend, patience!
—*Sherlock Holmes*[101]

By the time the study moved to this segment, more microfilmed and published county records were also available for searching: tax lists, deed records, court minutes and abstracts, and the like. Any "suspect" who (1) could be found in records after June 1846 or (2) had a wife other than Elizabeth between 1835 and 1846 could legitimately be removed from the list of candidates, for he no longer fit the profile. Over time, research into county records considerably narrowed the master suspect list.

The remaining Georgia candidates created a daunting task because many of them were named James, John, Thomas, or William. These common names are in most families and often require a detailed search to separate one John from all the others. Other suspects were known, so far, only by initials. Yes, some other veteran researchers may no doubt say, "I could have told you so, and you would not have spent all that time on a process that may be for naught. Why didn't you . . .?" Well, so be it. However, considering the knowledge and database of Robertsons now accumulated, it was not time wasted. The process was often frustrating, tiresome, and mentally demanding because the spelling variations of the surname are interchangeable in the records and there were thousands of pages of records to read.

As this phase of the search began, study of the Georgia map became imperative. The best map for this purpose was in Thorndale and Dollarhide's *Map Guide to the U.S. Federal Censuses, 1790–1920*. The given names of the remaining "suspects" from the 1840 census were penciled into each county on the 1840 map of Georgia. This provided a visual image of groups of candidates and neighboring counties in which to search for them. One man in Upson County in 1840 might well be found also in neighboring Pike or Talbot County records. Several "suspects" in counties bordering Alabama and South Carolina actually moved into those states and were identified in later censuses and records there.

TEXAS?

I confess that I am surprised and disappointed. I expected something definite by this time.
—*Sherlock Holmes* [102]

While the process of elimination continued in Georgia sources, the search persevered in Louisiana. A plan for a study such as this cannot be completely and minutely laid out all at once, at the beginning. A general idea, yes, can be outlined so that the project stays on target and remains focused. However, the searcher must be flexible to new ideas, newly available sources, and the discoveries made in the process. You have to plan your next move based on what you find or don't find.

Reminder

Because of the lack of evidence, instead of narrowing, this search branched out one more time. A major question remained with no answer: Where or how did Isaac and Elizabeth meet? They had to have been in the same location sometime prior to June 1846, the time of their marriage, and the only such place known at this point was Caddo Parish. It was not yet yielding answers. Were there other possibilities? Could they have met in Texas when Isaac lived there?

Hey, . . . this is all backward. We ought to be narrowing down the list of suspects, and here you go making it longer again.
—*Detective Richard LeJeune* [103]

Isaac Croom lived in Houston County, Texas, from about 1839 to 1844 and did receive a land certificate from the Republic of Texas. This land case file yielded the fact that he sold his certificate in May 1844.[104] (He bought land in Caddo Parish in July 1844.) Because the courthouse of Houston County burned, the earliest land books date from after the Civil War. Looking for rerecorded early deeds could be attempted if other efforts did not produce results. The Texas State Archives holds the early Houston County tax rolls, available on interlibrary loan. Would they reveal Robertsons during the period Isaac Croom lived in Houston County?

Unfortunately, the Houston County tax rolls for 1839 to 1844 did reveal six Robertsons (or variants), all men.[105] Only one of these could be conclusively eliminated through census records as a possible husband for Elizabeth Robertson Croom. The others had common names, such as James or William, which could mean years of trying to find them and distinguish them from others of the same names. It was decided that the remaining five could be filed for later study if the Georgia and Louisiana lists of candidates did not yield results. At this point, Miss Marple advised: "[E]xamine the simplest and most commonplace explanations first."[106] That meant Caddo Parish.

If the steps taken so far to place Isaac Croom and Elizabeth Robertson in the same place at the same time had not yielded substantial clues, was a different course of action feasible? On the one hand, the researcher had to ask the questions that were being addressed. On the other hand, was the search spinning its proverbial wheels? It was Hercule Poirot who stepped in to counsel: Leave the Texas question and stick to Louisiana and Georgia.

> You gave too much rein to your imagination. Imagination is a good servant, and a bad master. The simplest explanation is always the most likely.
> —*Hercule Poirot*[107]

THE WAKE-UP CALL

> It's still urgent, only I can't just see what must be perfectly plain.
> —*Miss Marple*[108]

The case simmered on the back burner for several years while other families got the research attention. Sometimes this is the best way. Nurse detective Hilda Adams knew the benefit of walking away and letting a mystery rest, or letting the brain rest: "I have had this happen before; I can puzzle over a thing until I am in a state of utter confusion, give it up, and then suddenly have the answer leap into my mind without any apparent reason."[109]

Research Tip

Was the Robertson case in a state of utter confusion? Not really. It was organized, but it was moving slowly and not yet producing the desired results. Perhaps it was time to pause and refocus. What would Miss Marple say under similar circumstances? She would probably answer with one of her signature statements: "[I]t must be quite simple really, mustn't it? . . . [T]here's really no need to make it all so difficult."[110] It's easy to hear this advice, wonder what she really meant, and argue back: Sure, it is simple once you know the answer, but until you know, you have to look at all kinds of possibilities and gather information accordingly. Yet, it was Miss Marple herself who explained her meaning when she faced a similar dilemma:

> [T]here was nothing *but* difficulty. Everything pointed in too many different directions at once. . . . The truth must be quite plain, if one could just clear away the litter. Too much litter, that's what's the matter.
> —*Miss Marple*[111]

Perhaps this case had collected too much litter. But what was unnecessary? What would Hercule Poirot advise at this juncture? In his own cases, he had said:

> The [clues] are all good in their way. The danger is they may assume undue importance. Most details are insignificant; one or two are vital. One must seek the truth within—not without. . . . Let us be calm. Let us reflect. Let us reason. Let us—*enfin!*—employ our little gray cells!
>
> —*Hercule Poirot* [112]

Poirot was right; it was time for reflection, with as much calm and reason as a frustrated genealogist could muster. The Robertson case had begun with the need to gather any evidence that could be found, starting in Louisiana. As information accumulated, the search had looked at a variety of scenarios and sought new data with which to study each possibility: (1) Elizabeth's husband may have died in Caddo Parish, leaving her a widow with two children; (2) perhaps Elizabeth had Robertson relatives in Caddo Parish or Madison County, Tennessee, or east Texas who could lead to her husband; (3) Elizabeth and her children must have been part of a family in Georgia in 1840; (4) maybe Isaac and Elizabeth met in Texas. The compiled details were voluminous. What were the most significant ones, Poirot's "vital" few?

Chronological Profile of Elizabeth Robertson Croom

Notes

It was time to review the facts now known about Elizabeth Robertson Croom. They were few and simple. Most of these items had been the basis for or results of research already. The first item could not be addressed without a more specific location or surname. The chronological profile contained eight items:

1. Elizabeth was reportedly born about 1808–1809 in Georgia.
2. She first married a man named Robertson (or variant).
3. She and at least two children arrived in Louisiana between about 1842 and 1845.
4. She remarried in 1846 in Caddo Parish, Louisiana, to Isaac Croom Sr.
5. She had three known living children in 1850, the two older ones apparently born in Georgia in about 1835–1836 and 1841–1842.
6. Louisiana records had not yet produced a single direct clue to a Robertson husband.
7. At least three Caddo Parish deed records gave her name as Elizabeth C. Croom.
8. She died between November 1857 and April 1868.

> Those are the main facts of the case, stripped of all surmise, and stated as baldly as possible.
>
> —*Sherlock Holmes* [113]

From these statements, could any inferences be made? Yes. As one sleuth had said, "The most difficult person to find is one who does not exist." [114] The Robertson husband was not showing up in Caddo Parish records because he probably was never there at all. Most likely, Elizabeth and her children came to Louisiana after he died. Apparently, they did not come with other Robertsons, since no others by the surname in the parish appeared to have any connection with them. They must have come with or at the invitation of someone else. Who? There was bound to be a clue there somewhere. There was.

RIGHT UNDER MY NOSE

It was there, all the time, under my nose. And because it was so near I could not see it. . . . It is to me a little reminder, Hastings. Never to despise the trivial—the undignified.

—*Hercule Poirot*[115]

Of the eight bald facts about the case, Elizabeth's first marriage had not been addressed. **Yes, identity of the husband had been addressed, but *marriage* had not been.** The idea knocked on the brain in the middle of one night. As Miss Marple said, "[W]hen one thinks of things just before going to sleep, quite often ideas come."[116] What kind of statewide record other than the federal census might help to identify husband candidates? Marriage records. Although the pool of data was much smaller and much less complete than the census, it would give first names of the women, which the 1830 and 1840 censuses did not. It was worth a try.

Brick Wall Buster

Furthermore, the newest fact about Elizabeth had not been tested. Was it Poirot's "trivial" tidbit right under the nose, her middle initial, *C*? Why not look in marriage records for any Robertson (or variant) man who married an Elizabeth, especially an Elizabeth C.?

Since the 1850 census had suggested an 1808–1809 birth for Elizabeth, her first marriage could have occurred between about 1824 and Ann's birth about 1835–1836. The four volumes of early Georgia marriage records compiled by Joseph T. Maddox had been out some years by the time this search created a new need for them.[117] (They had proved useful in other searches which had a groom's name and a short list of counties.) The volumes are not indexed. Instead, the entries appear alphabetically by county. Such a search for Robertsons would simply involve looking at all the reported counties (not all counties are included) for marriages between 1824 and 1835.

Did the *C* stand for a middle name, such as Catherine, or for a maiden name? The majority of middle initials in other families researched in the nineteenth century seemed to stand for a second given name, not a maiden surname. The researcher had to remain alert to both possibilities.

After matching entries for the published counties to the criteria, there were nine reported Elizabeths who had married a Robertson/Robinson husband during the 1824 to 1835 time period. Of these candidates, there was only one Elizabeth C.: Elizabeth C. Arnold, who married a Thomas Robertson in 1833 in Putnam County, Georgia.[118] The bride's name was right; the date was good; the groom's name was a positive sign in light of the son's name. Here was the first encouraging evidence in years of looking. The difficulty was suppressing the urge to dance on the table or turn cartwheels in the library aisle. Cautious optimism had to prevail. There was more work to do and eight other candidates to evaluate before any celebration.

Keep calm, my boy, keep calm. The situation is developing very nicely, but don't lose your head.

—*Anthony Eastwood to himself*[119]

Of these nine husbands, three were already on the master suspect list. Two of those had been eliminated through other county records. The one still on the Georgia master suspect list was this Thomas Robertson of Putnam County. He was now the only one on both lists. The other six grooms were "new" and had not been found, at least not recognizably, in the 1840 census study. And as luck would have it, of the grooms who now required study, two were named Thomas; two, William; one, James; and one, simply A. Why do families with common surnames give so many children common first names as well? Why not Salathiel or Septimus or the mother's maiden name?

The new grooms' names were combined with the Georgia master suspect list. After continued research in county records both in Georgia and neighboring Alabama and South Carolina, the list was gradually reduced to thirty-one. Reducing a list of 280 different individuals to thirty-one was progress, and 89 percent had been eliminated. To make a strong case for one, it was desirable to know that none of the remaining list posed threats with conflicting or contradictory evidence. In other words, the researcher needed convincing evidence that no others had a real chance of being the long-sought ancestor. Therefore, for the time being, as long as the potential prime suspect was only a suspect, the study of county records continued. Any other candidates who appeared in records after 1846 or had wives other than an Elizabeth could be eliminated from the list. However, none were because they were not found in the land, tax, and court records that were researched; probate records were the next option. Meanwhile, study began on Thomas Robertson of Putnam County.

NUMBER ONE SUSPECT EMERGES

Patience! Patience! . . . [T]hese little digressions of mine sometimes prove in the end to have some bearing on the matter.

—*Sherlock Holmes*[120]

The 1840 census for Putnam County had already revealed a Thomas Robinson family with both head of household and wife of age thirty to forty (a match with Elizabeth's age in 1850), three little girls under five, and a female adult slave.[121] The presence of three young girls was disconcerting since only one Georgia-born girl appeared with Elizabeth in 1850. She was Ann, then fourteen, born two to three years after this Thomas and Elizabeth married. Of the other two, perhaps only one, if older than Ann, could have been old enough to marry with parental consent by 1850. No such record has been found in Caddo Parish, Louisiana. It seemed more likely that Ann was the oldest (four in 1840) and the others both died before 1850. The six-year gap between the ages of Ann and T.J. in the 1850 census supports this possibility.

Because Elizabeth Robertson Croom's son was named Thomas James, it was feasible that he had been named for his father. One task ahead was to study Putnam County records to learn about Thomas Robertson, the number one suspect. The other task was to head back to Caddo Parish records to look again for Arnolds, for there was one among the remaining ten of Isaac Croom's cluster.

He was the James A. Arnold who witnessed the marriage bond in 1846 when Isaac Croom married Elizabeth Robertson. He had not appeared in the 1850 census or the other parish records studied. However, at Caddo Prairie, only seven census households away from Isaac and Elizabeth (in the Albany beat) in 1850 was Lucy A. Arnold, widow, age thirty-eight, born in Georgia, with four children: James K. (twelve), Georgiana (ten), Susan C. (nine), and Lucy A. (three).[122] The three older children were born in Georgia; young Lucy was born in Louisiana. These ages suggest that the family came to Louisiana between 1841 and early 1847. Was this James A. Arnold's family?

In fact, it was. The 1850 mortality schedule showed that James A. Arnold, planter of Caddo Prairie, age forty, a white male, born in Georgia, had died in May 1850.[123] The cause of death was "killed." Although cholera had been a frequent killer in the parish that year and other entries gave the cause of death as "accident," this one implied it was not disease or accident. This situation is still under investigation although no newspaper or court account has yet been found.

A third trip to Caddo Parish was the opportunity to revisit the parish succession files, this time for Arnolds. The files yielded several surprises. Lucy Porter (maiden name), widow of James A. Arnold, filed application in court on 1 June 1850 to be appointed administratrix and tutrix (guardian) of her four children by her husband: James, Georgiana, Catharine, and Lucy Anne.[124] Then, on 30 November 1853, Jacob C. Porter, "a near relative of Lucy Arnold and the only relation in the parish," was commissioned administrator of Lucy Arnold's estate.[125] He told the court that she had recently died, leaving *five* minor children: James, Georgiana, Catherine, Lucy, and Virginia, who must have been born after her father's death. Porter made his final report and accounting to the court in January 1859, after he had moved to neighboring DeSoto Parish.

What about Porter? The census records of 1850, 1860, and 1870 show his birth between 1815 and 1818 in Georgia, his wife's Alabama birth, and the births of all their children in Louisiana, the oldest born about 1842–1843.[126] As a note of interest, Lucy (Porter) Arnold's children were not with his family in either 1860 or 1870. (Were they with the Crooms? Neither the children nor the Crooms have turned up in 1860.) The census of 1840, showing Porter as a single man, age twenty to thirty, supports a birth between 1810 and 1820 and places him in Caddo Parish by June of that year. Marriage records reveal that Porter married Sarah Ann Garrett in Caddo Parish on 7 September 1841.[127] Compared with information known about the Arnold family, this data suggests that Porter came to Louisiana first and the Arnolds followed a year to several years later.

Where did the James A. Arnold family live in Caddo Parish? After Lucy Arnold's death, the court appointed neighbors or friends to attend a family meeting to deliberate the interests of the minor children and the propriety of selling the Arnold homestead. (No Croom or other Arnold was involved in this or any other part of the two successions.) This group decided that since the property was unoccupied and likely to decay, it was in the interest of the minors to sell it. The property sold at public auction on 18 March 1854 for $480.[128]

This land is the only known Caddo Parish residence of the Arnold family. Its proximity to the farm Isaac Croom bought in 1844 may well answer the question of how Isaac Croom and Elizabeth Robertson met. (See Figure 15.)

It is possible—very possible—and yet I have not my full material at present.

—*Sherlock Holmes*[129]

A page-by-page search had been made of the five volumes of Caddo Parish conveyances recorded between January 1841 and mid-1851 (well over 3000 pages). Neither they nor the conveyance indexes, 1839–1899, yielded evidence of James A. Arnold, either his purchase of the land his estate sold or his signing as a witness for someone else, not even Jacob C. Porter.[130] On the other hand, Porter appeared first in these deed records in September 1842 as a merchant (J.C. Porter and Company) to whom someone else owed $264. Porter sold land

	NE1/4 S34 T20N R16W James A. Arnold	S35		S36
	SE1/4 S34 vacant, 1850			
N1/2 S3 T19N R16W	NW1/4 S2 T19N R16W Isaac Croom 1844	NE1/4 S2 T19N R16W Isaac Croom 1844	NW1/4 S1 T19N R16W Isaac Croom 1852-53	

Figure 15 Land Belonging to James A. Arnold and Isaac Croom, 1850

in far southwest Caddo Parish in 1847 and served as a witness to two conveyance records in 1849 and three in 1850.[131]

A court case in which James A. Arnold was supposedly the plaintiff appeared in one court index but the court staff was unable to locate the file for study. Nevertheless, the succession records established the presence of James A. Arnold in Caddo Parish and at least one interaction (signing the marriage bond) with Elizabeth Robertson and Isaac Croom, apart from being their neighbor. The next challenge was to establish his presence in Georgia and determine whether he and Thomas Robinson/Robertson were associated in any way. Was he the missing link?

THE MISSING LINK?

> It'd be easier to make a case if we could find some solid evidence.
> —*Samuel Clemens*[132]

Another look at the Georgia marriages yielded a license and return for James A. Arnold and Lucy Ann Porter in Taliaferro County on 20 August 1832.[133] Taliaferro County is not a direct neighbor to Putnam County but only one county removed from it. However, the 1840 census showed both James A. Arnold and Thomas Robinson in Putnam County. Arnold's household included James, thirty to forty (thirty supports the 1850 mortality schedule); a female twenty to thirty (Lucy, twenty-eight); one male under five (James K., about two), a female under five (Georgiana, infant), and one young male slave.[134]

In the search for the missing link, the next Putnam County record consulted was the marriage book for the license of Thomas and Elizabeth. Thomas's surname appears on the license as Robertson and on the minister's return as Roberson. No witness was asked for or given.[135] Wouldn't you know!

The next best record to search for Arnold-Robertson interaction was the annual tax digests. The lists for 1824–1828 showed neither young man although several others of both surnames did appear. No digest survives for 1829. Thomas Robertson was the first to appear, in 1830, without land, as a defaulter in District 309.[136] His appearance on this year's list suggests that he had reached age twenty-one. If he was in fact on the missing 1829 list, his birth would be pushed back a year. Thus, we could estimate his birth year at about 1807–1809.

The tax roll for 1831 was encouraging.[137] In the same 309th District in the northern part of the county, James A. Arnold was listed for the first time as a taxable poll without land, and the fourth person down the list from him was Thomas Robinson, also a taxable poll without land. This seems to place them in close proximity to each other. The marriage records imply that both were single and thus were probably working for someone else or renting farms. The following two years, both appeared in the county but in separate districts, still without land. Only in 1833 did Thomas's entry indicate any land acquisition, ninety-five acres on Glady Creek.[138] (No deed record has been found.) Lists are missing for 1834–1835. Only Thomas appeared in 1836 and 1837, without land, first as Roberson, then as Robertson.[139]

Brick Wall Buster

The pivotal record was the 1838 tax list (Figure 16), showing Thomas *Robison* in District 375, without land, paying tax for himself and *as agent for* James A. Arnold, also one poll without land.[140] At last, there is evidence of the two men interacting with each other in a way usually reserved for relatives, administrators, executors, or guardians. Perhaps they were brothers-in-law.

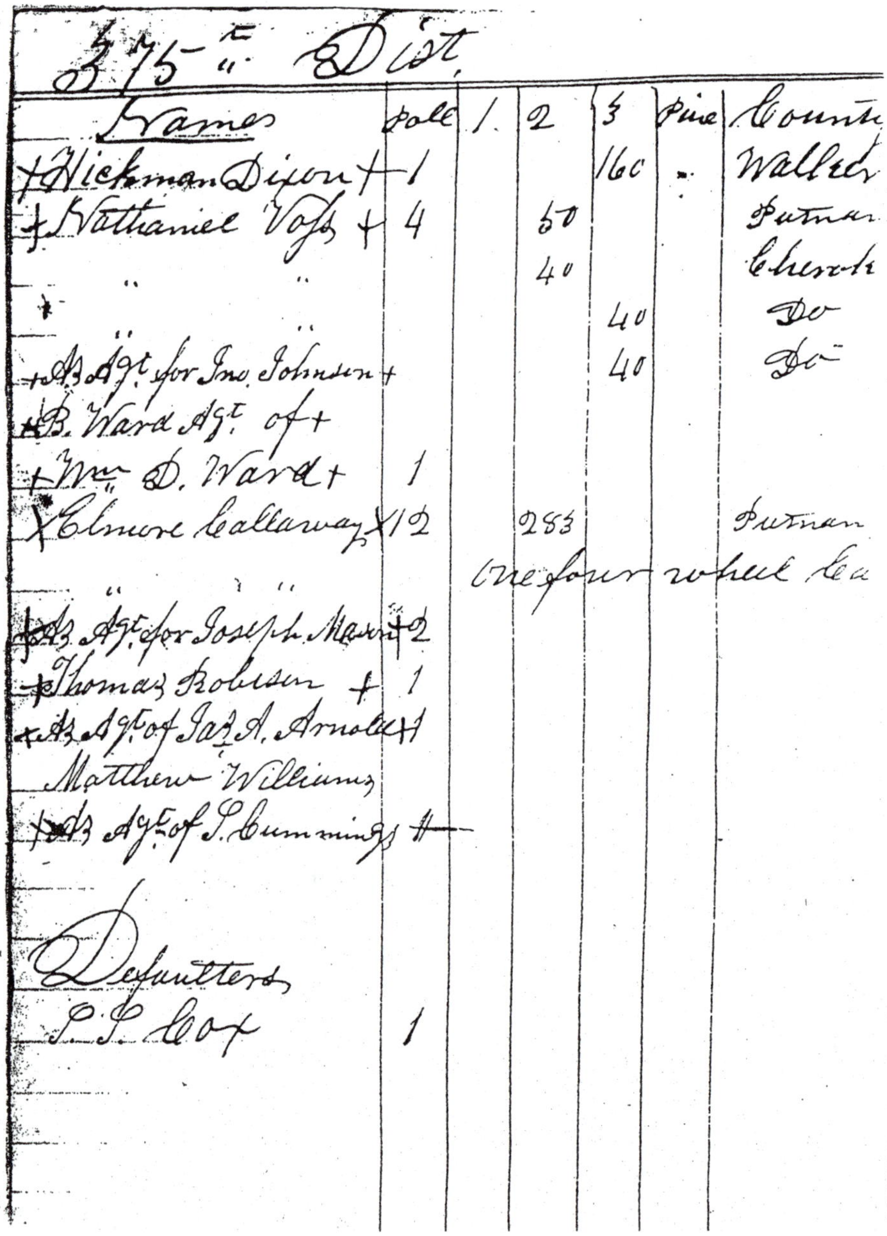

Figure 16 Putnam County, Georgia, Tax Digest, 1838

In 1839, 1840, and 1841 Arnold appeared in District 306, also on the northern edge of the county. No more than about nine miles away, Thomas Robertson/Roberson was in District 375 for two more tax years.[141] By 1841 tax time, he had moved back to District 309. These frequent moves from district to district were not uncommon among men who owned no land. Arnold's disappearance from the rolls in 1842 and beyond supports his move to Louisiana about this time. Thomas Roberson appeared for the last time in 1842, still as one poll without land or slaves. Tax digests do not exist for 1843, 1844, or 1847, but neither man was on the 1845, 1846, and 1848 lists.[142] (Lucy Arnold's "near relative," Jacob C. Porter, did not appear in any of these or other Putnam County records searched.)

Six county deed books of transactions recorded from 1827 to 1858 were searched page by page (over 3,300 pages) for mention of Arnold and Robertson. Although neither appeared in the deed records as grantor or grantee, both were witnesses to others' transactions but not together. Arnold (also Arnall) witnessed deeds written in August 1834 and August 1841; Robertson acted as a witness in December 1840 and January 1841.[143]

The last known evidence of Arnold in the county was a note for $575, dated 6 March 1840 and still unpaid on 11 January 1842. On this date, as security for payment of the note, Arnold "sold" to Josias and Elijah Boswell a seventeen-year-old slave named Harriett.[144] Perhaps he was trying to pay the debt in preparation for leaving the state; perhaps he was leaving regardless, knowing the young slave would satisfy the debt. The two documents of August 1841 and January 1842 tell us that the Arnolds had not moved to Caddo Parish, Louisiana, with Jacob C. Porter. Perhaps, they went *because of* him.

The Inferior Court Minutes for Putnam County between 1830 and 1846 show that Thomas Robertson was called for jury duty for the June 1837 term although he does not seem to have been drawn for actual jury service. However, for the mid-December 1841 term of court, both Robertson and James A. Arnold were sworn in to serve on Jury No. 2, twelve men from the larger pool of fifty.[145] This service represents another interaction of the two men, although in nonfamily circumstances. It also supports Arnold's residence in the county until early 1842.

The Superior Court Minutes for Putnam County between 1829 and 1846 showed jury service or court appearance for James A. Arnold in 1832 and 1834. Thomas Robinson/Robertson served on jury duty in 1835 and 1836. He was the plaintiff in two debt cases, which he won, in 1837 and 1838.[146]

Then on 24 March 1838, the Superior Court minutes indicated that "James A. Arnold, Thomas Robinson, and Elizabeth C., his wife," were in court asking for a "*ne exeat regus*" order against Chole [*sic*] C. Allen, that she not be allowed to leave the jurisdiction of the court (Figure 17, on page 198). A special jury called for the case decided in favor of the complainants "that the bond shall stand."[147] This language suggested that something had occurred previously that the researcher would want to find out about.

No further information appeared in the court record. The issue seemed to be a family matter of some kind since James A. Arnold and Elizabeth C. Robinson (nee Arnold) were both named. If it were a business affair among the men, Elizabeth would not be involved. Thomas seemed to be named because his wife was affected by the suit. At last, all three subjects were in the public records acting together in the same place at the same time.

This discovery prompted a telephone call to the Superior Court Clerk's office

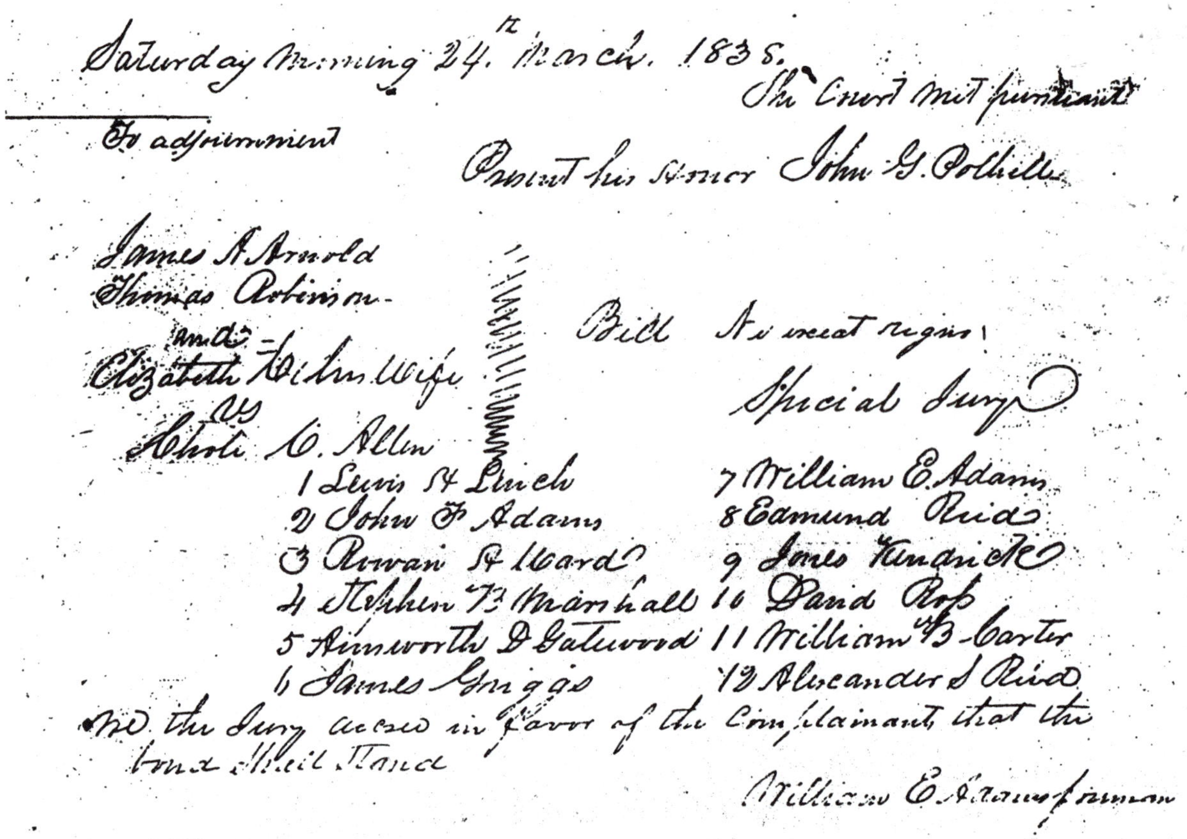
Saturday Morning 24th March. 1838.
The Court met pursuant
to adjournment
Present his Honor John G. Polhill

James A Arnold
Thomas Robinson
and
Elizabeth His Wife
vs
Chloe C. Allen

Bill Ne exeat regno
Special Jury

1 Lewis H Lunch 7 William E. Adams
2 John F Adams 8 Edmund Reid
3 Rowan H Ward 9 James Kendrick
4 Stephen B Marshall 10 David Ross
5 Ainsworth D Gatewood 11 William B. Carter
6 James Griggs 12 Alexander S Reid

We the Jury agree in favor of the Complainant that the bond shall stand

William E Adams foreman

Figure 17 Putnam County, Georgia, Superior Court Minutes, 24 March 1838

in Putnam County to ask about case files. The clerk's office could not say whether they had any further records on the case as all their old court files are in storage. So, the search turned to probate records after finding evidence that a Chloe Allen left a will in Putnam County.[148] Before that rented microfilm arrived, another important question was answered.

ONE MORE QUESTION ANSWERED

> I understand now. I understand quite well. The whole thing is really very simple, isn't it?
>
> —*Miss Marple*[149]

Thomas Robertson was not found in Caddo Parish, Louisiana, because he died in Putnam County, Georgia. His probate file contains a number of notes he had signed for value received, mostly from mercantile companies, that were unpaid at the time of his death.[150] The last one he signed on 27 March 1842 for $5.75. A temporary administrator's bond was filed in court on 8 October 1842. These documents narrow down the time of his death.

Two other documents in the probate file help pinpoint the death date more closely. One is a bill from a doctor, Martin G. Slaughter, for $9.25, dated 29

June 1842, for medicine and apparently a night visit.[151] The other is a receipt for payment to Sarah Tompkins of the $7.75 owed her by the estate for food-stuffs. The first item Tompkins charged to the estate was two barrels of corn, purchased 2 July 1842. This was not a note Thomas himself made; it was an account against the estate. It implies that Thomas had already died when the purchase was made. If so, his death can be narrowed down to the night of June 29, June 30, or July 1 of 1842.

This estate file makes two further implications. First, we cannot know how Thomas pronounced his name, but he signed all nine notes of debt in his probate file the same way: Thomas Roberson (Figure 18). Other documents in the file call him Robertson and Robinson about equally. Regardless of the actual name, all variations were used in documents and must, therefore, continue to be studied.

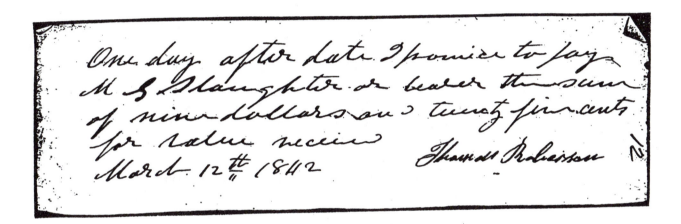

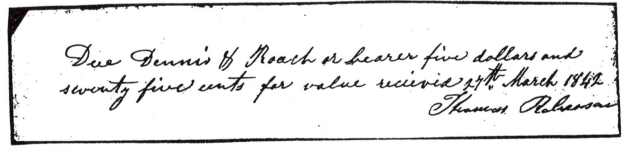

Figure 18 Thomas Roberson's Signature on Notes in Probate File

Second, the estate sale took place on 26 January 1843, with "Mrs. Robertson" purchasing most of the furniture and kitchen items, in addition to two cows and their calves.[152] This certainly suggests that she had not yet gone to Louisiana and perhaps was not planning an immediate removal. There was no evidence in the file of any Arnold or Porter involvement in the estate sale or settlement.

THE HYPOTHESIS

Let us, then, form the provisional theory. . . . This all hangs together, Watson! . . . It is more than [mere speculation]. It is the only hypothesis which covers the facts.

—*Sherlock Holmes*[153]

The working hypothesis had become that Elizabeth Robertson Croom's first husband was Thomas Robertson of Putnam County, Georgia. He died in mid-1842, and a year or so later, the widow and at least two children joined her brother, James A. Arnold, in Caddo Parish, Louisiana, where Elizabeth met and married Isaac Croom Sr. in June 1846.

The 1842 Putnam County tax roll had included Thomas Roberson but not James A. Arnold. Since Thomas lived at least until the end of June that year, we can imply that the tax lists were made during the first half of the year. (The tax list is not dated.) Arnold's absence from the 1842 roll, with his December 1841 jury service and January 1842 mortgage, suggests that he left during the first half of that year, before Thomas Roberson died.

The documents of Caddo Parish indicate that Jacob C. Porter was the first of this extended family to go to Louisiana, by early 1840. (Was the older Porter in the parish his father?) James A. and Lucy (Porter) Arnold apparently followed him there in the spring of 1842. Elizabeth (Arnold) Robertson and her children went between 1843 and 1845. As near neighbors to Isaac Croom, the Arnold and Robertson families would have known him and would have been aware of his wife's death in November 1844. Perhaps the Arnolds invited Elizabeth Robertson come to visit, knowing that the widower might be looking for a wife.

Another possibility is that Elizabeth Robertson tried to manage on her own for a while, at least until the spring of 1843. However, she owned no land and apparently no slaves. In addition, in the estate sale, others bought the seed cotton, tools and farming implements, oxcart, all the animals except two cows and two calves, the fodder, a lot of pork, and more than thirty barrels of corn.[154] The widow, it would appear, was not planning to raise another crop, but how could she manage for long?

Research continued (1) to try to eliminate other Robertson men remaining on the Georgia master suspect list to strengthen the case for Thomas, (2) to discover whether any other Caddo Parish, Louisiana, family was from Putnam County, Georgia, and (3) to learn whether any other Caddo Parish family was related to the Porters, Arnolds, or Robertsons. So far, no other candidate had presented evidence conflicting with or contradictory to the hypothesis, and Thomas Roberson of Putnam County had become the only and most likely first husband for Elizabeth C. Robertson Croom.

You sum up the difficulties of the situation succinctly and well. There is much that is still obscure, though I have quite made up my mind on the main facts.

—*Sherlock Holmes*[155]

THE CRITICAL LINK

I'm certain there's a link between the two . . ., something we just haven't found yet. You can't tell me it's pure coincidence.
—*Samuel Clemens*[156]

The researcher eagerly awaited the arrival of the microfilm containing Putnam County probate files. Chloe Allen's will and probate file yielded little other than the names of two daughters, Ann McGehee and Susan McFaddin.[157] However, the same roll of microfilm contained the probate files of other Allens, including James Allen, Chloe's husband. His will, written 21 September 1816 and proved in court 2 May 1818, named his wife as Chloe Collins Allen and named his children (Figure 19). Among his "three first children" was his daughter Elizabeth Arnold.[158] Yes! His probate file also contained the "missing" court document that solidified the relationships in question.

On 6 January 1837, a year before the record in the Superior Court minutes, Judge John G. Polhill of the Putnam County Chancery Court issued a writ to the sheriff of the county to require Chloe C. Allen, "defendant (amongst other things)," to give bond, with security, in the sum of twelve thousand dollars, to the complainants: James A. Arnold; Thomas Roberson; and Elizabeth C. Roberson, his wife.[159] According to the judge's explanation, the complainants had stated that Chloe Allen had a life estate in several slaves (not named here) under the will of James Allen, deceased, and that the complainants were entitled to an interest therein. The writ further explained that the complainants entertained "serious apprehensions that the said property will be removed beyond the limits of this State and that their rights will be impaired unless a remedy be afforded for the preservation thereof."

Five days later, Chloe Allen posted bond with at least two relatives signing with her: Green Allen (a son named in her husband's will) and William V. McGehee (the husband of her daughter Ann, as named in Chloe's will). The bond acknowledged the bill of *ne exeat regus* and the order that the slaves be "subject & accessible to the demand of the said James A. Arnold, Thomas Roberson & Elizabeth C his wife, according to the terms of the will of the said James Allen, decd."[160] This is the proof!

The only way James A. (Allen?) Arnold and Elizabeth C. Arnold had any claim to property under the will of James Allen was that they were brother and sister, the children of Elizabeth (Allen) Arnold, daughter of James Allen. The omission of their mother from the court proceeding suggests that she was deceased; otherwise, they would not yet have had any interest in the "property." No other Arnold siblings are mentioned or implied in these documents; so far, no others have been identified. The court and probate records do not name a relationship between Chloe and the three complainants. However, she was either grandmother or stepgrandmother, as the wife of their grandfather.

For the original question, her relationship is not an issue. That question now has an answer: Ann Maria (Robertson) Croom was the daughter of Elizabeth C.

For More Info

See chapter five for strategies for using probate records.

Figure 19 Portion of the Will of James Allen

Arnold and Thomas Rober(t)son, a granddaughter of Elizabeth (Allen) Arnold, and a great-granddaughter of James Allen, all of Putnam County, Georgia! Now, the research can take off into two new generations. If Ann's grandson, P.B. Croom, were alive today to hear about all these new ancestors, he would clap his forehead with his palm and utter one of his well-used exclamations: "Well, blow me down!"

And, of course, Hercule Poirot has something to say about the resolution of this case:

> [L]et me say this: To be sure means that when the right solution is reached, everything falls into place. You perceive that *in no other way* could things have happened.
> —*Hercule Poirot* [161]

Mr. Poirot, now I am sure.

Preparing for Adventure: An Overview of the Basics

O ne sleuth gave her reasons for getting involved in detective work. These can apply to genealogy as well. Near the beginning of the twentieth century, Mary Roberts Rinehart's character nurse Hilda Adams became a detective. Remembering her first assignment, she expressed what many genealogists come to feel: "I recall it all— . . . the prospect of adventure; the chance to pit my wits against other wits and perhaps win out. . . . I'll do it!"[1]

Notes

Endnotes for this appendix are on page 275.

AT THE BEGINNING

Start . . . at the beginning. Do not hurry yourself.
—*Hercule Poirot*[2]

Genealogical studies boil down to four basic components: names, dates, places, and relationships. We find these as we study the events and activities in an ancestor's life. In order to move backward in time from generation to generation, we need these details. They help define family members. They help us know that we have the right people at the right time and place. We start with ourselves, our parents and siblings, and our grandparents to accumulate vital statistics (birth, marriage, and death dates and places). We seek to prove the relationships that link these people to us and to each other. In other words, we begin with what we know and search to discover the unknown. With these components, we work our way back to the great-grandparent generation, then to their parents and grandparents, and so forth.

Do not hurry yourself. Building a solid foundation in research is likely to provide a better result. What is the foundation? At the very beginning, ideally before a first trip to the library or courthouse, the foundation includes

1. Vital statistics and other life events for several generations from family

sources, such as family Bible, letters, diaries, school records, newspaper clippings, photographs, military papers, memories, even family stories and oral tradition (used cautiously).

2. Any research into public records that is already provided on the individual or family.

3. Family group sheets, pedigree charts, and chronologies filled out and documented from these family papers and early research. These charts can be found in *The Unpuzzling Your Past Workbook* and in *Unpuzzling Your Past*.

4. A goal and a plan for continuing the search in a given lineage.

Research Tip

Do not hurry yourself. **One of the commandments of the genealogical process is "Thou shalt not try to skip back in time before thou hast done the necessary in-between work."** Back when census indexes were few and far between, many genealogists had a tendency to begin by heading straight for the published 1790 censuses and substitutes. If the surname was less common, such a tactic could give the searcher an idea of where the search might go some day. For a common name, the genealogist was better off not bothering, because it accomplished little. Either way, there were too many unknowns between the known (present) and 1790 to make 1790 a first target of research. One new researcher at the library, investigating a person who died in the 1970s, was, right off the bat, trying to collect information from the 1870s, working with a name only, without the links of dates and places. It doesn't work that way.

Do not hurry yourself. Any time a new ancestor is identified, the search comes to another beginning. This beginning is not usually an ancestor's birth. More often, it is a death or an event in adult life—a census, a deed or marriage record, a will, a military pension record—that triggers a light in the researcher's mind: "Ah, this may be the right ancestor!" We start with that clue and work from it step-by-step. We then accumulate enough information to allow us to move back in time with the right ancestor in the right place at the right time.

Do not hurry yourself. In our eagerness to convince ourselves that we have indeed found the next generation back in time, we can make mistakes. If we jump to conclusions, we make mistakes. If we make assumptions without adequate facts, we make mistakes. Upon finding two more people with the same name as the one he thought was his ancestor, one friend joked, "I should have stopped while I was ahead. I thought I had it nailed. Now I'm all confused again."

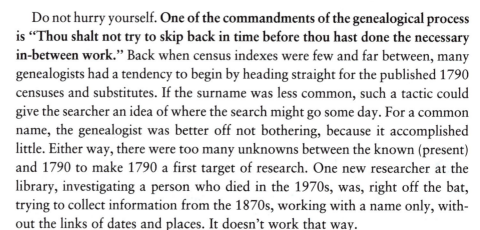

[A]lthough I am in the habit of using despatch in my business, I am never known to be in a hurry; hurry in affairs I take to be the especial mark of the slovenly and unpunctual.
—*said to detective Loveday Brooke*[3]

Do not hurry yourself. Eventually, every line of ancestors runs into snags. Specific birth and death information gets harder to find. A mother's maiden name is hiding. The family appears out of nowhere in 1840 and "nowhere" does not want to be identified. The parents for Great-Great-Grandmother could be the Abe and Nancy from the 1850 census, or maybe Sol and Sarah from an

1846 will, or maybe even Micajah and Demaris who married in the right place at the right time to qualify. Which ones are the right ones? Sherlock Holmes had it right: "Ah, that is a question that will take some time to answer."[4] Such searches simply will not let you hurry.

FOCUSING THE SEARCH

If the camera's not in focus, you get a blurry picture.
—*Conventional Wisdom*

Research has to have a focus. An historian does not start out to write in one lifetime a definitive history of the earth, including geological, meteorological, botanical, biological, and anthropological history, at least not nowadays. As scholars begin to focus on a topic of interest, they narrow the choice by setting subject, time, and place limits. They specialize in a much narrower field, such as the development of photography in the United States in the nineteenth century or immigration from Ireland to the United States during the infamous potato famine. Instead of writing about epidemics in the United States, one might choose the yellow fever epidemic in the fall of 1867 along the Gulf Coast or that epidemic as it affected Texas and Louisiana.

Likewise, genealogists cannot work effectively on all their lines at once. Each new generation doubles the number of potential lines (families) you have. By the time you discover all eight great-grandparents, including the maiden names of the wives, you have the potential of sixteen lines to work on just to find their parents. By that time, also, most genealogists run into some lines that are relatively easy to work and some that are more difficult. The perceived degree of difficulty often acts as a natural way of narrowing the focus. Some genealogists choose to focus their interest on the maternal line; some choose the paternal side first.

Focusing does not mean that we work only on one or two lines until we finish them, to the neglect of all the others. Sometimes, we put a few on the back burner to simmer while we think about what to do next or wait for interlibrary loan materials. Meanwhile, we work on another line. Nevertheless, we work best when we narrow the most active search to one or two persons or couples at a time.

Besides, genealogists never finish. We quit or we die, but we don't finish. People continually tell me they don't have to work on their paternal line because a cousin has already done it. I have to respond, "Perhaps, but your cousin did not finish. There is always one more wife or parent to identify or one more conclusion to document."

How do you choose a focus family? In selecting a focus family, ask yourself questions such as these. Out of the answers will emerge an ancestor ripe for study. Do you have

- A grandparent you never knew?
- An ancestor who led an unusually interesting life?

Idea Generator

205

- A great-grandparent who remains nameless?
- One who may give you success more readily than some others?
- An ancestor whose diary or scrapbook is available to you?
- One you know nothing about except for a single record?
- One similar to this character in one of nurse detective Hilda Adams's cases? "[T]here is one element which she has been mighty careful to keep out of her story. That's her family."[5] In genealogy, we'd say, "What's the matter with the family? Or with her? Why did she never mention them? What happened? I've got to find out."

REPOSITORIES OF GENEALOGICAL INFORMATION

I can only assure you, madame, that I am leaving no stone unturned.
—*Hercule Poirot*[6]

Genealogy research takes place in, or with materials from, libraries, courthouses, archives, cemeteries, and other repositories of records and documents. In looking for the many pieces of the genealogical puzzle, we frequently need to imitate Poirot's practice of "leaving no stone unturned." This can mean finding records created at different levels of government and found today in all kinds of repositories and research facilities.

A Word About Jurisdictions

Public sources available to genealogists abound and many are easily accessible. Many records on which genealogists rely were created as our ancestors interacted with one or more of the governmental authorities under whose jurisdiction they lived or served. These records are often still found within the governmental jurisdiction where they originated: town, county, state, or federal. City tax rolls, for example, may still be located at the city hall or city tax office, but the oldest records may have been transferred to a local museum or research center. In most states, the county is the jurisdiction that recorded ancestral vital registrations (births, marriages, and deaths), personal land transactions, civil lawsuits, probate settlements, and livestock marks and brands. The counties also collected taxes for the state government. In some areas, you may find old tax records at the county courthouse. In other places, surviving records may be at the state archives or historical society along with other old county records, collected for safekeeping.

Besides local and county records, genealogists also use records created at the state and federal levels of government. For the most part, you will not find federal records, such as military service and passport records, at a county courthouse. One exception is military discharge papers, mostly twentieth-century ones, which were created as service personnel left military or naval service and which were later brought voluntarily for filing by the veterans or their families. Another exception is copies of federal land tract books kept at the same office as the county deed records because they are useful in tracing land ownership. These land and military records were not placed at the courthouse for the convenience of genealogists, but we take advantage of their being there to study them.

Likewise, records created at the state level, such as state land grants and state pensions, including Confederate pensions, are not normally found at federal record repositories, such as the National Archives and its branches. Naturalization papers filed in federal courts can be found either at the federal court itself or where other federal court records are stored. Naturalization papers filed originally at a county court or state district court will be found with other records of those courts.

The process of creating records sometimes varied from state to state, but remembering the purpose for which they were created will help you determine the jurisdiction that may hold them today. Finding out about why records were created and about record-keeping responsibilities of the different jurisdictions is another reason to read books and articles on researching in a particular state.

Understanding why a record was created will also help you understand what you will find or will not find in the record itself. For example, the federal census records prior to 1850 named only the heads of household, not every person in the house. The purpose was a population count for the purpose of apportioning congressional districts, not a national directory of ancestors. As the government became interested in studying demographic information about the population for other reasons, such as public health, the census takers had to ask for more and more information.

Repositories

Genealogy does not take place in simply one location, but in many places. Genealogists conduct research anywhere there are records and information about people.

1. Public libraries often have genealogy collections of books, journals, and microfilm along with local and state history materials. Some public libraries are state or federal government documents depositories and may also house special collections of newspapers, city directories, maps, and other research sources and aids. Four of the numerous public libraries with large genealogy research collections are the Los Angeles Public Library; the Allen County Public Library in Ft. Wayne, Indiana; the Mid-Continent Public Library in Independence, Missouri; and the Clayton Library, Center for Genealogical Research, a branch of the Houston Public Library in Texas. Many state libraries have a genealogy and history division, in which researchers can work. Large public and state libraries often house law libraries, which can also be helpful to genealogists.

2. The national library, the Library of Congress, has a multitude of materials of use in genealogy. Refer to James C. Neagles's book *The Library of Congress: A Guide to Genealogical and Historical Research* (Salt Lake City: Ancestry, 1990) for details.

3. University libraries sometimes have local and state history or genealogy collections and government documents of many kinds. A number of university

libraries maintain special collections of manuscripts, maps, and newspapers. Academic libraries also have a variety of indexes and reference materials useful in genealogy. The universities with law schools also have, of course, law libraries, which do contain information on somebody's ancestors.

4. Some private libraries also house genealogy collections. The largest is the Family History Library in Salt Lake City, Utah. Open to the public, it houses millions of books and rolls of microfilm. Branches of this library, called Family History Centers, are scattered throughout the country. Other private libraries with excellent genealogy materials include the Newberry Library of Chicago and the libraries of such societies as the National Society, Daughters of the American Revolution in Washington, DC; the National Genealogical Society in Arlington, Virginia; and the New England Historic Genealogical Society in Boston.

5. Each state has a state archives or historical society that acts as an archive to house state government records from early periods. Many state documents and department records contain information on ancestors. These can include letters to the governor, petitions signed by citizens, individual business with state departments, Confederate military pension records, and, sometimes, state land records. For a number of years, some state archives have been gathering the earliest county record books for safekeeping, especially since many county courthouses are running out of storage space. Many of the state archives have published pamphlets or books about their holdings; try to get these publications for your research states. Local museums and libraries sometimes have archives departments for local and private manuscript collections.

6. Another major repository of records of use to genealogists is the National Archives in Washington, DC. Thousands of the records have been microfilmed, but many thousands more exist in the various National Archives buildings in Washington and around the country. Consult the National Archives publication *Guide to Genealogical Research in the National Archives*, revised edition (Washington, DC: National Archives Trust Fund Board, 1985) for an overview of holdings relevant to genealogy. The National Archives also has available a number of pamphlets about specific topics and catalogs of microfilm publications. **These catalogs are available online at <http://www.nara.gov/publicati ons/microfilm>. Also look at <http://www.nara.gov/genealogy>.**

Internet Source

7. Cemeteries are another place where genealogists find "records." Tombstone inscriptions preserve for the researcher names, dates, identities of spouses, sometimes birthplaces and marriage dates, sometimes parents' and children's names. At least, they preserve what someone once thought to be the correct information. (See "Research and Analysis: The Question of Rev. William Harrison's Death Date" on pages 119–121.) Miss Marple would want us to check out this information before we accept it as true. Sometimes this checking is possible, but the tombstone may be the only existing record of some of the information. Nevertheless, it behooves us to try to find the tombstones of all siblings in a given family, just as we try to get all birth and death certificates for sets of siblings. This effort helps us determine whether what we find is logical, even when we cannot determine whether it is completely accurate.

8. Families are repositories of much family history and genealogy. Even if you ask about family papers that could give you information on a focus ancestor, nongenealogist relatives usually have no idea what could be helpful: "All I have is a bunch of old letters." "Nobody ever wrote a family history." "I'm sure nothing I have would help you." If you had an opportunity to look for yourself, you would probably find things the relative had never seen or never considered of any use in genealogy and family history. The middle-name story in chapter four is an example of the kinds of records tucked away in family papers.

9. Other genealogical information can sometimes be found in local businesses, such as funeral homes, newspaper offices, church offices, abstract and title companies, and lawyers' files. Local sources can include people as well, whether in person or in the records they and their families kept. Hercule Poirot said, "Talk to the neighbours. . . . Let them talk to *you*. And from their conversation always, somewhere, you will find a clue. . . . Always somewhere there will be a word that sheds light."[7]

10. More and more transcriptions of records (tombstones, muster rolls, land grants, pension indexes, tax lists, and the like) appear on the Internet every year, and even graphic images of original records are becoming available. This "repository" is growing and is well worth using. Like any published book of abstracts and transcriptions, errors can occur in the copying process. Lord Peter Wimsey's comment on another set of records fits here as well: "Wonderful system they have there. But of course—being only human—it breaks down now and again—doesn't it?"[8]

A WORD ABOUT SOURCES

I suggest two categories. Public and private.
—*Investigator Jill Keller*[9]

The sources for research are quite varied. Research using both public and private (family) sources is illustrated throughout this book. Family sources sometimes are duplicated in public records but often exist only within the family. Thus, they can be very important to the genealogist.

Some documents and records in their original form exist in such varied places as archives, state historical societies, museums, courthouses, cemeteries, city halls, and special collections of libraries. If you need a vacation, plan a trip to the ancestral county courthouse and state archives to research on location. These visits may be necessary when working with some twentieth-century materials or certain kinds of courthouse files that are not always available on microfilm.

Record books in courthouses usually are copies of the original records, especially deeds, wills, and estate records. Copies of these and other records are often available for research on microfilm and microfiche. Collections in these different forms are accessible at numerous research libraries (public, private, and university), state libraries and archives, historical societies, the

Library of Congress, and at the main facility and regional branches of the National Archives.

Microfilm and microfiche can be borrowed on interlibrary loan from some libraries and state historical societies. Others can be rented for nominal fees from such facilities as the American Genealogical Lending Library in Bountiful, Utah (with annual membership, [800] 760-2455) and the Family History Library in Salt Lake City, Utah. Researchers can rent materials from the Family History Library at any of the hundreds of Family History Centers around the country. **To find a center near you, ask other researchers, check your telephone directory (under Church of Jesus Christ of Latter-day Saints), consult the Web site at <http://www.lds.org>, or call (800) 346-6044. To see the Family History Library catalog, visit a Family History Center or consult the Web site at <http://www.familysearch.org>.**

Sources

Often the most readily available version of the records is published abstracts or transcriptions of deeds, court records, newspaper entries, tombstone inscriptions, wills, and the like. An abstract is a summary of the facts in a document; a transcription is a handwritten or typed copy of the document itself. Frequently, genealogy collections in libraries have such published works. It is fortunate that so many genealogists have been willing to spend the time and effort to make these records available for the rest of us.

These abstracts and transcriptions are usually carefully prepared books and articles, but the two steps of the process (abstracting/transcribing and preparation for printing) allow the possibility of human error and make these sources two additional steps removed from the original record. If you have a specific reference for a record from an abstract, transcription, or published history, it is recommended that you obtain a photocopy from the appropriate office at the city hall, county courthouse, or archives.

SUGGESTIONS FOR EFFECTIVE RESEARCH

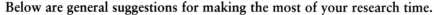

Are you a looker-upper?
—*Investigator Alan Grant*[10]

Timesaver

Below are general suggestions for making the most of your research time.

1. Write down all identifying information about a source before you use it. Record page numbers and applicable volume numbers as you take notes, as you turn the pages.

2. Dedicate each page of notes to one surname or one person, depending on how your files are organized. Write that name at the top of the page for ease of filing.

3. Know what you are looking for before you start each research session. Know why you need it or believe it will help. Check it off your research plan or record it on your research log when you finish. Make notes when you have new ideas for research.

4. Know that you are looking in the right time and place for the name(s) you are seeking. Or at least know why you are looking in the time and place you are.

5. Be as thorough as possible as you research any given record so that you do not have to repeat the effort. If your budget allows, photocopy what you can to save time and to aid in thoroughness: specific surname sections in indexes, census pages, copies of key documents or abstracts, and even title pages of books you use (to aid in documenting). Take change for copy machines.

6. Do not expect to find all your information in one research facility or one kind of source.

7. Do not skip a generation. Work backward one generation at a time.

8. Expect surnames to be spelled in various ways.

9. If you start with the census records, try vital registrations (birth and death certificates), marriage records, cemetery records, and wills next.

10. Include wives and mothers in the search; they are half of your ancestors.

11. Ask questions of the staff if you need help, but remember that, in court-houses especially, the staff is not there for the convenience of genealogists and, even in some libraries, many are not genealogists themselves.

12. As cheerfully as possible, observe the rules of the facility in which you research. Many require the use of pencils in taking notes.

DOCUMENTING RESEARCH
Citing Your Sources Means . . .

Important

1. Writing down enough detail about the source you are using that you can tell a year from now, or five years from now, whether you have already used the source, to keep you from duplicating your efforts. It also means writing down sources you use that do not yield information. They are still sources you have tried. You probably do not want to spend more time on them until you have another reason for doing so. Cite these sources, and in your notes write "no mention of the Powells" or "no marriage record under Powell, Poole, Polle, or other spellings."

2. Writing down enough detail about the source you are using that you or someone else can find the same information again to see whether you copied it correctly the first time. If one source tells you that Grandpa was born in 1864 and later you find a source that gives 1867, do you ignore the second and just consider it wrong because it is different from what you already have? Do you go back to your original source to see whether you copied it correctly the first time? Do you know where you got it the first time?

3. Writing down enough detail about the source you are using that you or someone else can find the same information again to copy down the rest of the information that you didn't think you needed the first time. Did Grandpa sign his name or make his mark? Who were the witnesses? What did the will be-queath to the sisters? What was the legal description of the land? We all will have a time when we have to go back to a source because we didn't think we

had a need or the time to write everything down the first time. Do you know where you got it the first time?

4. Getting enough detail about the source you are using that you or someone else can find the same information again to evaluate your notes. If a cousin shares family information with you and his list of Grandpa's brothers doesn't exactly match your own list, what do you do? Assume he is wrong? Assume your list is wrong? Combine the two lists and now Grandpa has nine brothers instead of five? Or do you look at the sources you and your cousin used to see if you interpreted the sources correctly? Do you know where you got it the first time?

5. Getting enough detail about the source you are using that you or someone else can evaluate the source. What kind of source is it? County record, family record, published county or family history? Is it an original document, a transcription, a microfilm copy, or something from the Internet? How close in time to the original event is the document? Who provided the information for this source? Someone with firsthand knowledge? How reliable is the source?

Footnotes

Footnotes (or endnotes) document, with page numbers, specific pieces of information. They may also contain explanations or parenthetical comments. In a formal presentation, notes are usually found at the bottom of the appropriate page, grouped at the end of a chapter, or grouped by chapter at the end of a book. Footnote form is what we use on family group sheets and chronologies, in our research notes, and in genealogy software to document events, names, dates, or places. It is important to read the footnotes or endnotes in any book or article you use, especially this book. See further discussion and examples in chapter four and appendix B.

Bibliography

A bibliography is the general list of the sources consulted in the preparation of a work or referred to in the work. Usually they are found at the end of the complete work. Some bibliographies include recommendations for further reading for those interested in going deeper into the subject.

The bibliography is useful in a book-length family history. It can help others identify sources for their own research. It informs your readers about materials you used. The bibliography is a capsule of all your sources. In turn, we need to read bibliographies that other researchers have prepared.

DATES IN OFFICIAL RECORD BOOKS

Most documents, such as wills, deeds, and marriage licenses, recorded in county (or town) courthouse books have at least two dates: the date of the document and the date of the filing with the court. The dates may be the same or a few days apart, but they may be years apart. The delay in filing may be due to many factors. For example, the grantee (buyer) did not get around to taking the deed to the courthouse for filing until he was ready to sell the property. The minister waited to return a marriage license until he had a stack of them. The minister forgot about them until years later. (Of course, the date of the actual marriage ceremony will be a third date in that record.) The testator made and signed the will on one date but lived another eighteen years, and the executor presented the will for probate several months after the death.

THE CALENDAR CHANGE

The Julian calendar went into use in Rome in the year we call 46 B.C. The Christian church adopted it in 325 A.D. Under that calendar, the year had twelve months, or 365 days, with an extra day added every four years, just as we have today. However, over many years, this man-made calendar was falling behind the sun's movement. By 1582 the spring equinox, the first day of spring, fell on March 11 by man's reckoning, not March 21 as the sun dictated. This discrepancy threw off the church's calculations for Easter, which are determined by the spring equinox. Pope Gregory XIII decided to change the calendar so that man's time would catch up with the sun's time. When Rome went to bed on 4 March 1582 and awoke the next morning, it was March 15 instead of March 5. Not everyone was happy with this change: Some thought it would shorten their lives by ten days!

The pope's mathematicians discovered that this was not a permanent solution because there would still be a loss of three days every 400 years. To rectify the problem, the pope authorized the omission of three leap years every 400 years to prevent the loss of those days. To simplify the calculations, he chose to eliminate leap year in the double-zero years that are not evenly divisible by 400. In other words, the year 1600 was leap year because it could be divided by 400 with no remainder, but 1700, 1800, and 1900 were not. The year 2000 is a leap year but not 2100, etc.

The other major change in the new, or Gregorian, calendar was to put New Year's Day on January 1 instead of March 25. Under the old, or Julian, calendar, the day after 24 March *1530* had been 25 March *1531*.

Important

Not everyone changed calendars at the same time. When Rome adopted the new calendar on 15 March 1582, it was still March 5 in London and other cities. Most of western Europe changed to the Gregorian calendar within a few years, but England clung stubbornly to the old dating for another 170 years. When 29 February 1700 came to London, it did not come to Rome, Paris, Madrid, Brussels, and most of the western world. This leap year put England eleven days behind instead of ten. Parliament finally decided in 1750 to take the plunge but gave everybody a two-year grace period to get used to the idea. Then, when England and her colonies went to bed on 2 September 1752, they woke up the next day to September 14.

Until that day in 1752, official record keepers in the British Isles and colonies usually adhered to the old calendar although many individuals had already begun using the new one. Thus, genealogists find evidence of the old calendar in many colonial records. The use of the Old Style and New Style calendars is discussed in chapter five.

STRATEGIES FOR EFFECTIVE CENSUS RESEARCH

Many researchers begin their research in the federal census records, a most valuable group of records. Some background in census strategies will help researchers new to these records. The census has been taken every ten years since 1790 for the purpose of apportioning seats in the U.S. House of Representatives among the states. Most census records still exist and are released for public use after seventy-two years. They are widely available on microfilm at research libraries. Many local libraries have the microfilm for their local area. You can also rent the film from the Family History Centers and the American Genealogical Lending Library. To use the censuses, it is best to know where your focus ancestor was in each census year.

The information you can get from the census varies from one census to the next. The more recent the census, the more information it will provide. Prior to 1850, only the heads of household were named. Everyone, slave and free, was listed in age brackets by sex. In 1850 and 1860, individual members of free households were listed by name, with other information such as age, sex, birthplace, and occupation; slaves were listed on a separate schedule individually by age and sex but not by name. Beginning in 1870, the first census after emancipation, all Americans were listed by name, with their age, sex, birthplace, occupation, and other information. Most of the 1890 census burned, but some fragments exist and are also on microfilm. A comprehensive discussion of the census records is in *The Genealogist's Companion & Sourcebook*.

Certain strategies in using census records will work to your advantage. Some are listed below; others are in chapter five.

See Also

Use Indexes Creatively

1. In most cases, start with the most recent census available and read backward in time for your focus ancestor. If you had several ancestors in the same county, read census entries for any who were in the county at the same time.

2. Whenever you have access to them, check the printed indexes first for your research state. This not only identifies a county in which to read for your target ancestors but also lists other people by the same surname in that county and/or surrounding counties for you to record as well. These may or may not be related to your ancestor, but collect their information while you are "in the county." You will likely need some of them as your search progresses.

3. If only a few entries of your ancestral surname appear in the index, note all of them and read them in the census itself.

4. Look in the indexes for variations of your ancestral names, both surnames and given names. One census may show the name of John W. Williamson, but another may enumerate him as John, J.W., Wesley, Wes, or Westly. We cannot know before reading the census just how the family named each member for the census taker or how the census taker reported them.

5. To guess at variations, try saying the names with regional or ethnic inflections, as the ancestors or their neighbors might have said them; try hurrying or slurring syllables together the way many people talk. Consider sounds which can be easily misunderstood for each other in English speech: *b* and *p*, *k* and hard *g*, *t* and *d*, *f* and *v*, *m* and *n*, *c* and *z*, and *ch* and *sh*. If the ancestors spoke English as a second language, their native language and accent need to be considered in guessing how a clerk or census taker could have heard their names.

6. Sometimes the discrepancy is a result of the indexing process. An indexer may not have been familiar with the family names in the county or may have had trouble reading the enumerator's handwriting. In this way, Lemuel and Samuel or David and Daniel were often misread for each other. Occasionally, the typist transposed letters or created other transcription errors: Thomas indexed as Thomsa. When William H. Hunter was indexed as Hunte,R William H., his name appeared before the Hunter list as a different name (Hunte,R) and not at the end of the list where we would normally look for him.

7. For the censuses of 1880, 1900, some of 1910, 1920, and some of 1930, the microfilmed index called Soundex is available. It is a system based on the sound of the surname. In order to look up your focus ancestor in the Soundex, you need a code number. The chart in chapter five on page 85 has a capsuled version of the Soundex coding system. Your local genealogists can also help you learn the system.

8. In using the Soundex or Miracode (some of 1910), write down all identifying information that you will need to find the family in the census: state, county, enumeration district (e.d.), and sheet number (in Miracode, the family number). Mark your notes clearly: which number is the e.d. number and which is the sheet or family number.

9. Armed with the index and Soundex entries, read the actual censuses. **The index is not a substitute for the real document.**

10. Be aware that censuses for some counties may be missing or lost, and some families were missed in each enumeration. However, if your family is not in the index, they may still be in the census. You may need to read the entire county to find them.

Important

Spelling Variations

Expect spelling variations in your ancestral surnames and given names. If the informant who talked to the census taker was illiterate and could not spell the family name, or did not spell it, the enumerator had to spell it his own way— the way he heard it and imagined it. For example, a girl appeared in one census as *Vertuas Mary*, possibly a creative way of spelling *Virtuous* Mary. Variant surname spellings may be minor but may still require the researcher to look in several parts of the index—for example, Rhodes and Roads, Robicheau and Robisho, Ingram and Enghram. Sometimes the difference is a simple matter of one letter: Berry, Barry, or Bury, Pie or Pye, Wright or Right.

Depending on regional speech patterns, the census taker may have heard sounds that are not part of the usual spelling of the name or heard an entirely different name: Orsborn for Osborn, Waters for Walter(s), Glassock for Glasscock. Given names have gone through the same mutations in census and other records: Hanner for Hannah, and Bertie for Verda. Cordelia and Adelia have been interchanged, as have Edward and Edmund.

Read the Census Thoroughly

Read several pages on each side of your family's entry to look for other relatives. Record everything in the family's entry, keeping spelling and ages as they appear there, even if you believe them to be incorrect. Why?

1. These pieces of information can suggest ideas for other sources to search: schools, occupational sources, veterans' records, land records if the head of household gave evidence of real estate value or home ownership, marriage licenses for new spouses or "missing" children, or probate files if the former head of household is missing.
2. People in the household with different surnames, even servants and boarders, may be relatives or may lead to other relatives.
3. We run the risk of sticking with names, ages, and birthplaces from the first census we find as if the subsequent ones, with different data, are wrong. We must think of all the data as evidence, not gospel truth.

Obviously, some entries are more accurate than others. Many researchers experience the amazement of finding a census record that must be the right family although much of the information is amiss. An 1870 example appears on page 166.

Study the handwriting of the census taker carefully. Reading one census entry, I was certain the husband's age was thirty-eight, until I began comparing the entry with ages reported for the same person in other censuses and comparing the handwriting with other entries on the page. At second glance, I realized the census taker made very distinctive eights and threes that looked like eights. I finally determined that the husband's age was truly written as thirty-three. I had misread a three for an eight until I studied other, more obvious, threes and eights on the page.

Read Every Available Census for Each Ancestor

Read every census available for each ancestor, in both federal and state enumerations. (Some states took their own censuses, too.) You never know what you will find. Not only do we gather evidence to corroborate or contradict data from other research, but we also learn about new wives, new children, elderly parents or grandchildren moving in, widowed children moving back home, children who may have died between censuses, changes in occupation or residence, and middle names or full names. In other words, we build a more complete picture of the family and therefore can make more accurate assessments.

Document Your Censuses

Write down in your extracts of census entries whatever identifying information is on the page, as well as the film and roll number: enumeration district number, sheet or page number, local post office or political division, date of enumeration, family and dwelling numbers. This is easier to do when you use good census extraction forms, such as the full-information ones in *The Unpuzzling Your Past Workbook*.

Why? Because (a) when you need to go back to the entry to check something, you will be able to find it again, (b) the information is the basis for a footnote or bibliographic citation documenting your findings, and (c) the name of the town, community, ward, or precinct, although not always given, may help locate the family's neighborhood within the county and provide clues for further study.

Usually Work Backward in Time

Generally, we work from the most recent census backward in time. Some circumstances require that we skip around or work forward.

Each enumeration missed some families and, sometimes, a whole neighborhood. If the error was in the copying process only, you may be able to find your family in the original enumeration at the state archives or state historical society. When your family was missed, you necessarily must go to the previous census. Thorndale and Dollarhide's *Map Guide to the U.S. Federal Censuses 1790–1920* identifies "lost" counties for each state in each census.

Research Tip

When you identify siblings of your ancestor, you often need to work forward again to find them with their own families and develop a family group sheet for each. This process helps sort out relatives with the same names and identify persons who may still be living and may communicate with you about the family.

Who Was the Informant?

We do not know exactly who gave the information to the census taker: an adult member of the family, a child, a boarder, even a neighbor. Some families appear very consistent in names and ages from one census to the next. Others vary greatly and for many reasons. It is common to find census ages for adults and children to be off by several years: a wife listed in three consecutive censuses as 24, 32, and 45. We do not know who furnished the information each time and why the discrepancies occurred. As students of the family, we must keep all the data as evidence until we have solid reasons to believe one is more accurate than another.

FOR FURTHER DISCUSSION

Chapter four and appendix B address the subject of documenting research. Chapter five discusses research in general and such specific record groups as

See Also

cemeteries, census, probate, land, and tax records. The progress report in chapter seven and the three studies in chapters nine through eleven illustrate the use of these and other kinds of sources on which genealogists rely.

The world is full of clues to everything, and if a man's mind is sharpened on any quest, he happens to notice and take advantage of what otherwise he would miss.

—*Edward Leithen.* [11]

Guide to Documentation: Examples of Style

Notes

Endnotes for this section are on page 275.

T his guide is a companion to chapter four and is placed near the end of the book for ease of use. It contains general information about citing typical categories of sources (books, articles, newspapers, CD-ROM material, documents, etc.) and reference examples of footnotes (or endnotes), shortened-form footnotes, and bibliography entries for each category. The general considerations at each section answer, with help from the style manuals, some of the frequent questions about citing works within that category. Refer to a style manual to answer other questions about form and details.

The first two sections below, on published books and articles, use a standard form found in most style books. The section on electronic sources is based on the fifth edition of Joseph Gibaldi's *MLA Handbook for Writers of Research Papers* (New York: Modern Language Association of America, 1999). Newspapers, interviews, and letters are sources genealogists often use. Although style manuals address the citing of these sources, genealogical standards often ask for more detail in the citations than most style manuals give. Thus, the section in this appendix uses genealogical examples of these sources. In some cases, "(Mills)," "(CMS)," or "(Lackey)" appears with a suggested format; such instances mean that the suggested format comes specifically from that reference. Otherwise, the format is generally based on these style manuals or is a genealogical application of the general principles of documenting.

The remaining section deals with types of genealogical sources not always, or not usually, addressed in style manuals. For ideas in citing family sources, see the examples in chapter four. As discussed in chapter four, genealogists have options in the ways they cite various records and documents. Whatever form you choose, the important thing is to use it regularly and consistently.

I. PUBLISHED BOOKS

And in detail if you please.

—*Hercule Poirot*[1]

Notes

General considerations for citing books:

- Basic standard elements of notes or bibliography entries are author, title, and publication information (place, publisher, year). *Author* may instead be an editor, compiler, translator, transcriber, or abstractor. Notes include the details of volume and page numbers from which specific information comes. Bibliographies omit page numbers.

- If no author, editor, or compiler, etc., is given on the title page and you cannot find the information in the introduction or library catalog, begin the citation with the title.

- If no place of publication, no publisher, or no publication date is given on the title page and you cannot find the information in the introduction or library catalog, insert "no place" or "n.p.," "no publisher" or "n.p.," or "no date" or "n.d." where that information would normally be found.

- If the author or compiler published the book, put "the author" or "the compiler" in the place for the publisher. If the book was privately printed as opposed to commercially published, and it is not clear who was responsible, put "privately printed" in the place for the publisher.

- If the place of publication is well known—such as Chicago, Baltimore, or New York—you do not need to include the name of the state in which it is located. If the town is not so widely known or if you are not sure how well known the city is, identify the state.

- To create shortened forms of the title, in citations after the first, use key words from the title, as shown in the examples below. This is not a rearranged or changed title. The short version needs to be so clear that the work is not confused with other similar titles or other works by the same author. Usually, titles of fewer than five words are not shortened.

- The shortened-form footnote gives the author's surname, the shortened but not changed title, and the page numbers.

- Many library catalogs are searchable online. You can often supply information missing from your notes by consulting catalogs of libraries with genealogical collections. Get the Web site addresses for the catalogs of your local public and university libraries and keep them handy for this and other uses.

- It seems to be a matter of personal or publisher choice whether to spell out or abbreviate *volumes (vols.)*, *editor (ed.)*, *edition (ed.)*, *revised edition (rev. ed.)*, *Company (Co.)* in a publisher's name, *United States (U.S.)*, and other such details. Consistency within the entire set of footnotes and bibliography is the important point. Spelling the full words is more formal and would be a better choice if there is any chance of confusion on the part of the reader.

- When citing a volume and page number, current usage suggests "5:45" for Vol. 5, p. 45.
- Current style books do not promote the use of *p.* or *pp.* before page numbers in footnotes or endnotes. However, the practice can be used (*The Chicago Manual of Style*, 14th ed., paragraph 15.189). Such usage would be a matter of choice in a genealogy primarily for the family and to prevent confusion on the part of readers not familiar with current styles, including those who learned different forms when they were in school. Again, consistency in usage is important.
- *Ibid.* (in the same place) can be used in the note immediately following a citation to refer to the same work (author and title) again. If more than one work is in a note, you cannot use *ibid.* in the following note.
- Elements of footnotes are generally separated by commas; elements of a bibliographic entry, by periods.

Book with one author
—footnote, first appearance

James W. Hagy, *Directories for the City of Charleston, South Carolina* (Baltimore: Clearfield Company, 1997), 52.

—shortened form for subsequent citations

Hagy, *Directories for the City of Charleston*, 67.

—repeat of same reference (same author and title) in the next note

Ibid., 45.

—bibliography entry

Hagy, James W. *Directories for the City of Charleston, South Carolina.* Baltimore: Clearfield Company, 1997.

Book with two authors
—footnote

Barbara R. Langdon and Shirley P. Langdon, *Chester County Marriages 1778–1879 Implied in Chester County, S.C. Probate and Equity Records* (Columbia, SC: Langdon & Langdon Genealogical Research, 1985), 120.

—shortened form

Langdon and Langdon, *Chester County Marriages*, 41–42.

—bibliography entry

Langdon, Barbara R., and Shirley P. Langdon. *Chester County Marriages 1778–1879 Implied in Chester County, S.C. Probate and Equity Records.* Columbia, S.C.: Langdon & Langdon Genealogical Research, 1985.

Book with compiler (comp.), editor (ed.), translator (trans.), etc.
—footnote, with explanatory note, such as is common in genealogical citations

Sherida K. Eddlemon, comp., *Genealogical Abstracts from Tennessee Newspapers 1791–1808* (Bowie, MD: Heritage Books, Inc., 1988), 154–155, from 24 May 1806, giving Wall's age as 24.

—shortened form
    Eddlemon, *Tennessee Newspapers*, 50.
—bibliography entry
    Eddlemon, Sherida K., comp. *Genealogical Abstracts from Tennessee Newspapers 1791–1808.* Bowie, MD: Heritage Books, Inc., 1985.

Book with organization as "author"
—footnote
    Hardeman County Historical Commission, *Hardeman County Historical Sketches* (Bolivar, TN: Hardeman County Historical Commission, 1979), 84.
—shortened form
    Hardeman County Historical Commission, *Historical Sketches*, 123.
—bibliography entry
    Hardeman County Historical Commission. *Hardeman County Historical Sketches.* Bolivar, TN: Hardeman County Historical Commission, 1979.

Book from multi-volume set
—footnote
    The Territorial Papers of the United States (Washington, DC: Government Printing Office, 1934–1975), 5 (Mississippi Territory):294.
—shortened form
    Territorial Papers, 16 (Illinois Territory):232.
—bibliography entry
    The Territorial Papers of the United States. 28 vols. Washington, DC: Government Printing Office, 1934–1975.

II. ARTICLES IN JOURNALS

How is this known?
    —*C. Auguste Dupin*[2]

Notes

General considerations:
- A typical note citing an article in a journal uses this standard form: author of article, title of article, title of journal, volume number, issue number or date of the issue, page number(s) referred to in the text.
- The bibliography entry gives the inclusive page numbers of the article.
- The bibliography entry uses the journal title, volume, issue or date, and inclusive pages as one element, not separated by periods. The journal title and volume number are not separated by commas, as in *Magazine* 55 (May 1907): 100–105. See examples below.
- Authors and titles are handled basically the same in citations for articles as in citations for books.

- If the journal is published in a foreign city or has a title similar to another journal, it is advisable to include the place of publication to prevent confusion. In genealogy, with so many journals published by local societies, it is helpful to identify the place of publication if it is not already in the title.
- If a title ends with its own punctuation mark (e.g., "Heavenly Days!") no comma or period would be necessary to separate the title from the next element of the citation.

Journal article with one author
—footnote

Nancy Simons Peterson, "Guarded Pasts: The Lives and Offspring of Colonel George and Clara (Baldwin) Bomford," *National Genealogical Society Quarterly* 86 (December 1998): 288.

—shortened form

Peterson, "Guarded Pasts," 293.

—bibliography entry

Peterson, Nancy Simons. "Guarded Pasts: The Lives and Offspring of Colonel George and Clara (Baldwin) Bomford." *National Genealogical Society Quarterly* 86 (December 1998): 283–305.

Journal article with place of publication
—footnote

Trevia Wooster Beverly, "Do You Have an 'Urban' Ancestor? Check out that City Directory!" *The CLF Newsletter* (Houston, Texas) 13 (February 1999): 8.

—shortened form

Beverly, "Do You Have an 'Urban' Ancestor?" 7.

—bibliography entry

Beverly, Trevia Wooster. "Do You Have an 'Urban' Ancestor? Check out that City Directory!" *The CLF Newsletter* (Houston, Texas) 13 (February 1999): 6–10.

Article in reference book or edited book
—footnote

Joseph W. McKnight, "Family Law," in *Encyclopedia of Southern Culture*, Charles Reagan Wilson and William Ferris, editors (Chapel Hill: The University of North Carolina Press, 1989), 807.

—shortened form

McKnight, "Family Law," 808.

—bibliography entry

McKnight, Joseph W. "Family Law." In *Encyclopedia of Southern Culture*, Charles Reagan Wilson and William Ferris, editors. Chapel Hill: The University of North Carolina Press, 1989. 806–809.

III. ELECTRONIC AND INTERNET SOURCES

Specifically, please.
—*Eleanor Roosevelt*[3]

The citations illustrated below basically follow the style suggested in the 1999 *MLA Handbook for Writers of Research Papers*. This work is cited as "MLA" when its formats are used below. The footnote styles have been adapted from the bibliography forms since this handbook uses parenthetical documentation instead of footnotes or endnotes in the text. Parenthetical documentation is inadequate for genealogy since it cites usually an author and page number that sends the reader to a list of works cited for details. The nature and quantity of genealogy citations makes this system unwieldy for our purposes. However, the *MLA Handbook* offers valid suggestions for the style of citations of electronic sources. In the first example, *TSHA* stands for the Texas State Historical Association.

Because items on the Internet come and go, it is wise to print out immediately whatever you find and want to keep. Otherwise, it may not be there when you need it again. At least you have your printout as your source.

Article in online book

—footnote (based on TSHA suggested form)

"Peter Powell," *The Handbook of Texas Online*, Texas State Historical Association, online <http://www.tsha.utexas.edu/handbook/online/articles/view/PP/fpo35.html>, accessed 31 May 1999.

—shortened form

"Peter Powell," *The Handbook of Texas Online.*

—bibliography entry (TSHA format)

"Powell, Peter." *The Handbook of Texas Online.* <http://www.tsha.utexas.edu/handbook/online/articles/view/PP/fpo35.html> [Accessed 31 May 1999].

Article from journal on CD-ROM

—footnote (based on MLA)

"Benjamin Fuller Bible Record," *National Genealogical Society Quarterly* 16 (March 1928): 11, *National Genealogical Society Quarterly, Vols. 1–85, 1600s–1900s,* CD-ROM, disc 1, Family Tree Maker's Family Archives CD #210 (Novato, CA: Brøderbund Software, 1998).

—shortened form

"Benjamin Fuller Bible Record," *National Genealogical Society Quarterly.*

—bibliography entry (based on MLA)

"Benjamin Fuller Bible Record." *National Genealogical Society Quarterly* 16 (March 1928): 11. *National Genealogical Society Quarterly, Vols. 1–85,*

1600s–1900s. CD-ROM. 2 discs. Family Tree Maker's Family Archives CD #210. Novato, CA: Brøderbund Software, 1998.

CD-ROM publication, previously published book
—footnote, source first

Genealogies of Virginia Families From the William and Mary College Quarterly Historical Magazine (Baltimore: Genealogical Publishing Co., 1982), 4:257, Ambrose Ransome will, CD-ROM, *Family History: Virginia Genealogies #2 1600s–1800s from GPC,* Family Tree Maker's Family Archives CD #186 (Novato, CA: Brøderbund Software, 1997).

—footnote, name first

Ambrose Ransome will, in *Genealogies of Virginia Families From the William and Mary College Quarterly Historical Magazine* (Baltimore: Genealogical Publishing Co., 1982), 4:257, CD-ROM, *Family History: Virginia Genealogies #2 1600s–1800s from GPC,* Family Tree Maker's Family Archives CD #186, (Novato, CA: Brøderbund Software, 1997).

—shortened form

Ambrose Ransome will, *Virginia Genealogies #2.*
[Note: If the short form citation refers to a different page, put the page number after the shortened title.]

—bibliography entry

Genealogies of Virginia Families From the William and Mary College Quarterly Historical Magazine. 5 vols. Baltimore: Genealogical Publishing Co., 1982. CD-ROM. *Family History: Virginia Genealogies #2 1600s–1800s from GPC.* Family Tree Maker's Family Archives CD #186. Novato, CA: Brøderbund Software, 1997.

CD-ROM publication, original publication
—footnote

Family Quest Archives, *Illinois 1870 Census Index,* CD-ROM, #ACD-0013 (Bountiful, UT: Heritage Quest, 1998), surname Nutter.

—shortened form

Illinois 1870 Census Index, CD-ROM.

—bibliography entry

Family Quest Archives. *Illinois 1870 Census Index.* CD-ROM. #ACD-0013. Bountiful, UT: Heritage Quest, 1998.

Database online
—footnote, name first

Nice Blaydes entry, *1798 Direct Tax, List 2a, Berkeley Parish, Spotsylvania County, Virginia,* online, Gary Stanton, comp., 21 July 1996, accessed 13 March 1999, <http://www.mwc.edu/~gstanton/hispinfo/1798l2a.htm>.

—shortened form, name first

Nice Blaydes entry, *1798 Direct Tax, List 2a. . . Spotsylvania County, Virginia,* online.

—bibliography entry

> *1798 Direct Tax, List 2a, Berkeley Parish, Spotsylvania County, Virginia.* Gary Stanton, comp. 1996. Accessed 13 March 1999. <http://www.mwc.edu/~gstanton/hispinfo/1798l2a.htm>.

E-mail message

—footnote (MLA)

> Jane Doe, "Bethel Primitive Baptist Church records," E-mail to author, 1 May 1999.

—shortened form

> Jane Doe, E-mail to author, 1 May 1999.

—bibliographic entry (MLA)

> Doe, Jane. "Bethel Primitive Baptist Church records." E-mail to author. 1 May 1999.

Social Security Death Index

—footnote, name first (Mills)

> Jane Doe, SS no. 123-45-6789, Social Security Death Index, *FamilySearch* (Salt Lake City: Family History Library), 1994.
> [Note: If using the SSDI from another source, cite that source.]

—shortened form (Mills)

> Jane Doe, no. 123-45-6789, Social Security Death Index, *FamilySearch*.

—bibliography entry (Mills)

> Social Security Death Index, *FamilySearch*. Salt Lake City: Family History Library, 1994.

IV. NEWSPAPERS, LETTERS, AND INTERVIEWS

Pray be precise as to details.
—*Sherlock Holmes*[4]

Two reasons for citing sources are (1) to show where you got your information and (2) to allow another researcher to find the same information. For many genealogical citations, there are no requirements for particular form. We must simply give enough information to achieve these two purposes. This section will illustrate several ways of creating these citations. The point is not to quibble over form; the point is to get all of us to document our research in a reasonable, meaningful way.

General considerations:

Notes

- In citing newspapers, use the complete date of the paper. If the newspaper published more than one edition a day, name the edition you used (morning, evening, city, etc.). If page numbers are not given, the researcher can count over to the referenced page and assign it a number, saying "pages not numbered but on third page." If the paper was published in sections, identify the section and page number.

- For a bibliography entry, use the newspaper name and date range of the issues you used: for example, 1850–1868. Individual news items are rarely shown in a bibliography. Clippings from unidentified newspapers could be cited by title or headline in the bibliography.

- Italicize the name of the city with the name of the newspaper for American newspapers. *The* at the beginning of a title, in English, is omitted in notes and bibliography. If the city is not widely known or could be confused with another city, add the name of the state, or Canadian province, italicized in parentheses: *Bolivar (Tennessee) Bulletin.* If this is awkward, given the name of the paper, the city and state can be identified after the name of the paper.

- For foreign papers, if the city is not part of the title, add the city in parentheses, not in italics. If the city is part of the title, italicize it along with the paper name.

- The city is omitted when citing national newspapers, such as the *Wall Street Journal.*

- Letters are identified by sender and receiver and date, if given. Further explanations can be made to authenticate the ownership and history of the document.

- For newspaper clippings and letters (as well as anything else), if the date is not given but can be determined, it can be cited in brackets. A note can be added to explain how the date was determined.

- Interviews are identified by the parties involved, medium, location, and date.

Because style books do not address all the sources genealogists need to cite, we make our own style based on what the style books do say and what we need to convey in our citations. Alternate forms in the examples below are based on the styles suggested primarily in CMS, MLA, and Mills, or combined ideas when these books give no form for the particular instance being cited. CMS and the others differ somewhat in bibliography entries. CMS would put the most specific identifying details only in the footnote and use the bibliography to list the more general identifying information. Lackey does not deal with bibliographies at all, but his footnote components can be applied to them.

Headlined clipping, article, or news item from identified newspaper
—footnote

    "Mrs. Fletcher E. Metcalfe, 83 former Georgetownite, dies Monday," *Williamson County Sun*, Georgetown, Texas, 30 December 1976, sec. 1, p. 9. Hereafter cited as Fletcher E. Metcalfe obituary.

—shortened form

    Fletcher E. Metcalfe obituary, *Williamson County Sun.*

—bibliography entry (Mills)

    "Mrs. Fletcher E. Metcalfe, 83 former Georgetownite, dies Monday." *Williamson County Sun*, Georgetown, Texas, 30 December 1976.

—bibliography entry (CMS)

Williamson County Sun, Georgetown, Texas, 30 December 1976.
[Note: CMS would put all other specific information in the first footnote.]

Undated clipping from unidentified or unnamed newspaper

—footnote

"H.O. Metcalfe Appointed Judge; Marfan Since 1917," clipping from unnamed newspaper [Marfa, Texas, January, 1941], p. 1, 8, original in possession of the author, Bellaire, Texas. The clipping mentions the January term of court beginning "here" on Monday, January 27, that Judge Metcalfe came in 1917 and has been "here more than twenty-three years," and that the judge was conducting the January term of court in Fort Davis within an hour after being sworn in. A perpetual calendar identifies the year as 1941 and supports the facts in the article.

—shortened form

"H.O. Metcalfe Appointed Judge," Marfa, Texas, newspaper.

—bibliography entry

"H.O. Metcalfe Appointed Judge; Marfan Since 1917." Undated clipping from unnamed newspaper [Marfa, Texas, January, 1941]. Original in possession of the author, Bellaire, TX.

News, advertisement, or other item from newspaper

—footnote

New-York Evening Post, 14 April 1821, 2nd page, col. 4. [Note: If using the paper at a research facility, you can mention that fact here and/or in the bibliography entry. Not required.]

—footnote

Houston Post, 14 April 1907, Society News, p. 40.

—bibliography entry

New-York Evening Post, 14 April 1821.

Letter in published book

—footnote

Emily Dickinson to Abiah [—], from Mount Holyoke Seminary, South Hadley, Massachusetts, 6 November 1847, in *The American Reader: From Columbus to Today*, Paul M. Angle, ed. (New York: Rand McNally & Company, 1958), 271–273, reprinted from Arthur C. Cole, *A Hundred Years of Mount Holyoke College* (New Haven: Yale University Press, 1940), 391–393. The letter is a delightful description of college life.

—shortened form

Emily Dickinson to Abiah [—], 272.

—bibliography entry (based on CMS)

Dickinson, Emily. Letter, 6 November 1847. In *The American Reader: From Columbus to Today*, Paul M. Angle, ed. New York: Rand McNally & Company, 1958. Reprinted from Arthur C. Cole, *A Hundred Years of Mount Holyoke College* (New Haven: Yale University Press, 1940), 391–393.

Letter in manuscript form
—footnote (Lackey)

Albert Croom to Dr. S.N. Hopper, 28 September 1902, original in possession of author.

[Note: If you use such sources at an archives facility, mention that fact here.]
—footnote with notes added

Letter from Albert Croom, Whiteville, Tennessee, to Dr. S.N. Hopper, Telephone, Texas, 28 September 1902, original in possession of the author, 1999, sent to author by Mary Jo Phillips, granddaughter of Dr. and Mrs. Hopper, about 1974. Mrs. Theodocia Hopper was Albert Croom's older half sister.
—shortened form (Mills)

Letter, Albert Croom to Dr. S.N. Hopper, 28 September 1902.
—bibliography entry (CMS)

Croom, Albert. Letter to Dr. S.N. Hopper, 28 September 1902.

[Note: CMS would put other specific details in the first footnote rather than the bibliography.]
—bibliography entry (Mills)

Croom, Albert, letter. 28 September 1902, from Whiteville, Tennessee, to Dr. S.N. Hopper, Telephone, Texas. Original in possession of the author, 1999.

[Note: If you use such sources at an archives facility, mention that fact here.]

Letter to author
—footnote (Lackey)

Virginia Guthrie Loyd to author, 11 February 1972, original in possession of the author.
—footnote

Letter from Virginia Guthrie Loyd, Natural Bridge Station, Virginia, to author, Houston, Texas, 11 February 1972.
—shortened form

Virginia Guthrie Loyd, letter to author, 11 February 1972.
—shortened form (Mills)

Letter, Virginia Guthrie Loyd to author, 11 February 1972.
—bibliography entry (CMS)

Loyd, Virginia Guthrie. Letter to author, 11 February 1972.

[Note: CMS would put other details in the first footnote.]
—bibliography entry (Mills)

Loyd, Virginia Guthrie, letter. 11 February 1972, from Natural Bridge Station, Virginia, to author, Houston, Texas. Held by author, 1999.

Interview or conversation by telephone (CMS)
—footnote

Henry Turner (H.T.) Coleman, Blanket, Texas, telephone conversation with the author, Bellaire, Texas, 26 August 1996. Notes of conversation held by the author.

—shortened form
 Coleman, telephone conversation, 26 August 1996.
—bibliography entry
 Coleman, Henry Turner (H.T.). Telephone conversation with the author, Bellaire, Texas, 26 August 1996.

Interview in person
—footnote (Mills)
 Interview with Claude Blalock, at Blalock home, near Whiteville, Tennessee, by Robert Shelby, 18 August 1997. Audiotape and transcription in Shelby's possession, Bellaire, Texas, 1999.
—footnote (Lackey)
 Interview with Claude Blalock, 18 August 1997, by Robert Shelby, near Whiteville, Tennessee, tape recording, owned by Shelby, Bellaire, Texas.
—shortened form
 Interview, Claude Blalock, 18 August 1997.
—bibliography entry (Mills)
 Blalock, Claude, interview. 18 August 1997, at Blalock home, near Whiteville, Tennessee. Audiotape and transcription held by interviewer, Robert Shelby, Bellaire, Texas, 1999.

Interview in person (CMS)
—footnote
 Sue Mood McMichael, interview by author, tape recording, Houston, Texas, 11 May 1980.
 [Note: If you use the tape at a research facility, mention that fact here.]
—shortened form
 McMichael, interview.
 [Note: Cite full name and date if interviewing more than one person of the same surname or if interviewing the same person more than once.]
—bibliography entry
 McMichael, Sue Mood. Interview by author. Tape recording. Houston, Texas, 11 May 1980.
 [Note: If you use the tape at a research facility, mention that fact here.]

V. PUBLIC OR UNPUBLISHED DOCUMENTS AND RECORDS

I've heard of reconstructing a crime, of course. . . . But I didn't know you were so particular about details.
  —*said to Hercule Poirot*[5]

The genealogical application of this comment is clear: I've heard of putting together a family history, of course, but I didn't know you were so particular about details. If we want to give our efforts credibility, even in the smallest details, we have to be particular—about our evidence and about our citing of it. For a more thorough consideration of the details of citing specialized genealogical sources, footnotes are discussed in this section. Bibliographies are addressed separately in section VII at page 247.

General considerations for footnotes and shortened-form notes:

Notes

- For notes citing documents, we use the name of the country (if other than U.S.), state, county or parish, city or town that issued or created the document, and in some cases the name of the agency within the government from which the document originated.

- Notes also include title or type of document, the date of its creation, and any other identifying details that help a researcher find it, especially volume and page numbers. Cite what you have actually used: a published abstract, an original document, a county-level copy in a county court record book (deeds, wills, court minutes, etc.), microfilm of a county record book, a document in an archives collection, etc.

- If the document used and cited is not widely available, include the facility, institution, or agency where researchers can find the document for research. Since microfilm materials are often available in facilities or on interlibrary loan, you would not necessarily need to cite where you used them.

- It is necessary in footnotes to include enough detail to find the record and identify it as a distinct entity, apart from other similar records. It is superfluous to include every conceivable detail in the citation unless (1) such detail is necessary to finding the record or (2) such detail is part of the discussion in the text. The superfluous items could include, for instance, the volume number for federal census records on microfilm. Since the microfilm is arranged by state and county, the volume number is not necessary to finding the correct roll of film.

- Examples in this book and others include a number of details. Not all sources of the same kind will include all the same details. Some pages of census microfilm give local post offices and others do not. You cannot always assume it is the same as what is on the previous or following page, because it may be different. Some tax rolls and court records are dated and others are not. Some tax rolls and court records have numbered pages and many do not. You cannot cite what is not on your record. Depending on the need and the situation, sometimes it is a good idea to mention what is missing, such as family numbers, the local post office name, or page numbers.

- Although not required, it is helpful to you and readers to include the name of the head of household or the parties to a deed or marriage record in your citation, especially when (1) you have a number of different citations of the same document type or the same people or (2) you want to make your meaning absolutely clear.

- Most footnote entries for books, articles, letters, and interviews (as discussed in previous sections) begin with the name of the author or person who created the record. Sometimes this form works well for genealogical documents and records. Sometimes, however, the note seems to read more smoothly and logically when it begins with the type of document. The examples below illustrate both formats. Consistency is important, in that all footnotes for books and articles use standard form, all citations of letters conform to the same style, and all census records maintain the same format.

- If your work is relatively short and you do not have a separate bibliography, you need to put all the finding material in the footnote. Refer to discussion below for bibliography ideas.

- Genealogists often create their own formats for such notes. Doing so is fine as long as the necessary details are provided and the format is consistent. That form may depend on how you file your own materials: first by name, first by type of document, or first by location. The form may also depend on what is logical to you. Some of the citations illustrated so far in this chapter have begun with the name of the person who created the document or caused it to be created. Some of the citations have begun with the type of source or record. Below are illustrations of both.

- If you cite more than one source in a footnote, it is common practice to separate the sources with a semicolon. It is common practice to separate the elements of each citation with commas. If you have several facts in one sentence that need citations, it is less cluttered and confusing to the reader to group the citations into a single footnote rather than have several footnote numbers interrupting the sentence. When such a footnote is necessary, you need to identify which source gives which piece of information. For example:

[23] Marriage license no. 234, dated 18 March 1874, New County, Texas, Marriage Book 2:12, County Clerk's Office, Courthouse, Newtown; *Five Corners (Texas) Star*, 25 March 1874, p. 3, col. 2, wedding story, adds the bride's middle name as Eugenia and the place of the wedding as the home of the bride's grandparents, Sam and Eliza Powell.

- Although many genealogists abbreviate words in their document citations, a formal presentation looks better when the key elements are spelled out. Many family histories are written for a broad, general audience of relatives as well as other researchers. We as presenters must make our citations as clear to the nongenealogist readers as to the genealogists who study our efforts. When in doubt, spell it out. If you use a large number of abbreviations, include a page to explain your abbreviations.

- A book-length work will have a number of citations. You can streamline the process by stating at the front whatever your readers will need to know in order to read your citations. For example, the following notes apply to the citation examples below:
1. Enumeration districts in census records will be abbreviated "e.d."
2. All federal census records cited are population schedules unless otherwise identified.

3. The National Archives in Washington, DC may be shortened to "National Archives" or "NARA."

4. The Family History Library in Salt Lake City will be abbreviated "FHL."

5. For purposes of illustration only, when two examples come from an identical source, the second one may begin in a different style and conclude with an ellipsis (. . .) to indicate that the rest of the citation remains the same as the previous example. This is a space-saving device for these examples. This is not the same as the use of *Ibid.* in actual footnotes. Use *Ibid.* to indicate that your own citation is from the same source as the previous one. An example is below.

Several styles of footnotes are illustrated below. Other styles are legitimate as well. Just as in the case of previous examples, the shortened form citations are for use in footnotes or endnotes when the same source is cited any time after the original note (footnote or endnote). The first citation is complete; subsequent citations give enough to identify the source and refer back to the first note. If the exact form illustrated comes from one of the three style books already mentioned (CMS, Lackey, Mills), the name will appear in parentheses.

American State Papers
—name first (based on CMS)

Alexander Armstrong entry, Land Claims in Mississippi Territory, 1806, *American State Papers* (Washington, DC: Gales and Seaton, 1832–1861), Class 8: *Public Lands, 1789–1837,* 1:1902.

—shortened form, for subsequent footnotes (CMS)

Alexander Armstrong, *American State Papers: Public Lands* 1:1902.

Archives document
—typical order: title and date of document, series title if applicable, name of collection if applicable, name of depository.

—document first

Petition to create a new county, 28 June 1870, from citizens of Falls, Robertson, and Limestone counties to Texas legislature (cover sheet labeled no. 87, Box 30, F), Texas State Archives, Austin, copy in author's possession.

—shortened form

Petition to create a new county (1870), Texas State Archives, Austin.

Birth record, county level
—document first

Birth record of David J. Coleman, Mills County, Texas, Birth Record Book 1:19, County Clerk's Office, Courthouse, Goldthwaite.

—document first, in record other than vital registration

Record of birth dates for Mary Ann and Joseph Mason, "Account of children returned for the year 1848," in the Poor School Records, 1825–

1859, no page or frame numbers, but under 1848 records, Court of Ordinary, Putnam County, Georgia, FHL microfilm 0401835.

—name first

David J. Coleman birth record, Mills County, Texas, . . . [continue as above]

—name first, microfilm record

Sarah Elizabeth LaMay birth record, 1888, Iron County, Michigan, Birth Index and Record, L-R, 1885–1971, p. 1, no. 306, County Clerk's Office, Courthouse, Crystal Falls, FHL microfilm 1017858.

—shortened form

David J. Coleman birth record, Mills County, Texas, Birth Record Book 1:19.

Birth record, state level

See Death record below.

Census record (federal) on microfilm, pre-1850

—document first

U.S. Census of 1810, Cumberland County, Virginia, National Archives microfilm M252, roll 68, p. 12, household of Elliott Coleman.

—name first

Elliott Coleman household, U.S. Census of 1810, Cumberland County, Virginia, National Archives microfilm M252, roll 68, p. 12.

—shortened form showing alternate style

1810 U.S. Census, Cumberland County, VA, p. 12.

Census record (federal) on microfilm, 1850–1870

—document first

U.S. Census of 1850, Talbot County, Georgia, National Archives microfilm M432, roll 83, p. 253, family/dwelling 422, household of Alfred Hudson.

—name first with alternate usages

Alfred Hudson household, 1850 U.S. Census, Talbot County, Georgia, NARA M432, roll 83, p. 253, family/dwelling 422.

—shortened form

1850 U.S. Census, Talbot County, Georgia, p. 253, family/dwelling 422.

—shortened form with explanatory note

Birth date estimated from 1850 U.S. Census, Greenup County, Kentucky, p. 224, family 85, household of Moses Bragg, showing Chaney, age 60.

Census record (federal) on microfilm, 1880 forward

—document first

U.S. Census of 1880, Grant Parish, Louisiana, National Archives microfilm T9, roll 453, e.d. 27, sheet 10, family 77, household of Mitchel Roston.

—name first with alternate format

    Louis Roshto household, U.S. Census of 1900, Grant Parish, Louisiana, Ward 7, e.d. 67, sheet 10, family 159, National Archives microfilm T9, roll 453.

—shortened form

    U.S. Census of 1880, Grant Parish, Louisiana, e.d. 27, sheet 10, family 77, Mitchel Roston household.

Census record (federal) on microfilm, supplemental schedule

—document first

    U.S. Census of 1850, Agriculture Schedule, Fayette County, Tennessee, district 2, National Archives microfilm T1135, roll 1, p. 853, line 1, farm of Isaac S. Patton.

—name first

    John L. Marshal, slave owner, U.S. Census of 1850, Slave Schedule, Monroe County, Alabama, National Archives microfilm M432, roll 22, p. 271 (pages not numbered consecutively).

—shortened form

    U.S. Census of 1850, Mortality Schedule, Caddo Parish, Louisiana, p. 89, Russell entry.

Census record (state) on microfilm

—document first

    1865 New York state census, Danby, Tompkins County, p. 2, visitation no. 17, family no. 17, lines 36–40, household of Noah Hollister, FHL microfilm 0856514.

—name first (Mills)

    Noah Hollister household, 1865 New York state census, Tompkins County, town of Danby, p. 2, lines 36–40, family no. 17, FHL microfilm 0856514.

—name first, supplemental schedule

    James H. McWhorter entry, 1865 New York state census, schedule for "industry other than agriculture," Tompkins County, town of Caroline, election district 2, p. 63, line 7, FHL microfilm 0856514.

—shortened form

    James H. McWhorter, 1865 New York state census, industry schedule, Tompkins County, Caroline, p. 63.

Church record (confirmation, membership, business)

—confirmation, document first

    Confirmation record of Elsie Mae Williamson Shelby, Records of the (Episcopal) Church of the Good Shepherd, Vol. 3:116 (1956), records held at St. Andrews Episcopal Church, 1819 Heights Blvd., Houston, Texas.

—membership, document first

    Membership list, 28 November 1817, Salem Baptist Church, Monroe

County, Alabama, photocopy of original minutes book, archives of the Monroe County Museum, Old Courthouse, Monroeville.

—church business, name first

Samuel D. Williamson, subject of church conference, 25 August 1832, Salem Baptist Church, Monroe County, Alabama, photocopy . . . [continue as above]

—shortened form

Salem Baptist Church, Monroe County, Alabama, minutes, 14 March 1833.

Church vital record (baptism, marriage, burial)

—baptism record, name first

Polly Steele McFadden baptism record, 1810, Fishing Creek Presbyterian Church, Records of the Session, 1799–1859, p. 29, facsimile reproduction in Brent H. Holcomb and Elmer O. Parker, compilers, *Early Records of Fishing Creek Presbyterian Church, Chester County, South Carolina 1799–1859* (Bowie, MD: Heritage Books, Inc., 1991).

—marriage record, document first

Marriage record, Elam Bennett to Marie Basco, 22 March 1866, St. John the Baptist Catholic Church, Cloutierville, Natchitoches Parish, Louisiana, Record Book 8:51, photocopy of original in Basco-McKinney collection, family file 16 (Bennett), Natchitoches Genealogical and Historical Association Library, Old Courthouse, Natchitoches, Louisiana.

—marriage record, microfilm

Marriage record, Bradford-Pemberton, 1703, Abington Monthly Meeting, Society of Friends, Montgomery County, Pennsylvania, in volume labeled *Miscellaneous Montgomery County Friends Meeting*, Records of Monthly Meeting–Abstract of Marriage Certificates, pages unnumbered, 8th page, Collections of the Genealogical Society of Pennsylvania, FHL microfilm 0383428.

—burial record, name first

C.C. Delhomme burial entry, June 1924, Book of Burials January 1922–September 1933, pages unnumbered but chronological, (Episcopal) Church of the Good Shepherd, Houston, Texas, records held at St. Andrews Episcopal Church, 1819 Heights Blvd., Houston.

—shortened form

Bradford-Pemberton marriage record, Abington Monthly Meeting, Montgomery County, Pennsylvania.

—shortened form, alternate

Bradford-Pemberton marriage record, Abington Monthly Meeting, Abstract of Marriage Certificates, 8th page.

City directory

—source first

The Charleston Directory; and Register, for 1835–6, in James W. Hagy, *Directories for the City of Charleston, South Carolina* (1835; reprint, Baltimore: Clearfield Company, 1997), 60, John C. Sigwald entry.

—name first

Rev. Elias Dibble entries, *Houston City Directory for 1866* (reprint, Dallas: R.L. Polk and Company, n.d.), 19, 112.

—shortened form

Dibble, *Houston City Directory for 1866*, 112.

City government record

—document first

Appointment of W.D. DeVolin as city commissioner, 18 January 1938, City Commission, The City of Marfa Minutes Book 4:2, City Secretary's Office, City Hall, Marfa, Texas.

—name first

W.D. DeVolin, appointment as city commissioner, 18 January 1938, City Commission, The City of Marfa Minutes Book 4:2, . . . [continue as above]

—shortened form

W.D. DeVolin, Marfa City Commission, Minutes Book 4:2.

City tax record

See Tax roll below.

Claims (state level)

—document first

Claim of Leeman Kelcey, administrator, on behalf of estate of Dr. Amos Pollard, claim no. 348, 2 January 1837, Audited Republic Claims Series, microfilm roll 083, frame 0664–0665, Texas State Library and Archives, Austin.

—name first

Leeman Kelcey, administrator of Dr. Amos Pollard, claim no. 348 (1837), . . . [continue as above]

—shortened form

Kelcey, claim 348, Audited Republic Claims Series.

Court records

(See also divorce record and legal case, both below.)

—name first

Benjamin W. McCarmack, application for letters of administration on the estate of Andrew J. Glasscock, Jasper County, Missouri, Probate Court Minutes, Vol. B (1851–1855):138, 5 October 1852, FHL microfilm 0932616.

—name first

Jacob J. Hollingsworth, defendant, Putnam County, Georgia, Superior Court Minutes, 21 September 1838, FHL microfilm 0400927, pages unnumbered but court sessions dated.

—name first

Thompson Robinson, Putnam County, Georgia, Court of Ordinary, Guardianship Records, FHL microfilm 1851814, frame 0433.

—document first

    Application of Benjamin W. McCarmack for letters of administration on the estate of Andrew J. Glasscock, Jasper County, Missouri, Probate Court Minutes, Vol. B (1851–1855):138, 5 October 1852, FHL microfilm 0932616.

—shortened form

    Benjamin W. McCarmack, Jasper County, Missouri, Probate Court Minutes, B:138.

Death record, county level

—name first

    N.W. Brelsford death record, Gonzales County, Texas, Death Register 4:99, County Clerk's Office, Courthouse, Gonzales.

—name first, microfilm record

    John G. Clawson death record (1871), Huron County, Ohio, Death Record, Vol. 1 (1867–1893):14, line 45, Probate Court, Norwalk, Ohio, FHL microfilm 0410483.

—shortened form

    John G. Clawson death record, Huron County, Ohio.

Death (or birth) record, state level

—death (or birth) certificate, document first

    Death certificate of Ruthan Benett [*sic*], no. 14206 (dated January 1924; died December 1923), Louisiana State Board of Health, Bureau of Vital Statistics, in Vital Records Section, Louisiana State Archives, Baton Rouge.

—death (or birth) certificate, name first

    Mary Liles, death certificate no. 6250 (1929), Texas Department of Health, Bureau of Vital Statistics, Austin.

—shortened form

    Ruthan Benett, Louisiana death certificate 14206.

Deed record

—document first

    Deed of gift, Allison to Allison, 3 June 1816, Shelby County, Kentucky, Deed Book N:400, County Clerk's Office, Courthouse, Shelbyville.

—names first

    Allison to Allison, deed of gift, 3 June 1816, Shelby County, Kentucky, Deed Book N:400, County Clerk's Office, Courthouse, Shelbyville.

—shortened form

    Shelby County, Kentucky, Deed Bk. N:400, Allison to Allison.

—shortened form

    Allison to Allison, Shelby County, Kentucky, Deed Bk. N:400.

—microfilm record, alternate form

    Irwin County, Georgia, Deed Book F:491, Rose to Bradberry, dated 1833, recorded 1888, FHL microfilm 0177098.

Divorce record

—in court minutes book

Sarah Heath vs. Guilford Heath, libel for divorce, Putnam County, Georgia, Superior Court Minutes, 1829–1839, March term of court, 1832 (pages unnumbered but terms are dated), carried over from March term, 1831, FHL microfilm 0400927, includes evidence of the missing husband's bigamy.

—in court case files

Angie Carpenter vs. Ed Carpenter, divorce case, District Court, Leon County, Texas, case no. 2228, 10 November 1896, case file in Court Clerk's Office, Courthouse, Centerville.

—shortened form

Carpenter vs. Carpenter, District Court, Leon County, Texas, case no. 2228.

Journal, autobiography, memoirs, diary, or scrapbook

—published

Stella M. Drumm, ed., *Down the Santa Fe Trail and Into Mexico: The Diary of Susan Shelby Magoffin 1846–1847* (1926; reprint, Lincoln: University of Nebraska Press, 1982), 67 (6 August 1846).

—unpublished manuscript

Sallie Glasscock Giberson (1884–1966), "A Record of My Family," unpublished journal and scrapbook, p. 71, in possession of her great-niece, Gay E. Carter, Houston, Texas.

—shortened form

Giberson, "A Record of My Family," 113.

Land grant or patent (state)

—document first

Conditional headright certificate of Isaac Croom, 2 December 1839, file NAC-3-527, Texas General Land Office, Archives and Records Division, Austin.

—name first

Isaac Croom, conditional headright certificate, 2 December 1839, file NAC-3-527, . . .

—shortened form

Isaac Croom, Texas General Land Office, file NAC-3-527.

Land patent file (federal)

—document first, with specific part of file cited

"Affidavit for Actual Settlement & Cultivation," dated 4 January 1860, in land entry case file 16123 of Michael Rosto, patented 1 October 1860, Natchitoches land office, Records of the Bureau of Land Management, Record Group 49, National Archives, Washington.

—name first

Michael Rosto, land entry case file 16123, 1 October 1860, Natchitoches land office, Records of the Bureau of Land Management, Record Group 49, National Archives, Washington.

—shortened form
> Rosto, land entry case file 16123.

Land patent index (federal)
—document first
> U.S. General Land Office, *Automated Records Project; Pre-1908 Homestead & Cash Entry Patents: Louisiana,* CD-ROM (Springfield, VA: Bureau of Land Management, Eastern States Office, 1993), Natchitoches land office (#04), William Robinson entry, land in S35 T15N R16W, certificate no. 2304, recorded 1 January 1846.

—name first
> William Robinson entry, U.S. General Land Office, *Automated Records Project; Pre-1908 Homestead & Cash Entry Patents: Louisiana,* CD-ROM (Springfield, VA: Bureau of Land Management, Eastern States Office, 1993), Natchitoches land office (#04), land in S35 T15N R16W, certificate no. 2304, recorded 1 January 1846.

—shortened form
> William Robinson, certificate 2304, Natchitoches land office, GLO, *Pre-1908 . . . Patents: Louisiana,* CD-ROM.

Lecture
—cited as author, title, date, location
> Mary McCampbell Bell, "Virginians on the Land: Patents, Probate, Taxes, Court Minute Books," lecture, 24 October 1998, Houston Genealogical Forum seminar, Houston, Texas, the compiler's notes.

Lecture tape
—cited as author, title, conference, location
> Eric G. Grundset, "17th Century Genealogical Research in Virginia: Special Sources & Indices," lecture at National Genealogical Society annual conference, Jacksonville, Florida, 1992, tape F116 (Hobart, IN: Repeat Performance, 1992).

Legal case
(See also divorce record above.)
—in minutes book, county level, with note
> *The State vs. Guilford Heath* (on charge of bigamy), Putnam County, Georgia, Superior Court Minutes, 1829–1839, March term of court, 1832, FHL microfilm 0400927; pages are unnumbered, but terms are dated; since any surviving records from this court from this period are in storage, not catalogued, and not readily accessible, the minutes may be the only information available on the case.

—shortened form
> *State vs. Guilford Heath,* Putnam County, Georgia, Superior Court, 1832.

Map
—in the order of a book with author (based on Mills)

Henry F. Walling, *Map of the town of Haverhill, Essex County, Mass.* (n.p.: A.B. Jacques, 1851), facsimile copy by unnamed publisher, 24″×29″, map no. Mass 5-1, at Clayton Library, Center for Genealogical Research, Houston, Texas.

—state map

Alabama Department of Archives and History, *Historic Roads and Trails* (Montgomery: State of Alabama Highway Department, 1975), 18″×24″, from Alabama Department of Transportation, 1409 Coliseum Blvd., Montgomery, AL 36130.

—county map

General Highway Map, Maury County, Tennessee (Nashville: Tennessee Department of Transportation, 1991), 18″×24″, from Tennessee D.O.T., James K. Polk Bldg., Suite 300, 505 Deaderick St., Nashville, TN 37243.

—shortened form

General Highway Map, Maury County, Tennessee.

—topographic map

Kendleton Quadrangle, Texas, topographic map, 7.5 minute series, U.S. Department of the Interior, U.S. Geological Survey, photo-revised 1981.

Marriage notice, newspaper
—document first

Marriage notice, S.H. Holmes and Nannie Brelsford, *Gonzales (Texas) Inquirer*, 10 December 1887, p. 3.

—name first

Holmes-Brelsford marriage notice, *Gonzales (Texas) Inquirer*, 10 December 1887, p. 3.

Marriage record, church
See Church vital record above.

Marriage record, county level
—document first

Marriage record of William Augustus Lowe and Rutha Ann Bennett, 5 October 1849, Natchitoches Parish, Louisiana, Notarial Record Book 41:48, Parish Clerk's Office, Courthouse, Natchitoches.

—names first

Lowe-Bennett marriage record, 5 October 1849, Natchitoches Parish, Louisiana, Notarial Record Book 41:48, . . . [same as above].

—original document

Marriage license of Bryant Bennett and Alice Carter, 2 February 1898, Natchitoches Parish, Louisiana, file of original licenses that survived a 1933 fire, Natchitoches Historical and Genealogical Society Library, Old Courthouse, Natchitoches.

—on microfilm

Robertson-Williams marriage record, 12 May 1836, Putnam County, Georgia, Marriage Book D:259, FHL microfilm 0394053.

—shortened form

Lowe-Bennett marriage record, Natchitoches Parish, Notarial Record Book 41:48.

Membership application, lineage society

—footnote (DAR format)

Membership application of Donna Jean Wilson (103778) on Elliott G. Coleman (c.1764–1823, Virginia), National Society, Children of the American Revolution, Office of the Registrar General, Washington, DC, n.d., copy sent to author by preparer, Thyrza McCollum, about 1971.

—shortened form

Membership application of Donna Jean Wilson (103778), NSCAR.

Military bounty land or pension application

See Pension below.

Military discharge record

—document first, public record

World War I military discharge, William Taylor Oldham (private, serial no. 1034675), Discharge Records, 1:375, County Clerk's Office, Courthouse, Franklin, Robertson County, Texas.

—name first, private family record

Isaac Heldreth, Civil War military discharge (private, Co. B, First Regiment of Engineers, Missouri Volunteers), original once in possession of his son, Frank Smith Heldreth, copy in possession of Dory (Heldreth) Graham, Houston, Texas.

Military service record

—name first, published record

Stephen J. Ford, compiled military service record (private, sergeant, Co. K, 1st Louisiana Cavalry), in Andrew Bradford Booth, comp., *Records of Louisiana Confederate Soldiers and Louisiana Confederate Commands*, 3 vols. in 4 (New Orleans: n.p., 1920), 2:893.

—name first, unpublished record

William T. Walter, compiled military service record (private, Co. K, 22nd Mississippi Infantry), *Compiled Service Records of Confederate Soldiers Who Served in Organizations from the State of Mississippi*, National Archives microfilm M269, roll 307 (22nd Infantry, S-We).

—shortened form (Mills)

William T. Walter, *Compiled Service Records . . . Confederate . . . Mississippi*, roll 307.

—shortened form, alternate

William T. Walter, compiled military service record.

Naturalization record
—document first

Petition for naturalization of Benjamin Wolf, 3 October 1911, Superior Court of Berkshire County, Massachusetts, Vol. 4, no. 422, Clerk of the Court, Courthouse, 76 East St., Pittsfield, MA 01201.

—name first

John Shannon, petition for naturalization, September court, 1832, Putnam County, Georgia, Superior Court Minutes, 1829–1839, pages unnumbered but terms of court dated, FHL microfilm 0400927.

—shortened form

John Shannon, petition for naturalization, Putnam County, Georgia.

Passenger list
—document first

Passenger Lists of Vessels Arriving at Baltimore, 1820–1891, list no. 110, arrivals 31 August 1847, on ship *Stephen Lurman* from Bremen, lines 8–13, Andrew Schmidt and family, National Archives microfilm M255, roll 6, FHL microfilm 0417388.

—name first

Andrew Schmidt and family, arrivals in Baltimore, 31 August 1847, on ship *Stephen Lurman* from Bremen, passenger list no. 110, lines 8–13, in Passenger Lists of Vessels Arriving at Baltimore, 1820–1891, National Archives microfilm M255, roll 6, FHL microfilm 0417388.

—shortened form, name first

Andrew Schmidt, passenger list no. 110 (1847), arrivals at Baltimore.

Pension application (state, Confederate)
—document first

"Widow's Application for Confederate Pension," no. 41387, for Elizabeth N. Shelby, 8 June 1925, Texas State Archives, Austin.

—name first

A. S. Coleman, Confederate pension application, no. 05762, 26 June 1899, Texas State Archives, Austin.

—name first

Elizabeth N. Shelby, "Widow's Application for Confederate Pension," no. 41387, 8 June 1925, Texas State Archives, Austin.

—shortened form

Elizabeth N. Shelby, "Widow's Application for Confederate Pension," no. 41387, Texas.

Pension and bounty land application (federal, military)
—document first

Revolutionary War pension application of John Blakeney (private, North Carolina), W2716, and Nancy Blakeney, his widow, BLWt 34506-160-55, Revolutionary War Pension and Bounty Land Warrant Application Files,

1800–1900, Records of the Veterans Administration, Record Group 15, National Archives, Washington, DC.

—name first (Mills and National Archives)

John Blakeney Revolutionary War pension application (private, North Carolina), W2716, Revolutionary War Pension and Bounty Land Warrant Application Files, 1800–1900, Records of the Veterans Administration, Record Group 15, National Archives, Washington.

—shortened form (Mills)

John Blakeney pension application, no. W2716, Veterans Administration, National Archives.

—shortened form, alternate

John Blakeney, Revolutionary War pension application, no. W2716.

Polling (voting) list

—document first

Poll Book, presidential election, 4 November 1868, First District, Caldwell County, Kentucky, p. 3, County Clerk's Office, Courthouse, Princeton.

—name first

Stephen Trent entry, poll for members to Congress, 24 April 1809, Cumberland County, Virginia, Deed Book 11:204, County Clerk's Office, Courthouse, Cumberland.

—shortened form

Poll Book, 1868, First District, Caldwell County, Kentucky.

Probate file, county record

—document first

Bill of Dr. C. McGarity to estate of E.G. Coleman, 1892, probate case 354, Hays County, Texas, County Clerk's Office, Courthouse, San Marcos.

—name first

Lizzie Brady, bill to estate of E.G. Coleman, 1892, probate case 354, Hays County, Texas, County Clerk's Office, Courthouse, San Marcos.

—shortened form

Lizzie Brady, Coleman estate, probate case 354, Hays County, Texas.

—shortened form, depending on the text being cited

Coleman estate, probate case 354, Hays County, Texas.

Probate file, microfilm

—document first

Temporary letters of administration for Isaac Robertson, administrator of Zachariah Robinson, 1818, probate file 105R, Putnam County, Georgia, FHL microfilm 03994042.

—name first

William Eakin, guardian, probate file 106R (1820), estate of James T. Robinson, Putnam County, Georgia, FHL microfilm 0394042.

—shortened form

James T. Robinson estate, probate file 106R, Putnam County, Georgia.

Probate file, other than death record

—document first

Record of insanity and arrest of Ora Shelby, 28 April 1911, case no. 1304, file 39, Probate Court files, Robertson County, Texas, County Clerk's Office, Courthouse, Franklin.

—name first

T.O. Shelby, appointment as guardian, May 1914, case 1441, file 43, Probate Court files, Robertson County, Texas, County Clerk's Office, Courthouse, Franklin.

—shortened form

T.O. Shelby, probate case 1441, file 43, Robertson County, Texas.

Serial Set document

—document first

Petition of Alfred Moore and Sterling Orgain, Senate Document 34 (18th Congress, 1st session), Vol. 2, Serial 90.

—name first

Alfred Moore and Sterling Orgain, petition and supporting documents, Senate Document 34 . . . [continue as above]

—shortened form, using standard Serial Set format

Moore and Orgain, S.doc. 34 (18-1) 90.

Social Security application

—document first

Social Security Application (SS-5) of Alfred Thomas King, 28 November 1936, microprint copy from Freedom of Information Office, Social Security Administration, Baltimore, Maryland, copy in author's possession.

—name first

Alfred Thomas King, Social Security Application (SS-5), 28 November 1936, . . . [continue as above]

—shortened form

Alfred Thomas King, Social Security Application.

Tax roll

—document first, original record

Tax roll for 1907, T.O. Shelby entry, City of Calvert, Levington Addition, block 115, lot 5, City Secretary's Office, City Hall, Calvert, Texas.

—name first, microfilm

George Nickerson entry, Tax Assessment Book, 1801, Dover, Kent County, Delaware, p. 42, FHL microfilm 0006497.

—shortened form

George Nickerson, 1801 tax assessment, Kent County, Delaware, p. 42.

Tombstone

—record first

Tombstone of Rebecca B. Cocke, Evergreen Cemetery, front section to right of gate, Vine at Red River Streets, Victoria, Texas, recorded by the author 18 June 1972.

—name first

Matilda W. Allison tombstone, Elmwood Cemetery, Owensboro, Kentucky, data copied by author, 11 July 1976.

—shortened form

Rebecca B. Cocke tombstone, Evergreen Cemetery, Victoria, Texas.

Vital registration in church record

See Church vital record above.

Vital registration, county or state level

See Birth record, Marriage record, and Death record, all above.

Will in probate file

—document first

Will of Chloe Allen, 23 June 1841, Putnam County, Georgia, Estate Records, case 46-A, frames 0198–0201, FHL microfilm 1832253.

—name first

Chloe Allen will, 23 June 1841, Putnam County, Georgia, . . . [continue as above]

—shortened form

Chloe Allen will, Putnam County, GA, frame 0198.

Will recorded in will book

—document first

Will of Elizabeth Daniel, dated 6 February 1800, probated 22 March 1802, Cumberland County, Virginia, Will Book 3:194, County Clerk's Office, Courthouse, Cumberland.

—document first

Will of Elizabeth Daniel (1800), Cumberland County . . .

[Note: Depending on the text being cited, you may not need the full dates.]

—source first

Cumberland County, Virginia, Will Book 3:194, will of Elizabeth Daniel, County Clerk's Office, Courthouse, Cumberland.

—name first (Mills)

Elizabeth Daniel will (1800), Cumberland County Will Book 3:194, County Clerk's Office, Courthouse, Cumberland, Virginia.

—shortened form, name first

Elizabeth Daniel will, Cumberland County, Virginia, Will Book 3:194.

World War I draft registration card

—document first

World War I draft registration card for Abe Goodman, 12 September 1918, Pittsfield, Massachusetts, National Archives microfilm M 1509, FHL microfilm no. 1674425.

—name first

    Abe Goodman, World War I draft registration card, 12 September
1918, . . . [continue as above]

—shortened form

    Abe Goodman, World War I draft registration card.

VI. SOURCES IN THE FAMILY

See chapter four.

VII. BIBLIOGRAPHY

General considerations:

Notes

- If you are writing a relatively short article, progress report, or family group
  sheet, you probably do not need a separate bibliography. Footnotes or
  endnotes may be quite sufficient.
- Bibliographies can make good master source lists, either on index cards
  or on sheets at the front or back of a file or notebook.
- Usually, a bibliography lists the general sources used and not the small
  details, such as page numbers or names of specific ancestors. Footnotes
  and endnotes give those details.
- If you are writing a book-length family history or long article or report,
  a bibliography is desirable as a master source list.
- Most style books use basically the same form for footnotes and bibliography except for punctuation. Elements in a footnote are usually separated
  by commas. Elements in a bibliography entry are separated by periods.
  Once you decide on your style, you can use your footnotes, such as the
  ones above, to create your bibliography entries.
- The example below illustrates part of a bibliography that came from a
  family history. The format was chosen to save space and to be convenient
  for the reader and the compiler to study. The first section of the bibliography is "Books and Articles Cited in the Text." The next section is "Letters
  and Interviews Cited in the Text." The third segment, part of which is
  shown below, is "Document Groups Cited in the Text." Documents were
  grouped by state for quick identification, and all census records were cited
  together.

Document Groups Cited in the Text [selected entries]

North Carolina

Jones County. Deeds. Book G. Microfilm 0386829. Family History Library.

North Carolina Marriages, 1741–1868. Microfiche. North Carolina Division
    of Archives and History. Raleigh.

North Carolina Wills, 1663–1789. Book RS. Office of the Secretary of State.
    North Carolina Division of Archives and History. Raleigh.

Tennessee

Bolivar Presbyterian Church Register. Transcript. Held by Mrs. Louise J. Mc-
Anulty (1972), Bolivar, Tennessee.

Crowder Cemetery. Whiteville, Tennessee. Headstone data recorded by author,
1972, 1997.

Death Certificates. Tennessee State Library and Archives. Nashville.

Fayette County. Inventory Book H. Microfilm 1003150. Family History
Library.

Hardeman County. Circuit Court. Minutes. Vol. 3. Court Clerk's Office. Courthouse. Bolivar.

Hardeman County. Executors and Administrators Settlements. Books 9-11.
County Clerk's Office. Courthouse. Bolivar.

Hardeman County. Marriages. Books A, 1, 3, 6–9, 11, 12, 14, 16. County
Clerk's Office. Courthouse. Bolivar.

*Records of the Assistant Commissioner for the State of Tennessee, Bureau of
Refugees, Freedmen, and Abandoned Lands, 1865–1869.* Record Group
105. National Archives microfilm M999. Roll 20-Indentures of Apprentice-
ship, 1865–1868, Hardeman County, Tennessee.

Texas

Coleman, Alfred S. Confederate Pension Application, no. 05762. Texas State
Archives. Austin.

Fannin County. Birth Records. Book 1. County Clerk's Office. Courthouse.
Bonham.

Hays County. Probate Records. Cases 256 and 354. County Clerk's Office.
Courthouse. San Marcos.

Virginia

Cumberland County. County Court Order Book, 1749–1751. Microfilm.
Library of Virginia. Richmond.

Cumberland County. Marriage Bonds. Photocopies. Library of Virginia, State
Archives. Richmond.

Census Records

U.S. Census of 1810. Population Schedule. National Archives microfilm M252.
Roll 40-Johnston County, NC. Roll 60-Chester County, SC. Roll 68-Cum-
berland County, VA.

U.S. Census of 1850. Agriculture Schedule. National Archives microfilm
T1135. Roll 1-Fayette County, TN. Roll 2-Hardeman County, TN.

U.S. Census of 1850. Free Schedule. National Archives microfilm M432. Roll
27-Johnson County, AR. Roll 377-Marshall County, MS. Roll 648-Warren
County, NC.

U.S. Census of 1850. Manufacturing Schedule. National Archives microfilm
T1132. Roll 4-Cumberland County, VA.

U.S. Census of 1850. Slave Schedule. National Archives microfilm M432. Roll 903-Fayette and Hardeman Counties, TN. Roll 986-Cumberland County, VA.

U.S. Census of 1850. Social Statistics. National Archives microfilm T1135. Roll 37-Hardeman County, TN.

U.S. Census of 1860. Mortality Schedule. National Archives microfilm T655. Roll 27-Hardeman County, TN.

U.S. Census of 1900. Population Schedule. National Archives microfilm T623. Roll 832-Washington County, MS. Roll 1568-Fayette County, TN. Roll 1615-Brown County, TX.

Endnotes

About the Citations

- The Family History Center in Salt Lake City, Utah, is called by its acronym, FHL.
- The National Archives and Records Administration in Washington, DC, is called simply National Archives. After the first citation, the abbreviation NARA (National Archives and Records Administration) is used.
- In citing census records from 1880 forward, *enumeration district* will be abbreviated *e.d.*
- All census records cited are the population or free schedules unless otherwise indicated.

Foreword

1 Agatha Christie, *Evil Under the Sun* (1941; reprint, New York: Berkley Books, 1991), 151.
2 Sir Arthur Conan Doyle, "The Adventure of the Missing Three-Quarter," *The Complete Sherlock Holmes* (Garden City, NY: Doubleday & Co., Inc., n.d.) 624.

Introduction

1 Doyle, "The Sign of Four," *The Complete Sherlock Holmes*, 123.
2 Doyle, "A Study in Scarlet," *The Complete Sherlock Holmes*, 37.
3 Agatha Christie, *The Mysterious Affair at Styles: Poirot's First Case* (1921; reprint, New York: Berkley Books, 1991), 171.

Chapter 1

1 Agatha Christie, "The Lemesurier Inheritance," *Hercule Poirot's Casebook* (New York: G.P. Putnam's Sons, 1984), 757.
2 Agatha Christie, *Elephants Can Remember* (New York: Berkley Books, 1984), 23.
3 Christie, "The King of Clubs," *Hercule Poirot's Casebook*, 771.
4 [Edgar Allan Poe], "The Purloined Letter," *Edgar Allan Poe Stories* (New York: Platt & Munk, 1961), 217.
5 Agatha Christie, "Problem at Sea," *The Regatta Mystery and Other Stories* (New York: Berkley Books, 1984), 212.
6 Christie, "The Kidnapped Prime Minister," *Hercule Poirot's Casebook*, 97.
7 Anita Blackmon, *Murder à la Richelieu* (1937), quoted in Jane Horning, comp., *The Mystery Lovers' Book of Quotations* (New York: The Mysterious Press, 1988), 22, #153.

8 Catherine Louisa Pirkis, "The Experiences of Loveday Brooke, Lady Detective: The Murder at Troyte's Hill" (1893), in Alan K. Russell, comp., *Rivals of Sherlock Holmes* (Secaucus NJ: Castle Books, 1978), 37–38.

9 Elliott Roosevelt, *The Hyde Park Murder* (New York: St. Martin's Press, 1985), 5.

10 Christie, "The Arcadian Deer," *Hercule Poirot's Casebook*, 456.

11 Josephine Tey, *The Daughter of Time* (New York: Collier Books, 1988), 120. Every genealogist should read this book.

12 Doyle, "The Adventure of the Veiled Lodger," *The Complete Sherlock Holmes*, 1096.

13 Tom and Ray Magliozzi, hosts of *Car Talk*, National Public Radio, 29 March 1997, KUHF radio, Houston, Texas. The Magliozzi brothers are sleuths of a different sort: car problems.

14 Agatha Christie, *The Clocks* (New York: Harper Paperbacks, 1991), 195. Readers will find a genealogical component in this story.

15 Doyle, "The Adventure of the Blue Carbuncle," *The Complete Sherlock Holmes*, 245.

Chapter 2

1 Agatha Christie, "Strange Jest," *Three Blind Mice and Other Stories* (New York: Dodd, Mead & Company, 1975), 97.

2 Christie, "The Tragedy at Marsdon Manor," *Hercule Poirot's Casebook*, 21.

3 Christie, "The Missing Will," *Hercule Poirot's Casebook*, 126.

4 Christie, "The Affair at the Victory Ball," *Hercule Poirot's Casebook*, 729.

5 Christie, "The Disappearance of Mr. Davenheim," *Hercule Poirot's Casebook*, 109.

6 Doyle, "The Adventure of the Sussex Vampire," *The Complete Sherlock Holmes*, 1034.

7 Ibid., 1037.

8 Peter J. Heck, *A Connecticut Yankee in Criminal Court: A Mark Twain Mystery* (New York: Berkley Prime Crime, 1996), 46.

9 Doyle, "The Hound of the Baskervilles," *The Complete Sherlock Holmes*, 669.

10 Christie, *The Clocks*, 140.

11 Doyle, "The Adventure of the Three Garridebs," *The Complete Sherlock Holmes*, 1047.

12 Heck, *A Connecticut Yankee in Criminal Court*, 218.

13 Ibid., 44–45.

14 Christie, "The Lernean Hydra," *Hercule Poirot's Casebook*, 433.

15 Christie, *Elephants Can Remember*, 129.

16 Doyle, "A Study in Scarlet," *The Complete Sherlock Holmes*, 38.

17 Pirkis, "The Murder at Troyte's Hill" (1893), in Russell, comp., *Rivals of Sherlock Holmes*, 45.

18 Peter Mark Roget, *Roget's International Thesaurus*, new ed., revised (New York: Thomas Y. Crowell Co., 1946), 303, note at #461; Bacon was an English philosopher and author.

19 Heck, *A Connecticut Yankee in Criminal Court*, 84.

Chapter 3

1 Phyllis Bentley, "Chain of Witnesses," *Ellery Queen's Mystery Magazine* (May 1954), in Horning, comp., *The Mystery Lovers' Book of Quotations*, 18, #126.

2 Heck, *A Connecticut Yankee in Criminal Court*, 59.

3 Ibid., 41–42.

4 Dorothy Sayers, "The Piscatorial Farce of the Stolen Stomach," *Lord Peter*, James Sandoe, comp. (New York: Avon Books, 1972), 190.

5 Sayers, "The Undignified Melodrama of the Bone of Contention," *Lord Peter*, 81.

6 Sayers, "The Fascinating Problem of Uncle Meleager's Will," *Lord Peter*, 35.

7 Agatha Christie, *Sleeping Murder* (New York: Bantam Books, 1977), 171; Reed was a main character in the novel.

8 Christie, *The Clocks*, 137.

9 [Poe], "The Murders in the Rue Morgue," *Edgar Allan Poe Stories*, 177.

10 Tey, *Daughter of Time*, 118.

11 Christie, *Elephants Can Remember*, 43.

12 Ibid., 28–30.

13 Christie, *The Clocks*, 180.

14 Nell Marion Nugent, ed., *Cavaliers and Pioneers: Abstracts of Virginia Land Patents and Grants, 1623–1800* (Richmond: Dietz Printing Co., 1934, Vol. 1; Richmond: Virginia State Library, 1977, 1979, 1992–, Vol. 2–3, 6–7); Dennis Ray Hudgins, ed., *Cavaliers and Pioneers: Abstracts of Virginia Land Patents and Grants, 1623–1800* (Richmond: Virginia Genealogical Society, 1994, Vol. 4–5).

15 Christie, *The Clocks*, 258.

16 Heck, *A Connecticut Yankee in Criminal Court*, 275.

17 U.S. Census of 1850, Natchitoches Parish, Louisiana, NARA microfilm M432, roll 233, p. 15, family 240, household of *Calep* Bennett.

18 U.S. Census of 1860, Natchitoches Parish, Louisiana, NARA microfilm M653, roll 414, p. 486, family 494, household of *Coley* Bennett.

19 Natchitoches Parish, Louisiana, Marriage Book 3:28, Bennett-Bennett marriage, Parish Clerk's Office, Courthouse, Natchitoches.

20 Natchitoches Parish, Louisiana, succession file 1463, Caleb Bennett, first dated 17 December 1866, Parish Clerk's Office, Courthouse, Natchitoches.

21 U.S. Census of 1900, Natchitoches Parish, Louisiana, NARA microfilm T623, roll 569, e.d. 81, sheet 22, family 441, household of John Bennett; Natchitoches Parish, Louisiana, Marriage Book 17:113, Ruth Ann Bennett to Ezra Carter, 30 January 1902.

22 Natchitoches Parish, Louisiana, Notarial Record 41:48, Bennett-Lowe marriage, Parish Clerk's Office, Courthouse, Natchitoches.

23 U.S. Census of 1850, Natchitoches Parish, Louisiana, p. 11, family 178, household of W.A. Low; the family was not shown in the index but was found by page-by-page reading of the parish.

24 U.S. Census of 1850, Natchitoches Parish, Louisiana, p. 15, family 239, household of Edmund Bennett; U.S. Census of 1860, Natchitoches Parish, Louisiana, p. 485, family 480, household of William Bennett (26); p. 495, family 591, household of William N. Bennett (27); the two households have the same names and middle initials of all members, the same ages for the wife and infant, similar ages for the other family members, the same occupation

(overseer) for William, the same birthplaces except for the wife, and similar amount of personal property; the neighbors are different in the two entries so it appears that the family may have moved.

25 U.S. Census of 1870, Grant Parish, Louisiana, NARA microfilm M593, roll 513, p. 130, family 101, household of Mitchel Rocheteau; U.S. Census of 1880, Grant Parish, Louisiana, NARA microfilm T9, roll 453, e.d. 67, sheet 2, family 27, household of Mitchel Roston.

26 U.S. Census of 1840, Talbot County, Georgia, NARA microfilm M704, roll 51, p. 228, household of Edmund Bennett; U.S. Census of 1830, Talbot County, Georgia, NARA microfilm M19, roll 20, p. 343, household of Edmund Bennett.

27 Natchitoches Parish, Louisiana, Miscellaneous Records, Book 44:411, Lowe-Rocherneau marriage.

28 U.S. Census of 1870, Grant Parish, Louisiana, p. 130, household of Mitchel Rocheteau.

29 U.S. Census of 1900, Grant Parish, Louisiana, NARA microfilm T623, roll 565, e.d. 67, sheet 2, family 27, household of Nicolas Lowe.

30 Land entry file 16263 for Michael Rosto, 1860, Pre-1908 Louisiana Land Entries, Natchitoches land office, Records of the Bureau of Land Management, Record Group 49, NARA; Land entry file 17236 for Edmund Bennett, 1860, Pre-1908 Louisiana Land Entries; Land entry file 16125 for Arthur Bennett, 1860, Pre-1908 Louisiana Land Entries.

31 U.S. Census of 1860, Natchitoches Parish, Louisiana, p. 488, family 575, household of Arthur Bennett.

32 Heck, *A Connecticut Yankee in Criminal Court*, 30, 41–42.

Chapter 4

1 Doyle, "The Adventure of Shoscombe Old Place," *The Complete Sherlock Holmes*, 1106.

2 Roosevelt, *The Hyde Park Murder*, 72.

3 Christie, "The Adventure of Johnnie Waverly," *Hercule Poirot's Casebook*, 645.

4 Christie, "The Disappearance of Mr. Davenheim," *Hercule Poirot's Casebook*, 102.

5 Elliott Roosevelt, *Murder and the First Lady* (New York: St. Martin's Press, 1984), 16.

6 Doyle, "A Study in Scarlet," *The Complete Sherlock Holmes*, 46.

7 Mary Roberts Rinehart, "The Buckled Bag," *Miss Pinkerton: Adventures of a Nurse Detective* (1914; reprint, New York: Rinehart & Co., 1959), 13.

Chapter 5

1 Tey, *Daughter of Time*, 89–91.

2 Christie, *Sleeping Murder*, 288.

3 Margaret Truman, *Murder in the White House* (New York: Arbor House, 1980), 36.

4 Christie, *The Clocks*, 253–254.

5 [Poe], "The Purloined Letter," *Edgar Allan Poe Stories*, 239.

6 Sayers, "The Vindictive Story of the Footsteps That Ran," *Lord Peter*, 148.

7 Christie, "The Under Dog," *Hercule Poirot's Casebook*, 673.

8 Elliott Roosevelt, *Murder in the East Room* (New York: St. Martin's Press, 1993), 140.

9 Truman, *Murder in the White House*, 32.

10 Heck, *A Connecticut Yankee in Criminal Court*, 54.

11 [Poe], "The Purloined Letter," *Edgar Allan Poe Stories*, 229.

12 Philip Dormer Stanhope, Earl of Chesterfield, 1746, in John Bartlett, *Familiar Quotations*, 13th and centennial ed. revised (Boston: Little, Brown and Co., 1955), 323a.

13 Cathryn Crawford, my high school English teacher for three years, Bellaire High School, Bellaire, Texas, who unraveled many mysteries of the English language for me and whose spirit hovers over me to this day as I write.

14 Christie, "The Arcadian Deer," *Hercule Poirot's Casebook*, 456.

15 Doyle, "The Sign of Four," *The Complete Sherlock Holmes*, 114.

16 Doyle, "The Adventure of the Mazarin Stone," *The Complete Sherlock Holmes*, 1014.

17 Christie, "The Plymouth Express," *Hercule Poirot's Casebook*, 724.

18 Doyle, "A Study in Scarlet," *The Complete Sherlock Holmes*, 30.

19 Roosevelt, *Murder and the First Lady*, 191.

20 Heck, *A Connecticut Yankee in Criminal Court*, 73.

21 Christie, "The Adventure of the Clapham Cook," *Hercule Poirot's Casebook*, 791.

22 Doyle, "The Adventure of the Speckled Band," *The Complete Sherlock Holmes*, 261.

23 Christie, *Sleeping Murder*, 252–253.

24 Truman, *Murder in the White House*, 36.

25 Tey, *Daughter of Time*, 146.

26 Heck, *A Connecticut Yankee in Criminal Court*, 220.

27 Christie, *Elephants Can Remember*, 129.

28 Doyle, "The Adventure of the Speckled Band," *The Complete Sherlock Holmes*, 269.

29 Heck, *A Connecticut Yankee in Criminal Court*, 31.

30 Doyle, "The Adventure of the Copper Beeches," *The Complete Sherlock Holmes*, 322.

31 John Dickson Carr, *The Arabian Nights Murder* (1936), in Horning, comp., *The Mystery Lovers' Book of Quotations*, 38, #261.

32 Charles A. Hanna, *Historical Collections of Harrison County, in the State of Ohio* (New York: privately printed, 1900), 419.

33 Harrison County, Ohio, Will Records, C:239, microfilm at Cadiz Public Library, Cadiz, Ohio.

34 Tey, *Daughter of Time*, 73.

35 Christie, *The Clocks*, 263.

36 [Poe], "The Murders in the Rue Morgue," *Edgar Allan Poe Stories*, introduction, 164.

37 [Poe], "The Purloined Letter," *Edgar Allan Poe Stories*, 221. The idea of the not-concealed-but-in-plain-view item also played a role in Dick Francis's *Straight* and Elliott Roosevelt's *Murder and the First Lady*.

38 Doyle, "The Resident Patient," *The Complete Sherlock Holmes*, 432.

39 Sayers, "The Vindictive Story of the Footsteps That Ran," *Lord Peter*, 138.

40 Doyle, "The Man With the Twisted Lip," *The Complete Sherlock Holmes*, 241.

41 Roosevelt, *Murder in the East Room*, 169.

42 H.C. Bailey, "The Little Dog," *Mr. Fortune's Casebook* (London, 1932), in John Ernst, ed., *Favorite Sleuths* (Garden City, NY: Doubleday & Co., 1965), 309.

43 Russell Cemetery, Bayou Derbanne, Montrose, Louisiana, and Pine Island Cemetery, Simpson, Louisiana, visited by author, 6 December 1998.

44 Christie, "In a Glass Darkly," *The Regatta Mystery and Other Stories*, 181.

45 Putnam County, Georgia, Deed Book P:233, FHL microfilm 0400941.

46 Irwin County, Georgia, Deed Book H:154, FHL microfilm 394615, index to deeds 1821–1900.

47 Jasper County, Missouri, Probate Court Minutes, Book B, 16 October 1852, FHL microfilm 0932616.

48 Cash entry file for Priscilla Speegle, certificate no. 12099 (1853), Springfield, Missouri, land office, for land in S27 and S28-T28N-R32W, Records of the General Land Office, Records of the Bureau of Land Management, Record Group 49, NARA, photocopy of file obtained from NARA.

49 Cumberland County, Virginia, Will Book 1:5, will of Daniel Johnson, microfilm from Library of Virginia, Richmond; all Cumberland County will and deed records hereafter cited are from Library of Virginia microfilm unless otherwise noted.

50 Archer Allen Bible Record, copied by Henry Archer Allen Jr. from Bible then in possession of William Archer Chambers of Richmond, Virginia, *William and Mary Quarterly*, Series 1, 22 (January 1914): 194–196.

51 [Poe], "The Purloined Letter," *Edgar Allan Poe Stories*, 225.

52 Roosevelt, *Murder in the East Room*, 107.

53 Elliott Roosevelt, *Murder in the Executive Mansion* (New York: St. Martin's Press, 1995), 21–22.

54 Roosevelt, *The Hyde Park Murder*, 135.

55 Doyle, "The Adventure of the Blue Carbuncle," *The Complete Sherlock Holmes*, 247.

56 U.S. Census of 1830, St. Joseph County, Michigan, NARA microfilm M19, roll 69, p. 180, household of Abiel Fellows.

57 Heck, *A Connecticut Yankee in Criminal Court*, 53.

58 U.S. Census of 1840, Maury County, Tennessee, 10th Civil District, NARA microfilm M704, roll 532, p. 323, line 26, household of Charles C. Frierson.

59 U.S. Census of 1850, Lafayette County, Mississippi, NARA microfilm M432, roll 375, p. 232, dwelling 109, household of Chas. C. Frierson.

60 U.S. Census of 1860, Lafayette County, Mississippi, NARA microfilm M653, roll 585, p. 107, dwelling 690, household of C. C. Frierson.

61 The Skipwith Historical and Genealogical Society, comp., *Lafayette County, Mississippi, Cemetery Records* ([Oxford, MS]: The Society, 1978), 1:39, tombstone inscription of Ada A. McClamrock, wife of Rev. S. McClamrock, College Hill Cemetery.

62 U.S. Census of 1840, Maury County, Tennessee, p. 323, line 2, household of Edwd. L. Frierson.

63 U.S. Census of 1850, Lafayette County, Mississippi, p. 232, dwelling 108, household of Edward L. Frierson.

64 U.S. Census of 1860, Lafayette County, Mississippi, p. 107, dwelling 691, household of Edward Frierson.

65 College Presbyterian Church Cemetery, College Hill Community, Lafayette County, Mississippi, data recorded by Gay E. Carter, October 1997.

66 Rinehart, "The Buckled Bag," *Miss Pinkerton*, 46.

67 Doyle, "A Study in Scarlet," *The Complete Sherlock Holmes*, 43.

68 Rinehart, "Miss Pinkerton," *Miss Pinkerton*, 199.

69 Gaius Marcus Brumbaugh, *Maryland Records: Colonial Revolutionary County and Church From Original Sources* (1915; reprint, Baltimore: Genealogical Publishing Co., 1967), 1:14.

70 Richard D. Mudd, *The Mudd Family of the United States* (Ann Arbor, MI: Edwards Brothers, Inc., 1951), 137–139.

71 Loudoun County, Virginia, Personal Property Tax Rolls, 1782–1816, pages unnumbered but years labeled, microfilm from Library of Virginia, Richmond.

72 Nelson County, Kentucky, Marriage Register 1:173, marriage of William Norton and Ezebel/Isabella Huston, solemnized 31 October 1810 by J. Ferguson; Nelson County, Kentucky, Tax Rolls, 1811, microfilm from the Kentucky State Archives.

73 Ruth Sparacio and Sam Sparacio, eds., *Will Abstracts of Loudoun County, Virginia, 1788–1793*, Virginia County Court Records (McLean, VA: The Antient Press, 1990), 61, Loudoun County, Virginia, Will Book D:254–256, will of Thomas Gregg Sr. dated 21 May 1792, probated 10 September 1792. One statement in the will was "my Wife is still to possess what she brought with her," which suggests she came to him as a widow.

74 Doyle, "A Study in Scarlet," *The Complete Sherlock Holmes*, 36.

75 Doyle, "A Case of Identity," *The Complete Sherlock Holmes*, 197.

Chapter 6

1 Rudyard Kipling, *From Sea to Sea: Letters of Travel* (New York: Doubleday & McClure, 1899), 2:180, from letter 37, an interview with Mark Twain.

2 H.C. Bailey, "The Little Dog," *Mr. Fortune's Casebook* (London: Ward Lock & Co., Ltd., 1932), reprinted in Ernst, ed., *Favorite Sleuths*, 288.

3 Paul Drake, *You Ought to Write All That Down: A Guide to Organizing and Writing Genealogical Narrative* (Bowie, MD: Heritage Books, Inc., 1998), 43.

4 Agatha Christie, "The Mirror Crack'd," *Five Complete Miss Marple Novels* (1962; reprint, New York: Avenel Books, 1980), 54, Inspector Dermot Craddock.

5 Paul Harding, *Red Slayer* (New York: Avon Books, 1994), 249; Father Anselm was the teacher of the fourteenth-century priest-detective Brother Athelstan.

6 Doyle, "A Case of Identity," *The Complete Sherlock Holmes*, 194.

7 Roosevelt, *Murder in the Executive Mansion*, 110.

8 Elsa Barker, *The C.I.D. of Dexter Drake* (1929), quoted in Horning, comp., *The Mystery Lovers' Book of Quotations*, 13, #92.

9 Doyle, "The Adventure of the Three Garridebs," *The Complete Sherlock Holmes*, 1045.

10 Ibid., 1051.

11 G.K. Chesterton, "The Queer Feet," *Father Brown Mystery Stories* (reprint, New York: Dodd, Mead & Co., 1966), 52, 51.

12 Christie, *The Mysterious Affair at Styles*, 35.

13 Rinehart, "The Buckled Bag," *Miss Pinkerton*, 13.

14 Christie, "Four-and-Twenty Blackbirds," *Hercule Poirot's Casebook*, 658.

15 Christie, "Miss Marple Tells a Story," *The Regatta Mystery and Other Stories*, 129–130.

16 Doyle, "A Study in Scarlet," *The Complete Sherlock Holmes*, 32.

17 Christie, *The Clocks*, 255.

18 Doyle, "The Adventure of the Blanched Soldier," *The Complete Sherlock Holmes*, 1011.

19 Doyle, "The Boscombe Valley Mystery," *The Complete Sherlock Holmes*, 204.

20 Rinehart, "Miss Pinkerton," *Miss Pinkerton*, 156.

21 Christie, "The Affair at the Victory Ball," *Hercule Poirot's Casebook*, 738.

22 [Poe], "The Purloined Letter," *Edgar Allan Poe Stories*, 216.

23 Christie, *The Mysterious Affair at Styles*, 34.

24 Doyle, "The Hound of the Baskervilles," *The Complete Sherlock Holmes*, 683.

25 Doyle, "The Sign of Four," *The Complete Sherlock Holmes*, 135.

26 Truman, *Murder in the White House*, 36.

27 Roosevelt, *Murder in the Executive Mansion*, 141.

28 Rinehart, "Miss Pinkerton," *Miss Pinkerton*, 143.

29 Christie, *The Mysterious Affair at Styles*, 114.

30 Heck, *A Connecticut Yankee in Criminal Court*, 29.

31 Doyle, "The Adventure of the Norwood Builder," *The Complete Sherlock Holmes*, 503.

32 Christie, *The Mysterious Affair at Styles*, 111.

33 Tey, *Daughter of Time*, 172.

34 [Poe], "The Murders in the Rue Morgue," *Edgar Allan Poe Stories*, 184–185.

35 Erle Stanley Gardner, "The Case of the Demure Defendant," *The Perry Mason Omnibus* (1955; reprint, New York: William Morrow & Co., n.d.), 463.

36 Doyle, "The Adventure of the Speckled Band," *The Complete Sherlock Holmes*, 273.

37 Christie, "Nemesis," *Five Complete Miss Marple Novels*, 330.

38 Anthony Berkeley, *Trial and Error* (1937), quoted in Horning, comp., *The Mystery Lovers' Book of Quotations*, 19, #130.

39 Christie, "The King of Clubs," *Hercule Poirot's Casebook*, 774.

40 Christie, *The Mysterious Affair at Styles*, 112.

41 Christie, *The Clocks*, 135.

42 Douglas Adams, *Dirk Gently's Holistic Detective Agency* (1987), quoted in Horning, comp., *The Mystery Lovers' Book of Quotations*, 1, #5.

43 Christie, "The Veiled Lady," *Hercule Poirot's Casebook*, 134.

44 Rinehart, "Miss Pinkerton," *Miss Pinkerton*, 136.

45 Heck, *A Connecticut Yankee in Criminal Court*, 28.

46 Rinehart, "Miss Pinkerton," *Miss Pinkerton*, 109.

47 Pirkis, "The Murder at Troyte's Hill" (1893), in Russell, comp., *Rivals of Sherlock Holmes*, 46.

48 Christie, "The Mirror Crack'd," *Five Complete Miss Marple Novels*, 41.

49 [Poe], "The Murders in the Rue Morgue," *Edgar Allan Poe Stories*, 198.

50 Christie, "The Mirror Crack'd," *Five Complete Miss Marple Novels*, 121.

51 Christie, "How Does Your Garden Grow?" *The Regatta Mystery and Other Stories*, 68.

52 Truman, *Murder in the White House*, 174.

53 Christie, "The Adventure of Johnnie Waverly," *Hercule Poirot's Casebook*, 647.

54 Roosevelt, *The Hyde Park Murder*, 73.

55 Doyle, "The Adventure of the Veiled Lodger," *The Complete Sherlock Holmes*, 1101.

56 Christie, "The Capture of Cerberus," *Hercule Poirot's Casebook*, 611.

57 Truman, *Murder in the White House*, 64.

58 Christie, "How Does Your Garden Grow?" *The Regatta Mystery and Other Stories*, 71.

59 Doyle, "The Adventure of the Golden Pince-Nez," *The Complete Sherlock Holmes*, 608.

60 Sue Grafton, *"A" Is for Alibi* (New York: Holt, Rinehart and Winston, 1982), 20.

61 Doyle, "A Scandal in Bohemia," *The Complete Sherlock Holmes*, 163.

62 Sayers, "The Vindictive Story of the Footsteps That Ran," *Lord Peter*, 148.

63 Tey, *Daughter of Time*, 123.

64 Christie, "Dead Man's Mirror," *Hercule Poirot's Casebook*, 210.

65 Doyle, "The Sign of Four," *The Complete Sherlock Holmes*, 114.

66 Christie, *The Mysterious Affair at Styles*, 77.

67 Doyle, "The Adventure of Black Peter," *The Complete Sherlock Holmes*, 570.

68 Christie, "The Mystery of the Bagdad Chest," *The Regatta Mystery and Other Stories*, 45.

69 Christie, "The Mirror Crack'd," *Five Complete Miss Marple Novels*, 132.

70 Heck, *A Connecticut Yankee in Criminal Court*, 276.

71 Doyle, "The Adventure of the Norwood Builder," *The Complete Sherlock Holmes*, 502.

72 Rinehart, "Miss Pinkerton," *Miss Pinkerton*, 197.

73 Ibid., 167.

74 Bartlett, *Familiar Quotations*, 897b.

75 Doyle, "The Reigate Puzzle," *The Complete Sherlock Holmes*, 407.

76 Doyle, "The Naval Treaty," *The Complete Sherlock Homes*, 467–468.

77 Christie, *The Mysterious Affair at Styles*, 35.

78 Truman, *Murder in the White House*, 36.

79 Tey, *Daughter of Time*, 160.

80 Doyle, "The Adventure of the Blanched Soldier," *The Complete Sherlock Holmes*, 1066.

81 Doyle, "The Sign of Four," *The Complete Sherlock Holmes*, 110.

82 Roosevelt, *The Hyde Park Murder*, 76.

83 Heck, *A Connecticut Yankee in Criminal Court*, 61.

84 Ibid., 226.

85 Roosevelt, *Murder and the First Lady*, 187.

86 Christie, "The Mirror Crack'd," *Five Complete Miss Marple Novels*, 143.

87 Tey, *Daughter of Time*, 85–86.

88 Roosevelt, *Murder in the East Room*, 169.

89 Standard line of Sergeant Joe Friday, *Dragnet*, radio and television show.

90 Doyle, "The Adventure of the Blanched Soldier," *The Complete Sherlock Holmes*, 1011.

91 Erle Stanley Gardner, "The Case of the Crying Swallow" (1947) in Ernst, ed., *Favorite Sleuths*, 283.

92 Truman, *Murder in the White House*, 198.

93 Tey, *Daughter of Time*, 133.

94 Christie, "The Mirror Crack'd," *Five Complete Miss Marple Novels*, 111.

95 Christie, *The Clocks*, 135.

96 Doyle, "The Adventure of Black Peter," *The Complete Sherlock Holmes*, 568.

97 H.C. Bailey, "The Little Dog," *Mr. Fortune's Casebook*, in Ernst, ed., *Favorite Sleuths*, 299.

98 Doyle, "The Adventure of the Noble Bachelor," *The Complete Sherlock Holmes*, 294.

99 Blandford Church, Petersburg, Virginia, visited by the author, June 1973.

100 Petersburg, Virginia, Hustings Court, Will Book 2 (1805–1827):91, will of William Harrison, FHL microfilm 0033402.

101 Ibid., 2:117.

102 Letter to author from Mrs. Marie M. Barnett, Librarian, Grand Lodge of Virginia, Richmond, Virginia, 31 January 1992.

103 Petersburg City, Virginia, Land Tax Rolls, 1788–1817, microfilm from Library of Virginia, dates for 1801, 1803, 1807 appear on the first frame of each year, frame 589 (1813 entry for Harrison), frame 613 (1814 for Harrison estate), all entries in earlier years appear alphabetically by surname, Harrison's entries on frames 377, 393, 416, 442, 491, 516, 539, 565.

104 Petersburg City, Virginia, Personal Property Tax Rolls, 1800–1833, microfilm from the Library of Virginia, names roughly alphabetical under each year, dates varying at the beginning or end of the lists, Harrison's entries of 1813 and 1814 on frames 403 and 431 respectively.

105 Christie, "The Italian Nobleman," *Hercule Poirot's Casebook*, 121.

Chapter 7

1 Christie, "The Plymouth Express," *Hercule Poirot's Casebook*, 724.

2 Doyle, "A Study in Scarlet," *The Complete Sherlock Holmes*, 43.

3 Christie, "The Adventure of Johnnie Waverly," *Hercule Poirot's Casebook*, 647.

4 Tey, *Daughter of Time*, 142.

5 Ibid., 133.

6 Heck, *A Connecticut Yankee in Criminal Court*, 93.

7 Rinehart, "The Buckled Bag," *Miss Pinkerton*, 10.

8 Christie, *The Mysterious Affair at Styles*, 155.

9 Doyle, "The Greek Interpreter," *The Complete Sherlock Holmes*, 436.

10 Doyle, "A Study in Scarlet," *The Complete Sherlock Holmes*, 44.

11 Tey, *Daughter of Time*, 168.

12 Cumberland County, Virginia, Will Book 4:43, will of William Coleman, photocopy from County Clerk's Office, Courthouse, Cumberland.

13 Ibid., Book 4:307.

14 Cumberland County, Virginia, Personal Property Tax Rolls, 1782–1836, for the year 1811, pages unnumbered, microfilm, Library of Virginia, Richmond, hereafter cited as Cumberland County Personal Property Tax Rolls.

15 William Waller Hening, *Statutes at Large, Laws of Virginia* (Philadelphia PA: 1823), 12:143 (1785).

16 U.S. Census of 1850, Cumberland County, Virginia, NARA microfilm M432, roll 941, p. 285, family 41, household of Ferdinand G. Coleman; U.S. Census of 1860, Cumberland County, Virginia, NARA microfilm M653, roll 1341, p. 973, household of F.G. Coleman.

17 U.S. Census of 1820, Cumberland County, Virginia, NARA microfilm M33, roll 130, p. 99 (p. 347), Ferdinand G. Coleman, single; U.S. Census of 1830, Cumberland County, Virginia, NARA microfilm M19, roll 192, p. 185, household of Ferdinand G. Coleman.

18 U.S. Census of 1840, Cumberland County, Virginia, NARA microfilm M704, roll 554, p. 7, household of Ferdinand G. Coleman.

19 Cumberland County Personal Property Tax Rolls, 1815.

20 Cumberland County, Virginia, Land Tax Rolls, 1782–1824, for the year 1812, pages unnumbered, microfilm, Library of Virginia, Richmond, hereafter cited as Cumberland County Land Tax Rolls.

21 Hening, *Statutes at Large*, 12:193 (1785).

22 Cumberland County, Virginia, Marriage Bonds, file 1789–32, Library of Virginia, Richmond, photocopy in author's possession.

23 Hening, *Statutes at Large*, 6:83 (1748).

24 Cumberland County Personal Property Tax Rolls, 1782–1787.

25 Cumberland County, Virginia, Will Book 4:43, will of William Coleman.

26 Cumberland County Personal Property Tax Rolls, 1804.

27 Cumberland County, Virginia, Deed Book 10:15, polling list, April 1805.

28 Cumberland County, Virginia, Will Book 2:4, will of Daniel Coleman, dated 29 August 1763, probated 22 January 1770.

29 Sherrianne Coleman Nicol, *The Coleman Family of Mobjack Bay, Virginia* (Bradenton, FL: the author, 1998), 2:486, giving the birth year for William, son of Daniel Jr., as 1752.

30 Cumberland County, Virginia, Will Book 2:41, will of Patience Coleman, dated 18 July 1771, probated 26 August 1771.

31 Cumberland County Personal Property Tax Rolls, 1782.

32 U.S. Census of 1820, Cumberland County, Virginia, NARA microfilm M33, roll 130, p. 100, household of Gulielmus Coleman.

33 Cumberland County, Virginia, Will Book 7:204, will of Elene [Eleanor] Coleman, dated 24 September 1823, probated 24 February 1824; Will Book 8:709, estate settlement, 1830; Cumberland County, Virginia, Deed Book 11:23 (Gulielmus Coleman to "his son Edward Turner Coleman"), 25 (Gulielmus Coleman to William Guthrey), both September 1807.

34 Laurence R. Guthrie, *American Guthrie and Allied Families* (Chambersburg, PA: n.pub., 1933), 523, family chart submitted by Gulielmus's descendant, Judge Benjamin W. Coleman, giving this Elizabeth's birthdate as 25 August 1783 and her husband as William Guthrie/Guthrey, and also giving Eleanor's father's name, Thomas Turner.

35 Cumberland County, Virginia, Deed Book 11:23, Gulielmus Coleman to Edward Turner Coleman.

36 Hening, *Statutes at Large*, 12:141 (1785).

37 Cumberland County, Virginia, Deed Book 11:204, polling list for 24 April 1809.

38 Hening, *Statutes at Large*, 12:120 (1785), voting qualifications.

39 Cumberland County Land Tax Rolls, 1810.

40 Katherine B. Elliott, *Marriage Records, 1749–1840, Cumberland County, Virginia* (South Hill, VA: [the author], 1969), 34.

41 Cumberland County, Virginia, Will Book 2:41, will of Patience Coleman.

42 Cumberland County Personal Property Tax Rolls, 1784.

43 Cumberland County, Virginia, Will Book 8:815.

44 Cumberland County Personal Property Tax Rolls, 1784–1789, 1791, 1793–1797.

45 Cumberland County, Virginia, Deed Book 4:54 (Eli Noell to Daniel Coleman, 170 acres on Bear Creek and south side of Willis River, 1765) and 349

(Thomas Coleman to William Coleman, 170 acres on Barr Creek, with similar adjoining neighbors).

46 Cumberland County Personal Property Tax Roll, 1788.

47 Christie, "The Body in the Library," *Five Complete Miss Marple Novels*, 646.

Chapter 8

1 Tey, *Daughter of Time*, 163.

2 Manning Coles, "Handcuffs Don't Hold Ghosts," *Nothing to Declare* (1946), in Ernst, ed., *Favorite Sleuths*, 213, Chief Superintendent Bagshott of Scotland Yard.

3 Doyle, "A Study in Scarlet," *The Complete Sherlock Holmes*, 43.

4 Bartlett, *Bartlett's Familiar Quotations*, 121b, from *Of Studies*.

5 Doyle, "The Sign of Four," *The Complete Sherlock Holmes*, 119.

6 Doyle, "The Adventure of Charles Augustus Milverton," *The Complete Sherlock Holmes*, 582.

7 Christie, "The Kidnapped Prime Minister," *Hercule Poirot's Casebook*, 96.

8 Doyle, "The Hound of the Baskervilles," *The Complete Sherlock Holmes*, 670.

Chapter 9

1 Christie, "The Kidnapped Prime Minister," *Hercule Poirot's Casebook*, 94.

2 Frank Smith Heldreth, *The Heldreth Family History* (the compiler: typescript, ongoing project, 1940s to 1960s, as births, marriages, and deaths occurred in the families of Isaac Heldreth's children), 1, booklet in possession of Dory (Heldreth) Graham, Houston, Texas.

3 Christie, *Sleeping Murder*, 36.

4 Heldreth, *Heldreth Family History*, 1.

5 Civil War military discharge for Isaac Heldreth (private, Co. B, First Regiment of Engineers, Missouri Volunteers, Union), original once in possession of his son Frank Smith Heldreth, copy in possession of Dory (Heldreth) Graham.

6 Heldreth, *Heldreth Family History*, 1.

7 Tey, *Daughter of Time*, 96.

8 Isaac Heldreth, death certificate no. A6545, Scott County, Iowa, Death Records, Book 10:31, County Clerk's Office, Davenport; Heldreth, *Heldreth Family History*, 1.

9 Rinehart, "Miss Pinkerton," *Miss Pinkerton*, 111.

10 Ibid., 118.

11 U.S. Census of 1870, Pike County, Illinois, Chambersburg, NARA microfilm M593, roll 269, p. 59, line 21 (Isaac Heldreth); p. 53B, family/dwelling 110 (Nancy Hildreth) and 112 (John Winegar).

12 Earle H. Morris, ed., *Marriage Records, Harrison County Virginia (West Virginia) 1784–1850* (Ft. Wayne, IN: Ft. Wayne Public Library, 1966), 149; Wes Cochran, *Harrison County West Virginia Marriages, 1785–1894* (Parkersburg, WV: the author, 1985), 64 (gives date as 21 December *1827*).

13 U.S. Census of 1900, Pike County, Illinois, Griggsville, NARA microfilm T623, roll 337, e.d. 115, sheet 7 (p. 107), line 20, Isaac Heldreth, age 60; U.S. Census of 1910, McDonough County, Illinois, Colchester, NARA microfilm T624, roll 305, e.d. 47, sheet 6, family 379, household of Isaac Heldreth, age 70; U.S. Census of 1920, Scott County, Iowa, Davenport, NARA microfilm T625, roll 513, e.d. 170, sheet 21, line 4, Isaac Heldreth, age 80; the 1910 and 1920 were read when they became available.

14 Heck, *A Connecticut Yankee in Criminal Court*, 305.

15 U.S. Census of 1850, Greenup County, Kentucky, NARA microfilm M432, roll 202, p. 223, dwelling 84, family 86, household of Uriah Hildreth.

16 Family Quest Archives, *Illinois 1870 Census Index*, CD-ROM, #ACD-0013 (Bountiful, UT: Heritage Quest, 1998), surname Hildreth, 31 hits.

17 Doyle, "The Adventure of the Creeping Man," *The Complete Sherlock Holmes*, 1076.

18 Harrison County, West Virginia, Marriage Book 1:39, Uriah Heldreth-Nancy Nutter, marriage license 18 December 1826, solemnization 21 December 1826 by Jesse Flowers, J.P., County Clerk's Office, Courthouse, Clarksburg.

19 Deed of trust, Uriah Hildreth to Jesse Cain, Wood County, (West) Virginia, Deed Book 12:406–407 (12 September 1842), County Clerk's Office, Courthouse, Parkersburg; Uriah Hildreth, grantee, in Willard Rouse Jillson, comp., *The Kentucky Land Grants: A Systematic Index to All of the Land Grants Recorded in the State Land Office at Frankfort, Kentucky, 1782–1924* (1925; reprint, Baltimore: Genealogical Publishing Company, 1971), Vol. 1, Part 2, Chapter X (Grants in the County Court Orders, 1836–1924), p. 1345, survey date 23 December 1844, 50 acres in Greenup County.

20 U.S. Census of 1850, Greenup County, Kentucky, p. 223, household of Uriah Hildreth; U.S. Census of 1870, Pike County, Illinois, p. 53, household of Nancy Hildreth; U.S. Census of 1860, Daviess County, Missouri, Salem Township, NARA microfilm M653, roll 617, p. 419, family 125, household of Nancy Hildreth; William Hildreth tombstone, Brown Cemetery, Chambersburg, Pike County, Illinois, gives his birth date as 4 April 1844.

21 Harrison County, Virginia, Will Book 4:391, Frazier Heldreth will (dated 11 May 1831, recorded 5 November 1831), County Clerk's Office, Courthouse, Clarksburg.

22 U.S. Census of 1830, Harrison County, Virginia, NARA microfilm M19, roll 190, p. 364 (all four families).

23 U.S. Census of 1840, Wood County, Virginia, NARA microfilm M704, roll 579, p. 152, household of Uriah Heldrett.

24 Sayers, "The Vindictive Story of the Footsteps That Ran," *Lord Peter*, 150.

25 Frances Terry Ingmire, *Greenup County, Kentucky, Death Records*, Kentucky Vital Records, Series 3, Vol. 45 (St. Louis, MO: the author, 1985), 2 (Uriah Hildreth entry).

26 U.S. Census of 1860, Daviess County, Missouri, p. 419, family 125, household of Nancy Hildreth, living near a married Hildreth daughter, Lavina, and her husband Boon Eldridge, family 134, which included a son Uriah; Lavina Hildreth and Richard Boone Elledge married 30 January 1856, Pike County, Illinois, Marriage Book 1:224, County Clerk's Office, Courthouse, Pittsfield.

27 Civil War military service record for Isaac Heldreth (private, Co. D, 25th Regiment of Infantry, Missouri Volunteers, and Cos. A and B, First Missouri Engineers, Union), photocopy of file from National Archives, in possession of Dory (Heldreth) Graham.

28 Christie, *The Mysterious Affair at Styles*, 155.

29 U.S. Census of 1880, Chambersburg, Pike County, Illinois, NARA microfilm T9, roll 242, e.d. 181, sheet 25, family 43 (household of Isaac Heldreth), and sheet 24, family 37 (household of John and Sarah Todd) and family 38 (household of Nancy Hildreth), which was actually a continuation of the Todd

household, as Nancy was listed as "mother" and her son William, as "brother"; marriage of Sarah Hildreth and John Todd also shown in Bible record in possession of William Heldreth Harms of Evansville, Indiana, thought to have belonged to a daughter of William Hildreth and Dora Brubaker, listing the siblings of this William Hildreth (son of Uriah and Nancy), copy in possession of Dory (Heldreth) Graham.

30 Civil War Union Army pension file for Isaac N. Heldreth (Co. D, 25th Regiment, Missouri Infantry, Union), "Declaration for Invalid Pension," dated 14 July 1890, Invalid Certificate No. 550,657, Can No. 12037, Bundle 15, National Archives, Washington, DC, photocopy in possession of Dory (Heldreth) Graham.

31 Ibid., "Declaration for Pension" dated 16 February 1926; by this time, Isaac was living in Davenport, Iowa.

32 Ibid., affidavit dated 4 October 1909.

33 Ibid., affidavit dated 15 October 1909.

34 They appear in Daviess County, Missouri, in the 1860 census. See note 26 above.

35 Doyle, "The Adventure of the Creeping Man," *The Complete Sherlock Holmes*, 1081.

Chapter 10

1 Christie, "Nemesis," *Five Complete Miss Marple Novels*, 407.

2 Figured from census numbers reported in Henry F. Graff and John A. Krout, eds., *The Adventure of the American People*, 2nd ed. (Chicago: Rand McNally, 1968), 818.

3 Figured from census numbers reported in J. G. Randall and David Donald, *The Civil War and Reconstruction* (Boston: D.C. Heath, 1961), 5, 61, 68, 75.

4 Jack Temple Kirby, "Plantations," in *Encyclopedia of Southern Culture*, Charles Reagan Wilson and William Ferris, editors (Chapel Hill: The University of North Carolina Press, 1989), 27; Randall and Donald, *Civil War and Reconstruction*, 67 (showing that in 1850, less than .5 percent of slave owners had more than 100 slaves), 68 (showing that less than 27 percent of white families owned any slaves in 1860).

5 Kirby, "Plantations," 27.

6 Tey, *Daughter of Time*, 98.

7 Doyle, "The Adventure of the Retired Colourman," *The Complete Sherlock Holmes*, 1116.

8 U.S. Census of 1880, Soundex for Mississippi, Code D120, NARA microfilm T757, roll 15, Archie Davis card; U.S. Census of 1880, Claiborne County, Mississippi, Beat 2, NARA microfilm T9, roll 644, e.d. 66, sheet 26, family 417, line 35, household of Archie Davis.

9 U.S. Census of 1900, Claiborne County, Mississippi, Beat 3, NARA microfilm T623, roll 804, e.d. 160, sheet 1, family 7, line 25, household of Archie Davis Sr.

10 U.S. Census of 1910, Claiborne County, Mississippi, NARA microfilm T624, roll 735, e.d. 37, sheet 1, line 29, family 6 (household of Arch Davis Sr.) and family 7 (household of Archie Davis Jr.), microfilmed pages were dark, with the top and right sides of the pages too dark to decipher.

11 U.S. Census of 1920, Claiborne County, Mississippi, NARA microfilm T625, roll 872, e.d. 39, sheet 9, line 10, household of Arch Davis Sr.

12 Christie, "The Adventure of Johnnie Waverly," *Hercule Poirot's Casebook*, 649.

13 U.S. Census of 1870, Claiborne County, Mississippi, Grand Gulf District, NARA microfilm M593, roll 726, p. 572, family 231, line 8, household of Nella Davis.

14 Ibid., p. 571, family 228, line 26, household of Archie Davis.

15 Christie, "Nemesis," *Five Complete Miss Marple Novels*, 306.

16 U.S. Census of 1870, Claiborne County, Mississippi, Grand Gulf District, p. 571, family 227, line 20, household of Jesse Humphreys; p. 572, family 230, line 1, household of James Humphreys.

17 Heck, *A Connecticut Yankee in Criminal Court*, 219.

18 Visit with Sylvia Lee Boines Smith and Georgia Helen Boines Rucker, by Franklin Smith, at the Rucker home, Grand Gulf, Claiborne County, Mississippi, March 1996.

19 Visit with Johnnie Johnson, by Franklin Smith, at the Johnson home, Port Gibson, Claiborne County, Mississippi, July 1997; Mrs. Johnson was a great-granddaughter of Martha and Archie Davis Sr. and granddaughter of Harriett Davis; she confirmed that Lucinda Haywood was the sister of Martha Davis.

20 Haywood-Humphreys marriage, 12 October 1870, Claiborne County, Mississippi, in Automated Archives, *Marriage Records: Arkansas, Mississippi, Missouri, Texas*, CD-ROM, #CD5 (General Research System, now Novato, CA: Brøderbund, 1993), grooms listed alphabetically.

21 U.S. Census of 1870, Claiborne County, Mississippi, Grand Gulf District, p. 583, family 437, line 4, household of Willoughby Humphreys.

22 Rinehart, "Miss Pinkerton," *Miss Pinkerton*, 218.

23 [Poe], "The Murders in the Rue Morgue," *Edgar Allan Poe Stories*, 185.

24 Doyle, "The Adventure of the Creeping Man," *The Complete Sherlock Holmes*, 1079.

25 [Poe], "The Murders in the Rue Morgue," *Edgar Allan Poe Stories*, 185.

26 U.S. Census of 1870, Claiborne County, Mississippi, Grand Gulf District, p. 572, family 233, line 16, household of John P. McIntyre.

27 U.S. Census of 1880, Claiborne County, Mississippi, Beat 2, e.d. 66, sheet 26, family 415, line 21, household of J.P. McIntyre.

28 U.S. Census of 1880, Claiborne County, Mississippi, Beat 2, e.d. 66, sheet 28, line 11 (household of James Humphreys) and line 15 (household of Willoughby Humphreys).

29 U.S. Census of 1860, Free Schedule, Claiborne County, Mississippi, Police District 3, NARA microfilm M653, roll 580, p. 55, family 14, household of Dr. E. Pollard; U.S. Census of 1860, Slave Schedule, Claiborne County, Mississippi, NARA microfilm M653, roll 596, p. 440, slaves of Jno. McIntyre.

30 U.S. Census of 1850, Free Schedule, Claiborne County, Mississippi, NARA microfilm M432, roll 370, p. 123, family 316, line 1, household of A.C. McIntyre; U.S. Census of 1850, Slave Schedule, Claiborne County, Mississippi, District 2, NARA microfilm M432, roll 384, pages not numbered, 6 September 1850, A.C. McIntyre entry.

31 U.S. Census of 1840, Claiborne County, Mississippi, NARA microfilm M704, roll 213, p. 72, line 17, household of D.H. McIntyre (30–40), with 48 slaves; p. 72, line 31, household of Peter McIntyre (60–70), probably father of D.H., with 72 slaves; U.S. Census of 1830, Franklin County, Mississippi, NARA microfilm M19, roll 70, p. 166, line 1, household of D.H. McIntyre (30–40),

with 13 slaves; p. 153, line 11, household of Peter McIntyre (50–60), with 24 slaves; Claiborne County, Mississippi, Record of Probate, Book 1849–1851:2, widow A.C. McIntyre received her dower as part of the estate of D.H. McIntyre, 1849, Chancery Court Clerk's Office, Courthouse, Port Gibson; all Claiborne County records hereafter cited are from the same office unless otherwise noted.

32 Claiborne County, Mississippi, Record of Probate, Book K:40ff, 1842 inventory and appraisal of estate of Duncan H. McIntyre, showing the plantations Caledonia and Beeches and naming 102 slaves.

33 Chesterton, "The Blue Cross," *Father Brown Mystery Stories*, 13.

34 Claiborne County, Mississippi, Deed Book R:347 (Duncan H. McIntyre from Josiah B. Sugg) and Book R:453 (Peter McIntyre from Josiah B. Sugg); D.H. and Peter McIntyre entries in the 1830 and 1840 censuses, cited above, show they were of age to be father and son; further indication of that relationship comes from Claiborne County, Mississippi, Deed Book V:64, Peter McIntyre deeding all his property to D.H. McIntyre (1841), including the two plantations that then appear in D.H.'s estate in 1842, Caledonia and Beeches.

35 Dorris D. Hendrickson and Paul L. Hisaw, *From a Sow or a Sparrow: A History of the Sugg Family* ([Fayetteville, AR: D.D. Hendrickson], 1988), 352, Sugg-McIntyre marriage.

36 Claiborne County, Mississippi, Deed Book EE:192 (John P. McIntyre from W.R. Sugg); Hendrickson, *Sugg Family*, 351, citing Claiborne County Marriage Book 5:151, marriage of William Robert Sugg to Mary Adeline McIntyre; according to Hendrickson (p. 351), she was barely fourteen when she married and was a daughter of Duncan H. and Adeline Catherine Evans McIntyre; therefore she was a sister of John P. McIntyre.

37 Claiborne County, Mississippi, Land Tax Rolls, 1848, p. 17, microfilm, Record Group 29, Records of the Auditor of Public Accounts, Mississippi Department of Archives and History, Jackson.

38 U.S. Census of 1830, Claiborne County, Mississippi, NARA microfilm M19, roll 70, p. 73, household of Josiah B. Sugg, which includes a female 60–70, possibly his mother, and p. 81, household of Margaret Sugg with 14 slaves; see next paragraph and footnotes for identity of Margaret Sugg.

39 U.S. Census of 1840, Claiborne County, Mississippi, p. 85, line 4, household of W.R. Sugg, single with 21 slaves.

40 Claiborne County, Mississippi, Orphans Court Records, Book C (1822–1826):238–239 (27 December 1824), inventory and appraisal of William Sugg's estate; Orphans Court Records, Book of July 1829–June 1832:38 (report of William Sugg's estate, 11 August 1829).

41 U.S. Census of 1830, Claiborne County, Mississippi, p. 81, household of Margaret Sugg.

42 Claiborne County, Mississippi, Orphans Court Records, Book of July 1829–June 1832:310–312 (inventory and appraisal of Margaret Sugg's estate, 25 March 1831).

43 Claiborne County, Mississippi, Orphans Court Records, Book of July 1829–June 1832:352 (inventory of William R. Sugg's estate by his guardian Josiah B. Sugg, 16 January 1832).

44 U.S. Census of 1870, Claiborne County, Mississippi, p. 572, household of James Humphreys, with child Sampson (age nine).

45 Claiborne Parish, Mississippi, Record of Probate, Book K:17, dated 26 January 1842.

46 Hendrickson, *Sugg Family*, 353, indicating the children of Josiah Bryan Sugg and Elizabeth McIntyre were born in Bossier Parish, Louisiana.

47 Christie, "The Under Dog," *Hercule Poirot's Casebook*, 669.

48 Hendrickson, *Sugg Family*, 351, giving his birthday as 4 December 1822 and his marriage date as 4 April 1844.

49 Claiborne County, Mississippi, Deed Book EE:192.

50 Heck, *A Connecticut Yankee in Criminal Court*, 264.

51 Claiborne County, Mississippi, Deed Book A:55–56, Bryan and Sugg to the Sugg brothers, dated and recorded 21 January 1804; Hendrickson, *Sugg Family*, 350.

52 Claiborne County, Mississippi, Papers of Decedents Estates, file B-11, inventory and appraisal of Britton Bryan's estate, 31 May 1804.

53 *Heads of Families at the First Census of the United States Taken in the Year 1790: North Carolina* (Washington, DC: Government Printing Office, 1908; reprint by Baltimore: Genealogical Publishing Co., 1966), 54.

54 Rinehart, "The Buckled Bag," *Miss Pinkerton*, 15.

Chapter 11

1 Christie, *Sleeping Murder*, 72–73.

2 Heck, *A Connecticut Yankee in Criminal Court*, 24.

3 Letter from Albert Croom, Whiteville, Tennessee, to Dr. S.N. Hopper, Telephone, Texas, 28 September 1902, written as he and his wife were preparing to move to Texas, original sent to author by Mary Jo Phillips, granddaughter of Dr. and Mrs. Hopper, about 1974; the letter begins "Mr. Sam N & Docia Hopper, Dear Bro & Sister."

4 Christie, *Elephants Can Remember*, 152.

5 U.S. Census of 1850, Madison County, Tennessee, District 17, NARA microfilm M432, roll 889, p. 354, family 899 (next to Isaac Croom), household of Stringer Croom, showing Isaac, age 21.

6 Madison County, Tennessee, Loose Marriage Records, 1846–1866, p. 86, Isaac N. Croom to Mary F. Mays, license dated 19 May 1856, microfilm; letter to author, February 1991, from Alison (Croom) Cowling, great-granddaughter of Isaac N. Croom Sr., with information on second wife, Rachel Carruthers; U.S. Census of 1860, Henderson County, Tennessee, NARA microfilm M653, roll 1256, p. 31, family 183, household of Isaac N. and Mary F. Croom; U.S. Census of 1880, Henderson County, Tennessee, NARA microfilm T9, roll 1262, e.d. 58, sheet 6, family 1, household of Isaac N. and Rachel C. Croom; Madison County, Tennessee, Guardian Renewal bonds, 1868–1879, p. 49, James G. Mays, guardian of Mary Ada Ann Croom, child of Mary D. (should be F.) Croom, microfilm; telephone conversation with Alison (Croom) Cowling of Guilderland, NY, about this family, 21 June 1999; telephone conversation with Carol Liedmann of Oklahoma City, another great-granddaughter of Isaac N. Croom Sr., about this family, 26 June 1999.

7 Madison County, Tennessee, Marriage Book B:15, Catherine Croom to Sterling M. Watlington, license 16 May 1866 (no return); Book D:116, #230, Laura Croom to John G. Haynes, 17 February 1870; Book F:341, Samuel N. Hopper to Theodocia E. Croom, 8 February 1876, microfilm; U.S. Census of 1880, Madison County, Tennessee, NARA microfilm T9, roll 1270, e.d. 103, sheet 21, family 178 (Thomas A. and Susan Haynes), shows the wife, Susan, as age 36, suggesting birth in 1843–1844, and the eldest child, Sarah, as age

13, suggesting birth in 1866–1867 and parents' marriage prior to that; U.S. Census of 1900, Madison County, Tennessee, NARA microfilm T623, roll 1586, e.d. 114, sheet 13, household of Susan Haynes, giving birth date as December 1843 and daughter Sallie Moore, with birth date of November 1866. Together with the court case cited below for Isaac's heirs and the 1860 census for Isaac's household, we can suggest that Susan married between 1860 and 1866.

8 U.S. Census of 1850, Madison County, Tennessee, District 17, p. 354, family 900, household of Isaac Croom.

9 U.S. Census of 1860, Madison County, Tennessee, District 17, Jackson, NARA microfilm M653, roll 1263, p. 196B, dwelling 1838, family 1872, household of Isaac Croom.

10 U.S. Census of 1870, Madison County, Tennessee, 17th District, near Jackson, NARA microfilm M593, roll 1545, p. 380, dwelling/family 88, household of I. and A. Croom.

11 U.S. Census of 1880, Madison County, Tennessee, e.d. 103, p. 24, dwelling 202, family 206, household of Isaac Croom; e.d. 103, sheet 23, family 195, S.M. and Catherine Watlington; e.d. 103, sheet 21, family 178, Thomas A. and Susan Haynes; e.d. 103, sheet 28, Charles E. Croom, listed as son-in-law in the household of W.F. Gardner; e.d. 87, sheet 46–47, family 386, Napoleon B. and Ella Croom; John G. and Laura J. Haynes have not been found in 1870 and 1880, but the 1900 census gives her age as 52 and birth date as November 1847: U.S. Census of 1900, Madison County, Tennessee, e.d. 88, sheet 3, household of John G. Haynes; Madison County, Tennessee, Marriage Book F:341, Hopper-Croom; Book F:140, Napoleon B. Croom to Ella E. Gardner, (license) 19 May 1873, no return, microfilm.

12 U.S. Census of 1880, Mortality Schedule, Madison County, Tennessee, NARA microfilm T655, roll 29, Madison County entries.

13 Sayers, "The Fascinating Problem of Uncle Meleager's Will," *Lord Peter*, 35.

14 Madison County, Tennessee, Deed Book 97:182, sale of land of Isaac Croom by the heirs per court decree, 12 October 1891, Office of Register of Deeds, Courthouse, Jackson; Madison County, Tennessee, Probate Court Minute Book 18:140 (request for administrator, 15 July 1889), 156 (request for homestead for minors, 2 Sept 1889), 158, 435, 502, 582 (court order to sell homestead, list of heirs, 7 May 1891), 602, 612–615, County Clerk's Office, Courthouse, Jackson.

15 U.S. Census of 1880, Madison County, Tennessee, e.d. 87, sheet 46–47, family 386, household of Napoleon B. Croom.

16 *Cemetery Records of Madison County Tennessee: The Southern Half of County* (Jackson, TN: Mid-West Tennessee Genealogical Society, 1995), I:24, 28, 30, 32, 34, corroborates dates and spouses of Isaac Croom's first set of children: Catherine, Susan E., Charles E., Napoleon Bonaparte, Laura Jane, and Clarkey F.; Napoleon Bonaparte Croom indeed died in 1882. The Madison County marriage records, previously cited, also support the court record.

17 Doyle, "The Adventure of the Dancing Men," *The Complete Sherlock Holmes*, 515.

18 Madison County, Tennessee, Marriage Book A:40, license 211 (Isaac Croom Jr. to Elizabeth Sturdevant), copy of page in possession of author; Susan K. Croom Bible, in 1966 in possession of Lacy Price, Jackson, Tennessee, transcribed by Faye Tennyson Davidson of Bolivar, Tennessee, and sent to author, Houston, Texas, 3 August 1966.

19 Caddo Parish, Louisiana, Marriage Book 1:484, Isaac Croom Jr. to Ann Maria Robertson, the bond and license, 16 May 1856; Book 2:10, Isaac Croom Jr. to Maria Ann [sic] Robertson, the solemnization by Rev. John McCain, 15 September 1856, Parish Clerk's Office, Courthouse, Shreveport; Caddo Parish records hereafter cited are from this office unless otherwise noted.

20 Caddo Parish, Louisiana, Marriage Book 1:143 (Isaac Croom to Mrs. Elizabeth Robinson); Olive Godwin Croom tombstone, Old Mooring Cemetery, Caddo Parish, in *Caddo Parish, Louisiana, Cemeteries*, alphabetical in 4 vols. (no publisher, date, compiler, or page numbers; bound photocopies of card file), in Shreve Memorial Library, Shreveport, Louisiana; also in *Louisiana Tombstone Inscriptions* (n. p.: Louisiana Society, D.A.R., 1954–1960), 10:127 (Old Mooring Cemetery, Caddo Parish, tombstone of Olive Godwin Croom, "mother of C.S. Croom") and 132 (Mooringsport Cemetery, Caddo Parish, tombstone of Calvin Stewart Croom, "son of Isaac and Olive Godwin Croom"); *Biographical and Historical Memoirs of Northwest Louisiana* (Nashville: The Southern Publishing Co., 1890, p. 59, biographical sketch of Calvin S. Croom; Caddo Parish, Louisiana, Donation Book A:14, gift of 240 acres from Isaac Croom to his son Calvin Stewart Croom, 5 January 1853.

21 Sayers, "The Image in the Mirror," *Lord Peter*, 299.

22 U.S. Census of 1850, Caddo Parish, Louisiana, Albany beat, NARA microfilm M432, roll 230, p. 358, dwelling 51, family 54, household of Isaac Croom.

23 U.S. Census of 1860, Shreveport, Caddo Parish, Louisiana, NARA microfilm M653, roll 409, p. 13, dwelling/family 87, household of C.J. Miller, which included Calvin Croom and family.

24 Rinehart, "Miss Pinkerton," *Miss Pinkerton*, 123.

25 Doyle, "The Boscombe Valley Mystery," *The Complete Sherlock Holmes*, 204.

26 Doyle, "The Adventure of the Copper Beeches," *The Complete Sherlock Holmes*, 317.

27 Doyle, "A Study in Scarlet," *The Complete Sherlock Holmes*, 28, 32.

28 Caddo Parish, Louisiana, Marriage Book 2:10 (Croom-Robertson), 367 (Robertson-Gerrald); *Biographical and Historical Memoirs of Northwest Louisiana*, 80, biographical sketch of James B. McCain reports his father, John McCain, was a Baptist minister.

29 Caddo Parish, Louisiana, Conveyance Book P:975, Isaac Croom to Louisiana Harris, wife of John H. Harris, 24 April 1868.

30 *Biographical and Historical Memoirs of Northwest Louisiana*, 46, report of epidemics; *Shreveport Southwestern*, 4 September through 13 November 1867 with weekly reports on the yellow fever spread, microfilm.

31 U.S. Census of 1870, Panola County, Texas, NARA microfilm M593, roll 1601, dwelling/family 1484, household of Isaac Croom; Panola County, Texas, Marriage Book C:22, Isaac Croom to Mary N. Jones, 15 November 1868, photocopy in author's possession; Caddo Parish, Louisiana, Conveyance Book P:975, 24 April 1868, deed of gift from Isaac Croom to his daughter Louisiana, wife of Jno. H. Harris of Caddo Parish.

32 U.S. Census of 1880, Caddo Parish, Louisiana, Ward 3, NARA microfilm T9, roll 449, e.d. 14, sheet 2, family 19, household of J.H. Harris; U.S. Census of 1900, Caddo Parish, Louisiana, NARA microfilm T623, roll 559, e.d. 29, sheet 3, family 62, household of J.H. Harris; Caddo Parish, Louisiana, Conveyance Book 67:500, will of Lou Harris, dated 1 May 1911, recorded 19 July 1911.

33 Tey, *Daughter of Time*, 165.

34 U.S. Census of 1910, Marshall County, Mississippi, NARA microfilm T624, roll 751, e.d. 44, sheet 11A, household of Thomas N. Jones.

35 U.S. Census of 1900, Chester County, Tennessee, NARA microfilm T623, roll 1561, e.d. 11, sheet 9, family 144, household of Major Croom; U.S. Census of 1920, Crockett County, Tennessee, NARA microfilm T625, roll 1736, e.d. 7, sheet 1, family 10, household of M.L. Croom.

36 U.S. Census of 1900, Hardeman County, Tennessee, NARA microfilm T623, roll 1586, e.d. 145, sheet 1, family 9, household of Albert S. Croom; U.S. Census of 1910, Mills County, Texas, NARA microfilm T624, roll 1578, e.d. 208, sheet 17A, household of Albert S. Croom; U.S. Census of 1920, Angelina County, Texas, NARA microfilm T625, roll 1773, e.d. 6, sheet 17, family 379, household of Albert S. Croom.

37 Death Certificate for Albert Sidney Croom, State File No. 31305 (1954), Texas Department of Heath, Bureau of Vital Statistics, Austin, copy in author's possession.

38 U.S. Census of 1900, Marshall County, Mississippi, NARA microfilm T623, roll, 820, e.d. 66, sheet 9, household of O.P. Armour; U.S. Census of 1910, Chickasaw County, Mississippi, Buena Vista, NARA microfilm T624, roll 735, e.d. 47, sheet 15, household of O.P. Armour.

39 Rinehart, "Miss Pinkerton," *Miss Pinkerton*, 203.

40 Heck, *A Connecticut Yankee in Criminal Court*, 307.

41 Rinehart, "The Buckled Bag," *Miss Pinkerton*, 21.

42 Roosevelt, *Murder and the First Lady*, 191.

43 U.S. Census of 1850, Caddo Parish, Louisiana, pp. 321–322, 325, 326, 330, 331, 332, 335, 346; those who could be found in 1860 were double-checked.

44 U.S. Census of 1850, Madison County, Tennessee, pp. 231, 256, 257, 267, 278, 280, 287, 291, 329, 358.

45 Caddo Parish, Louisiana, succession file 241 for Archibald Robinson and file 176 for R.M. Robinson; Caddo Parish, Louisiana, Conveyance Book G:69, Archibald Robinson's widow to daughter, photocopy in author's possession; Caddo Parish, Louisiana, Marriage Book 1:128 and 137, Susan J. Robinson to Cicero C. Bates; Book 1:194, Mary Robinson to William Wooldridge, photocopies in author's possession.

46 Caddo Parish, Louisiana, Assessments, 1865–1871, microfilm roll 6-206, from Louisiana State Archives and Records Commission, at Shreve Memorial Library, Shreveport, Louisiana.

47 Heck, *A Connecticut Yankee in Criminal Court*, 308.

48 U.S. General Land Office, *Automated Records Project; Pre-1908 Homestead & Cash Entry Patents: Louisiana*, CD-ROM (Springfield, VA: Bureau of Land Management, Eastern States Office, 1993), Natchitoches land office, entries for the four named individuals; this was also the source of the "no hits" on the other names; land location was then plotted on parish maps.

49 U.S. General Land Office, *Pre-1908 . . . Patents: Louisiana*, CD-ROM, Natchitoches land office, John Robinson entries, land in S31 and S32-T12N-R14W, S6-T11N-R14W, certificates 2375 (recorded 1 January 1846), 2187 and 2188 (recorded 1 April 1843); land in S5, S6, S7, S8 all in T11N-R14W, certificates 3250, 3291, 4649, 4650, and 4651, all recorded 1 September 1849; land in S33-T12N-R14W, certificate 3141, recorded 7 May 1848; land in S28-T13N-R15W, certificates 4157 and 4727, both recorded 1 September 1849.

50 U.S. Census of 1850, DeSoto Parish, Louisiana, NARA microfilm M432, roll 23, p. 202, family 604, household of John Roberson, Sen.

51 Caddo Parish, Louisiana, Marriage Book 1:48, 50, photocopies in author's possession.

52 U.S. General Land Office, *Pre-1908 . . . Patents: Louisiana, CD-ROM,* Natchitoches land office, Aaron Robinson entry, land in S28-T13N-R15W, certificates 2376 and 2377, recorded 1 January 1846.

53 U.S. Census of 1850, DeSoto Parish, Louisiana, p. 197, family 538, household of Aaron Roberson.

54 Caddo Parish, Louisiana, Marriage Book 1:19, 46, photocopies in author's possession.

55 U.S. General Land Office, *Pre-1908 . . . Patents: Louisiana, CD-ROM,* Natchitoches land office, William Robinson entry, land in S35-T15N-R16W, certificate 2304, recorded 1 January 1846.

56 Caddo Parish, Louisiana, Marriage Book 1:19, William Robinson to Mary Blout [*sic*], 9 January 1840, Elias Blout, surety, photocopies in author's possession; U.S. Census of 1840, Caddo Parish, Louisiana, NARA microfilm M704, roll 127, p. 40, household of William Robertson, male 20–30 and female 15–20.

57 Caddo Parish, Louisiana, Conveyance Book D:555–556, Mary Blount, wife of William Robinson, grantor, 25 January 1849, photocopies in author's possession.

58 U.S. Census of 1840, Claiborne Parish, Louisiana, NARA microfilm M704, roll 127, p. 112, household of Archibald Robison.

59 U.S. General Land Office, *Pre-1908 . . . Patents: Louisiana, CD-ROM,* Natchitoches land office, Archibald Robinson, certificates 945 and 803, recorded 1 April 1843 and 9 March 1844; Caddo Parish, Louisiana, Conveyance Book A:548–550, dated 28 November 1840, sale of the patented land, photocopies in author's possession.

60 Caddo Parish, Louisiana, Marriage Book 1:194 (Robinson-Wooldridge), photocopy in author's possession; Caddo Parish, Louisiana, succession file 241.

61 Caddo Parish, Louisiana, Conveyance Book N:598–599, photocopies in author's possession; collateral Croom research in land, marriage, and cemetery records show Bickham as a brother-in-law to Calvin S. Croom.

62 U.S. Census of 1850, Caddo Parish, Louisiana, p. 363, family 129, household of Samuel Jarrell.

63 U.S. Census of 1860, Caddo Parish, Louisiana, p. 2, family 11, household of Samuel Gerreal.

64 Doyle, "The Adventure of Shoscombe Old Place," *The Complete Sherlock Holmes,* 1103.

65 Caddo Parish, Louisiana, Conveyance Book L:194, Isaac Croom to James Christian, 5 November 1857.

66 Caddo Parish, Louisiana, Conveyance Book P:975, Isaac Croom to Louisiana Harris, wife of John H. Harris, 24 April 1868; Panola County, Texas, Marriage Book C:22.

67 Caddo Parish, Louisiana, Conveyance Book S:721, Isaac Croom to John H. Harris, 25 October 1871.

68 Caddo Parish, Louisiana, Conveyance Book S:855, Thomas J. Robertson to John H. Harris, 16 December 1871.

69 Caddo Parish, Louisiana, Conveyance Book 51:585 (receipt of John H. Harris

for advance royalty paid by Gulf, 23 December 1908), 690–693 (documents of ratification of the mineral leases).

70 Caddo Parish, Louisiana, Conveyance Book 57:163, A.S. Croom and his wife, L.E. Croom, of Mills County, Texas, to W.C. Dew of Mills County, Texas, 5 April 1909.

71 Christie, *The Clocks*, 257.

72 Ongoing correspondence and E-mail between the author and Robert Carson McCain of Shreveport, a descendant of Rev. John McCain, beginning 29 December 1996; McCain lived near a community called Albany, no longer in existence.

73 U.S. Census of 1850, Caddo Parish, Louisiana, Albany beat, p. 358, Isaac Croom; Caddo Parish, Louisiana, map, Louisiana Department of Transportation and Development, Traffic and Planning Division, Baton Rouge, revised 1989; E-mail message to author from Robert C. McCain of Shreveport, 19 June 1999.

74 Caddo Parish, Louisiana, Conveyance Book C:225, 227 (Croom from Allen and Belton, 5 July 1844).

75 Certificate no. 8984 for Isaac Croom, patent for land in S1-T19N-R16W, receipt dated 2 February 1852, recorded 11 September 1853, Natchitoches land office, Pre-1908 Land Patents, Records of the General Land Office, Record Group 49, photocopy from National Archives.

76 Caddo Parish, Louisiana, Conveyance Book H:478 (Croom from Mooring, 7 January 1853), 488 (Croom to Mooring, 7 January 1853); Donation Book A:14 (Croom to son Croom, 5 January 1853).

77 Caddo Parish, Louisiana, Conveyance Book L:194 (Croom to Christian, 5 November 1857), 248 (Philyaw to Croom, 7 December 1857), 250 (Christian to Croom, 7 December 1857).

78 Certificates no. 14518 (receipt dated 16 April 1859) and no. 14577 (receipt dated 4 May 1859) for Isaac Croom, patents for land in S32-T20N-R15W, both recorded 1 June 1860, Natchitoches land office, Pre-1908 Land Patents, Records of the General Land Office, Record Group 49, photocopy from National Archives.

79 U.S. Census of 1850, Caddo Parish, Louisiana, p. 358, family 56, household of Joseph Allen; U.S. Census of 1860, Caddo Parish, Louisiana, p. 18, family 120, household of Joseph Allen, corroborates the Tennessee birthplaces; family also in U.S. Census of 1840, Caddo Parish, p. 46.

80 U.S. General Land Office, *Pre-1908 . . . Patents: Louisiana*, CD-ROM, certificate 1289, Joseph Allen, NW4-S2-T19-R16, finalized 1 April 1843.

81 U.S. Census of 1850, Caddo Parish, Louisiana, p. 359, family 76, household of Joseph B. [*sic*] Belton.

82 U.S. Census of 1830, Thomas County, Georgia, NARA microfilm M19, roll 21, p. 16, line 3, household of Joseph R. Belton.

83 U.S. Census of 1840, Caddo Parish, p. 46.

84 U.S. General Land Office, *Pre-1908 . . . Patents: Louisiana*, CD-ROM, certificate 893, Joseph R. Betton [*sic*], NE1/4-S2-T19-R16, recorded 1 September 1846 (although Croom bought it from him July 1844).

85 U.S. Census of 1850, Caddo Parish, Louisiana, p. 358, family 57, household of Timothy Mooring.

86 *Biographical and Historical Memoirs of Northwest Louisiana*, 59, sketch of Calvin S. Croom.

87 U.S. Census of 1850, Madison County, Tennessee, p. 331, family 592, household of James Christian [with Pherelize (48), Thomas H. (15), Sarah (17), and James M. (18), and Mary A. Jones (2)].

88 Wanda Volentine Head, comp., *Caddo Parish, Louisiana, Newspaper Gleanings 1844–1865* (Shreveport: J&W Enterprises, 1992), 43.

89 Caddo Parish, Louisiana, Conveyance Book L:194, dated 5 November 1857, Croom to Christian.

90 Head, *Caddo Parish, Louisiana, Newspaper Gleanings*, 79.

91 U.S. Census of 1860, Caddo Parish, Louisiana, p. 14, family 93, household of James Christian; in this part of the parish the enumerator recorded the year of marriage for each couple and each widow or widower; four households away from James Christian was M.J. Christian, 25, Tennessee, who could well be the James M. Christian (18) in the 1850 census household above.

92 Caddo Parish, Louisiana, Marriage Book 1:414, Christian-Kerley marriage, photocopy in author's possession.

93 U.S. Census of 1850, Madison County, Tennessee, p. 331, family 592, household of James Christian, and family 593, household of M. Milam.

94 Caddo Parish, Louisiana, Marriage Book 2:10, solemnization of marriage, Isaac Croom Jr. and Maria Ann [*sic*] Robertson, 15 September 1856; Marriage Book 2:126, marriage of M.B./Mark Milam and Sarah Harris, 30 March 1859, photocopies in author's possession.

95 U.S. Census of 1850, Caddo Parish, Louisiana, p. 361, family 98, household of Thomas Phillshaw.

96 Caddo Parish, Louisiana, Conveyance Book L:248, Thomas Philyaw to Isaac Croom; this family has not been located in 1860 and 1870.

97 Caddo Parish, Louisiana, Marriage Book 2:367.

98 Christie, "The Mirror Crack'd," *Five Complete Miss Marple Novels*, 67.

99 Rinehart, "The Haunted Lady," *Miss Pinkerton*, 268.

100 Christie, *Sleeping Murder*, 36.

101 Doyle, "A Study in Scarlet," *The Complete Sherlock Holmes*, 49.

102 Doyle, "The Sign of Four," *The Complete Sherlock Holmes*, 128.

103 Heck, *A Connecticut Yankee in Criminal Court*, 275.

104 Conditional headright certificate and file of Isaac Croom, 2 December 1839, file NAC-3-527, Texas General Land Office, Archives and Records Division, Austin.

105 Houston County, Texas, Tax Rolls, 1838–1846, microfilm roll 693, Texas State Library, Austin, obtained through interlibrary loan.

106 Christie, *Sleeping Murder*, 36.

107 Christie, *The Mysterious Affair at Styles*, 75.

108 Christie, "A Caribbean Mystery," *Five Complete Miss Marple Novels*, 246.

109 Rinehart, "Miss Pinkerton," *Miss Pinkerton*, 151.

110 Christie, "Strange Jest," *Three Blind Mice and Other Stories*, 96, 105.

111 Christie, "A Caribbean Mystery," *Five Complete Miss Marple Novels*, 246.

112 Christie, "The Disappearance of Mr. Davenheim," *Hercule Poirot's Casebook*, 103; Christie, "The Veiled Lady," *Hercule Poirot's Casebook*, 135–136.

113 Doyle, "Silver Blaze," *The Complete Sherlock Holmes*, 338.

114 Ernest Bramah, "The Holloway Flat Tragedy," *Max Carrados Mysteries* (1927), in Horning, comp., *The Mystery Lovers' Book of Quotations*, 29, #201, Max Carrados.

115 Christie, "The Dream," *The Regatta Mystery and Other Stories*, 168; Christie, "The Adventure of the Clapham Cook," *Hercule Poirot's Casebook*, 795.

116 Christie, "Nemesis," *Five Complete Miss Marple Novels*, 285.

117 Joseph T. Maddox and Mary Carter, comp., (1) *37,000 Early Georgia Marriages* (1975), (2) *40,000 Early Georgia Marriages* (1976), (3) *Early Georgia Marriage Roundup* (1976), and (4) *Early Georgia Marriages, Book 4* (1980) (probably Irwinton, GA: Joseph T. Maddox).

118 Maddox and Carter, *37,000 Early Georgia Marriages*, p. 226, Putnam County.

119 Christie, "The Mystery of the Spanish Shawl," *The Witness for the Prosecution and Other Stories* (New York: Berkley Books, 1984), 151.

120 Doyle, "The Adventure of the Three Garridebs," *The Complete Sherlock Holmes*, 1045.

121 U.S. Census of 1840, Putnam County, Georgia, NARA microfilm M704, roll 49, p. 176, household of Thomas Robinson.

122 U.S. Census of 1850, Caddo Parish, Louisiana, p. 357, family 46, household of Lucy A. Arnold.

123 U.S. Census of 1850, Mortality Schedule, Caddo Parish, Louisiana, NARA microfilm T655, roll 21, p. 89.

124 Application for letters of administration, Caddo Parish, Louisiana, succession file 343 (1850) for James A. Arnold.

125 Administrator's bond and appointment, Caddo Parish, Louisiana, succession file 506 (1853) for Lucy A. Arnold.

126 U.S. Census of 1850, Caddo Parish, Louisiana, p. 328, family 135, household of Jacob C. Porter; U.S. Census of 1860, DeSoto Parish, Louisiana, NARA microfilm M653, roll 410, p. 841, family 120, household of J.C. Porter; U.S. Census of 1870, Natchitoches Parish, Louisiana, NARA microfilm M593, roll 518, p. 406, family 201, household of Jacob Porter.

127 U.S. Census of 1840, Caddo Parish, Louisiana, Shreveport, p. 44, household of J.C. Porter; Caddo Parish, Louisiana, Marriage Book 1:45, 49, bond and marriage respectively, photocopy in author's possession.

128 Record of family meeting, Caddo Parish, Louisiana, succession file 506 for Lucy A. Arnold; Caddo Parish Conveyance Book H:672, Porter as administrator to Gillies, 1854.

129 Doyle, "The Adventure of the Creeping Man," *The Complete Sherlock Holmes*, 1076.

130 Caddo Parish, Louisiana, Conveyance Books B-F, 1841-1851, FHL microfilm 0265868–0265871.

131 Caddo Parish, Louisiana, Conveyance Book B:517; Book D:377, 622; Book E:19 (Porter's sale); Book F:253, 284, 612, FHL microfilm 0265868 (B), 0265870 (D-E), and 0265871 (F).

132 Heck, *A Connecticut Yankee in Criminal Court*, 195.

133 Maddox and Carter, *37,000 Early Georgia Marriages*, Taliaferro County, p. 243; Taliaferro County, Georgia, Marriage Book A:61, license and return for Arnold-Porter marriage (no witnesses asked for or given), photocopy in author's possession.

134 U.S. Census of 1840, Putnam County, Georgia, District 306, p. 186, household of James A. Arnold; District 375, p. 176, household of Thomas Robinson.

135 Putnam County, Georgia, Marriage Book D:206, showing marriage date of 18 August 1833, FHL microfilm 0394053.

136 Putnam County, Georgia, Tax Digests, 1824–1828, FHL microfilm 0401836, and 1830–1833, 1836–1839, FHL microfilm 0401837, pages not numbered on either roll. The roll for the 1820s first contains a tax book for a year marked "1820?," to which someone added a note that it might be 1840. In fact, at least for the 375th district, it is an almost exact copy in the same handwriting as the 1838 list. The page breaks are slightly different, but everyone appears in the same order and with the same information. A few appear in this copy as initials instead of full names and one man is missing from the copy.

137 Putnam County, Georgia, Tax Digests, 1830–1833, 1836–1839.

138 Ibid., 1833.

139 Ibid., 1836–1837.

140 Ibid., 1838.

141 Ibid., 1839; Putnam County, Georgia, Tax Digests, 1840–1842, 1845–1846, 1848, FHL microfilm 0401838; General Highway Map, Putnam County, Georgia, 1985, Georgia Department of Transportation, No. 2 Capitol Square, Atlanta, Georgia, 30334; map shows the boundaries of the militia districts.

142 Putnam County, Georgia, Tax Digests, 1840–1842, 1845–1846, 1848.

143 Putnam County, Georgia, Deed Book O:302; Book P:450–451, 511, 544, FHL microfilm 0400941.

144 Putnam County, Georgia, Deed Book O:556.

145 Putnam County, Georgia, Inferior Court Minutes Book for 1826–1846, FHL microfilm 0394032, pages unnumbered; Inferior Court Minutes Book A (1819–1831) on the same microfilm yielded no evidence of Robertson or Arnold between 1828 and 1831.

146 Putnam County, Georgia, Superior Court Minutes Book for 1829–1839, pages unnumbered, March term 1832, 15 September 1834, 17 March 1835, 21 March 1836, 20 September 1835, 23 March 1838, FHL microfilm 0400927.

147 Putnam County, Georgia, Superior Court Minutes, 1829–1839, 24 March 1838.

148 Jeannette Holland Austin, *Index to Georgia Wills* (1985; reprint, Baltimore: Clearfield Company, 1998), 2.

149 Christie, "The Mirror Crack'd," *Five Complete Miss Marple Novels*, 142.

150 Putnam County, Georgia, probate file 101R (1842), Thomas Robertson, 27 March 1842 note (frame 032) and temporary administrator's bond (frame 058), FHL microfilm 1851587.

151 Ibid., bill from Slaughter (frame 029), receipt from Tompkins (frame 036); U.S. Census of 1850, Cobb County, Georgia, NARA microfilm M432, roll 66, p. 90, family 15, household of Martin G. Slaughter, identifies him as a physician. The bill in the probate file implies but does not state that he was the doctor; it was scribbled and made sense only if he were the doctor. The census simply confirmed his identity. The Putnam County, Georgia, Inferior Court Minutes 1826–1846, cited above, show that he was called to serve as a physician on a special jury in November 1845 to determine whether a county resident was a lunatic and should be committed to the state asylum.

152 Putnam County, Georgia, probate file 101R, Thomas Robertson, estate sale inventory, frames 041–046.

153 Doyle, "The Adventure of the Creeping Man," *The Complete Sherlock Holmes*, 1079; Doyle, "The Sign of Four," *The Complete Sherlock Holmes*, 120.

154 Putnam County, Georgia, probate file 101R, Thomas Robertson, estate sale inventory, frames 041–046; Putnam County, Georgia, Tax Digests, 1840–1842.

155 Doyle, "A Study in Scarlet," *The Complete Sherlock Holmes*, 33.

156 Heck, *A Connecticut Yankee in Criminal Court*, 216.

157 Putnam County, Georgia, probate file 46A (1841), Chloe Allen, will, dated 2___? June 1834, probated 15 November 1841, frames 198–204, FHL microfilm 1832253.

158 Putnam County, Georgia, probate file 42A (1818), James Allen, will, dated 21 September 1816, probated 2 May 1818, frames 210–211, FHL microfilm 1832253.

159 Ibid., writ to sheriff, frames 212–213; the surname used is clearly Roberson.

160 Ibid., bond of Chloe C. Allen, frames 237–239.

161 Christie, *The Clocks*, 253.

Appendix A

1 Rinehart, "The Buckled Bag," *Miss Pinkerton*, 10.

2 Christie, "The Arcadian Deer," *Hercule Poirot's Casebook*, 456.

3 Pirkis, "The Experiences of Loveday Brooke, Lady Detective: The Black Bag Left on a Door-Step" (1893), in Russell, comp., *Rivals of Sherlock Holmes*, 19.

4 Doyle, "The Musgrave Ritual," *The Complete Sherlock Holmes*, 397.

5 Rinehart, "The Buckled Bag," *Miss Pinkerton*, 148.

6 Christie, "The Incredible Theft," *Hercule Poirot's Casebook*, 257.

7 Christie, *The Clocks*, 137.

8 Sayers, "The Image in the Mirror," *Lord Peter*, 297.

9 Truman, *Murder in the White House*, 35.

10 Tey, *Daughter of Time*, 73.

11 John Buchan, Lord Tweedsmuir, *The Power House* (1916), in Horning, comp., *The Mystery Lovers' Book of Quotations*, p. 32, #222, Edward Leithen.

Appendix B

1 Christie, "The Adventure of Johnnie Waverly," *Hercule Poirot's Casebook*, 640.

2 [Poe], "The Purloined Letter," *Edgar Allan Poe Stories*, 218.

3 Roosevelt, *Murder and the First Lady*, 211.

4 Doyle, "The Adventure of the Speckled Band," *The Complete Sherlock Holmes*, 261.

5 Christie, "The Affair at the Victory Ball," *Hercule Poirot's Casebook*, 735.

Bibliography

Bibliography of Sleuths

Bartlett, John, comp. *Familiar Quotations*. 13th ed. Boston: Little, Brown and Co., 1955.

Car Talk. National Public Radio. KUHF, Houston, Texas. 29 March 1997.

Chesterton, G.K. *Father Brown Mystery Stories*. New York: Dodd, Mead & Co., 1966.

Christie, Agatha. *The Clocks*. New York: HarperPaperbacks, 1991.

———. *Elephants Can Remember*. New York: Berkley Books, 1984.

———. *Evil Under the Sun*. New York: Berkley Books, 1991.

———. *Five Complete Miss Marple Novels*. New York: Avenel Books, 1980.

———. *Hercule Poirot's Casebook*. New York: G.P. Putnam's Sons, 1984.

———. *The Mysterious Affair at Styles: Poirot's First Case*. New York: Berkley Books, 1991.

———. *The Regatta Mystery and Other Stories*. New York: Berkley Books, 1984.

———. *Sleeping Murder*. New York: Bantam Books, 1977.

———. *Three Blind Mice and Other Stories*. New York: Dodd, Mead & Co., 1975.

———. *The Witness for the Prosecution and Other Stories*. New York: Berkley Books, 1984.

Doyle, Sir Arthur Conan. *The Complete Sherlock Holmes*. Garden City, NY: Doubleday & Co., n.d.

Ernst, John, ed. *Favorite Sleuths*. Garden City, NY: Doubleday & Co., 1965.

Gardner, Erle Stanley. *The Perry Mason Omnibus*. New York: William Morrow & Co., n.d.

Grafton, Sue. *"A" Is for Alibi*. New York: Holt Rinehart & Winston, 1982.

Harding, Paul. *Red Slayer*. New York: Avon Books, 1994.

Heck, Peter J. *A Connecticut Yankee in Criminal Court: A Mark Twain Mystery*. New York: Berkley Prime Crime, 1996.

Horning, Jane, comp. *The Mystery Lovers' Book of Quotations*. New York: The Mysterious Press, 1988.

Kipling, Rudyard. *From Sea to Sea: Letters of Travel*. Vol. 2. New York: Doubleday & McClure, 1899.

[Poe, Edgar Allan]. *Edgar Allan Poe Stories*. New York: Platt & Munk, 1961.

Rinehart, Mary Roberts. *Miss Pinkerton: Adventures of a Nurse Detective*. New York: Rinehart & Co., 1959.

Roget, Peter Mark. *Roget's International Thesaurus*. New ed. Revised. New York: Thomas Y. Crowell Co., 1946.

Roosevelt, Elliott. *The Hyde Park Murder*. New York: St. Martin's Press, 1985.

———. *Murder and the First Lady*. New York: St. Martin's Press, 1984.

———. *Murder in the East Room*. New York: St. Martin's Press, 1993.

———. *Murder in the Executive Mansion*. New York: St. Martin's Press, 1995.

Russell, Alan K., comp. *Rivals of Sherlock Holmes*. Secaucus, NJ: Castle Books, 1978.

Sayers, Dorothy. *Lord Peter*. James Sandoe, comp. New York: Avon Books, 1972.

Tey, Josephine. *The Daughter of Time*. New York: Collier Books, 1988.

Truman, Margaret. *Murder in the White House*. New York: Arbor House, 1980.

Bibliography of Selected Works Mentioned in the Text or for Further Reference

American State Papers: Documents Legislative and Executive of the Congress of the United States. 38 vols. Washington: Gales and Seaton, 1832–1861. Class 8: *Public Lands*. Class 9: *Claims*.

Atlas & Gazetteer Series. Yarmouth, ME: DeLorme. (207) 846-7000. Web site: <http://www.delorme.com>.

Barsi, James C. *The Basic Researcher's Guide to Homesteads & Other Federal Land Records*. Colorado Springs, CO: Nuthatch Grove Press, 1994.

Berry, Ellen T., and David A. Berry. *Our Quaker Ancestors: Finding Them in Quaker Records*. Baltimore: Genealogical Publishing Co., 1987.

Bockstruck, Lloyd DeWitt. *Revolutionary War Bounty Land Grants Awarded by State Governments*. Baltimore: Genealogical Publishing Co., 1996.

Black, Henry Campbell. *Black's Law Dictionary*. 5th or other ed. St. Paul, MN: West Publishing Co., 1979.

Carmack, Sharon DeBartolo. *A Genealogist's Guide to Discovering Your Female Ancestors*. Cincinnati: Betterway Books, 1998.

———. *Organizing Your Family History Search*. Cincinnati: Betterway Books, 1999.

Carter, Clarence E., comp., ed. *The Territorial Papers of the United States*. 28 vols. Washington, DC: Government Printing Office, 1934–1975. There are several additional sets of similar papers available on microfilm.

Cerny, Johni, and Arlene Eakle. *Ancestry's Guide to Research: Case Studies in American Genealogy*. Salt Lake City: Ancestry, 1985.

Colletta, John P. *They Came in Ships: A Guide to Finding Your Immigrant Ancestor's Arrival Record*. 2nd ed. Salt Lake City: Ancestry, 1993.

County Maps. Lyndon Station, WI: County Maps, unit of Thomas Publications. (608) 666-3331.

Croom, Emily Anne. *The Genealogist's Companion & Sourcebook.* Cincinnati: Betterway Books, 1994.

————. *Unpuzzling Your Past: A Basic Guide to Genealogy.* 3rd ed. Cincinnati: Betterway Books, 1995.

————. *The Unpuzzling Your Past Workbook.* Cincinnati: Betterway Books, 1996.

Davis, Robert Scott, Jr., comp. *Research in Georgia.* Greenville, SC: Southern Historical Press, 1981.

Dollarhide, William. "It's About Time: Calendars and Genealogical Dates." *Genealogy Bulletin* 15 (March/April 1999): 1, 6–13.

Drake, Paul. *What Did They Mean By That? A Dictionary of Historical Terms for Geneaologists.* 2 Vols. Bowie, MD: Heritage Books, 1994, 1998.

————. *You Ought to Write All That Down: A Guide to Organizing and Writing Genealogical Narrative.* Bowie, MD: Heritage Books, 1998.

Eichholz, Alice, ed. *Ancestry's Red Book: American State, County & Town Sources.* Rev. ed. Salt Lake City: Ancestry, 1992.

Evans, Barbara Jean. *A to Zax: A Comprehensive Dictionary for Genealogists & Historians.* 3rd ed. Alexandria, VA: Hearthside Press, 1995.

Everton, George B., Sr., ed. *The Handy Book for Genealogists.* Logan, UT: The Everton Publishers, latest edition.

Filby, P. William. *Passenger and Immigration Lists Index.* Detroit: Gale Research, 1981–.

Greenwood, Val D. *The Researcher's Guide to American Genealogy.* 2nd. ed. Baltimore: Genealogical Publishing Co., 1990.

Guide to Genealogical Research in the National Archives. Rev. ed. Washington, DC: National Archives Trust Fund Board, 1985.

Harris, Maurine, and Glen Harris. *Ancestry's Concise Genealogical Dictionary.* Salt Lake City: Ancestry, 1989.

Hatcher, Patricia Law. *Producing a Quality Family History.* Salt Lake City: Ancestry, 1996.

Hawkins, Kenneth, comp. *Research in the Land Entry Files of the General Land Office: Record Group 49.* Washington, DC: National Archives and Records Administration, 1997. General Information Leaflet Number 67.

Hone, E. Wade. *Land & Property Research in the United States.* Salt Lake City: Ancestry, 1997.

Hudgins, Dennis Ray, ed. *Cavaliers and Pioneers: Abstracts of Virginia Land Patents and Grants, 1623–1800.* Richmond: Virginia Genealogical Society, 1994, Vol. 4–5.

Jacobus, Donald Lines. *Genealogy as Pastime and Profession.* 2nd ed. revised. Baltimore: Genealogical Publishing Co., 1968.

Kemp, Thomas Jay. *International Vital Records Handbook.* Baltimore: Genealogical Publishing Co., 1990 or latest edition.

Lackey, Richard S. *Cite Your Sources: A Manual for Documenting Family Histories and Genealogical Records.* Jackson: University Press of Mississippi, 1980.

Lainhart, Ann S. *State Census Records.* Baltimore: Genealogical Publishing Co., 1992.

Lucas, S. Emmett, Jr., comp. *The Third or 1820 Land Lottery of Georgia.* Easley, SC: Southern Historical Press, 1986.

McMullin, Phillip W., comp. *Grassroots of America: A Computerized Index to the American State Papers: Land Grants and Claims (1789–1837).* Salt Lake City: Gendex Corp., 1972.

Mills, Elizabeth Shown. *Evidence! Citation & Analysis for the Family Historian.* Baltimore: Genealogical Publishing Company, 1997.

Mississippi Road Atlas. Jackson: University Press of Mississippi, 1997.

Neagles, James C. *The Library of Congress: A Guide to Genealogical and Historical Research.* Salt Lake City: Ancestry, 1990.

———. *U.S. Military Records: A Guide to Federal and State Sources.* Salt Lake City: Ancestry, 1994.

Nugent, Nell Marion, ed. *Cavaliers and Pioneers: Abstracts of Virginia Land Patents and Grants, 1623–1800.* Richmond: Dietz Printing Co., 1934, Vol. 1; Richmond: Virginia State Library, 1977, (Vol. 2), 1979 (Vol. 3), 1992– (Vol. 6–7). These and other Virginia records can be accessed on the Library of Virginia Web site at <http://www./lva.lib.va.us/dlp> (through the Digital Library Program) or <http://image.vtls.com/collections>.

Remington, Gordon L. "Quaker Preparation for the 1752 Calendar Change." *National Genealogical Society Quarterly* 87 (June 1999): 146–150.

The Roads of [State Name]. Atlas. Fredericksburg, TX: Shearer Publishing. (800) 458-3808.

Rubicam, Milton. *Pitfalls in Genealogical Research.* Salt Lake City: Ancestry, 1987.

Salmon, Marylynn. *Women and the Law of Property in Early America.* Chapel Hill: The University of North Carolina Press, 1986.

Schaefer, Christina K. *Guide to Naturalization Records of the United States.* Baltimore: Genealogical Publishing Co., 1997.

———. *The Hidden Half of the Family: A Sourcebook for Women's Genealogy.* Baltimore: Genealogical Publishing Co., 1999.

Shammas, Carole, Marylynn Salmon, and Michel Dahlin. *Inheritance in America: From Colonial Times to the Present.* New Brunswick, NJ: Rutgers University Press, 1987.

Stevenson, Noel C. *Genealogical Evidence.* Rev. ed. Laguna Hills, CA: Aegean Park Press, 1989.

Stratton, Eugene A. *Applied Genealogy.* Salt Lake City: Ancestry, 1988.

Stryker-Rodda, Kenn, ed. *Genealogical Research: Methods and Sources.* Vol. 2. Rev. ed. Washington, DC: The American Society of Genealogists, 1983.

Tepper, Michael. *American Passenger Arrival Records.* Updated and enlarged ed. Baltimore: Genealogical Publishing Co., 1993.

Thaxton, Donna B., ed. *Georgia Indian Depredation Claims.* Americus, GA: Thaxton Co., 1988.

Thorndale, William, and William Dollarhide. *Map Guide to the U.S. Federal Censuses, 1790–1920.* Baltimore: Genealogical Publishing Co., 1987.

Woodtor, Dee Parmer. *Finding a Place Called Home: A Guide to African-American Genealogy and Historical Identity.* New York: Random House, 1999.

Index